D1540135

REVOLUTION!

ALSO BY PETE AYRTON

NO MAN'S LAND
¡NO PASARÁN!

REVOLUTION!

WRITINGS FROM RUSSIA, 1917

EDITED BY PETE AYRTON

PEGASUS BOOKS
NEW YORK LONDON

Revolution!

Pegasus Books Ltd.
148 West 37th Street, 13th Floor
New York, NY 10018

Selection, introduction, and editorial matter copyright © 2017 by Pete Ayrton
Further copyright information is to be found on pages 362–364

First Pegasus Books hardcover edition September 2017

All rights reserved. No part of this book may be reproduced in whole or in
part without written permission from the publisher, except by reviewers who
may quote brief excerpts in connection with a review in a newspaper, magazine,
or electronic publication; nor may any part of this book be reproduced, stored in a retrieval
system, or transmitted in any form or by any means electronic, mechanical, photocopying,
recording, or other, without written permission from the publisher.

ISBN: 978-1-68177-520-3

10 9 8 7 6 5 4 3 2 1

Printed in the United States of America
Distributed by W. W. Norton & Company, Inc.

Contents

This book is dedicated to
JOHN BERGER
whose optimism was both
life-affirming and lucid.

Acknowledgements

Special thanks to Julian Evans, Robert Chandler, Boris Dralyuk and Lesley Chamberlain for sharing their knowledge of the literature of the period. To Stephen Smith, historian of the Russian Revolution, for generously giving me time and wisdom. To Jeremy Beale at Harbour Books and Claiborne Hancock at Pegasus Books for their publishing wisdom and support. To Edmund Fawcett, Sarah Martin, Malcolm Imrie and Ruthie Petrie who read and suggested improvements to the introduction. To Sarah, Carla and Oscar, for their enthusiasm and support that made compiling this anthology all the more worthwhile.

Introduction

The Russian Revolution took place one hundred years ago, in October 1917[1] – a crucial event of the twentieth century for all sides of the political divide. The revolutionary process began with the overthrow of the Tsar in February and ended with the seizure of power in October by the Bolshevik Party through the Soviets,[2] which saw themselves as organs of revolutionary government. In the months between February and October, the Bolsheviks increased their influence in the Soviets by adopting a position of total opposition to further Russian participation in the 1914–18 War and support for the transfer of land from the land-owning class to the peasants. The Provisional Government, led by Kerensky who had become Prime Minister in July, and backed by all the political parties except the Bolsheviks and the Left Socialist Revolutionaries, found its support ebbing away as Russia faced mounting war casualties. The Bolshevik slogan 'Bread, Peace and Land' brilliantly captured popular sentiment; the soldiers, many of whom came from the countryside, wanted to stop fighting and get back to work on the land. The promise to end the fighting brought the Bolsheviks an enormous popular following. The seizure of power by the Soviets in October was not violent – on 24 October, bridges and railway stations

---

1   On 1 February 1918, the Bolsheviks changed the Julian calendar, which was thirteen days behind that of the West, to the Western Calendar. The October Revolution (24–5 October 1917) thus took place on 6–7 November 1917 according to the Western calendar.
2   The Soviets saw themselves as organs of 'revolutionary democracy' – they were directly elected by those they represented and directly accountable. By October there were Soviets mainly in the cities – more peasant Soviets were formed by the end of the year. The Soviets initially were supported by the Bolsheviks as organs of dual power. See S. A. Smith, *Russia in Revolution: An Empire in Crisis, 1890–1928*, Oxford 2017, an invaluable source in providing the historical material for this introduction.

were under Soviet control and Kerensky escaped to the front to seek military support. By the morning of 25 October only the Winter Palace, the headquarters of the Provisional Government, remained to be taken by revolutionary forces. That afternoon Lenin appeared in public for the first time since July, proclaiming to the Congress of the Petrograd[3] Soviet that the Provisional Government had been overthrown. 'In Russia we must now set about building a proletarian socialist state.' At 10.40 p.m. the Second Congress of Soviets, which had been postponed since 20 October, finally opened against the sound of the distant artillery bombardment of the Winter Palace. At the news of the 'Storming of the Winter Palace' the non-Bolshevik parties walked out of the Congress of Soviets. A Bolshevik government with Lenin as chairman was established, with its first priority being to end the war. Armistice negotiations began in Brest-Litovsk in November and the Treaty with Germany was signed in March 1918; extremely punitive, it took away from Russia territory that included a third of the population, over half of its industrial production and nine-tenths of its coal mines. Defeated in turn by the Western Allies, Germany signed an Armistice in November 1918 and abandoned the gains made in Eastern Europe and Russia. In the ensuing fight over these now contested territories, White Russian armies led by Yudenich and Denikin attacked Soviet forces. In October 1919, the White armies almost took Petrograd. However, by the next year the Red Army led by Trotsky was victorious and the Civil War was coming to an end.

These momentous events provide the background to the contributions in *Revolution!* In showing that liberation was possible, they brought great hope and exhilaration to people the world over. The autocratic Tsar had been replaced by a government speaking for the people, a government committed to ending the war, to expropriating factories and land and to introducing a new era of human dignity. Over the next ten years, many of those hopes were to be disappointed.

---

3   At the outbreak of World War I it was thought that St Petersburg sounded too German so the city's name was changed to Petrograd. After Lenin's death in 1924 it was changed again to Leningrad and in 1991 after the fall of the Soviet Union the city reverted to its original name of St Petersburg.

But it is impossible to overestimate the expectations vested in the Soviet government that came to power in October 1917 – expectations that inspired revolutionary movements all over the world during the twentieth century.

The extracts included in *Revolution! Writings from Russia, 1917* come from three different sources:

1. **Foreign writers and intellectuals** who visited the Soviet Union after the Revolution and wrote about their experiences: sympathetic to the Revolution, they came from all over the world. They included **Arthur Ransome**[4] and **H. G. Wells** from Britain, **John Reed, Louise Bryant** and **Langston Hughes** from the USA, **Victor Serge** from France, **Walter Benjamin** from Germany, **Claude McKay** from Jamaica, **Panaït Istrati** from Romania.

2. **Russian writers who stayed in the Soviet Union** and wrote under conditions of increasing censorship. In the first decade after the Revolution, the Bolshevik government allowed different interpretations of what art and literature should be to coexist. So there was room for **Isaac Babel, Mikhail Zoshchenko, Alexandra Kollontai, Ilf and Petrov** and **Lev Lunts**. By the end of the 1920s, Stalin had strengthened his grip on power and socialist realism became the only permissible literature.

3. **Russian émigré writers** who, after the Revolution, did not feel in sympathy with developments in the Soviet Union and emigrated before 1925 while it was still possible to leave. **Teffi, Edith Sollohub** and **Nina Berberova** were among the many who followed this path.

Foreign Writers and Intellectuals

The expectations raised by October 1917 were on a truly epic scale. As the international ruling classes feared, the Russian Revolution showed working-class and peasant movements all over the world that rapid change was possible. While the most acute revolutionary uprisings were in Europe – in countries with a developed working class like Germany and Italy, there were also revolutionary upheavals in Egypt,

4   Names in bold indicate featured writers.

Mexico and India, among others. The Bolshevik government in Russia had quickly fulfilled its commitment to end Russian involvement in the war. It had confiscated land and factories from the owners and embarked on a series of progressive social measures. Not surprisingly, this enthusiasm brought to the Soviet Union in the years following October 1917 many progressive sympathisers who wanted to see for themselves how the promised land was faring: many of the pieces in *Revolution!* capture what they saw. There were those, such as Beatrice and Sidney Webb, whose faith in Communism and the Soviet Union never wavered. However, the majority of contributors featured here found at some point or other that the discrepancies between what they had been led to believe was happening and what was actually happening were too great; their early enthusiasm was curbed or revised. For most, the moment of reckoning was postponed by the Civil War: they accepted that in a war it was legitimate for a government to curtail freedoms such as freedom of the press, of political opposition and of the right to strike. When the dangers of the Civil War receded and the Bolshevik government showed no signs of reintroducing the suspended freedoms, many early sympathisers were forced to take stock.

For Victor Serge, it was the Kronstadt Uprising that was decisive. In March 1921, the sailors of Kronstadt had mutinied in support of the striking workers of Petrograd. Their demands were for a renewal of the programme of the 1917 Revolution: elections to the Soviet by secret ballot, freedom of the press for all revolutionary parties and groups, the release of revolutionary political prisoners. The Bolsheviks refused to negotiate and after ten days of heavy fighting the uprising was defeated with bloody force and Kronstadt taken back. Serge writes about the period immediately after Kronstadt:

> The truth was that emergent totalitarianism had already gone half-way to crushing us. 'Totalitarianism' did not yet exist as a word; as an actuality it began to press hard on us, even without our being aware of it . . .
>
> 'What with the political monopoly, the Cheka[5] and the Red

5 The first Soviet state security organisation. Between October 1917 and

Army, all that now existed of the 'Commune-State' of our dreams was a theoretical myth. The war, the internal measures against counter-revolution, and the famine (which has created a bureaucratic rationing apparatus) had killed off Soviet democracy.[6]

Serge accepted that a revolutionary government had the right to curtail freedoms when under military threat but should not do so when that was no longer the case:

I am well aware that terror has been necessary up till now in all great revolutions, which do not happen according to the tastes of well-intentioned men, but spontaneously, with the violence of tempests: that the individual has as much weight as straw in a hurricane; and that the duty of revolutionaries is to employ the only weapons that history affords us if we are not to be overwhelmed through our own folly. But the perpetuation of terror, after the end of the Civil War and the transition to a period of economic freedom, was an immense and demoralising blunder. I was and still am convinced that the new regime would have felt a hundred times more secure if it had henceforth proclaimed its reverence, as a Socialist government, for human life and the rights of all individuals without exception.[7]

For **Emma Goldman** and **Alexander Berkman**, two well-known anarchists who had arrived in Russia from the United States in January 1920 to support the Revolution, Kronstadt was also their breaking point. Their appeal to the Petrograd Soviet to offer their services in an attempt to bring about an end to the conflict with the sailors fell on deaf ears and the mutiny was crushed. Emma Goldman considered it time to leave: 'The idea that I might want to leave Russia had never before entered my mind. I was startled and shocked by the mere thought of it. I to leave Russia to her Calvary! Yet I felt that I would

---

February 1922, Cheka executions were on a very large scale – Smith puts the number at 140,000 (Smith, op. cit., p. 199).

6 *Memoirs of a Revolutionary*, New York, 2012, p. 155

7 ibid., p. 179

even take that step rather than become a cog in the machinery, an inanimate thing to be manipulated at will.'⁸

Many of the sympathisers who came in these years were radicals for whom the Soviet Union was a litmus paper by which to judge the conditions in their home countries; this was true of Claude McKay, the Jamaican writer, and Langston Hughes, the African-American writer, who both visited the Soviet Union and wrote at length about their visits in their respective autobiographies *A Long Way from Home* and *I Wonder as I Wander*. They went hoping to find a new social order in which racial inequality was on the way to being eliminated – in marked contrast to the situation prevailing in America and Europe where it showed no sign of diminishing.

In 1932, Langston Hughes visited Soviet Central Asia and took with him his collection of jazz records. It was the sounds of jazz that attracted Arthur Koestler and encouraged him to introduce himself to Hughes in Ashkhabad, the capital of Turkmenistan. A chance meeting of two very adventurous minds. Touring together, Hughes and Koestler discussed how where they came from determined how they assessed their experiences; Koestler looked at things only from a class perspective, for Hughes, it was a question of race; 'I was trying to make [Arthur Koestler] understand why I observed the changes in Soviet Asia with *Negro* eyes. To Koestler, Turkmenistan was simply a *primitive* land moving into twentieth-century civilisation. To me it was a *coloured* land moving into orbits hitherto reserved for whites.'⁹ As Hughes succinctly put it: 'After all, I suppose, how anything is seen depends on whose eyes look at it.'

Walter Benjamin went to Russia in the winter of 1926–7. He went not to make up his mind about Russia but rather to better understand the Berlin he was coming from:

> More quickly than Moscow itself, one gets to know Berlin through Moscow. For someone returning home from Russia the city seems freshly washed. There is no dirt but no snow, either. The streets

8 *Living My Life*, London, 2006, pp. 506–7
9 *I Wonder as I Wander*, New York, 1956, p. 116

seem in reality as desolately clean and swept as in the drawings of
Grosz. And how true-to-life his types are has become more obvious.
What is true of the image of the city and its people applies also to
the intellectual situation: a new perspective of this is the most
undoubted gain from a stay in Russia. However little one may
know Russia, what one learns is to observe and judge Europe with
the conscious knowledge of what is going on in Russia. This is the
first benefit to the intelligent European in Russia. But, equally, this
is why the stay is so exact a touchstone for foreigners. It obliges
everyone to choose his standpoint.'[10]

Benjamin visited Moscow after the end of the Civil War at a time when
the government was consolidating its power and clamping down on
dissent in all its forms – political, social and artistic. It was in the process
of forming an obedient bureaucracy, which was to include artists.
Becoming a state functionary was of very limited appeal to Benjamin!

It should be remembered that visitors to Soviet Russia faced many
obstacles in coming to an understanding of what exactly they were
witnessing. For some there was the problem of language, for others
there was the problem of being allowed to see only what the authorities
wanted to show. H. G. Wells writes about being shown round a
school where, when asked who their favourite writer was, the students
replied H. G. Wells, ahead of Shakespeare, Dickens and Milton.
Repelled by this obvious manipulation, Wells surprised his hosts the
next day and insisted on visiting another school unannounced. Here
there were no books by him in the library and none of the students
had heard of him; Wells went away a happy man!

The All-Union Society for Cultural Relations with Foreign
Countries (VOKS) existed to make sure that important cultural guests
were given tailor-made, red-carpet treatment. Only determined
visitors, who knew exactly what they did and did not want to be
shown, and whom they did or did not want to meet, could refuse the
programme of rallies at railway stations, welcoming speeches, trips to
the Bolshoi, and official banquets that VOKS had planned for them.

10 'Moscow', in *Reflections*, New York, 1987, p. 97

Russian Writers Who Stayed in the Soviet Union

In the years immediately after the Revolution, the government had not fully consolidated its power and had no option but to give artists and writers some leeway in their artistic production. The Bolshevik leadership had a clear idea of its preferred art but it was also prepared to accept art from 'fellow-travellers' as long as this did not question the basic tenets of Bolshevik rule. The description of a fellow-traveller comes from Trotsky:

> Between bourgeois Art, which is wasting away either in repetitions and in silences, and the new art which is as yet unborn, there is being created a transitional art, which is more or less organically connected with the Revolution, but which is not, at the same time, the Art of the Revolution . . . They are not artists of the proletarian Revolution, but her artist 'fellow-travellers' . . .
>
> As regards a 'fellow-traveller', the question always comes up – How far will he go? This question cannot be answered in advance, not even approximately. The solution of it depends not so much on the personal qualities of this or that 'fellow-traveller' but mainly on the objective trend of things during the coming decade.[11]

Foremost among the fellow-travellers were the Serapion Brothers, a loosely knit group that took its name and inspiration from the writings of E. T. A. Hoffman. In his collection of stories, *The Stories of the Serapion Brothers*, Hoffman describes the meeting of old friends who dispense with all literary rules and regulations and meet to read one another their works. The theorist of the Serapion Brothers was Lev Lunts and its most popular writer Mikhail Zoshchenko.

Deeply serious but also flamboyantly provocative, Lunts wrote:

> The Serapion Brothers as a school never existed. What we have in common is not a manner of writing but an attitude towards what is written, an acceptance of any work of literature, if only it be organic, a hatred of any socio-political intolerance. We argue with

11 *Art and Revolution*, Chapter 2, 1923. 'Objective trend' allows many interpretations.

each other as writers and not as social thinkers. We recognise both Sinclair and Kipling, a Communist and an Imperialist, because they are good writers.

At a time when Soviet critics were questioning whether Shakespeare should be available on the grounds that though 'he was an interesting, bright and valuable poet', he was a bard of 'lords and kings' and his relationship to the plebs suspicious, Lunts's answer was:

> I would like to pose a question that has long interested me. We have the excellent stories of Kipling, for example. They are saturated – from beginning to end – with the preaching of imperialism, they praise the rule of England over the oppressed Hindus. What am I to do with these stories? Comrade Kogan advises to struggle against them. Agreed. I will unmask their ideology in the eyes of all those who have already read Kipling. But should I give these stories to children who are beginning to read? They are harmful. Burn them? This would deprive the children of a great pleasure. What is more important in a work of art, its political action on the masses or its aesthetic value?[12]

Even in an ideological climate of relative tolerance Lunts was asking for trouble. Unable to get his plays performed in the Soviet Union, he moved to Germany in 1923 to join his parents who had emigrated there in 1921.

If Lunts was the Serapions' theorist, Mikhail Zoshchenko was, then, its most popular writer, in fact the most popular of Soviet writers. His wry, satirical tales captured the mood of the times. Much of the best writing reflects the conditions people were living in – shortages of all kinds, a lack of heating, the petty (and not so petty) aggravations of communal living, the frustrations of dealing with an inflexible bureaucracy. Much of the contemporary literary landscape is devoted to queues, shortages and the question of which books to burn to keep warm.

12 from 'Ideology and Publicistic Literature', an essay published in 1922 and included in *The Serapion Brothers*, an anthology edited by Gary Kern and Christopher Collins, Ann Arbor, 1975

Krokodil, the satirical magazine that Zoshchenko mainly wrote for, was one of the many that flourished during the NEP (New Economic Policy) period; it is estimated that in the years 1922–8, the seven leading satirical magazines of Moscow and Petrograd/ Leningrad had a combined print run of over half a million copies. In 1926–7, 700,000 copies of Zoshchenko's books alone were sold. His enormous popularity was in part due to his finding a style accessible to a working-class readership – he rightly considered himself a proletarian writer or at least a faux proletarian writer:

> The thing is that I'm a proletarian writer. Or rather in my stuff I'm parodying the sort of imaginary but genuine proletarian writer who might exist in the present-day environment . . .
>
> 'I'm just parodying. I'm a temporary substitute for the proletarian writer. That's why the themes of my stories are so full of a naïve philosophy that is just the right level for my readers.' [13]

If Zoshchenko found the right tone to appeal to a working-class readership, he also found the right subject matter. Many of the ideas for his stories came from readers' letters to newspapers. Zoshchenko valued these so much that in 1929 he published a collection of such letters, *Letters to a Writer*. Beneath the satire and irony, it is clear that he felt strongly about the everyday oppressions and humiliations that the system put his subjects through. Such empathy was not likely to find favour with Glavlit (the Central Directorate for Matters of Literature and Publishing), an institution of Soviet censorship founded in 1922 that was beginning to flex its muscles. As Stalin consolidated his grip on power, there was less and less room for dissent and that included the satirical press. Zoshchenko refused to self-censor his writings and found it more and more difficult to get published. Like many other Soviet writers of his generation, he was reduced to silence as state control of the arts spread. In *Hope Against Hope*, Nadezhda Mandelstam writes:

> On the first of our two visits to Leningrad we went out to see

---

13   from his 1927 essay 'About myself, my critics and my work', quoted in Jeremy Hicks's excellent introduction to Zoshchenko's *The Galosh and Other Stories*, London, 2000

Zoshchenko in Sestroretsk (or it may have been Razliv). Zoshchenko had a weak heart and beautiful eyes. *Pravda* had commissioned a story from him and he had written something about the wife of the poet Kornilov, who was refused work and turned away from every door as though she were the wife of an arrested man. The story wasn't printed, of course, but in those years only Zoshchenko would have dared to do something so provocative. It is amazing he got away with it – though it must immediately have gone down on the 'account' which he later had to pay.[14]

Russian Émigré Writers

Many writers left Russia in the first years after the Revolution: they departed for political reasons but with very different politics. Some were Tsarist and in favour of the return of the monarchy, other were in favour of bourgeois democracy, still others like Teffi were in favour of socialism but were fiercely opposed to the Bolshevik one-party state: 'Leninists, Bolsheviks, anarchists and communists, thugs, registered housebreakers – what a muddle! What a satanic vinaigrette! What immense work – to raise once more and cleanse from all this garbage the great idea of socialism!'

Almost all the émigré writers thought that the Bolshevik regime would be short-lived and they would soon be able to return. However, by 1925, it had become clear that the regime was far from temporary and the émigrés had to reconcile themselves to permanent exile. Initially, the centre for the émigré community was Berlin, but by the early 1920s, Paris had taken pride of place and many of the émigré writers found themselves in a dialogue with French intellectual life – all the more necessary since relationships among the Russians were fraught:

> We – *les russes*, as they call us – live the strangest of lives here, nothing like other people's. We stick together, for example, not like planets, by mutual attraction, but by a force quite contrary to the laws of physics – mutual repulsion. Every *lesrusse* hates all the others – hates them just as fervently as the others hate him.[15]

14   *Hope Against Hope*, London, 1999, p. 317
15   from Teffi's 'Que Faire?', in the collection *Subtly Worded*, London, 2014

As the pieces in *Revolution!* show, much of their writing was about Russia in a deliberate attempt to keep alive the memories and traditions of the country they had left. But even if these writers had escaped Soviet state censorship by leaving, they had not escaped censorship by publishers. During the first years of the revolution, the poet Marina Tsvetaeva kept a set of diaries, which she tried to get published under the title *Earthly Signs*; in February 1923, it was rejected by Helicon, the émigré publishing house, because of its political nature. Helicon exported books to the Soviet Union and, not wanting to lose this important market, demanded the deletion of all passages that contained what it called 'politics'. Outraged at this censorship for economic reasons, Tsvetaeva withdrew her manuscript. Later she commented on the incident: 'There is no *politics* in the book: there is *passionate* truth: the partisan truth of cold, of hunger, of anger, of the *Year*! My youngest girl died of hunger in a children's home – that's also "politics" (the home was Bolshevik).'[16]

From 1925, Tsvetaeva lived for fourteen years in and around Paris. In 1939, she decided to return to the Soviet Union with her son. Her husband and her surviving daughter Alya had gone back two years earlier. She went with no illusions about what awaited her there: she knew she would be condemned to silence. And indeed, after her husband and daughter had been arrested and taken away, Tsvetaeva, alone with her son, committed suicide in August 1941. By then, a whole generation of Soviet writers, dead or alive, had been reduced to silence.

As Nina Berberova, another Russian émigré, writes in her moving autobiography *The Italics are Mine*:

Now, looking back at those months, I see that destruction of the intelligentsia came not in a straight path but in a tortuous one, through a period of brief flowering; that the way was not simple through that flowering, that some people at the same time both flowered and perished, and made others perish, without being

16 See the excellent introduction to *Earthly Signs* (New Haven, 2002) by Jamey Gambrell, p. xix. Reference is also made to Simon Karlinsky's *Marina Tsvetaeva*, Cambridge, 1985.

themselves aware of it; that a little later there would be hundreds of sacrifices and later still tens of thousands: from Trotsky through Vororsky, Pilnyak, the formalists and fellow travellers to the futurists and young workers and peasant poets who bloomed to the very end of the twenties, serving the new regime wholeheartedly. From bearded elders, members of the Philosophical Society of the beginning of the century, to the members of the Association of Proletarian Writers, who had invented, at the right time it then seemed, the slogan about the debasement of culture but were killed like everybody else. Destruction came not personally to each one who was being destroyed, but as a group destruction of a whole profession, carefully planned.

It is clear that the hopes and expectations raised by the first socialist revolution were immense – the revolution showed there was nothing inevitable about how society had until then been arranged. It showed that a new world and new ways of living were possible – that the inequality and cruelty of capitalism could be replaced by something better – a system, communism, that replaced exploitation with equality and fairness. When it became clear, in the decade after 1917, that such a transition was not going to happen, that the dream had turned to nightmare, the disillusion was all the more painful. Historians will continue to debate the relative weight to ascribe to the different causes of this failure; the absence of world revolution, the allied support for the Whites in Civil War, the Bolshevik interpretation of the dictatorship of the proletariat, the degree to which the tyranny of Stalinism was prefigured in the decisions taken by Lenin before his death in 1924. In this period, many of the contributors to *Revolution!* experienced this disillusionment – for some it was a matter of life or death. I hope that taken collectively their contributions convey both the intense exhilaration as well as the despair of individuals caught up in a political whirlwind that they could, at best, understand intermittently. A hundred years later, despite everything that has happened and despite the many lost hopes, the sense that our present condition is not inevitable and that fundamental change for the better remains possible lives on.

Leon Trotsky

Born Lev Davidovich Bronstein, **Leon Trotsky** (1879-1940) was a leading figure of the October Revolution. Having recently joined the Bolshevik Party, Trotsky was at the beginning of October 1917 elected Chairman of the Petrograd Soviet and it was in this position that he played so prominent a role in the overthrow of the Provisional Government and the seizure of power by the Bolsheviks. Trotsky's organisational and motivational skills were immense; having made a decision, he did not vacillate and was always able to get the best out of those under his command; he was a ruthless commander who did not tolerate dissent. After the Revolution, Trotsky founded the Red Army and became People's Commissar of Military and Naval Affairs, he led the Red Army to victory in the Civil War which lasted from 1918 to 1922; this brought him immense prestige in the Party and in the country as a whole. Like those of many other revolutionary leaders (eg. Fidel Castro, Mao), Trotsky's skills were best suited to periods of war and conflict. He was much less adroit in the political infighting that took place in the Bolshevik Party after the Civil War and ended with Stalin seizing power and eliminating – in one way or another – his political opponents. Trotsky was expelled from the Party in 1927, exiled to Alma-Ata in 1928 and from the Soviet Union in 1929; he remained in exile for the rest of his life. In exile, Trotsky had the time to write the books of this period that make him one of the great historians of the Russian Revolution: *My Life* (1930), *The Permanent Revolution* (1930) and *The Revolution Betrayed: What is the Soviet Union and Where is It Going* (1937). In August 1940, Trotsky was assassinated in Mexico City where he had lived since January 1937. His killer was Ramon Mercader, a Spanish-born Soviet agent sent by Stalin. Since his death, Trotsky has become an inspiration to revolutionaries the world over. They are inspired by his refusal to capitulate to Stalin and to advocate permanent revolution and seem less worried by his lifetime fidelity to the dictatorship of the proletariat and one-party rule.

The Deciding Night

from *My Life* by Leon Trotsky

The twelfth hour of the revolution was near. The Smolny was being transformed into a fortress. In its garret there were a dozen or two machine guns, a legacy from the old Executive Committee. Captain Grekov, commandant of the Smolny, was an undisguised enemy. On the other hand, the chief of the machine-gun company came to tell me that his men were all on the side of the Bolsheviks. I instructed someone – perhaps Markin – to inspect the machine guns. They proved to be in poor condition as a result of continuous neglect – the soldiers had grown slack because they had no intention of defending Kerensky. I had a new and more reliable machine-gun detachment brought to the Smolny.

The twenty-fourth of October, a grey morning, early, I roamed about the building from one floor to another, partly for the sake of movement and partly to make sure that everything was in order and to encourage those who needed it. Along the stone floors of the interminable and still half-dark corridors of the Smolny, the soldiers were dragging their machine guns, with a hearty clangour and tramping of feet – this was the new detachment I had summoned. The few Socialist-Revolutionists and Mensheviks still in the Smolny could be seen poking sleepy, frightened faces out at us. The music of the guns was ominous in their ears, and they left the Smolny in a hurry, one after the other. We were now in full command of the building that was preparing to rear a Bolshevist head over the city and the country.

Early in the morning, two workers, a man and a woman, panting after the run from the party printing-works, bumped into me on the staircase. The government had closed down the central organ of the party and the paper of the Petrograd Soviet. Government agents, accompanied by military students, had put seals on the printing-works. For a moment the news startled us; such is the power exercised over the mind by legal formality.

'Couldn't we break the seals?' the woman asked.

'Break them,' I answered, 'and to make it safe for you we will give you a dependable escort.'

'There is a battalion of sappers next door to us; the soldiers are sure to back us,' said the woman printer, confidently.

The Military-Revolutionary Committee immediately ordered: (1) the printing-works of revolutionary newspapers to be reopened; (2) the editorial staffs and compositors to be invited to continue publishing the papers; (3) the honorary duty of protecting the revolutionary printing-works from counter-revolutionary attacks to be entrusted to the gallant soldiers of the Litovsky regiment and the Sixth Sapper Reserve Battalion. And from that time on, the printing-works ran without interruption, and both newspapers continued publication.

On the 24th, there was difficulty at the telephone exchange. Military students had entrenched themselves there, and under their protection the telephone operators went into opposition to the Soviet and refused to make our connections. This was the first sporadic instance of sabotage. The Military-Revolutionary Committee sent a detachment of sailors to the telephone exchange, and the detachment placed two small guns at the entrance. The telephone service was restored. Thus began the taking over of the organs of administration.

On the third floor of the Smolny, in a small corner room, the Committee was in continuous session. All the reports about the movements of troops, the attitude of soldiers and workers, the agitation in the barracks, the designs of organisers of pogroms, the intrigues of the bourgeois politicians and the foreign embassies, the happenings in the Winter Palace – all these came to this centre, as did the reports of the conferences of the parties formerly in the Soviet. Informants came from all sides – workers, soldiers, officers, porters, socialist military students, servants, wives of petty officials. Many of them told us utter rubbish, but some supplied us with serious and very valuable information.

All that week I had hardly stepped out of the Smolny; I spent the nights on a leather couch without undressing, sleeping in snatches, and constantly being roused by couriers, scouts, messenger-cyclists, telegraphists and ceaseless telephone calls. The decisive moment was close at hand. It was obvious that there could now be no turning back.

On the night of the 24th, the members of the Revolutionary Committee went out into the various districts, and I was left alone. Later on, Kamenev came in. He was opposed to the uprising, but he had come to spend that deciding night with me, and together we stayed in the tiny corner room on the third floor, so like the captain's bridge on that deciding night of the Revolution.

There is a telephone booth in the large empty room adjoining us, and the bell rings incessantly about important things and trifles. Each ring heightens the alertness of the silence. One can readily picture the deserted streets of Petrograd, dimly lit, and whipped by the autumn winds from the sea; the bourgeois and officials cowering in their beds, trying to guess what is going on in those dangerous and mysterious streets; the workers' quarters quiet with the tense sleep of a war-camp. Commissions and conferences of the government parties are exhausting themselves in impotence in the Tsar's palaces, where the living ghosts of democracy rub shoulders with the still hovering ghosts of the monarchy. Now and again the silks and guildings of the halls are plunged into darkness – the supplies of coal have run short. In the various districts, detachments of workers, soldiers and sailors are keeping watch. The young proletarians have rifles and machine-gun belts across their shoulders. Street pickets are warming themselves at fires in the streets. The life of the capital, thrusting its head from one epoch into another on this autumn night, is concentrated about a group of telephones.

Reports from all the districts, suburbs and approaches to the capital are focused in the room on the third floor. It seems that everything has been foreseen; the leaders are in their places; the contacts are assured; nothing seems to have been forgotten.

Once more, let us go over it in our minds. This night decides. Only this evening, in my report to the delegates of the second congress of the Soviets, I said with conviction: 'If you stand firm, there will be no civil war, our enemies will capitulate at once, and you will take the place that belongs to you by right.' There can be no doubt about victory; it is as assured as the victory of any uprising can be. And yet, these hours are still tense and full of alarm, for the coming night decides. The government, while mobilising cadets yesterday, gave orders to the cruiser *Aurora* to steam out of the Neva. They were the same Bolshevik sailors whom Skobelev, coming hat in hand, in August begged to protect the Winter Palace from Kornilov. The sailors referred to the Military-Revolutionary Committee for instructions, and consequently the *Aurora* is standing tonight where she was yesterday. A telephone call from Pavlovsk informs me that the government is bringing up from there a detachment of artillery, a battalion of shock troops from Tsarskoye Selo,[17] and student-officers from the Peterhof military school. Into the Winter Palace Kerensky has drawn military students, officers and the women shock troops. I order the commissaries to place dependable military defences along the approaches to Petrograd and to send agitators to meet the detachments called out by the government. All our instructions and reports are sent by telephone and the government agents are in a position to intercept them. But can they still control our communications?

'If you fail to stop them with words, use arms. You will answer for this with your life.'

I repeat this sentence time and time again. But I do not yet believe in the force of my order. The Revolution is still too trusting, too generous, optimistic and light-hearted. It prefers to threaten with arms rather than really use them. It still hopes that all questions can be solved by words, and so far it has been successful in this – hostile elements evaporate before its hot breath. Earlier in the day (the 24th) an order was issued to use arms and to stop at nothing at the first sign of street pogroms. Our enemies don't even dare think of the streets; they have gone into hiding. The streets are ours; our commissaries are watching all the approaches to Petrograd. The officers' school and the gunners have not responded to the call of the government. Only a section of the Oraniembaum military students have succeeded in making their way through our defences, but I have been watching their movements by telephone. They end by sending envoys to the Smolny. The government has been seeking support in vain. The ground is slipping from under its feet.

17 Russian royal family's summer palace, fifteen miles from St Petersburg

The outer guard of the Smolny has been reinforced by a new machine-gun detachment. The contact with all sections of the garrison is uninterrupted. The companies on duty are on watch in all the regiments. The commissaries are in their places. Delegations from each garrison unit are in the Smolny, at the disposal of the Military-Revolutionary Committee, to be used in case the contact with that unit should be broken off. Armed detachments from the districts march along the streets, ring the bells at the gates or open the gates without ringing, and take possession of one institution after another. Nearly everywhere these detachments are met by friends who have been waiting impatiently for them. At the railway terminals, specially appointed commissaries are watching the incoming and outgoing trains, and in particular the movement of troops. No disturbing news comes from there. All the more important points in the city are given over into our hands almost without resistance, without fighting, without casualties. The telephone alone informs us: 'We are here!'

All is well. It could not have gone better. Now I may leave the telephone. I sit down on the couch. The nervous tension lessens. A dull sensation of fatigue comes over me.

'Give me a cigarette,' I say to Kamenev. (In those years I still smoked, but only spasmodically.) I take one or two puffs, but suddenly, with the words, 'Only this was lacking!' I faint. (I inherited from my mother a certain susceptibility to fainting spells when suffering from physical pain or illness. That was why some American physician described me as an epileptic.) As I come to, I see Kamenev's frightened face bending over me.

'Shall I get some medicine?' he asks.

'It would be much better,' I answer after a moment's reflection, 'if you got me something to eat.' I try to remember when I last had food, but I can't. At all events, it was not yesterday.

Next morning I pounced upon the bourgeois and Menshevik-Populist papers. They had not even a word about the uprising. The newspapers had been making such a to-do about the coming action by armed soldiers, about the sacking, the inevitable rivers of blood, about an insurrection, that now they simply had failed to notice an uprising that was actually taking place. The press was taking our negotiations with the general staff at their face value, and our diplomatic statements as signs of vacillation. In the meantime, without confusion, without street-fights, almost without firing or bloodshed, one institution after another was being occupied by detachments of soldiers, sailors and the Red Guards, on orders issuing from the Smolny Institute.

The citizen of Petrograd was rubbing his frightened eyes under a new regime. Was it really possible that the Bolsheviks had seized the power? A delegation from the municipal Duma called to see me, and asked me a few inimitable questions. 'Do you propose military action? If so, what, and when?' The Duma would have to know of this 'not less than twenty-four hours in advance'. What measures had the Soviet taken to ensure safety and order? And so on, and so forth.

I replied by expounding the dialectic view of the Revolution, and invited the Duma to send a delegate to the Military-Revolutionary Committee to take part in its work. This scared them more than the uprising itself. I ended, as usual, in the spirit of armed self-defence: 'If the government uses iron, it will be answered with steel.'

'Will you dissolve us for being opposed to the transfer of power to the Soviets?'

I replied: 'The present Duma reflects yesterday: if a conflict arises, we will propose to the people that they elect a new Duma on the issue of power.' The delegation left as it had come, but it left behind it the feeling of an assured victory. Something had changed during the night. Three weeks ago we had gained a majority in the Petrograd Soviet. We were hardly more than a banner – with no printing-works, no funds, no branches. No longer ago than last night, the government ordered the arrest of the Military-Revolutionary Committee, and was engaged in tracing our addresses. Today a delegation from the city Duma comes to the 'arrested' Military-Revolutionary Committee to enquire about the fate of the Duma.

The government was still in session at the Winter Palace, but it was no more than a shadow. Politically, it had ceased to exist. During the day of the 25th, the Winter Palace was being surrounded on all sides by our troops. At one o'clock midday, I made a statement of the situation to the Petrograd Soviet. The newspaper account reports it as follows: 'On behalf of the Military-Revolutionary Committee, I declare that the Provisional Government is no longer existent. [Applause.] Some ministers have been arrested. ['Bravo.'] Others will be arrested in the course of a few days or hours. [Applause.] The revolutionary garrison, at the disposal of the Military-Revolutionary Committee, has dissolved the session of the Pre-Parliament. [Loud applause.] We have been on the watch here throughout the night and have followed the detachments of revolutionary soldiers and the workers' guards by telephone as they silently carried out their tasks. The citizen slept in peace, ignorant of the change from one power to another. Railway-stations, the post-office, the telegraph, the Petrograd Telegraph Agency, the State Bank, have been occupied. [Loud applause.] The Winter Palace has not yet been taken, but its fate will be decided during the next few minutes. [Applause.]'

This bare account may give a wrong impression of the mood of the gathering. My memory supplies these particulars. When I reported the change of power effected during the night, there was tense silence for a few seconds. Then applause began, a not very stormy, rather thoughtful applause. The assembly was feeling intensely and waiting. While they were preparing for the struggle, the working class had been seized by an indescribable enthusiasm, but when we stepped over the threshold of power, this unthinking enthusiasm gave way to a disturbed thoughtfulness. A sure historical instinct revealed itself here. Ahead of us there was probably the greatest resistance from the old world; there were struggle, starvation, cold, destruction, blood and death. 'Will we overcome all this?' many asked themselves. That was the cause of the moments of disturbed reflection. 'We will overcome it!' they all answered. New dangers were looming in the far distance. But now we felt a sense of a great victory, and it sang in our blood. It found its expression in the tumultuous welcome accorded to Lenin, who at that meeting made his first appearance after a four months' absence.

Late that evening, as we were waiting for the opening of the congress of the Soviets, Lenin and I were resting in a room adjoining the meeting-hall, a room entirely empty except for chairs. Someone had spread a blanket on the floor for us; someone else, I think it was

Lenin's sister, had brought us pillows. We were lying side by side; body and soul were relaxing like over-taut strings. It was a well-earned rest. We could not sleep, so we talked in low voices. Only now did Lenin become reconciled to the postponement of the uprising. His fears had been dispelled. There was a rare sincerity in his voice. He was interested in knowing all about the mixed pickets of the Red Guards, sailors and soldiers that had been stationed everywhere. 'What a wonderful sight: a worker with a rifle, side by side with a soldier, standing before a street fire!' he repeated with deep feeling. At last the soldier and the worker had been brought together!

Then he started suddenly. 'And what about the Winter Palace? It has not been taken yet. Isn't there danger in that?' I got up to ask, on the telephone, about the progress of the operations there, but he tried to stop me. 'Lie still, I will send someone to find out.' But we could not rest for long. The session of the congress of the Soviets was opening in the next hall. Ulyanova, Lenin's sister, came running to get me.

'Dan is speaking. They are asking for you.'

In a voice that was breaking repeatedly, Dan was railing at the conspirators and prophesying the inevitable collapse of the uprising. He demanded that we form a coalition with the Socialist-Revolutionists and the Mensheviks. The parties that had been in power only the day before, that had hounded us and thrown us into prison, now that we had overthrown them were demanding that we come to an agreement with them.

I replied to Dan and, in him, to the yesterday of the revolution: 'What has taken place is an uprising, not a conspiracy. An uprising of the masses of the people needs no justification. We have been strengthening the revolutionary energy of the workers and soldiers. We have been forging, openly, the will of the masses for an uprising. Our uprising has won. And now we are being asked to give up our victory, to come to an agreement. With whom? You are wretched, disunited individuals; you are bankrupts; your part is over. Go to the place where you belong from now on – the dustbin of history!'

This was the last retort in that long dialogue that had begun on 3 April, with the day and hour of Lenin's arrival in Petrograd.

John Reed
&
Louise Bryant

Known to modern audiences through the film *Reds*, **John Reed** (1887–1920) and **Louise Bryant** (1885–1936) were American journalists sympathetic to the Russian Revolution. Married in 1916, they went to Russia in 1917 and wrote classic accounts of their experiences: Reed's *Ten Days that Shook the World* and Bryant's *Six Red Months in Russia*. The chapter taken from Reed's book is entitled 'The Fall of the Provisional Government' – it captures that moment when power was taken from the Provisional Government by the Soviets and then from the Soviets by the Bolsheviks; the transitions occurred with surprisingly little violence. Reed's account captures the unsettling uncertainty of these days whilst making clear that the Bolsheviks saw the seizing of power as the first stage of a world revolution – inspired by the Russian Revolution, the working classes of the more advanced European nations (e.g. Germany, France) would form soviets led by the local Communist Party and take power from their bourgeoisies. Although very sympathetic to the Bolsheviks, Reed makes clear that they were quite prepared to ride roughshod over decisions taken democratically if these did not suit their plans. *Six Red Months in Russia* is more anecdotal but just as powerful. Sent by Bell Syndicate, to cover the Revolution 'from a woman's point of view', Bryant in her writing shows great empathy for her subjects including the women soldiers.

John Reed and Louise Bryant returned to Russia in 1920. Reed contracted typhus in Baku where he was attending the First Congress of Peoples of the East as a representative of the American Communist Party. He died on 17 October and was given a state funeral. In keeping with Russian custom, Bryant walked alone behind the hearse, at the head of the funeral procession:

A grey sky overhanging Moscow, rain steadily drizzling its melancholy tune, and artificial wreaths that had served at other funerals were Jack's farewell in the Red Square. No beauty for the man who had loved it so, no colour for his artist-soul. No spark of the red-white flame of the fighter to inspire those who in bombastic speeches claimed him as their comrade. Alexandra Kollontai alone came close to the spirit of John Reed and found the words that would have pleased him most. During her simple and beautiful tribute to Jack, Louise crumpled to the ground in a dead faint just as the coffin was being lowered into the grave.

(Emma Goldman, Living My Life)

The Fall of the Provisional Government

from *Ten Days that Shook the World* by John Reed

When we came into the chill night, all the front of Smolny was one huge park of arriving and departing automobiles, above the sound of which could be heard the far-off slow beat of the cannon. A great motor-truck stood there, shaking to the roar of its engine. Men were tossing bundles into it, and others receiving them, with guns beside them. 'Where are you going?' I shouted.

'Downtown – all over – everywhere!' answered a little workman, grinning, with a large exultant gesture.

We showed our passes. 'Come along!' they invited. 'But there'll probably be shooting –' We climbed in: the clutch slid home with a raking jar, the great car jerked forward, we all toppled backward on top of those who were climbing in: past the huge fire by the gate, and then the fire by the outer gate, glowing red on the faces of the workmen with rifles who squatted around it, and went bumping at top speed down the Suvorovsky Prospect, swaying from side to side . . . One man tore the wrapping from a bundle and began to hurl handfuls of papers into the air. We imitated him, plunging down through the dark street with a tail of white papers floating and eddying out behind. The late passer-by stooped to pick them up; the patrols around bonfires on the corners ran out with uplifted arms to catch them. Sometimes armed men loomed up ahead, crying '*Stoi!*' and raising their guns, but our chauffeur only yelled something unintelligible and we hurtled on . . .

I picked up a copy of the paper, and under a fleeting street-light read:

TO THE CITIZENS OF RUSSIA!

The Provisional Government is deposed. The State Power has passed into the hands of the organ of the Petrograd Soviet of Workers' and Soldiers' Deputies, the Military Revolutionary Committee, which stands at the head of the Petrograd proletariat and garrison.

The cause for which the people were fighting: immediate proposal of a democratic peace, abolition of landlord property-rights over the land, labour control over production, creation of a Soviet Government – that cause is securely achieved.

LONG LIVE THE REVOLUTION OF WORKMEN, SOLDIERS AND PEASANTS!

Military Revolutionary Committee
Petrograd Soviet of Workers' and Soldiers' Deputies

A slant-eyed, Mongolian-faced man who sat beside me, dressed in a goatskin Caucasian cape, snapped, 'Look out! Here the provocators always shoot from the windows!' We turned into Znamensky Square, dark and almost deserted, careened around Trubetskoy's brutal statue and swung down the wide Nevsky, three men standing up with rifles ready, peering at the windows. Behind us the street was alive with people running and stooping. We could no longer hear the cannon, and the nearer we drew to the Winter Palace end of the city the quieter and more deserted were the streets. The City Duma was all brightly lighted. Beyond that we made out a dark mass of people, and a line of sailors, who yelled furiously at us to stop. The machine slowed down, and we climbed out.

It was an astonishing scene. Just at the corner of the Ekaterina

Canal, under an arc-light, a cordon of armed sailors was drawn across the Nevsky, blocking the way to a crowd of people in a column of fours. There were about three or four hundred of them, men in frock coats, well-dressed women, officers – all sorts and conditions of people. Among them we recognised many of the delegates from the Congress, leaders of the Mensheviki and Socialist Revolutionaries; Avksentiev, the lean, red-bearded president of the Peasants' Soviets, Sarokin, Kerensky's spokesman, Khinchuk, Abramovich; and at the head white-bearded old Schreider, Mayor of Petrograd, and Prokopovich, Minister of Supplies in the Provisional Government, arrested that morning and released. I caught sight of Malkin, reporter for the *Russian Daily News*. 'Going to die in the Winter Palace,' he shouted cheerfully. The procession stood still, but from the front of it came loud argument. Schreider and Prokopovich were bellowing at the big sailor who seemed in command.

'We demand to pass!' they cried. 'See, these comrades come from the Congress of Soviets! Look at their tickets! We are going to the Winter Palace!'

The sailor was plainly puzzled. He scratched his head with an enormous hand, frowning. 'I have orders from the Committee not to let anybody go to the Winter Palace,' he grumbled. 'But I will send a comrade to telephone to Smolny . . . '

'We insist upon passing! We are unarmed! We will march on whether you permit us or not!' cried old Schreider, very much excited.

'I have orders –' repeated the sailor sullenly.

'Shoot us if you want to! We will pass! Forward!' came from all sides. 'We are ready to die, if you have the heart to fire on Russians and comrades! We bare our breasts to your guns!'

'No,' said the sailor, looking stubborn, 'I can't allow you to pass.'

'What will you do if we go forward? Will you shoot?'

'No, I'm not going to shoot people who haven't any guns. We won't shoot unarmed Russian people . . . '

'We will go forward! What can you do?'

'We will do something!' replied the sailor, evidently at a loss. 'We can't let you pass. We will do something.'

'What will you do? What will you do?'

Another sailor came up, very much irritated. 'We will spank you!' he cried energetically. 'And if necessary we will shoot you too. Go home now, and leave us in peace!'

At this there was a great clamour of anger and resentment. Prokopovich had mounted some sort of box, and waving his umbrella, he made a speech:

'Comrades and citizens!' he said. 'Force is being used against us! We cannot have our innocent blood upon the hands of these ignorant men! It is beneath our dignity to be shot down here in the streets by switchmen –' (What he meant by 'switchmen' I never discovered.) 'Let us return to the Duma and discuss the best means of saving the country and the Revolution!'

Whereupon, in dignified silence, the procession marched around and back up the Nevsky, always in their column of fours. And taking advantage of the diversion we slipped past the guards and set off in the direction of the Winter Palace.

Here it was absolutely dark, and nothing moved but pickets of soldiers and Red Guards grimly intent. In front of the Kazan Cathedral a three-inch field-gun lay in the middle of the street, slewed sideways from the recoil of its last shot over the roofs. Soldiers were standing in every doorway talking in loud tones and peering down towards the Police Bridge. I heard one voice saying: 'It is possible that we have done wrong . . . ' At the corners patrols stopped all passers-by – and the composition of these patrols was interesting, for in command of the regular troops was invariably a Red Guard . . . The shooting had ceased.

Just as we came to the Morskaya somebody was shouting: 'The *yunkers* [18] have sent word that they want us to go and get them out!' Voices began to give commands, and in the thick gloom we made out a dark mass moving forward, silent but for the shuffle of feet and the clinking of arms. We fell in with the first ranks.

Like a black river, filling all the street, without song or cheer we poured through the Red Arch, where the man just ahead of me said in

[18] students of the yunker schools in Petrograd who mutinied against the Bolsheviks

a low voice: 'Look out, comrades! Don't trust them. They will fire, surely!' In the open we began to run, stooping low and bunching together, and jammed up suddenly behind the pedestal of the Alexander Column.

'How many of you did they kill?' I asked.

'I don't know. About ten . . . '

After a few minutes huddling there, some hundreds of men, the Army seemed reassured and without any orders suddenly began again to flow forward. By this time, in the light that streamed out of all the Winter Palace windows, I could see that the first two or three hundred men were Red Guards, with only a few scattered soldiers. Over the barricade of firewood we clambered, and leaping down inside gave a triumphant shout as we stumbled on a heap of rifles thrown down by the *yunkers* who had stood there. On both sides of the main gateway the doors stood wide open, light streamed out, and from the huge pile came not the slightest sound.

Carried along by the eager wave of men we were swept into the right-hand entrance, opening into a great bare vaulted room, the cellar of the east wing, from which issued a maze of corridors and staircases. A number of huge packing cases stood about, and upon these the Red Guards and soldiers fell furiously, battering them open with the butts of their rifles, and pulling out carpets, curtains, linen, porcelain, plates, glassware . . . One man went strutting around with a bronze clock perched on his shoulder; another found a plume of ostrich feathers, which he stuck in his hat. The looting was just beginning when somebody cried, 'Comrades! Don't take anything. This is the property of the People!' Immediately twenty voices were crying, 'Stop! Put everything back! Don't take anything! Property of the People!' Many hands dragged the spoilers down. Damask and tapestry were snatched from the arms of those who had them; two men took away the bronze clock. Roughly and hastily the things were crammed back in their cases, and self-appointed sentinels stood guard. It was all utterly spontaneous. Through corridors and up staircases the cry could be heard growing fainter and fainter in the distance, 'Revolutionary discipline! Property of the People . . . '

We crossed back over to the left entrance, in the west wing. There order was also being established. 'Clear the Palace!' bawled a Red Guard, sticking his head through an inner door. 'Come, comrades, let's show that we're not thieves and bandits. Everybody out of the Palace except the Commissars, until we get sentries posted.'

Two Red Guards, a soldier and an officer, stood with revolvers in their hands. Another soldier sat at a table behind them, with pen and paper. Shouts of 'All out! All out!' were heard far and near within, and the Army began to pour through the door, jostling, expostulating, arguing. As each man appeared he was seized by the self-appointed committee, who went through his pockets and looked under his coat. Everything that was plainly not his property was taken away, the man at the table noted it on his paper, and it was carried into a little room. The most amazing assortment of objects were thus confiscated; statuettes, bottles of ink, bedspreads worked with the Imperial monogram, candles, a small oil-painting, desk blotters, gold-handled swords, cakes of soap, clothes of every description, blankets. One Red Guard carried three rifles, two of which he had taken away from *yunkers*; another had four portfolios bulging with written documents. The culprits either sullenly surrendered or pleaded like children. All talking at once the committee explained that stealing was not worthy of the people's champions; often those who had been caught turned around and began to help go through the rest of the comrades.

Yunkers came out in bunches of three or four. The committee seized upon them with an excess of zeal, accompanying the search with remarks like, 'Ah, provocators! Kornilovists! Counter-revolutionists! Murderers of the People!' But there was no violence done, although the *yunkers* were terrified. They too had their pockets full of small plunder. It was carefully noted down by the scribe, and piled in the little room . . . The *yunkers* were disarmed. 'Now, will you take up arms against the People any more?' demanded clamouring voices.

'No,' answered the *yunkers*, one by one. Whereupon they were allowed to go free.

We asked if we might go inside. The committee was doubtful, but the big Red Guard answered firmly that it was forbidden. 'Who are you anyway?' he asked. 'How do I know that you are not all Kerenskys?' (There were five of us, two women.)

'*Pazhal'st*', *tovarishchi!* Way, comrades!' A soldier and a Red Guard appeared in the door, waving the crowd aside, and other guards with fixed bayonets. After them followed single file half a dozen men in civilian dress – the members of the Provisional Government. First came Kishkin, his face drawn and pale, then Rutenberg, looking sullenly at the floor; Tereshchenko was next, glancing sharply around; he stared at us with cold fixity . . . They passed in silence; the victorious insurrectionists crowded to see, but there were only a few angry mutterings. It was only later that we learned how the people in the street wanted to lynch them, and shots were fired – but the sailors brought them safely to Peter-Paul . . .

In the meanwhile unrebuked we walked into the Palace. There was still a great deal of coming and going, of exploring new-found apartments in the vast edifice, of searching for hidden garrisons of *yunkers* which did not exist. We went upstairs and wandered through room after room. This part of the Palace had been entered also by other detachments from the side of the Neva. The paintings, statues, tapestries and rugs of the great state apartments were unharmed; in the offices, however, every desk and cabinet had been ransacked, the papers scattered over the floor, and in the living-rooms beds had been stripped of their coverings and wardrobes wrenched open. The most highly prized loot was clothing, which the working people needed. In a room where furniture was stored we came upon two soldiers ripping the elaborate Spanish leather upholstery from chairs. They explained it was to make boots with . . .

The old Palace servants in their blue and red and gold uniforms stood nervously about, from force of habit repeating, 'You can't go in there, *barin*! It is forbidden –' We penetrated at length to the gold and malachite chamber with crimson brocade hangings where the Ministers had been in session all that day and night, and where the *shveitzari* had betrayed them to the Red Guards. The long table covered with green baize was just as they had left it, under arrest. Before each empty seat was pen, ink and paper; the papers were scribbled over with beginnings of plans of action, rough drafts of proclamations and manifestos. Most of these were scratched out, as their futility became evident, and the rest of the sheet covered with absent-minded geometrical designs, as the writers sat despondently listening while Minister after Minister proposed chimerical schemes. I took one of these scribbled pages, in the handwriting of Konovalov, which read, 'The Provisional Government appeals to all classes to support the Provisional Government – '

All this time, it must be remembered, although the Winter Palace was surrounded, the Government was in constant communication with the front and with provincial Russia. The Bolsheviki had captured the Ministry of War early in the morning, but they did not know of the military telegraph office in the attic, nor of the private telephone line connecting it with the Winter Palace. In that attic a young officer sat all day, pouring out over the country a flood of appeals and proclamations; and when he heard the Palace had fallen, put on his hat and walked calmly out of the building . . .

Interested as we were, for a considerable time we didn't notice a change in the attitude of the soldiers and Red Guards around us. As we strolled from room to room a small group followed us, until by the time we reached the great picture-gallery where we had spent the afternoon with the *yunkers*, about a hundred men surged in upon us. One giant of a soldier stood in our path, his face dark with sullen suspicion.

'Who are you?' he growled. 'What are you doing here?' The others massed slowly around, staring and beginning to mutter. '*Provocatori!*' I heard somebody say, 'Looters!' I produced our passes from the Military Revolutionary Committee. The soldier took them gingerly, turned them upside down and looked at them without comprehension. Evidently he could not read. He handed them back and spat on the floor. '*Bumagi!* Papers!' said he with contempt. The mass slowly began to close in, like wild cattle around a cow-puncher on foot. Over their heads I caught sight of an officer, looking helpless, and shouted to him. He made for us, shouldering his way through.

'I'm the Commissar,' he said to me. 'Who are you? What is it?' The others held back, waiting. I produced the papers.

'You are foreigners?' he rapidly asked in French. 'It is very dangerous . . . ' Then he turned to the mob, holding up our documents. 'Comrades!' he cried. 'These people are foreign comrades – from America. They have come here to be able to tell their countrymen about the bravery and the revolutionary discipline of the proletarian army!'

'How do you know that?' replied the big soldier. 'I tell you they are provocators! They say they came here to observe the revolutionary discipline of the proletarian army, but they have been wandering freely through the Palace, and how do we know they haven't got their pockets full of loot?'

'*Pravilno!*' snarled the others, pressing forward.

'Comrades! Comrades!' appealed the officer, sweat standing out on his forehead. 'I am Commissar of the Military Revolutionary Committee. Do you trust me? Well, I tell you that these passes are signed with the same names that are signed to my pass!'

He led us down through the Palace and out through a door opening on to the Neva quay, before which stood the usual committee going through pockets . . . 'You have narrowly escaped,' he kept muttering, wiping his face.

'What happened to the Women's Battalion?' we asked.

'Oh – the women!' He laughed. 'They were all huddled up in a back room. We had a terrible time deciding what to do with them – many were in hysterics, and so on. So finally we marched them up to the Finland Station and put them on a train to Levashovo, where they have a camp . . . '

We came out into the cold, nervous night, murmurous with obscure armies on the move, electric with patrols. From across the river, where loomed the darker mass of Peter-Paul, came a hoarse shout . . . Underfoot the sidewalk was littered with broken stucco from the cornice of the Palace where two shells from the battleship *Aurora* had struck; that was the only damage done by the bombardment.

It was now after three in the morning. On the Nevsky all the street-lights were again shining, the cannon gone, and the only signs of war were Red Guards and soldiers squatting around fires. The city was quiet – probably never so quiet in its history; on that night not a single hold-up occurred, not a single robbery.

But the City Duma Building was all illuminated. We mounted to the galleried Alexander Hall, hung with its great gold-framed, red-shrouded Imperial portraits. About a hundred people were grouped around the platform, where Skobeliev was speaking. He urged that the Committee of Public Safety be expanded, so as to unite all the anti-Bolshevik elements in one huge organisation to be called the Committee for Salvation of Country and Revolution. And as we looked on, the Committee for Salvation was formed – that Committee which was to develop into the most powerful enemy of the Bolsheviki, appearing, in the next week, sometimes under its own partisan name, and sometimes as the strictly non-partisan Committee of Public Safety . . .

Dan, Gotz, Avksentiev were there, some of the insurgent Soviet delegates, members of the Executive Committee of the Peasants' Soviets, old Prokopovich, and even members of the Council of the Republic – among whom were Vinaver and other Cadets. Lieber cried that the convention of the Soviets was not a legal convention, that the old Tsay-ee-kah was still in office . . . An appeal to the country was drafted.

We hailed a cab. 'Where to?' But when we said 'Smolny', the *izvozchik* shook his head. *'Niet!'* said he, 'there are devils . . . ' It was only after weary wandering that we found a driver willing to take us – and he wanted thirty roubles, and stopped two blocks away.

The windows of Smolny were still ablaze, motors came and went, and around the still-leaping fires the sentries huddled close, eagerly asking everybody the latest news. The corridors were full of hurrying men, hollow-eyed and dirty. In some of the committee-rooms people lay sleeping on the floor, their guns beside them. In spite of the seceding delegates, the hall of meetings was crowded with people roaring like the sea. As we came in, Kameniev was reading the list of arrested Ministers. The name of Tereshchenko was greeted with thunderous applause, shouts of satisfaction, laughter; Rutenberg came in for less; and at the mention of Palchinsky, a storm of hoots, angry cries, cheers burst forth . . . It was announced that Chudnovsky had been appointed Commissar of the Winter Palace.

Now occurred a dramatic interruption. A big peasant, his bearded face convulsed with rage, mounted the platform and pounded with his fist on the presidium table.

'We, Socialist Revolutionaries, insist on the immediate release of the Socialist Ministers arrested in the Winter Palace! Comrades! Do you know that four comrades who risked their lives and their freedom fighting against tyranny of the Tsar, have been flung into Peter-Paul prison – the historical tomb of Liberty?' In the uproar he pounded and yelled.

Another delegate climbed up beside him and pointed at the presidium. 'Are the representatives of the revolutionary masses going to sit here quietly while the *Okhrana* of the Bolsheviki tortures their leaders?'

Trotsky was gesturing for silence. 'These "comrades" who are now caught plotting the crushing of the Soviets with the adventurer Kerensky – is there any reason to handle them with gloves? After the 16th and 18th July they didn't use much ceremony with us!' With a triumphant ring in his voice he cried, 'Now that the *oborontsi* and the faint-hearted have gone, and the whole task of defending and saving the Revolution rests on our shoulders, it is particularly necessary to work – work – work! We have decided to die rather than give up!'

There followed him a Commissar from Tsarskoye Selo, panting and covered with the mud of his ride. 'The garrison of Tsarskoye Selo is on guard at the gates of Petrograd, ready to defend the Soviets and the Military Revolutionary Committee!' Wild cheers. 'The Cycle Corps sent from the front has arrived at Tsarskoye, and the soldiers are now with us; they recognise the power of the Soviets, the necessity of immediate transfer of land to the peasants and industrial control to the workers. The Fifth Battalion of Cyclists, stationed at Tsarskoye, is ours . . .'

Then the delegate of the Third Cycle Battalion. In the midst of delirious enthusiasm he told how the cycle corps had been ordered *three days before* from the south-west front to the 'defence of Petrograd'. They suspected, however, the meaning of the order; and at the station of Peredolsk were met by representatives of the Fifth Battalion from Tsarskoye. A joint meeting was held, and it was discovered that 'among the cyclists not a single man was found willing to shed the blood of his fathers, or to support a government of bourgeois and landowners!'

Kapelinsky, for the Mensheviki Internationalists, proposed to elect a special committee to find a peaceful solution to the civil war. 'There isn't any peaceful solution!' bellowed the crowd. 'Victory is the only solution!' The vote was overwhelmingly against, and the Mensheviki Internationalists left the Congress in a whirlwind of jocular insults. There was no longer any panic fear . . . Kameniev from the platform shouted after them, 'The Mensheviki Internationalists claimed "emergency" for the question of a "peaceful solution", but they always voted for suspension of the order of the day in favour of declarations of factions which wanted to leave the Congress. It is evident,' finished Kameniev, 'that the withdrawal of all these renegades was decided upon beforehand!'

The assembly decided to ignore the withdrawal of the factions, and proceed to the appeal to the workers, soldiers and peasants of all Russia.

TO WORKERS, SOLDIERS AND PEASANTS

The Second All-Russian Congress of Soviets of Workers' and Soldiers' Deputies has opened. It represents the great majority of the Soviets. There are also a number of Peasant deputies. Based upon the will of the great majority of the workers, soldiers and peasants, based upon the triumphant uprising of the Petrograd workmen and soldiers, the Congress assumes power.

The Provisional Government is deposed. Most of the members of the Provisional Government are already arrested.

The Soviet authority will at once propose an immediate democratic peace to all nations, and an immediate truce on all fronts. It will assure the free transfer of landlord, crown and monastery lands to the Land Committees, defend the soldiers' rights, enforcing a complete democratisation of the Army, establish workers' control over production, ensure the convocation of the Constituent Assembly at the proper date, take means to supply bread to the cities and articles of first necessity to the villages, and secure to all nationalities living in Russia a real right to independent existence.

The Congress resolves: that all local power shall be transferred to the Soviets of Workers', Soldiers' and Peasants' Deputies, which must enforce revolutionary order.

The Congress calls upon the soldiers in the trenches to be watchful and steadfast. The Congress of Soviets is sure that the revolutionary Army will know how to defend the Revolution against all attacks of Imperialism, until the new Government shall have brought about the conclusion of the democratic peace which it will directly propose to all nations. The new Government will take all necessary steps to secure everything needful to the revolutionary Army, by means of a determined policy of requisition and taxation of the propertied classes, and also to improve the situation of the soldiers' families.

The Kornilovitz-Kerensky, Kaledin, and others, are endeavouring to lead troops against Petrograd. Several regiments, deceived by Kerensky, have sided with the insurgent People.

Soldiers! Make active resistance to the Kornilovitz-Kerensky! Be on guard!

Railway men! Stop all troop-trains being sent by Kerensky against Petrograd!

Soldiers, Workers, Clerical employees! The destiny of the Revolution and democratic peace is in your hands!

Long live the Revolution!

> *The All-Russian Congress of Soviets of*
> *Workers' and Soldiers' Deputies.*
> *Delegates from the Peasants' Soviets*

It was exactly 5.17 a.m. when Krylenko, staggering with fatigue, climbed to the tribune with a telegram in his hand.

'Comrades! From the Northern Front. The Twelfth Army sends greetings to the Congress of Soviets, announcing the formation of a Military Revolutionary Committee which has taken over the command of the Northern Front!' Pandemonium, men weeping, embracing each other. 'General Chermissov has recognised the Committee – Commissar of the Provisional Government Voitinsky has resigned!'

So. Lenin and the Petrograd workers had decided on insurrection; the Petrograd Soviet had overthrown the Provisional Government, and thrust the *coup d'état* upon the Congress of Soviets. Now there was all great Russia to win – and then the world! Would Russia follow and rise? And the world – what of it? Would the peoples answer and rise, a red world-tide?

Although it was six in the morning, night was yet heavy and chill. There was only a faint unearthly pallor stealing over the silent streets, dimming the watch-fires, the shadow of a terrible dawn grey-rising over Russia . . .

Odds and Ends of Revolution

from *Six Red Months in Russia* by Louise Bryant

There were many little incidents I came across in Russia that while of themselves are of no particular importance, yet gathered together may give the reader more atmosphere than a deliberate attempt at a picture. Now that I am home again and must depend for information largely on the reports sent out by Berlin or Vienna and meant to prejudice us against Russia, or by those of my colleagues who make it a business to write sensational stories, it seems but fair that I should tell of my own experiences and those of my friends in this supposed violent Russia. It is a great pity that all our correspondents are not as well balanced and as intelligent as Mr Arthur Ransome, whose despatches appear in the London *Daily News*, New York *Times* and the *New Republic*. Mr Ransome is an Englishman who has lived in Russia for a number of years and knows his ground well, he writes as an observer and not for or against any party in power, and that seems to me the only reasonable conduct for a reporter. No more clear-headed comment on the political situation in Russia has been publicly made than that which appeared in his 'Letter to the American People' in which he said, 'Remember any non-Soviet government in Russia would be welcomed by Germany and, reciprocally, *could not but regard Germany as its protector. Remember that the revolutionary movement in Eastern Europe, no less than in the American and British navies, is an integral part of the Allied blocade of the Central Empires.*' If one goes to Russia and finds that the Soviet government is the expression of the people, it is quite necessary to say so, no matter what one may feel personally concerning the Soviet government.

If one expects to find nothing but bloodshed and one finds that there is much else, that one can go about in a fur coat without the least hindrance, that theatres, the ballet, movies and other more or less frivolous institutions still flourish, it may subdue the tone of one's tale, but it is highly necessary to note the fact. It is silly to defend the revolution by claiming there has been no bloodshed and it is just as silly to insist that the streets are running blood. We must use logic in deciding the truth of widely varying statements. There is, for example, that careful, scientific observer, Professor Albert Ross, who travelled 20,000 miles in Russia and 'never saw a blow struck' and 'instead of agitation and tumult, found habit still the lord of life', in comparison to a prejudiced reporter like Herman Bernstein who somehow managed to see everywhere the wildest confusion, murders and robberies in broad daylight, cars falling off the tracks, the dead unburied and so on *ad infinitum*. No one can predict what will happen before the problem of a new government is settled in Russia, but up to the present moment the actions of the mass, so long mistreated and suppressed and now suddenly given liberty, has been surprisingly gentle.

If all the things that are supposed to be done are really done, I think some of them would have happened to me. I am a woman, not noticeably old, and I often travelled alone in Russia. I did not have one unpleasant, ugly experience. I was followed by spies, I was in battles, but in the first instance I was treading on dangerous ground and in the second instance it was because I chose to be in the centre of action. A few days ago I read with some amazement about a brave reporter who travelled all the way from Petrograd to Moscow and back to Petrograd again. It was the first time that I realised it *was* a brave thing. I did it many times, when the train was packed with hungry soldiers. Once I tried to divide my sandwiches with one. He had been standing up in the aisle all night and looked weary and miserable. He refused the food. 'Eat it yourself, little comrade,' he said, 'it will be many hours before we reach the end of the journey.'

A San Francisco newspaper woman, who was in Russia when I was there and who travelled home with me, often remarked with indignation on the exaggerations of conditions in Russia. She tells an amusing tale about an encounter she had with a Cossack shortly after her arrival at the Astoria Hotel in Petrograd. She had been filled with tales of the brutality of Cossacks and so she was quite naturally alarmed one evening to have a tall, handsome Cossack rap sharply on her door. When she opened it, he stepped into the room, closed the door, made a bow and took from his pocket a green sash. Miss B – recognised it as her own. She realised at once that she must have dropped the sash going to or coming from dinner. She wanted to thank the Cossack, but she did not speak Russian and she did not speak German. It occurred to her that many Russians speak French. She had a smattering of French. '*Merci-pour-cette*,' she murmured, taking the sash and pointing to her waist. The Cossack came closer, touched her dress and smiled. 'Ah,' he remarked in perfect English. 'I understand, you do not wear corset.' Then he added politely: 'That is very interesting. Good-night, mademoiselle.' And making another formal little bow he went out.

Tales of violence of the most dastardly character were spread everywhere in Petrograd and produced, for a while, a mild hysteria in the foreign colonies. Hysteria always produces ludicrous situations. An Englishman managed to get aboard a crowded car one evening and was obliged to stand on the back platform. He was very nervous and imagined that one neatly dressed little man avoided his eyes. Reaching down for his watch, he found it missing. Just after that the little man got off the car. The Englishman followed quickly and the little man began to run. The Englishman finally caught him in a yard hiding behind a pile of wood. He said in a commanding voice: 'Watch! watch!' The little man promptly handed over a watch. Safe at home the Englishman found his own watch on his dresser where he had carelessly left it in the morning and a strange watch in his pocket. Very much upset by what he had done, he advertised in the papers and in due time the little man appeared. The Englishman began an elaborate apology; but the little man shut him off. 'It's quite all right,' he said, 'what worried me that night was that I was carrying 3000 rubles and I was afraid you would demand those.'

The Soviet government tried to do away with many outworn or difficult customs. They paused in the midst of civil war to change the calendar which up until 7 February was thirteen days behind the corresponding dates in all other countries.

And they abolished classes of society, planned people's theatres, reformed the marriage laws and even the spelling.

The old caste system enforced in Russia since the time of Peter the Great, in the middle of the eighteenth century, was never formally annulled until November 25, 1917. The decree reads as follows:

> All classes of society existing up to the present time in Russia and all divisions of citizens, all class distinctions and privileges, class organisations and institutions and also all civil grades are abolished.
>
> All ranks – nobleman, merchant, peasant; all titles – prince, count, etc., and denominations of civil grades (private, state and other councillors) are abolished and the only denomination established for all the people of Russia is that of *citizens of the Russian republic*.

Lunarcharsky, Minister of Education, is one of the most picturesque figures in Russia, and for years has been known as the Poet of the Revolution. He is an extremely cultured man and could very possibly have held the same office under any regime. He does not believe in mixing art and politics. It was his idea to turn the old palaces into people's museums, just as they are in France. It was his idea to organise the Union of Russian Artists. These artists, made up of all classes, rich and poor, have charge of the precious art treasures of the nation. They have decreed that no art objects over twenty-five years of age shall be taken out of the country.

Lunarcharsky is a fervid Bolshevik, but when he heard that the Kremlin was razed to the ground he took to his bed and resigned his position. He appeared at his post a few days later when he found that it was a false report.

Right in the middle of the fiercest fighting he got out a decree simplifying the spelling, dropping the superfluous letters out of the alphabet. And he established the School of Proletarian Drama. Like mushrooms, overnight almost, dozens of theatres came into being. Plays were given in factories, in barracks. And they chose good plays by the best authors – Gogol, Tolstoy, Shakespeare . . . There is so much romance in this whole proletarian movement, such magnificent and simple gestures, it is not surprising that it caught the imagination of an impressionable man like Lunarcharsky. Lunarcharsky and Professor Pokrovsky, who holds the chair of history in the University of Moscow, and is another ardent Bolshevik, are both true types of the old intelligentsia who have thrown in their lot with the Soviets.

As for the new marriage laws so widely discussed abroad and mis-understood by various indignant and righteous public characters: instance, Mrs Pankhurst's latest outburst against certain elements in Russia, in which she claimed that women over eighteen have been made public property and proved it by a decree published in a French newspaper. I was present at the meeting when the decree of the Soviets regarding marriage was passed and have the correct data. The decree which fell into the hands of Mrs Pankhurst was gotten out by persons of absolutely no authority, a little remote group of Anarchists in Odessa. There was no reason at all to get excited about it. Groups of Anarchists all over the world have held strange and outlandish opinions – there are some in America that do, but that doesn't prove theirs is the will of the American people.

According to the marriage laws passed early in January, nothing but civil marriages are recognised. Civil marriages do not mean common-law marriages, but those that have been legalised by process of law. All the contracting parties have to do is to go before the Department of Marriage and Divorce and register. No ceremony is necessary. Divorce is equally easy. Either or both of the parties can swear they find it impossible to live together any more, and they are legally free. If there are children the affair is a little more complicated and the one who has the most money, either the man or the woman, must give the most financial aid. The same decree declared all divorces pending in the churches to be null and void.

Declarations of marriage are not accepted from persons of close relationship or those in direct line. No bigamy is allowed. The age at which marriages are legalised in Great Russia is eighteen for the males and sixteen for the females. In the Trans-Caucasian countries the ages are lowered to sixteen and thirteen respectively.

Just before the vote was taken on this decree one soldier arose and said that he thought the government should limit the divorces to three. Another soldier got up and denounced him, saying: 'Why should we, who believe in freedom, tell any man how many times he should wed?' So the discussion was dropped. It is interesting to note that with marriage and divorce as easy to get as a cup of tea there has been no great rush to the bureau. With the removal of all kinds of suppression immorality notably lessens. Russia with all these lax laws can boast of less immorality than any country in the world.

One of the most puritanical acts of the Bolsheviki was to raid all the gambling houses, to confiscate the money and turn it over to the army and the poor. They went even further and posted notices giving the names of all persons who frequented these places.

Women's magazines are not popular in Russia, equality of the sexes is too settled a thing. The only interesting woman's magazine I came across was edited by Madame Samoilova and was contributed to solely by factory women. It has a circulation of twenty-five thousand. Children's magazines have reached a high stage of development. They publish one called *Our Magazine*. All the illustrations and stories and poems are the work of small children. Most of the great Russian artists are interested in it and some fascinating numbers have been produced. Civil war and the last German invasions, of course, have temporarily stopped all this delightful spirit of play.

Russians are not very happy away from their own country. Many of the rich Russians, no longer comfortable at home, now seek our shores or go to Sweden or Norway, France or England. But they are not content; they are not at all like the old exiles who fled away from the tyranny of the Tsar. Russia has a strong hold on all of her children. Eventually they will have to go back and work it all out together, as we did in our Civil War, as they did in France . . .

Pogroms among the Jews have almost ceased. This anti-Semitic feeling, like all race hatred, is artificial and has to be artificially stimulated. With the fall of the monarchy and the discrediting of the reactionaries, the Jews ceased to be segregated according to religion and became Russian citizens. Many of them did excellent work in reorganising. This was especially true of those exiles who had lived a long time in America and had become acquainted with American efficiency. William Shatoff became a member of the famous Military

Revolutionary Committee, organiser of the Printers' Union and a member of the Executive Committee of the Factory Shop Committee. He has lately been reported to be governor of Karkov. Voskoff became head of the Factory Shop Committee at Sestroretz, and was one of the chief inventors of that ingenious institution. Under the old regime one of the chief causes for pogroms was the crowding together of Jews in the Pale so that they were forced in self-defence to combine against the Gentiles. Now there is absolutely no occasion for these hideous performances and none can occur, except those invited by the Black Hundred who are working to put back a Tsar on the throne. The high place and the respect accorded Trotsky give evidence of the real feeling of the people.

Owing to the terrific scarcity of paper in Russia, ordinary postage stamps were used for kopecks, minus the glue.

The one-ruble notes were pasted together again and again until finally they became very rare. And there was absolutely no metal money. We had to use forty- and one hundred-ruble notes, and as the merchants had no change we had to establish credits. In the restaurants where we ate most frequently, we either gave them the money in advance or they trusted us.

When I read absurd stories of Russia I always am reminded of the experience of the *Evening Post*'s correspondent who was down the Volga, last summer, absorbing atmosphere. He said one afternoon he sat in a one-roomed peasant's hut jotting down impressions. He wrote: 'Rough wooden table and benches – large bowl in the centre of the table from which the whole family eats – woman and dirty baby . . . ' But just then he was interrupted, the baby put his feet on the table and the mother scolded it sharply. 'Remember you are not in America,' she said.

Arthur Ransome

Arthur Ransome (1884–1967) is best know as the author of the *Swallows and Amazons* series of children's books. In 1913, Ransome went to Russia with his first wife – from this trip came the book *Old Peter's Russian Tales*, a collection of folktales, and an enduring love for the country. During the First World War, Ransome became a foreign correspondent for the radical *Daily News* and, in 1917, he went back to Russia to cover the Revolution; he returned again in 1919 this time for the *(Manchester) Guardian*. His sympathies were with the Bolsheviks and he knew personally Lenin, Trotsky, Bukharin and Radek. When Ransome met her, Evgenia Shelepina, who later became his second wife, was Trotsky's personal secretary. While reporting on the Revolution, Ransome provided MI5 with information[19] – according to Bruce Lockhart, who defended Ransome from charges of being a Soviet spy, the latter was ' a sentimentalist who could always be relied on to champion the underdog, and a visionary whose imagination had been fired by the Revolution. He was on excellent terms with the Bolsheviks and frequently brought us information of the greatest value.' It should be added that one reason Lockhart came to Ransome's defence was because they shared a love of fishing – 'As an ardent fisherman, who had written some charming sketches on angling, he made a warm appeal to my sympathy, and I championed him resolutely against the secret-service idiots who later tried to denounce him as a Bolshevik agent.'

19 An MI5 note written in 1927 says: 'At a later stage in 1918 it appeared that Ransome was quite loyal and willing to help the British by giving information, and that the appearance of his working against us was due to his friendship with Bolshevik leaders, not by any means to any sympathy with their regime. It was decided to give him a chance to prove whether or not he was reliable.' British spy, double agent or Bolshevik spy – the jury is still out on Ransome.

The unique quality of *Six Weeks in Russia in 1919* comes from the fact that Ransome did not report on the Revolution through the filter of an ideology. The extracts show how fine a journalist Ransome was. 'An Ex-Capitalist' tells how workers and bosses keep to the old ways of doing things while satisfying the government officials' demands for change and taxes! And the interview with Bukharin is revealing – the latter gulps his tea down as he expounds tales of worldwide proletarian conquest. A heady brew for Ransome who listens and sips in silence.

An Ex-Capitalist

from *Six Weeks in Russia in 1919* by Arthur Ransome

13 February

I drank tea with an old acquaintance from the provinces, a Russian who, before the revolution, owned a leather-bag factory which worked in close connection with his uncle's tannery. He gave me a short history of events at home. The uncle had started with small capital, and during the war had made enough to buy outright the tannery in which he had had shares. The story of his adventures since the October Revolution is a very good illustration of the rough and ready way in which theory gets translated into practice. I am writing it, as nearly as possible, as it was told by the nephew.

During the first revolution, that is from March till October 1917, he fought hard against the workmen, and was one of the founders of a Soviet of factory owners, the object of which was to defeat the efforts of the workers' Soviets.[20] This, of course, was smashed by the October Revolution, and, 'Uncle, after being forced, as a property owner, to pay considerable contributions, watched the newspapers closely, realised that after the nationalisation of the banks resistance was hopeless, and resigned himself to do what he could not to lose his factory altogether.'

He called together all the workmen, and proposed that they should form an *artel* or co-operative society and take the factory into their

20 by agreeing upon lock-outs, etc.

own hands, each man contributing a thousand roubles towards the capital with which to run it. Of course the workmen had not got a thousand roubles apiece, 'so uncle offered to pay it in for them, on the understanding that they would eventually pay him back'. This was illegal, but the little town was a long way from the centre of things, and it seemed a good way out of the difficulty. He did not expect to get it back, but he hoped in this way to keep control of the tannery, which he wished to develop, having a paternal interest in it.

Things worked very well. They elected a committee of control. 'Uncle was elected president, I was elected vice-president, and there were three workmen. We are working on those lines to this day. They give uncle 1,500 roubles a month, me a thousand, and the bookkeeper a thousand. The only difficulty is that the men will treat uncle as the owner, and this may mean trouble if things go wrong. Uncle is forever telling them, "It's your factory, don't call me Master," and they reply, "Yes, it's our factory all right, but you are still Master, and that must be." '

Trouble came fast enough, with the tax levied on the propertied classes. The uncle, very wisely, had ceased to be a property owner. He had given up his house to the factory, and been allotted rooms in it, as president of the factory Soviet. He was therefore really unable to pay when the people from the District Soviet came to tell him that he had been assessed to pay a tax of sixty thousand roubles. He explained the position. The nephew was also present and joined in the argument, whereupon the tax-collectors consulted a bit of paper and retorted, 'A tax of twenty thousand has been assessed on you too. Be so good as to put your coat on.'

That meant arrest, and the nephew said he had five thousand roubles and would pay that, but could pay no more. Would that do?

'Very well,' said the tax-collector, 'fetch it.'

The nephew fetched it.

'And now put your coat on.'

'But you said it would be all right if I paid the five thousand!'

'That's the only way to deal with people like you. We recognise that your case is hard, and we dare say that you will get off. But the Soviet has told us to collect the whole tax or the people who refuse to pay it, and they have decreed that if we come back without one or the other, we shall go to prison ourselves. You can hardly expect us to go and sit in prison out of pity for you. So on with your coat and come along.'

They went, and at the militia headquarters were shut into a room with barred windows, where they were presently joined by most of the other rich men of the town, all in a rare state of indignation, and some of them very angry with the uncle, for taking things so quietly. 'Uncle was worrying about nothing in the world but the tannery and the leather-works, which he was afraid might get into difficulties now that both he and I were under lock and key.'

The plutocracy of the town being thus gathered in the little room at the militia-house, their wives came, timorously at first, and chattered through the windows. My informant, being unmarried, sent word to two or three of his friends, in order that he might not be the only one without someone to talk with outside. The noise was something prodigious, and the head of the militia finally ran out into the street and arrested one of the women, but was so discomfited when she removed her shawl and he recognised her as his hostess at a house where he had been billeted as a soldier that he hurriedly let her go. The extraordinary parliament between the rich men of the town and their wives and friends, like a crowd of hooded crows, chattering outside the window, continued until dark.

Next day the workmen from the tannery came to the militia-house and explained that the uncle had really ceased to be a member of the propertied classes, that he was necessary to them as president of their Soviet, and that they were willing to secure his release by paying half of the tax demanded from him out of the factory funds. The uncle got together thirty thousand, the factory contributed another thirty, and he was freed, being given a certificate that he had ceased to be an exploiter or a property owner, and would in future be subject only to such taxes as might be levied on the working population. The nephew was also freed, on the grounds that he was wanted at the leather-works.

I asked him how things were going on. He said, 'Fairly well, only Uncle keeps worrying because the men still call him "Master".'

Otherwise, he is very happy because he has persuaded the workmen to set aside a large proportion of the profits for developing the business and building a new wing to the tannery.'

'Do the men work?'

'Well,' he said, 'we thought that when the factory was in their own hands they would work better, but we do not think they do so, not noticeably, anyhow.'

'Do they work worse?'

'No, that is not noticeable either.'

I tried to get at his political views. Last summer he had told me that the Soviet government could not last more than another two or three months. He was then looking forward to its downfall. Now he did not like it any better, but he was very much afraid of war being brought into Russia, or rather of the further disorders which war would cause. He took a queer sort of pride in the way in which the territory of the Russian republic was gradually resuming its old frontiers. 'In the old days no one ever thought the Red Army would come to anything,' he said. 'You can't expect much from the government, but it does keep order, and I can do my work and rub along all right.' It was quite funny to hear him in one breath grumbling at the revolution and in the next anxiously asking whether I did not think they had weathered the storm, so that there would be no more disorders.

Knowing that in some country places there had been appalling excesses, I asked him how the Red Terror that followed the attempt on the life of Lenin had shown itself in their district. He laughed.

'We got off very cheaply,' he said. 'This is what happened. A certain rich merchant's widow had a fine house, with enormous stores of all kinds of things, fine knives and forks, and too many of everything. For instance, she had twenty-two samovars of all sizes and sorts. Typical merchant's house, so many tablecloths that they could not use them all if they lived to be a hundred. Well, one fine day, early last summer, she was told that her house was wanted and that she must clear out. For two days she ran hither and thither trying to get out of giving it up. Then she saw it was no good, and piled all those things, samovars and knives and forks and dinner services and tablecloths and overcoats (there were over a dozen fur overcoats) in

59

the garrets, which she closed and sealed, and got the president of the Soviet to come and put his seal also. In the end things were so friendly that he even put a sentinel there to see that the seal should not be broken. Then came the news from Petrograd and Moscow about the Red Terror, and the Soviet, after holding a meeting and deciding that it ought to do something, and being on too good terms with all of us to do anything very bad, suddenly remembered poor Maria Nicolaevna's garrets. They broke the seals and tumbled out all the kitchen things, knives, forks, plates, furniture, the twenty-two samovars and the overcoats, took them in carts to the Soviet and declared them national property. National property! And a week or two later there was a wedding of a daughter of one of the members of the Soviet, and somehow or other the knives and forks were on the table, and as for samovars, there were enough to make tea for a hundred.'

A Theorist of Revolution

from *Six Weeks in Russia in 1919* by Arthur Ransome

13 February

After yesterday's talk with a capitalist victim of the revolution, I am glad for the sake of contrast to set beside it a talk with one of the revolution's chief theorists. The leather-worker illustrated the revolution as it affects an individual. The revolutionary theorist was quite incapable of even considering his own or any other individual's interests and thought only in terms of enormous movements in which the experiences of an individual had only the significance of the adventures of one ant among a myriad. Bukharin, member of the old economic mission to Berlin, violent opponent of the Brest peace, editor of *Pravda*, author of many books on economics and revolution, indefatigable theorist, found me drinking tea at a table in the Metropole.

I had just bought a copy of a magazine which contained a map of the world, in which most of Europe was coloured red or pink for actual or potential revolution. I showed it to Bukharin and said, 'You cannot be surprised that people abroad talk of you as of the new Imperialists.'

Bukharin took the map and looked at it.

'Idiotism, rank idiotism!' he said. 'At the same time,' he added, 'I do think we have entered upon a period of revolution which may last fifty years before the revolution is at last victorious in all Europe and finally in all the world.'

Now, I have a stock theory which I am used to set before revolutionaries of all kinds, nearly always with interesting results. I tried it on Bukharin. I said: 'You people are always saying that there will be revolution in England. Has it not occurred to you that England is a factory and not a granary, so that in the event of revolution we should be immediately cut off from all food supplies? According to your own theories, English capital would unite with American in ensuring that within six weeks the revolution had nothing to eat. England is not a country like Russia, where you can feed yourselves somehow or other by simply walking to where there is food. Six weeks would see starvation and reaction in England. I am inclined to think that a revolution in England would do Russia more harm than good.'

Bukharin laughed. 'You old counter-revolutionary!' he said. 'That would be all true, but you must look further. You are right in one thing. If the revolution spreads in Europe, America will cut off food supplies. But by that time we shall be getting food from Siberia.'

'And is the poor Siberian railway to feed Russia, Germany and England?'

'Before then Pichon and his friends will have gone. There will be France to feed too. But you must not forget that there are the cornfields of Hungary and Romania. Once civil war ends in Europe, Europe can feed herself. With English and German engineering assistance we shall soon turn Russia into an effective grain supply for all the working men's republics of the Continent. But even then the task will be only beginning. The moment there is revolution in England, the English colonies will throw themselves eagerly into the arms of America. Then will come America's turn, and, finally, it is quite likely that we shall all have to combine to overthrow the last stronghold of capitalism in some South African bourgeois republic. I can well imagine,' he said, looking far away with his bright little eyes through the walls of the dark dining-room, 'that the working men's republics of Europe may have to have a colonial policy of an inverse kind. Just as now you conquer backward races in order to exploit them, so in the future you may have to conquer the colonists to take from them the means of exploitation. There is only one thing I am afraid of.'

'And what is that?'

'Sometimes I am afraid that the struggle will be so bitter and so long drawn out that the whole of European culture may be trampled under foot.'

I thought of my leather-worker of yesterday, one of thousands experiencing in their own persons the appalling discomforts, the turn over and revaluation of all established values that revolution, even without death and civil war, means to the ordinary man; and, being perhaps a little faint-hearted, I finished my tea in silence. Bukharin, after carelessly opening these colossal perspectives, drank his tea in one gulp, prodigiously sweetened with my saccharin, reminded me of his illness in the summer, when Radek scoured the town for sweets for him, curing him with no other medicine, and then hurried off, fastening his coat as he went, a queer little De Quincey of revolution, to disappear into the dusk, before, half running, half walking, as his way is, he reached the other end of the big dimly lit, smoke-filled dining-room.

Robert Bruce Lockhart

Robert Bruce Lockhart (1887–1970) was the author of the
international best-seller *Memoirs of a British Agent*, published in 1932.
His life was lived during times when diplomacy and spying were never
far from champagne, mistresses and Cuban cigars. A fluent speaker of
Russian, Bruce Lockhart was sent to Russia in 1918 with the official
brief of Head of Special Mission to the Soviet Government; his
unofficial role was to coordinate the activities of the British spies sent
by MI6 to bring about the overthrow of the Bolshevik government; to
fund this he was given diamonds worth £650! The plan was to use
disaffected Latvian troops who protected the Bolshevik government
to arrest the Bolshevik leadership at a Central Committee meeting to
be held on 28 August 1918. The Cheka became aware of the plot and
the British agents including Bruce Lockhart were taken to the Lubyanka
Prison in Moscow. *Pravda* declared Lockhart the main organiser of
the plot and wrote that he was ' . . . a diplomatic representative
organising murder and rebellion on the territory where he is
representative. This bandit in dinner jacket and gloves tries to hide
like a cat at large, under the shelter of international law and ethics. No,
Mr Lockhart, this will not save you. The workmen and poorer peasants
are not idiots enough to defend murderers, robbers and highwaymen.'
In October, the British government arranged for Lockhart to be
exchanged for captured Soviet officials, including Maxim Litvinov who
held in the UK on behalf of the Soviet government a position similar
to Lockhart's. At the plotters' trial, those still in Russia were condemned
to death; it was noted that Lockhart had fled and would be shot if ever
found on Soviet soil. On his debriefing on his return to London,
Lockhart found that his views were deemed by the Foreign Office to
be too sympathetic to the Bolsheviks. Lockhart left the Foreign Office
in 1922. One of his last acts in office was to protect his friend Arthur
Ransome from accusations of being a Bolshevik sympathiser. Lockhart

had been very friendly with Ransome in Moscow and, in fact, had helped Ransome bring Trotsky's secretary, Evgenia Shelepina, to England. During World War II, Lockhart was the Director-General of the Political Warfare Executive, coordinating British propaganda against the axis powers. After the war, he became the editor of the *London Evening Standard*'s Londoner's Diary – where his talents for gossip and flirtatious banter served him well.

'Perhaps it is for the Best'

from *Memoirs of a British Agent* by Bruce Lockhart

In one sense I was glad to be back in Moscow. I knew nearly every stone of its cobbled streets. It was almost my home. I had spent more years of my life inside its walls than in any other city in the world.

Yet it was a new Moscow that I found. Many of my old Russian and English friends had left. Chelnokoff had fled to the South. Lvoff was in hiding. Most of the fine houses of the rich merchants were occupied by Anarchists, whose outrages were even more daringly executed than in St Petersburg. The city, too, was abnormally gay with a gaiety that shocked me. The bourgeoisie was awaiting the Germans with impatience and was already celebrating in advance the hour of its relief. Cabarets flourished. There was even one in the Elite Hotel, which was now our headquarters. Prices were high, especially for champagne, but there seemed no lack of money among the guests, who nightly thronged the tables until the early hours.

I had, however, little time for moralising. Within twenty-four hours of my arrival I was plunged into a whirlpool of turbulent activity. I found Robins and his Red Cross Mission at the Elite, where between us we had secured comfortable suites with sitting-rooms and bathrooms. General Lavergne and a large French military mission had also made Moscow their headquarters. General Romei was there with a smaller Italian mission. Major Riggs represented American military interests. If there was not to be the wildest confusion of opinion, it was essential that we should coordinate our efforts.

I called on all the Allied representatives, and at Romei's suggestion we had a daily conference in my rooms, at which Lavergne, Romei, Riggs and myself were always present. Robins also attended frequently. We succeeded in establishing a remarkably smooth co-operation. Almost to the bitter end we were in complete agreement regarding policy. We were watching the situation from the inside, and we realised that without Bolshevik consent military intervention would result only in a civil war, which, without very large Allied forces, would be disastrous to our prestige. Intervention with Bolshevik consent was the policy which we sought to carry out, and within ten days of my arrival we passed a common resolution condemning Japanese intervention as futile. In self-defence I should make it plain that all our actions were influenced by the situation on the Western Front, where the great German March offensive was in full swing. We knew that the burning anxiety of the Allied High Command was to detach as many German soldiers from the West as possible. But taking every factor into consideration, we could not believe that this object could be attained by support of Alexeieff or Korniloff, who were at that time the forerunners of Denikin and Wrangel. These generals, like Skoropadsky, who was installed by the Germans as head of a White Government in Kieff, were not immediately interested in the war in the West. They may have been sincere in their desire to reconstitute an Eastern front against Germany, but, before they could do so, they had to deal with the Bolsheviks. Without strong foreign aid they were not powerful enough for this task. Outside the officer class – and it, too, was demoralised – they had no support in the country. Although we realised that the Bolsheviks would fight only if they were forced into war by German aggression, we were convinced that this situation might easily develop and that by a promise of support we might help to shape events in the form we desired. We could understand the resentment of the Allied Governments against the Bolsheviks. We could not follow their reasoning.

In this miniature Allied council Romei and I were independent. Romei reported direct to the Italian General Staff. He was not under the Italian Embassy. Since the departure of our own Embassy, I was alone. Lavergne, although the head of a military mission, was also military attaché. He was directly under the control of his Ambassador.

Riggs was in an even more subordinate position. And the Allied Ambassadors were at Vologda, a little provincial town, hundreds of miles away from the centre of events. It was as if three foreign Ambassadors were trying to advise their governments on an English cabinet crisis from a village in the Hebrides. They were, too, strangely ill-fitted for their task. Francis, the American Ambassador, was a charming old gentleman of nearly eighty – a banker from St Louis, who had left America for the first time to be plunged into the vortex of the revolution. Noulens, the French Ambassador, was also a new arrival. He was a professional politician, whose attitude was determined by the prevailing policy of his own Party in the French Chamber. Lavergne, too, had a Socialist on his staff – Captain Jacques Sadoul, the well-known French barrister and former Socialist deputy. Sadoul, who was on friendly terms with Trotsky, was a legacy of Albert Thomas. He served Lavergne well and faithfully, but to Noulens he was like a red rag to a bull. Politician mistrusted politician. There was continual friction. Noulens held up Sadoul's correspondence with Thomas, and in the end his obstinacy and his oppression drove the unfortunate Sadoul into throwing in his lot with the Bolsheviks. Torretta, the Italian chargé d'affaires, knew Russia well and spoke the language. His Russia, however, was the Russia of the old regime. Even had he wished to do so, he was morally incapable of standing up against the virile and aggressive Noulens. Moreover, he had had that desperate interview with Lutsky. There was not much to be hoped for from Torretta.

Vologda, even more than London and Paris, lived on the wildest anti-Bolshevik rumours. Rarely a day passed without Lavergne's being ordered by his Ambassador to investigate some new evidence of Bolshevik pro-Germanism. Romei and I roared with laughter when Lavergne asked us if we had heard anything of a German Control Commission in St Petersburg. At the head of it was Count Frederiks, the former Court Minister of the Tsar. It was working behind the scenes, but it had complete control over the Bolshevik Foreign Office, and not a single foreigner could leave Russia without its permission. 'Another telegram from Vologda!' we said. But Lavergne did not laugh. These little excitements of M. Noulens had to be taken seriously, and, while Lavergne made enquiries on his own, down would go Sadoul to Trotsky to register an official protest against the establishment of such a mission. Trotsky would look blank. Sometimes he would be angry. At other times he would laugh and offer to write out a bromide prescription to calm the nerves of their Excellencies of Vologda. His father had been a chemist, and his acquaintance with a drugstore had enriched his vocabulary. Lavergne had to take the tedious journey to Vologda fairly frequently. Romei and I went only once. Romei's comment was, 'If we had put all the Allied representatives there in a cauldron and stirred them up, not one drop of common sense would have come out of the whole boiling.'

The month of March 1918 was the period during which the Bolsheviks were most amenable to an understanding with the Allies. They were afraid of further German aggression. They had little confidence in their own future. They would have welcomed the assistance of Allied officers in training the new Red Army which Trotsky was now forming.

A coincidence of misfortune had provided us with a remarkable opportunity of supplying the Bolshevik War Minister with the Allied officers whom he required. A large French military mission, headed by General Berthelot, had just arrived in Moscow from Romania. Holding the view that it was better that the Red Army should be trained by Allied officers than by Germans, we proposed to Trotsky that he should make use of General Berthelot's services. The Red leader, who had already shown his goodwill by appointing a committee of Allied officers to advise him, accepted the proposal with alacrity. At the first meeting of this new committee, which was composed of General Romei, General Lavergne, Major Riggs and Captain Garstin, Trotsky made a formal request for help. General Lavergne accepted the invitation, and it was agreed that General Berthelot's mission should remain. We seemed to have secured a tactical advantage.

Two days later the whole scheme was wrecked. M. Noulens had intervened. General Lavergne was hauled over the coals for exceeding his powers, and General Berthelot and his staff of officers were ordered to return immediately to France. The barometer of Trotsky's temperament suffered a severe depression, and the *Izvestia* came out with a leading article declaring that 'only America had known how to treat the Bolsheviks decently and it was the Allies themselves who, by disregarding the wishes of the Russian people, were preventing the creation of a pro-Ally policy'.

If General Lavergne had his troubles, my own were just as great. With the help of our secret-service agents the British Government had discovered a new pro-German scare. According to the reports it had received, Siberia was teeming with German regiments composed of war prisoners, who had been armed by the Bolsheviks. They were in control of a vast area. Here was a further proof that the Bolsheviks were handing over all Russia to the enemy. I received a querulous telegram pointing out the difference between my reports and the actions of the Bolsheviks.

I referred the matter to my Allied colleagues in Moscow. Common sense told me that the story was a mare's nest. Siberia, however, was far away. We could not quote the evidence of our own eyes. Robins and I, therefore, went down to the Commissariat for War to interview Trotsky. His reply was unequivocal. It was no use his issuing a denial. We should not believe him. We must go – and see for ourselves. There and then he offered full facilities to anyone we liked to send to carry out an investigation on the spot.

Ill as I could spare him, I decided to send Hicks, my most reliable assistant. He left that night together with Captain Webster, an officer of the American Red Cross Mission. Trotsky carried out his promise. He gave to both officers a personal letter instructing the local Soviets to give them the fullest assistance. They were to be allowed to go anywhere and to see everything.

Hicks was not to return for six weeks. During that time he travelled all over Siberia, inspecting the prison camps and carrying out his investigations with great thoroughness. His telegrams to me contained some startling information, especially regarding Semenoff, the Cossack general, who behind the Chinese frontier was waging a brigand warfare against the Bolsheviks. But of armed German or Austrian war-prisoners in Siberia he had seen no trace.

I paraphrased his reports and ciphered them to the War Office.

The immediate reaction of London was a telegram from the War Office ordering Hicks to return to England at once. I was in a quandary. I had a shrewd idea why Hicks had been recalled. Moreover, I could not spare him. I had already more work than I could cope with, and no one on my staff was an expert cipherer. At the end of a long day's work I had to sit up late and take a hand in the ciphering myself. I sent a telegram to the Foreign Office pointing out my difficulties. At the same time I added that Hicks had been sent to Siberia on my responsibility and that, if he were to be recalled, there was no other course than for me to ask for my own recall. I received a private telegram from George Clerk, whose kindness and patience with my shortcomings I remember with gratitude, informing me that Hicks could remain.

The incident closed, but it did not increase my popularity in London. Within four days I received two alarming telegrams from my wife. The second ran as follows: 'Have fullest information. Do nothing rash. Am anxious about your future career. I understand your personal feelings but hope to see you soon. Would be better for you. Please acknowledge immediately, also wire about no sympathy here.'

The meaning was unmistakable. I knew from whom my wife had received her information. I was to throw in my hand and come home. I kept a stiff upper lip and my troubles to myself.

Quite apart from the major question of policy, life at this moment was full of minor excitements. There were perpetual pinpricks between the British and Russian Governments – pinpricks which served to confuse the real issue. We had small missions all over Russia, and each mission had a different policy. At the same time we were making every kind of protest against the Bolshevik confiscation of Allied property. The Bolsheviks retaliated by attacks on the war aims of the Allies and attempts to influence British Labour in their favour. Litvinoff, in particular, was making himself a nuisance in London. In this game of protest and counter-protest I was a sadly battered shuttle-cock between the battledores of the two Governments.

Nevertheless, there were rays of light in this murky situation. The German successes on the Western Front had alarmed the Bolsheviks. They were prepared to go so far as to agree to Allied intervention in the event of renewed aggression by the Germans. The atmosphere in Moscow at this stage may best be illustrated by the fact that in its account of the March fighting on the Western Front the Bolshevik press suppressed all German bulletins. The bourgeois press published them in full.

The Germans, too, seemed to be playing into our hands in Russia. Their attitude towards the Bolsheviks was truculent and overbearing. They made numerous protests against our presence at Murmansk, which we still occupied, and for form's sake the Bolshevik Foreign Office sent me several notes, which in accordance with its practice of so-called open diplomacy were published in the official press. I took the notes to Chicherin. 'What am I to do with them?' I asked. He replied that it would help if we would take the local Soviet into greater consideration. 'Otherwise,' he said cynically, 'you can put them in your wastepaper basket.'

Trotsky, although almost in despair over the attitude of the Allies, was no less friendly. 'Just when we are on the verge of going to war,' he said, 'the Allied governments do everything they can to help the Germans.' In the history of the Jews, which at that time was – not without reason – my bedside literature, I found the prayer of Bar Cochba, the Jewish 'Son of the Star', in his struggle against the Romans in AD 132. 'We pray Thee not to assist our enemies: us Thou needst not help.' The words were almost the same as those which Trotsky addressed to me daily.

It was at this time that Trotsky gave me one remarkable proof of his physical courage. I was talking to him in the Commissariat for War in the square behind the Cathedral of the Saviour. Suddenly, a startled assistant burst into the room in a state of panic. There was a large crowd of armed sailors outside. They had not been paid or their pay was insufficient. They wanted to see Trotsky. If he did not come, they would storm the place.

Trotsky rose at once, his eyes blazing, and went down into the square. I watched the scene from the window. He made no attempt to satisfy the sailors. Instead, he lashed them with a withering blast of invective. They were dogs totally unworthy of the Fleet, which had played such a glorious part in the Revolution. He would look into their complaints. If they were justified, they would be rectified. If not, he would brand them as traitors to the Revolution. In the meantime they were to go back to their barracks or he would disarm them and take away their privileges. The sailors slunk away like beaten curs, and Trotsky returned to me to resume his conversation where he had left off. Was Trotsky another Bar Cochba? At any rate he was very bellicose.

Lenin, whom Robins saw frequently, was more guarded, but he, too, was prepared to go a long way to secure the friendly co operation of the Allies.

Nor were the other Commissars behindhand in their evidence of friendliness. I had established smooth-working relations with Karachan, who, together with Chicherin and Radek, formed a kind of triumvirate at the Bolshevik Foreign Office. An Armenian, with dark, waving hair and a well-trimmed beard, he was the Adonis of the Bolshevik Party. His manners were perfect. He was an excellent judge of a cigar. I never saw him in a bad temper, and during the whole period of our contact, and even when I was being denounced as a spy and an assassin by his colleagues, I never heard an unpleasant word from his lips. This is not to imply that he was a saint. He had all the guile and craft of his race. Diplomacy was his proper sphere.

Radek, however, was our chief delight among the Commissars. A Jew, whose real name is Sobelsohn, he was in some respects a grotesque figure. A little man with a huge head, protruding ears, clean-shaven face (in those days he did not wear that awful fringe which now passes for a beard), with spectacles, and a large mouth with yellow, tobacco-stained teeth, from which a huge pipe or cigar was never absent, he was always dressed in a quaint drab-coloured Norfolk suit with knickers and leggings. He was a great friend of Ransome, the correspondent of the *Manchester Guardian*, and through Ransome we came to know him very well. Almost every day he would turn up in my rooms, an English cap stuck jauntily on his head, his pipe puffing fiercely, a bundle of books under his arm and a huge revolver strapped to his side. He looked like a cross between a professor and a bandit.

Of his intellectual brilliance, however, there was no doubt. He was the virtuoso of Bolshevik journalism, and his conversation was as sparkling as his leading articles. Ambassadors were his game and Foreign Ministers his butts. As Assistant Commissar for Foreign Affairs he received the Ambassadors and Ministers in the afternoon, and the next morning, under the thinly-disguised pseudonym of Viator, he attacked them in the *Izvestia*. He was a Puck full of malice and with a delicious sense of humour. He was the Bolshevik Lord Beaverbrook.

When the German Embassy arrived, he sorely tried the patience of the Kaiser's representatives. For, in those days, at any rate, this little man was violently anti-German. He had been at Brest-Litovsk, where he had taken an impish delight in puffing the smoke of his vile cheroot into General Hofmann's face. He had voted on every occasion against peace. Hot-headed and impulsive, he chafed under the restraint which from time to time had to be placed on his conduct by his more cautious colleagues. And, when he came to us and was rewarded with a half-pound tin of navy tobacco, he would air his grievances with scintillating abandon. His satirical shafts were aimed at all and sundry. He spared nobody – not even Lenin, and certainly not the Russians. When the peace was ratified, he exclaimed, almost in tears: 'My God, if we had had any other race but Russians behind us in this struggle, we should have upset the world.' He had a poor opinion of both Chicherin and Karachan. Chicherin was an old woman. Karachan he described as the *osel klassicheskoi krasoty* – the donkey of classical beauty. He was an amusing and entertaining comedian and, kept in proper check, the most dangerous propagandist that the Bolshevik movement has so far produced.

During our first two months in Moscow Robins and I enjoyed a privileged position. We had no difficulty in seeing the various Commissars. We were even allowed to be present at certain meetings of the Central Executive Committee. On one occasion we went to hear the debate on the new army. In those early days the Bolshevik Parliament held its meetings in the main restaurant of the Metropole Hotel, which had been renamed the 'First House of Soviets'. The deputies were seated in chairs set out in rows as for a concert. The various speakers spoke from the little pulpit from which formerly

Konchik, the leader of the orchestra, had stirred countless bourgeois souls with the sobbing of his violin. On this particular occasion the chief speaker was of course Trotsky. As a demagogic orator Trotsky is wonderfully effective until he loses his temper. He has a fine command of language, and the words stream from his mouth in a torrent, which never seems to abate. At its highest pitch his voice sounds almost like a hiss.

That night he was at his best. He was the man of action reporting the first progress of his great achievement – the creation of the Red Army. There was just sufficient opposition (in March and April there were still several Mensheviks in the Central Executive Committee) to rouse him to a great effort but not to make him lose his control, and he demolished his opponents with vigour and obvious relish. The enthusiasm he aroused was remarkable. His speech was like a declaration of war. He himself was an incarnation of belligerent hate.

Before the debate began, Robins and I were given tea and biscuits and were introduced to various Commissars whom we had not yet met: the mild-mannered and silky-tongued Lunacharsky; Bukharin, diminutive in size but a man of great personal courage and the only Bolshevik who was not afraid to criticise Lenin or to cross swords with him in a dialectical duel; Pokrovsky, the eminent Bolshevik historian; Krylenko, an epileptic degenerate, the future Public Prosecutor, and the most repulsive type I came across in all my connections with the Bolsheviks. These four men, together with Lenin and Chicherin, represented the purely Russian element in a hotch-potch of Jews, Georgians, Poles and other nationalities.

During the debate we sat at a side table with Radek and Gumberg, Robins's Jew-American assistant. Lenin came into the hall several times. He sat down and chatted with us for a few minutes. He was, as usual, in a good humour – indeed, I think of all the public figures I have met he possessed the most equable temperament – but he took no part in the debate. The only attention he paid to Trotsky's speech was to lower his voice slightly in his own conversation.

There were two other Commissars whom I met that night for the first time. One was Derjinsky, the head of the Cheka and a man of correct manners and quiet speech but without a ray of humour in his character. The most remarkable thing about him was his eyes. Deeply sunk, they blazed with a steady fire of fanaticism. They never twitched. His eyelids seemed paralysed. He had spent most of his life in Siberia and bore the traces of his exile on his face. I also shook hands with a strongly-built man with a sallow face, black moustache, heavy eyebrows, and black hair worn *en brosse*. I paid little attention to him. He himself said nothing. He did not seem of sufficient importance to include in my gallery of Bolshevik portraits. If he had been announced then to the assembled Party as the successor of Lenin, the delegates would have roared with laughter. The man was the Georgian Djugashvilli, known today to the whole world as Stalin, the man of steel.

Of these new acquaintances the one who made the deepest impression on me was Lunacharsky. A man of brilliant intellect and wide culture, he has been more successful than anyone in converting bourgeois intellectuals to Bolshevism or to tolerance of the Bolshevik regime. It was he who brought back Gorky to the Bolshevik fold, to which, perhaps without knowing it, he had always belonged. It was he, too, who insisted on the preservation of the bourgeois arts, who provided protection for the treasures of the Russian museums, and who is primarily responsible for the fact that today Moscow has still its opera, its ballet and its famous Art Theatre. It was also Lunacharsky, who, as an original adherent to the Orthodox Faith, started the 'Bolshevising' movement inside the Russian Church. A brilliant speaker, he advanced many original arguments in support of his revised religion. It was during that first year of Bolshevism that he made his famous speech in which he compared Lenin's persecution of the capitalists with Christ's expulsion of the money-lenders from the Temple, finishing with the startling peroration that 'if Christ were alive today, he would be a Bolshevik'.

Robins and I had one more thrilling experience during this period of March and April, 1918. One of Trotsky's first tasks as Commissar for War had been to rid Moscow of the Anarchist bands who were terrorising the city. At three in the early morning of 12 April he carried out a simultaneous raid on the twenty-six Anarchist nests. The venture was a complete success. After a desperate resistance the

Anarchists were evicted from the houses they had occupied, and all their machine guns, their rifles, their ammunition and their loot were captured. Over a hundred were killed in the fighting. Five hundred were arrested. Later in the day on Derjinsky's invitation, Robins and I made a tour of the different fighting areas. We were given a car and an armed escort. Our cicerone was Peters, Derjinsky's Lettish assistant and my future gaoler-in-chief.

The Anarchists had appropriated the finest houses in Moscow. On the Povarskaia, where the rich merchants lived, we entered house after house. The filth was indescribable. Broken bottles littered the floors, the magnificent ceilings were perforated with bullet-holes. Wine stains and human excrement blotched the Aubusson carpets. Priceless pictures had been slashed to strips. The dead still lay where they had fallen. They included officers in guards' uniform, students – young boys of twenty – and men who belonged obviously to the criminal class and whom the Revolution had released from prison. In the luxurious drawing-room of the House Gracheva, the Anarchists had been surprised in the middle of an orgy. The long table which had supported the feast had been overturned, and broken plates, glasses, champagne bottles, made unsavoury islands in a pool of blood and spilt wine. On the floor lay a young woman, face downwards. Peters turned her over. Her hair was dishevelled. She had been shot through the neck, and the blood had congealed in a sinister purple clump. She could not have been more than twenty. Peters shrugged his shoulders. 'Prostitutka,' he said. 'Perhaps it is for the best.'

It was an unforgettable scene. The Bolsheviks had taken their first step towards the establishment of discipline.

Edith Sollohub

Edith Sollohub (1886–1965) was the daughter of a Russian diplomat and professor, part of the group of Baltic Germans who served the Tsar and occupied a privileged position in Russian society. First published in 2009, her memoir, *The Russian Countess*, is an magical account of childhood – she dreamed of 'remaining a child as long as possible' – of hunting with her father on the family estates, of becoming engaged in 1906 to Count Alexander Sollohub, a friend from the skating rink and tennis court. Three sons are born during a happy eleven years as the couple live the elegant life of the upper classes of the times. All this ends with the Revolution; in September 1918, Count Alexander goes south to join the White Army: he is killed fighting the Bolsheviks later that year. Leaving her three sons in German-occupied Estonia, Edith returns alone to Petrograd to sell off possessions before they are nationalised or looted; by a stroke of luck, Ivan, her father's former coachman, has been appointed 'Communist Commandant' of her apartment building. To avoid her having to share her apartment with strangers, he suggests registering people who have recently died in the building as her tenants – her apartment really is filled with Dead Souls! In spring 1920, after assuming a Polish identity, Edith Sollohub is arrested and imprisoned. Freed after several weeks, she changes her identity papers once again and begins moving westwards, working as a language tutor, a violinist and an assistant Red Army nurse. Stationed in Volkovysk (now in Belarus), she deserts as the town is recaptured by the Polish Army in September 1920. Once again a free person she is reunited with her sons in Estonia. *The Russian Countess* ends with their arrival in Paris in October 1922. In this elegant memoir, Edith Sollohub recognises that her survival is due to many acts of kindness by individuals, some known, some unknown to her. Her subtle writing allows the reader to enter into and share these generous moments.

Alone in Petrograd

from *The Russian Countess* by Edith Sollohub

By Christmas it was clear to me that there was no way, at present, to escape. On Christmas Eve I was alone – and this was hard, very hard. Needless to say my thoughts wandered to the boys, as I wondered where they were and how they were, and thousands more questions. No news from them since the middle of November – it seemed very long. When and how could I join them? So many, many uncertainties and difficulties grew up around me day after day. The house empty, bleak, terribly silent – and everything so black around me. I looked wistfully at the furniture of the various rooms, at the Italian pictures on the walls, the Gobelins and Japanese tapestries. It had taken decades to assemble all these works of art. Already it was almost impossible to imagine that these rooms had been full of laughter, that music had sounded from the grand piano, and the rooms had been warm and well lit which now stood cold and dim and dusty.

It was December 24th by the newly reformed calendar, but the Russian Church did not recognise the new dates and therefore the celebration of Christmas in most churches was to take place thirteen days later. However, the Catholic churches were celebrating Christmas now and I decided to get a small tree and make my study look festive, with a few white wax candles on the tree and one silver star at its point.

A real winter gale was blowing as I left the house some time after 10 o'clock to go to the midnight mass at St Catherine's – the large Catholic church on the Nevsky. The streets were only dimly lit by one lantern here, another there – no carriages, no sleighs – here and there a hurrying dark figure disappearing rapidly in the darkness. It was a long walk, and I hurried through the snow hiding my face in my high fur collar and endeavouring to keep my hands warm. The less familiar streets looked even darker and certainly more terrifying; this was the right setting to remind me of all the cases of robbery, which were becoming very frequent at the time. It all looked so empty and dead – it was hard to believe that there were people behind these silent walls, behind the dark blank windows and dark entrance doors against which the snow had drifted high – as if no one ever went in or out of them.

Figures began to appear, hurrying in the same direction; I guessed they were also bound for the church – and I felt less lost in this black stillness. Figures going up the broad steps, stamping the snow off their felt boots, shaking it off their coats and caps – a few words of greeting between friends – Polish talk mostly, with here and there some other Slav language. The doors of the church swung open and bright light streamed out – light from many candles, from a Christmas tree – light spread over human faces tired and worn but full of inner quiet. Another world – a world of peace.

Midnight mass had begun, music, singing, people kneeling and praying in the flickering light of the candles. A crowd lost in prayer – prayer, a word despised now by the new rulers, a word laughed at and hated by them. For once I was happy in a crowd – happy because this crowd had forgotten selfish motives, put aside hatred and bitterness, and felt the presence of God in light and peace – in spite of all the evil, hatred and brutality outside.

Mass finished and the crowd moved reluctantly towards the doors. A gust of biting cold wind made us shrink into the protecting fur of coats and caps. Night everywhere, muffled steps in the soft snow, people streaming out of the church and hurrying away, first in groups and then singly – all were silent, as if afraid of losing the bit of light and happiness we had all just experienced.

In the lonely streets again a feeling of terror seized me. I saw two women who were going in the same direction on the other side of the street. I crossed and asked whether I might join them. A muffled voice, a vague answer – and I said thank you in Polish. 'Ah, you also come from the church?' was the quick reply. 'Yes, it was a beautiful mass,' I answered. One woman murmured something – the other nodded her head, covered by a thick shawl over a fur cap. 'Yes – a beautiful mass – how happy we are to have that still . . . ' We walked on in silence as far as my street corner. They had at least another half-hour's walk before them.

'God's blessing be with you – and happy Christmas,' said my companions, and they disappeared in the white darkness of the drifting snow. And so it was, that that Christmas Eve remains in my memory as a quaint contrast of dark and light – if I can put it in these simple words – of oppressing darkness and misery and of vivid light of inner simple faith. The light side of the picture prevails – why? I don't know – probably because inner joys last when dangers are forgotten.

I was alone in the apartment, except for Masha, my former maid, who had chosen to stay on. She had a friend in the neighbourhood, a black-whiskered chauffeur, and together they made a living out of selling illicit alcohol. (He supplied her with motor fuel and she distilled it in some primitive way to make an evil-smelling strong drink.) I was alone to handle all the new problems which cropped up daily, often urgent, often unexpected and without any precedent. Every day there were new Communist 'decrees' and ordinances. A 'Communist Commandant' was appointed for each apartment block. I knew that I must face an interview with the Commandant of our particular block, that I must control my real feelings and appear calm and indifferent in his presence. Thus, summoning up my courage and conscious that I must do all in my power to keep the flat as a home for my family, I went down the three flights of stairs and across the yard to the small door which had been pointed out to me as the dwelling of the new Communist House Commandant. I knocked at the door, which was immediately opened by a small boy of about twelve. In the back of the room sat an older man bent over a pair of boots that he was polishing vigorously.

'Could I speak to the House Commandant?' I asked the boy.

The man turned round abruptly, and I gazed in amazed recognition at the red beard and the beaming smile.

'Edinka! Countess! Yes, here I am now, times have changed . . . Yes, I am the Commandant . . . who would have thought it . . . ?' and he stood there with his broad smile and a strange sorrowful expression in the eyes of old Ivan, my father's former coachman.

I was so taken aback that I could not think what to say, how to address him. In a few words he told me how he had been appointed by the 'new authorities' because his daughter-in-law knew them all (I quickly noted this for it meant I must keep well out of the way of that daughter in-law) and he wound up by saying, 'Times have changed, no carriages to drive, no horses to care for, I can just as well be a Communist and be in the old house!'

This was an unexpected conclusion but Ivan was here, Ivan could not have changed much and I could talk to him – probably – without fear. Cautiously I sketched out the situation, avoided mentioning my husband, who as an officer would evidently be 'suspect' and it was better for us both that Ivan should know nothing. Ivan only nodded his head, ordered his boy to note down what I wanted and what my problems were, frowned and stroked his beard, repeating: 'We will see to it . . . we'll manage . . . ' But this first meeting was inevitably somewhat strained, and I left soon fearing some stranger might call. As Ivan opened the door for me, he patted my shoulder and smiling childishly from under his bushy eyebrows said swiftly, 'Come to me whenever you want help – I'll find the way to wriggle out!'

How relieved I felt and what an utterly unexpected surprise it had been to see old Ivan, in this exalted position, after all the years that I had lost sight of him. Was it too much to hope that he would remain, as before, a devoted old friend?

Ivan kept his word and helped me in a quiet, unnoticeable way throughout the year and a half that I remained in my house in Petrograd. He was really my 'guardian angel', helpful and clever in getting me on the right side of the 'new law'. And this he did even though he was illiterate; it was his little son who had to read out aloud every new decree, every new ordinance which came out, for the old man to ponder over. But by the time I had read the paper and came down to ask him for advice, Ivan had already found an answer to the new difficulties.

Thus, one morning, instructions were issued according to which so many square yards per head were allowed as living space, the surplus being put at the disposal of the municipal authorities. In many well-to-do houses of the residential quarters, entire families of factory workers or groups of soldiers and sailors had already been billeted upon the owners, who were strictly assigned their own small 'living space'.

Worried by this prospect, as three rooms only were occupied in my sixteen-room apartment, I went for advice to Ivan. He met me with a knowing smile which meant 'I know what you have come for!' and added that he had just worked out a plan for me and was already carrying it out. Pointing to his boy who was bending over house books and papers, Ivan said in a triumphant tone: 'You see – Vaska is copying out of the house-book the names of suitable people who died here in the course of the last few years. You see – I will say they are alive and all live in your house. They are registered now as your tenants. Will that do? . . . '

I was aghast, and then I understood. 'Dear Ivan, but this is marvellous! Shall I learn their names?'

'No, you go home and put some sort of bed in all the rooms, and then hang up here a skirt and there a pair of trousers – well, you know, to show someone lives there – and if the authorities turn up, I will talk to them, that will be better . . . '

As I thanked him effusively, he gave me one of his broad placid smiles and said: 'There it is, you'll have to live with the dead souls, they are not bad people – And very quiet tenants.'

They certainly were – and I never knew their names; but in putting down coats and trousers, hats and shoes, stray brushes and shawls near the bedsteads arranged all over the place, I pictured to myself who these dead souls were and soon imagined their names and occupations as I thanked them in my thoughts for the good turn they were doing me. True to his word, Ivan did all the necessary intro-ductions when Communist search parties appeared – searching for people hiding, for money, jewels, firearms, photographic cameras, and anything else which might momentarily interest the individuals making the search. Ivan walked in with the head of the search party and rattled off by heart name after name of my 'tenants' as he led the way from room to room. I was always referred to by Ivan as the 'hostess' and as being the wife of 'a very good Red Air Force man now in Moscow'. Once or twice I heard him explain the absence of my tenants, saying that several of them worked in a night shift in a factory, while others had been sent to the provinces on a government job, and someone was having a baby in hospital. So it all worked to perfection: the house search went its very unpleasant way, opening cupboards, pulling out drawers, unlocking boxes, throwing clothes out of cupboards to see whether weapons were hidden in the depths of these enormous old-fashioned linen and clothes cupboards. And after four or five hours of search they would walk away with a sleepy Ivan talking ponderously and patiently, unperturbed, unruffled, probably having to accompany the search party to some other part of the building. What I marvelled at was Ivan's readiness on the spot with suitable answers, something one would least expect from an elderly man who had spent his working life as a coachman and who could not even read or write.

*   *   *

Once I had accepted the unwelcome fact that escape from Petrograd would not be possible for some months (especially during the cold of the winter), I began to ask myself how I should occupy my time. There was work to be had in the state service, but many of us could not bring ourselves to work for a regime opposed to all our ideas of justice and right. The choice of independent occupations was very limited since all commercial and industrial activities had come under the complete control of the state, all enterprise was nationalised and any private trade was thus 'illegal'.

I was just turning these problems over in my mind when a friend, a Red Cross nurse, dropped in to ask me to help her bring back from the office some food supplies she had received there as payment in kind. She had a small sledge with her and we managed to get the heavy load of pumpkins safely home. The friend then insisted on my sharing her ration of rye bread 'in payment for the work' as she jokingly put it. Here was an idea – why not earn my living by driving a sledge, by joining the transportation business? It would suit me to perfection since it was an independent occupation, and it would leave me free to choose my own hours and places, and keep me free from too close contact with other people.

Without wasting any time, I sent a message to my old gamekeeper Ivan Ivanovich and a week later he came to my house with a nice, comfortable country sledge.

'Here is the sledge you ordered, my lady. It must be right – I polished the runners and they run easily,' he said, lifting the sledge for me to admire his work.

'It looks excellent, just what I wanted to have. Thank you so much, Ivan Ivanovich. It is a fine sledge and of birch wood too.'

'May I ask – is my lady going to use it at once? I might carry what is needed – I can take the evening train home.'

'No, thank you – it is not for today . . . it is for me to earn my living with,' and I saw his eyes getting round with astonishment. 'Well, I have no money left and am going to take luggage from the station to private addresses – something like a porter, you know?'

A look of dismay, then of deep sorrow came into his face. He looked away and murmured: 'So this is what we have come to . . . with their rights and liberties . . . shame on Russia.' Then turning to me quickly he said: 'Godspeed – and don't overwork yourself, my lady – I had better go now . . . '

He went, and the sledge was leaning against the wall with its smell of fresh birch wood, and I felt that Kamenka's friendly presence was still with me. The next morning I set out on my first attempt in the career I had chosen.

The Nikolayevsky railway station, which was the main station for the line connecting Petrograd with Moscow and central Russia, was the nearest to the centre of the town, so I walked off there cheerfully pulling my sledge behind me. In front of the station a small group of luggage drivers had already assembled. I must say, the looks of my new colleagues rather terrified me. They seemed to be the very outcasts of society – queer-looking individuals, men and half-grown boys, ragged, dirty, long-armed and slouching, growling abuse or shouting at each other, occasionally coming to blows. They made me think of a pack of snarling dogs. I am afraid I would not have withstood for long their evil side-glances in my direction, but at that moment a long-distance train came in and as the passengers with luggage appeared on the steps, the crowd I had been looking at rushed with howls and gesticulations at these victims of their professional appetite. I stood well out of the way, waiting for some lucky passenger who might be able to escape this attack.

From a side gate came a tall soldier with two boxes and a square basket and, catching sight of me, he beckoned me to approach. As I helped him tie the things on the sledge and asked him where they had to be taken, he looked at me attentively and, having given the address, added: 'I suppose I'll have to make use of the services of a member of the intelligentsia today,' and smiled ironically. I did not answer but was amused at this remark.

Off we went, the man striding along the pavement with his hands in the pockets of his short leather jacket, and I on the road – dragging the heavily laden sledge, walking as fast as I could in my thick felt boots. Fortunately my shooting coat was light, but the high grey astrakhan cap and the *bashlyk* on my shoulders soon felt much too warm. The way was long, a good walk across the town, through the snow lying deep in the unswept streets – and the pace was more a trot than a walk. I did my best to keep up with the man, and when we finally arrived at the given address the soldier paid me the fare I had asked and, smiling gently, added a three-rouble note 'for driving so fast'.

I was so proud of my first earnings – and of my first tip – that I took it easy for the rest of the day and allowed myself the luxury of a real dinner at an 'illegal' private restaurant. But I did not spend that three-rouble note which I kept as a souvenir of my first success in my new career.

However, not all excursions to the station in search of clients were as successful as my first experience. I remember one day standing over two hours in the blizzard, with snow drifting along the streets, whirling in clouds in the open square, the wind howling dismally and cutting my face. And no passenger appeared for me; the few who came were immediately snatched off by the rushing, gibbering crowd of luggage drivers – like dogs or monkeys dashing for a good morsel, I always thought.

Suddenly I felt a slap on my shoulder: 'Hello, youngster, will you undertake a job for me?' I turned round to see the face of an old man, long-bearded, black-eyed, crooked-nosed. He looked at me in some surprise. 'Oh, I thought you were a boy! However, the job may suit you anyhow. A little wood is to be driven from a shed across the yard to another place – that's all. Will you come? It's right here near the station.'

'All right, but what will you pay?' – I was trying to be businesslike.

'Don't worry, I'll be generous and the work is but a trifle, about one cubic metre of fuel wood to drag across. Ten roubles will be a real present for it.'

Tired of standing in the cold, I agreed and followed the old man. We reached his house in five minutes and here I found that first I was expected to climb into the loft, to throw the wood down from there, then to drag it across the yard and carry it upstairs to the third floor. And besides, there was much more than one cubic metre – all scattered about the loft. Still, I had agreed, it was late afternoon and no more long-distance trains would be coming in – and the work would warm me up. So I started with set teeth – I was dismally cold – and two hours later, when the large stack of wood was piled up in the stuffy entrance hall and kitchen of the old man's flat, I received my ten roubles and went off as hot as after two hours of tennis on a July afternoon.

I ran home, my soaked gloves freezing stiff now in the severe cold, and I laughed heartily at myself for having made such a bad bargain. The next day, however, I could scarcely move being so stiff . . . and the ten roubles were enough to buy just two buns!

Little by little my reputation as a transportation agent spread among friends – and strangers – and I received daily so many private orders that trips to the station in search of customers were no longer necessary. Some of the requests addressed to me were most amusing, while some were almost impossible. Once I was asked to move the entire contents of a four-roomed flat, including sideboards, chests-of-drawers, etc. Another time the widow of a well-known admiral asked me to take her boxes and luggage from her flat to that of some friends, insisting on my taking all the six or seven trunks at one time – so that she need pay for one trip only. It was physically impossible to do this, but I was so amused at her insistence – and parsimony – that I agreed to do so on the condition that she would sit on the top of these trunks, 'to keep the balance' as I explained to her. I could just picture myself with the dignified and very stiff old lady with highly powdered nose, a lorgnon in her right hand and a miniature portrait of her late husband adorning her jacket, perched on a pyramid of trunks on top of my small sledge. She finally refused my suggestion with sour politeness, having realised that I was joking.

Having become something of a specialist by now, I began to enjoy undertaking the delivery of 'illegal' goods such as typewriters, sewing machines, etc. In order not to be stopped by the Cheka I had to take certain precautions. Besides the usual ropes, I would take a rug or blanket, a big pillow and an iron kettle. I would then wrap up the typewriter so skilfully into a parcel with the pillow sticking out on one side and the kettle fixed on the top, that the bundle looked exactly like the luggage of any peasant woman going off on a journey by train. I was never stopped although I frequently passed Cheka agents combing the streets.

Transportation of food-stuffs was as a rule quite pleasant, as the fee was frequently paid in kind and this meant so much less hunting for food. However, I remember one journey of that kind which was most unpleasant – except for the comic side which made me laugh at the same time.

I had been asked to take some horse meat from a co-operative organisation to a school. On approaching the store rooms of the co-operative organisation I was struck by the most unpleasant smell of the place, and when the bags of horse meat were carried out and put on my sledge I knew where the smell came from. Nothing to be done, I thought, and as I am a horse myself and run in front of the sledge, the smell will not disturb me too much. Off I went quite cheerfully, though apprehensive of any payment in kind this time.

Scarcely had I come out into the street when a kind of forlorn fox terrier who was busy gnawing a bone by the roadside looked up, sniffed the air, abandoned his bone and dashed after me and my sledge. Poor little beast, I thought, one of those thousands of abandoned dogs roaming about the town – and I smiled at it with sympathy. But the smile was wasted on it – all its senses, all its attention, were concentrated in the black, shiny nose which sniffed and sniffed the air at the back of my sledge.

When I looked back again to see whether my companion had

abandoned me, I saw two black noses sniffing the air and I laughed at the funny picture they made. Evidently these two dogs awakened the interest of all the other dogs we met, and soon enough I found my sledge being followed and surrounded by a pack of the most disreputable looking dogs – all breeds, all colours, all sniffing violently, all lean and mangy. I began to be rather anxious about the safety of my load and the increasing snarls and growls made me think that sooner or later some of the more enterprising creatures would not be content with sniffing but would bring their teeth into action. I stopped once or twice and tried to scatter the crowd by swinging my spare rope in a circle round me. The effect was good as none of the dogs had spirit enough to oppose me – they were all so scared, so much beaten, so starved that they darted aside with their tails between their legs. But the moment I resumed my course, the whole pack reassembled and renewed its concert of sniffs and growls. We must have looked a very comic procession, but I was glad when I reached at last my destination with the load untouched. I felt sorry for the children, whose faces must have worn a different expression from the faces of the dogs when the time came for those children to sniff the dinner that I had brought them. But perhaps they were too hungry to care?

Some people, if they saw a horse falling in the streets, would wait for it to die, and then run to cut meat from the carcass. Such was the plight of horses in Petrograd in 1919. I like to believe that, in the same way that some people have a way with plants – 'green fingers' as it is called – so too there can be a mysterious connection between a human and an animal. I felt that I had a special way with animals; I felt it particularly as a child and later also as a married woman dealing with the horses and dogs in the country. My attention turned now towards the horses to be seen in the streets of Petrograd, whose sufferings were so hopeless and cruel. The city was by now on the brink of famine: we all had the smallest possible rations to live on, and even the black market in illegal goods was highly insufficient and badly organised. People, especially the old and the very young, walked like shadows in the streets and frequently some peasant woman would stop one, offering some coffee or lard hidden carefully under her apron, illegal goods carried across the border from Finland. All this was bad enough for humans, and few people had thoughts to spare for the half-starved horses who were falling like flies in the snow-covered streets of the town. Not a day passed without my having seen two or three collapsing in their shafts.

One day, unable to bear any longer the sight of a miserable animal endeavouring to rise to its feet, hampered by the harness and beaten pitilessly by his driver, I came up to the man and said to him with an assurance I had never had before: 'Let me raise the horse. I know the trick!' The man looked at me with an evil smile but stopped beating the horse, probably ready to rest. 'You? Lift the horse to its feet? – We'll see that! . . . ' and he laughed with a sneer.

I patted the horse's nose and spoke closely into its face, wondering what I could do to help it. The first thing was to loosen the strap across its back, and in spite of the man's sneers I managed to do this. By then the horse had quietened down, its breathing was more regular. I took it by the bridle and spoke soothingly close to its head, ashamed of the man hearing my endearing words. The horse seemed to understand, and as I began to lift the bridle and collar it gave a jerk and stood up on its knotted trembling legs. I tightened the strap, gave a final pat and walked away, leaving the man muttering something into his beard. A few seconds later I heard the regular, slow and muffled sound of my horse pulling the sledge with its load of wood.

This first attempt gave me courage and from then on I never hesitated to approach a horse in difficulties. I did not always succeed, but it was worth trying and often both horse and driver seemed grateful for my help. Once I saw a sledge with a heavy load trying to get up the raised approaches of a vaulted bridge over one of the canals. The snow had been driven into drifts along the sides, and the middle of the road was covered with a bluish surface of ice. The horse was a relatively well-fed beast – not all of its ribs were showing, and the sinews of its neck did not stand out too starkly. The man was shouting, swinging his short whip, but was also leaning his shoulder against the curved front of the sledge trying to help push it off the icy spot. The horse's legs could not grip the ice and were sliding apart in all directions. It looked hopeless, but why not try? As I approached, the man stopped shouting, the horse stood still. 'Can I help your horse?'

'You, miss? Your help won't be of much use,' answered the man, but with quite a friendly smile. 'Look at the ice. The horse sees it and he won't pull – he knows it's useless – he is a clever, cunning old horse, I know him.'

I was patting the flank, then the head of the animal, talking softly to it, and wondering what to do. Just then I noticed an axe stuck under the seat of the sledge.

'Let me have the axe . . . and pull the horse back, just a little . . . I'll roughen the ice. He is a clever horse, he'll understand that it's less slippery . . . let me try.'

A minute later I was chopping at the ice, making the surface irregular, the man looking on and smiling, the horse looking on too and perhaps smiling in his own way. People passing turned round and smiled, and I began to laugh about the picture myself.

'Now, this must do the trick. Come on, Vanka!' I said, throwing down the axe and pulling by the bridle. The horse put his feet hesitatingly on the roughened surface as if to test it, and having a more secure foothold he suddenly gave a pull and dragged the load up the short slope with the man running and shouting encouragement on one side and me clinging to the shaft on the other. We stopped on the top of the bridge, red, hot and pleased.

'Here is your axe,' I said, 'and really your Vanka is a clever one – how he tested his footing before he pulled. Good luck to you both!'

The man touched his cap. 'Goodbye, miss, and thank you. Vanka and I won't forget your help. Well, I certainly never expected it from a girl like you.'

It was a nice day full of smiles.

Konstantin Paustovsky

Konstantin Paustovsky (1892–1968) is best known for his six-volume autobiography, *Story of a Life*, which covers the turbulent years of World War 1, the rise of the Soviets, the Revolution of 1917 and the Civil War. The autobiography was written over a period of eighteen years from 1945 to 1963. A journalist by profession, Paustovsky's great talent is to get behind the headlines; he is always aware of a small detail that captures the flavour of the event he is describing. In 'Blockade', the extract that follows, the incident he writes about throws a new light on the events that took place in and around Odessa when Allied fleets were anchored in the outer harbours of Odessa and Sebastopol. In the winter of 1920–1, fraternisation took place between the Allied sailors and soldiers and Bolshevik workers which unsettled the Allied high command who saw clearly the appeal of Bolshevik ideas to their troops. The decision was swiftly taken to evacuate Odessa. This retreat did not prevent a large-scale mutiny in the French fleet which had sailed from Odessa to Sebastopol to halt the advancing Red Army. The mutiny which was only punished when the French ships returned to France made it very clear to the Allied commanders that they had to end their intervention in the Black Sea. Their soldiers and sailors had shown that they could not be relied on to continue the war against Soviet Russia. At the end of his life, Paustovsky edited literary collections that published writers suppressed during the Stalin years. He died in Moscow in 1968.

Blockade

from *Story of a Life: Years of Hope* by Konstantin Paustovsky
(translated by Manya Harari and Andrew Thomson)

Memory plays many unaccountable tricks on us.

Our recollection of great events can be as hazy as that of a grey uneventful day.

I have tried to avoid this danger in my writing, but I am not sure of having been completely successful. The image we retain of a period can be subjective even though it seems to us objective and accurate. How otherwise account for the fact that, amid all the resounding and amazing events of the time, our life in Odessa at the end of 1920 and in 1921 seems to me in retrospect a relatively peaceful interlude?

Odessa was deserted. Many workers had left with the first Red Army units – supply divisions and sailors' detachments – before the arrival of Denikin and the Interventionists. Many other people had fled to the country, to escape hunger and mobilisation by the Whites.

The city had hardly any important industries. The largest were the jute and canning factories and the dry docks. The town was dominated by the port and its poor – dockhands, tramps and layabouts – while the stubborn and resourceful middle class had dug in on the outskirts of the city.

During the Intervention, the workers who had stayed in Odessa gave every assistance to the Bolshevik underground.

The Bolsheviks were in hiding in the quarries, right inside the town. In spite of arrests and shootings, their daring was such that, even during the joint French and Denikin occupation, they held a regional Bolshevik conference, regularly published an underground paper, *Communist*, distributed leaflets, helped the printers and the telegraph and tramway workers who were on strike, blew up a train carrying supplies for the Interventionists, and ended by forming a war-revolutionary committee which provisionally took over the administration when the Soviet troops occupied Odessa.

Shortly before this, when already there was fighting in the suburbs, nine young underground Bolsheviks were caught by Denikin's counter-intelligence and shot after being horribly tortured. The account of these medieval tortures shook even the hardened population of Odessa.

I remember the stories about Ida Krasnoshchekina who bore the brunt of the fury of the Whites and showed unbelievable firmness and courage.

Before their death the prisoners wrote, in a letter to their free comrades: 'We are dying but we have triumphed.' These simple and moving words hold all the passion and boundless faith in victory which have become the hallmark of young revolutionaries.

By the end of Denikin's second occupation, there were even fewer workers left in the city. Nearly all the factories had shut down. The port was derelict. Life was at a standstill. Only black-marketeering raged like a bush fire.

In addition there was a wide rift in outlook between those who came from the north, and were living a third year of the Revolution, and the Odessans for whom the Revolution was only a few months old.

I, too, experienced not one but three October Revolutions – in 1917 in Moscow, in 1918 in Kiev and in 1920 in Odessa.

The Revolution not only brought with it to Odessa the new political and social structure developed in the north, it also brought new men, trained by the Revolution and alien to the mentality and practical experience of the average Odessan.

Resolute and ruthless men appeared (all referred to, indiscriminately, as 'Commissars') who knew exactly what to do to ensure the triumph of the revolutionary outlook in the minds of the mixed southern population, impulsive and prone to anarchical acts.

One reason for the seeming quiet of our life was the blockade which lasted through the winter of 1920 and all through 1921. For months the sea lay flat and lifeless, without a trace of smoke from a ship's funnel. At the same time, blocked railways, blown-up bridges, bandit gangs and the 'wild lands' which knew no law, cut Odessa off from the north.

All this accounts for the singularity of Odessa's way of life at that time.

I often woke up on the Professor's couch and listened to the night. This had become my favourite hobby.

The night gradually filled with silence. I listened to its approach, and the occasional faint sound of distant gunfire. It came from the French gunboat *La Scarpe* which regularly shelled Ochakov by night.

The heavy silence and the echoing shots were signs of the blockade. Until then I had only read the word in history books and in adventure stories as old as green oxide on bronze. Still, I had a fairly clear image of it.

'Blockade' meant an empty sea swept by fast patrol ships; naval guns trained on suburban vegetable gardens; extinct lighthouses; a blown-up transport ship showing the tip of its mast at the harbour entrance; a distant searchlight probing the milky way; and a feeling of lightness brought on by hunger.

If these were signs of blockade, the blockade of Odessa ran true to type. They all appeared in our daily life, though sometimes fantasy and reality were so mixed up that it was hard to tell one from the other.

In spite of hunger, the cold, damp lodge, the devastation and the loneliness (in spring Yasha went to live in town and I was left on my own) I was sometimes unaccountably filled with elation. I ascribed this to my youth; not that I was so young – I would soon be getting on for thirty – but I felt as though I were eighteen. I was against everything adult, positive and sensible – against it, though sometimes also scared of it like a schoolboy.

I reacted in this childish way to everything in Odessa, even to the long spring and summer of the blockade.

'Blockade' meant an empty sea – and the sea was empty, and I liked it.

It was as empty as in the days before man had even learned to build a raft. You could watch it for weeks and months on end from the Boulevard, and never see anything except the sun flashing on the ripples.

Occasionally a squadron of strange ships appeared on the horizon, advancing haughtily under taut white sails, but as they drew nearer they turned into menacing, snow-covered mountains that suddenly thundered and flashed lightning at the darkened waves.

The sea responded to the voices of the clouds, turning a single clap of thunder into a multitude of reverberating peals that shook the watery expanse in all directions.

Every time I had a day off I went to the country, usually to the far end of Great Fountain.

Spring had come. In the steppe along the sea, it was more touching than in places rich in vegetation – perhaps because here you noticed every separate flower that struggled from under the rusty rails of the disused tramline, and every butterfly that fluttered, drying its wings, in a stream of warm sea air.

That warm air rose in steady, powerful exhalations from the foot of the steep red cliffs, from the beaches which the war had cluttered up with the wreckage of steamers and sailing boats. It seemed even to come from the hull of the minesweeper *Xanthe*. Wrecked off the shore of Great Fountain, she had wedged herself into the rocks and no one had so much as tried to re-float her.

Water gurgled, flowing in and out of her cabins and holds, and crabs climbed confidently up her sides, to warm themselves on the riveted metal plates of her deck.

And still the sea remained a desert, and I think we would not have been surprised to catch sight of coloured Phoenician sails or of bronze prows of Greek triremes, long since vanished from the world.

The idea of ancient times goes with that of wilderness. There were, after all, very few people in the world in the days of the triremes, so the continents and seas were largely deserts.

But the reason why the Black Sea was a desert was partly the blockade, and partly that, when the Whites had fled from Odessa, they had taken with them the whole of the so-called merchant fleet – all the tugs, barges, cutters and passenger and cargo ships belonging to the Volunteer Navy, the Black Sea-Danube Company and the ROPIT (Russian Passenger and Cargo Line).

The fleet was taken to various Mediterranean ports where the White Command was selling it to foreign companies.

The Whites had taken privately owned ships as well, even the junk that had belonged to the notorious ship-owner Shay Kropotsky. Shay had been the laughing stock of all seafaring Odessa. His meanness and his double dealing were a legend. Not even a cab-driver would give him credit. Only down-and-outs agreed to serve on his ships, and they had literally to shake him for their pay – take him by the scruff of the neck and shake him. Shay had owned the antediluvian paddle-steamer *Turgenev* which plied between Odessa and Ackerman and which Katayev described in his *White Sail* – though some native Odessans dispute this and assert that the *Turgenev* belonged to the firm of Mishures and Sons.

Lost in the ships' graveyard among the rubbish dumps at the back of the oil port were a few old wrecks waiting to be broken up, among them, rusted through and through, the *Dimitry*, which had also belonged to Shay. That ship was very nearly to cost me my life.

The harbour was as calm as a lagoon. Its proper function lost, it had become a breeding pool for bullheads and mackerel, and the favourite resort of aged fishermen.

Oats (from spilled grain) and sweet-smelling yellow camomile grew on the breakwaters. The mooring posts were so thick with rust that you could scarcely see the name of the manufacturers – Bellino-Fenderikh – engraved on the metal.

The harbour watchmen grew vegetables on the wide piers.

Of all the countless vegetable plots I have seen, these were the most attractive. Amid the jungle of tomato plants each owner placed a packing case to serve as a seat. There you could sit and smoke and listen to conversation of every sort.

Every plot had its scarecrow to keep away the sparrows. They were made to look like tramps in sailors' vests and bell-bottoms made of sacking. A battered bowler hat or a child's quilted bonnet covered the rag-doll head. The bowler, set at a rakish angle, gave the scarecrow a shameless appearance, as though at any moment it might break into a *danse macabre* or a can-can.

The one that was most admired stood on watchman Dukonin's plot on Quarantine Pier. It represented a drunken skipper with a bottle of vodka in his hand and was known as 'Dukonin's George'. Instead of vodka the bottle was full of sea-water but the habitués of the port were none the less delighted with George and always gave a noisy welcome to his owner.

There were other anti-sparrow devices: little windmills with plywood sails that drummed on splinters of glass hanging on twine – this made a pleasant melodious tinkle which the sparrows could not abide; and coloured rags that fluttered from bamboo sticks, furling and unfurling in the wind.

All these things, including scarecrows in the port, were secondary signs of the blockade, which, for the time being, operated fairly peacefully (even the *La Scarpe* had moved away from the shore at the beginning of summer) and therefore encouraged the Odessans' peaceful and even idyllic pursuits.

The Polish war hadn't reached Odessa. All was quiet. Only rarely did the roar of gunfire come from the sea, always from the side of Ochakov and the Kinburn Spit. This happened when Vrangel's cruiser, *Kagul*, came from the Crimea and shelled the coast at random. Our shore batteries drove it off and it turned readily back with an air of mission accomplished – belching smoke, rolling mountains of shining spray and flying a faded St Andrew's flag from its gaff.

Another sign of the blockade was the fact that a tiny piece of hard maize-bread and ten apricots were considered a sufficient diet.

Working at Oprodkomgub, we knew the superhuman effort needed to supply the town at all; it was like feeding its thousands on the five loaves of the Gospel parable.

Bread was issued against ration cards – or, as they were called, 'by letters'. The cards were marked with all the letters of the alphabet from A to Z, each denoting the category to which the consumer belonged. The As got most, the Zs about enough to feed a canary. I belonged to category K.

I liked standing in the long queues. The life of a queue, though brief, was interesting. It lived on fantastic rumours, anecdotes, sudden panics, arguments and jokes about some bit of worldly wisdom someone had dropped, and of course on rows. The rows blew up as suddenly as rockets, but took a long time to die down, like dust after an explosion.

Fights were rare and took the harmless form of people pushing each other in the chest with the flat of the hand.

Once I witnessed a scene of which the verbal economy and effective pantomime deeply impressed me.

Standing in the queue was a short, old, Jewish gentleman in a dusty bowler and a worn black coat reaching to his ankles. Smiling and nodding benevolently, he observed the queue through unusually thick spectacles. Now and then he took out of his pocket a small black book with the Star of David embroidered in gold on the cover, read a page or two and returned the book to his pocket.

He must surely be a scholar, I thought, perhaps even a *tsaddic*, an old philosopher from Portofrank Street, his tranquil spirit unshaken, his kindliness unchilled and the smile in his blue, childlike eyes undimmed by the misfortunes of a lifetime.

Watching the queue from the side was a young man with an impudent air, a black skullcap and down-at-heel but shiny, canary-coloured shoes.

Leather shoes were a great rarity. People went about in clogs. The town echoed to their drumming. In the morning, when everyone was hurrying to work, if you shut your eyes you could imagine that the entire population of Odessa was dancing to castanets. So the queue watched the impudent young man's canary-coloured shoes with deep envy and admiring looks and sighs.

The young man was wondering how to jump the queue without causing a fuss and a row. He saw the old gentleman with the book, and naturally took him for the very embodiment of mildness and non-resistance to evil. Making up his mind, he skilfully inserted his shoulder between him and his neighbour in the queue and, pushing the old man, muttered casually: 'Excuse me.'

Still with the same smile, the old man bent his sharp little elbow, drew it back, took aim and, dealing the young man a swift and forceful blow in the chest, right under the heart, said politely: 'Not at all. Excuse *me*.'

The young man grunted and flew back, hitting an acacia tree. His cap fell off his head. He picked it up and walked away without looking back. Only at the corner did he turn and shake his fist at the old man, whimpering: 'Jailbird! Bandit!'

The queue was silent – its collective thought had not had time to crystallise and find expression – while the old man took his book out of his pocket and immersed himself in it, evidently searching for some

97

kernel of truth which he would later discuss with his cronies in the quiet of Portofrank Street.

If the weeks and months of the blockade could seem peaceful and untroubled to a part of the population, this was only because it knew nothing of what was happening outside the town. In reality, the situation was grim and the new administration had need of all its resourcefulness and self-reliance to cope with the danger to the city.

After the flight of Denikin's main army, a force of some seventy thousand of his officers and men had been left behind and were concentrated in the various German settlements – Liebenthal, Lustdorf, Marienthal – on the outskirts of the town.

The Allies relied on them to promote an uprising in Odessa, which they on their side would then support with artillery fire from their ships.

Apart from this, there were, at a conservative estimate, some two thousand bandits, burglars, thieves, forgers, fences and other shady characters living in the suburbs of Moldavanka, Bugayevka, Slobodka-Romanovka and Inner and Outer Mills. Their mood was uncertain. As a general rule, bandits tend to be hysterical and unstable in their attachments. No one could tell what they would do if there were an uprising.

There were very few Soviet troops in Odessa. Meanwhile an Allied squadron was already cruising offshore, having sent the Italian mine sweeper *Raccia* ahead on reconnaissance.

But an event took place which sharply changed the situation. The *Raccia* struck a mine when it was beam-on to the Great Fountain lighthouse. All we heard of it in town was the faint echo of an explosion at sea, which alarmed no one.

By order of the Provincial Committee, fishermen from Golden Shore, Great Fountain, the Kovalevsky estate and Lustdorf – all experienced and level-headed men – went out in their barges, picked up the survivors and the bodies of the dead, and brought them ashore before the squadron had had time to reach the scene of the shipwreck.

The bodies of the dead were taken to Odessa, and a signal was sent to the commander of the squadron. It informed him that the city was grieved by the disaster and wished to assume the burden of a solemn funeral for the gallant victims, and it invited him to attend the ceremony and to send sailors' units to form a guard of honour.

The admiral agreed – there was not much else he could do.

Next morning, unarmed Soviet soldiers and sailors formed up all along the way from the port to Kulikov Field where a common grave had been dug. Mourning flags hung on all the houses, and the way was strewn with flowers and branches of thuya.

A hundred thousand Odessans – almost the entire population at that time – attended the funeral.

Dock workers carried the coffins. After them came sunburnt Italian sailors, rifles pointing down.

The bands of the foreign ships played, as well as the combined Odessa band. Ours did not disgrace itself, and the heart-rending strains of Chopin's Funeral March made the sensitive Odessan women wipe away their tears with their shawls.

The bells tolled mournfully from New Athos Church. The roofs were black with watching crowds.

Speeches were made at the grave. The Italians listened and presented arms. Then the distant sound of a salvo at sea mingled with that of a volley of rifle-shots on Kulikov Field. A pyramid of flowers rose over the grave.

After the funeral the foreign sailors were given supper at the former Frankoni café. Comrade Agin dipped into the sacred food reserve for the occasion, and used up most of it.

After such a funeral, how could there be any question of bombardment or of uprising? The sailors of the foreign ships would not have stood for it. They were grateful for the honour paid their fallen comrades and for the warmth of their own reception.

The old admiral (who looked like Giuseppe Verdi) decided that the game was up and ordered the squadron back to Constantinople. It vanished into the gloom of the evening, leaving Denikin's officers to their fate.

By allowing armed foreign sailors into the town, the Provincial Committee had taken a huge risk, but it was an honourable one, and the funeral proved a bloodless victory over the Interventionists.

Soon afterwards, the blockade was lifted, and the first bargeloads of apricots sailed into the port from Kherson.

Then, on a cloudless morning, two Turkish feluccas from Skutari, colourful as a picture, tied in at the Quarantine Pier – they were the first cargo ships to reach Odessa.

Next day the papers announced triumphantly that two feluccas had arrived from Turkey with a kilo of flints for cigarette lighters, glass beads, gilt bracelets and a small barrel of olives.

What mattered, of course, was not the kilo of flints, but the fact that the sea was free again. This seemed to me suddenly to alter its appearance: gay under a gusty wind, it shone with such snow-white spray as I had never seen on it before.

Any day now, we would see, in the blue distance to the south-west, the mighty hulls and yellow funnels and strange flags of ocean-going craft, and would hear whistles and rumbling anchor-chains – a sound which promised those who sailed the seas a well-earned rest in a beautiful though foreign land.

Dmitriy Furmanov
&
Mikhail Sholokhov

The literary ideology most associated with post-revolutionary Russia is Socialist Realism. Although not formulated as a doctrine until the 1930s, Socialist Realism has a pedigree that goes back to Lenin's 1905 article 'Party Organisation and Party Literature'. In the 1920s, Socialist Realism was one of many competing literary ideologies but with Stalin's support it became the dominant one.

The first use of the term is attributed to Ivan Gronsky, at the time editor of *Izvestia* and Stalin's unofficial commissar for literature: 'The basic demand that we make on the writer is: write the truth, portray truthfully our reality that is in itself dialectic. Therefore the basic method of Soviet Literature is the method of Socialist Realism.'

By the time of the First Writers' Congress in 1934, Socialist Realism, like all correct ideas, had become the invention of Stalin. Zhdanov made this clear:

> 'Comrade Stalin has called our writers engineers of human souls. What does this mean? What duties does the title impose on you? [. . .]
>
>   The truthfulness and historical concreteness of the artistic portrayal should be combined with the ideological remoulding and education of the working people in the spirit of socialism. This method in literature and in literary criticism is what we call the method of Socialist Realism.'[21]

In fact, writers had been writing according to Socialist Realist

---

21 quoted in *The Soviet Writers' Congress, 1934*, Lawrence and Wishart, London, 1977, p. 21

principles since immediately after the Revolution and it is no surprise that the first classics of Socialist Realism are set in the Civil War – Furmanov's *Chapaev* and Serafimovich's *The Iron Flood*. A period when dashing acts of individual heroism (e.g. a lightning charge through the White cavalry) had not yet given way to the more sober, collective tasks of rebuilding the economy – another Socialist Realist classic is Gladkov's *Cement* which celebrates the victory of the masses over obstructive bureaucrats in a cement factory.

Dmitriy Furmanov (1891–1926) was a nurse in the First World War. He joined the Bolsheviks in 1918 and went to fight with Chapaev, the celebrated commander of the Red Army's 25th Rifle Division. In September 1919, the division's headquarters near Lbishchensk (now Chapaev) in Kazakhstan was surrounded and Chapaev drowned in the Ural River trying to swim to safety. Furmanov in the meantime had been transferred to Tashkent. He returned to Moscow in 1921 and was made an editor in the State Publishing House. Published in 1923, *Chapaev* was an instant success, reprinted many times and made, in 1934, into a very successful film.

Originally a non-fiction memoir, *Chapaev* is a brilliant epic that captures the dilemma facing Klychkov, the party commissar. He must rein in Chapaev's individualism and lack of class consciousness – he has no idea how a collective farm works! – while at the same time not undermining the latter's charismatic power over his soldiers – he knows how to spur them on to victory.

Mikhail Sholokhov (1905–1984) was awarded the Nobel Prize for Literature in 1965; he best known work is *And Quietly Flows the Don* (aka *The Quiet Don*). His whole life, apart for short stays in Moscow, was spent in the Don region. In 1926, he moved to Veshenskaya where he lived until his death. That year he published his first collection of stories, *Tales from the Don*, which includes 'Family Man'. It is a devastating story about the demands a civil war can make on an individual – in this case infanticide. One of the few Soviet writers to write sympathetically about the peasantry, Sholokhov played an active part in the 1930s collectivisation programme of the Don Valley. Befriended by Stalin, Sholokhov became part of the Soviet literary establishment.

Chapaev

from *Chapaev* by Dmitriy Furmanov
(translated by Nicholas Luker)

Early in the morning, about five or six o'clock, somebody knocked firmly on Fedor's door. He opened it and saw a stranger.

'Good-day. I am Chapaev!'

Every vestige of drowsiness vanished from Fedor's face. He was wide awake at once. He threw a quick glance at Chapaev and held out his hand – the gesture was somehow too hasty though he tried hard to keep calm.

'Klychkov's my name. When did you arrive?'

'Just come down from the station. My men are there. I have sent horses for them.'

Fedor was examining him rapidly with piercing eyes; he was anxious to memorise every lineament of his face, to see and understand what kind of man he was.

'An ordinary, spare man, of middle height and not particularly powerful build, with delicate, almost feminine hands; his thin, dark hair clings in wisps to his forehead; his nose is thin and sensitive; his eyebrows are narrow, they look as if they had been traced with a pencil; his lips are thin, his teeth clean and shining, his chin clean-shaven, his moustaches bushy like those of a noncom. His eyes . . . they are light blue, almost green – quick, intelligent, unblinking. His face is pale, but fresh, without spots or wrinkles. He wore a field-grey jacket, navy blue trousers, and top boots of deer-hide with the fur on. His cap had a red band and he held it in his hand. There was a bandolier slung around his shoulders and a revolver hung on his right hip. He threw down his silver-hilted sword and long-skirted green coat on the table.'

That is what Fedor wrote in his diary on the evening of the day he first saw Chapaev.

Everyone wants a drink of tea after a journey. But Chapaev declined the offer of tea and did not even sit down. He sent a runner to the brigade commander to tell him to go at once to headquarters where he, Chapaev, would join him shortly. Soon the men who had come with him arrived, and noisily invaded Fedor's room, depositing their baggage in all four corners; they littered the tables, chairs and windowsills with their caps, gloves and bandoliers, laid down their revolvers anywhere; some of them unslung the white, bottle-necked bombs they were carrying and shoved them recklessly down on the heap of caps and gloves. Their tanned faces looked stern and courageous, their hair was rough and thick, their gestures and speech rude, free, uncouth, but impressive and convincing. Some had such a strange way of speaking that you might have thought they were simply swearing all the time; they questioned you in sharp, barking tones, and when questioned themselves, answered gruffly, as if in a rage. They shoved and threw things about anyhow. The whole house re-echoed with their loud talk; they very quickly invaded all the rooms with the exception of Ezhikov's, which he had locked from the inside.

They had not been there two minutes before one of them was sprawling on Fedor's untidy bed, with his legs against the wall, lighting a cigarette and deliberately flicking the ash on Klychkov's suitcase, which stood beside the bed. Another leaned with all his weight against the rickety washstand, breaking one of its legs, so that it keeled over on its side. Another smashed the window pane with the butt-end of his revolver, yet another threw his stinking sheepskin on the bread that had been left on the table, so that it smelt loathsome when you came to eat it. With this horde, and as if heralding its coming, a gust of strong, noisy talk had come bursting into the room. It went on unceasingly, without changing in volume – a ceaseless din of shouting voices. That was the ordinary manner of speaking among these free people of the steppe. It was impossible to make out who was chief and who subordinate among them. Nothing to distinguish the one from the other; they all behaved in the same forceful way, all had equally rough manners – the same colourful assertive speech, primitive and wholesome as the steppe itself. They formed a united family! But there were no outward indications of any affection between one member and another, no vestige of considerateness, no bothering or caring about one another, even in the most trifling matters. And all the same you could see and feel that they were all indissolubly linked together. The bond between these men had been cemented by the perils of nomadic warfaring, by their courage, personal hardihood, contempt for privations and dangers, and by true, deep-rooted solidarity, unwavering loyalty to one another, by their arduous and many-coloured life, lived together, shoulder to shoulder, in the ranks and on the battlefield.

Chapaev stood out among them. He had already acquired something of culture, looked less uncouth than his companions, behaved differently; he was like a proud horse of the steppe who voluntarily obeyed the bridle, and he was treated as one apart from and above the rest. Have you ever watched a fly crawling across the window-pane? It crawls boldly, bumps into other flies, climbs over them or gets entangled with them, and it does not seem to mind, it disentangles itself and crawls on. But if it happens to blunder into a wasp, it starts away in terror and flies off. So it was with the followers of Chapaev. While they were among themselves, they felt entirely at their ease, could say anything that came into their heads, bang one another with their caps or spoons, kick, splash hot water out of glasses into one another's faces, but the moment they crossed Chapaev's path, such liberties ceased. Not from fear, not from a feeling of inferiority, but because of the respect he commanded.

'He's one of us, to be sure, but he's something out of the ordinary; you can't put him quite on a level with us.'

You could feel this subtle distinction all the time, however freely the men behaved in his presence, however much noise they made, however heartily they swore. The moment they came in contact with him, their demeanour changed at once. Such was the love and respect in which they held him.

'Petka, off with you to the commandant's office!' ordered Chapaev.

Petka jumped up at once and ran off on his errand without a word. He was a thin little man, who acted as a sort of 'aide-de-camp'.

'I start in two hours, mind the horses are ready on time. Send the cavalry horses first, then a sledge for Popov and myself. Be quick! Popov, you are coming with me.'

Chapaev nodded authoritatively to a sallow-faced round-shouldered fellow of about thirty-five. He had kind, laughing grey eyes and a voice that croaked like a crow's. He was powerful and thick-set, but he had a strangely lithe and sinuous way of moving, like a girl.

Popov had evidently been telling some funny story to his comrades, but as soon as he heard Chapaev's order, the expression of his face immediately sobered, the twinkle died out of his grey eyes, like a flame that is quenched. He looked Chapaev straight in the face and his whole attitude seemed to say: 'At your orders!'

Chapaev continued: 'That's all. Wait, the commissar is coming too, and with him three mounted men. The rest will follow us to Talovka. Ride easy, spare the horses. Be there early in the evening!'

'Listen, you . . . ' Chapaev turned round, then realised that the man he wanted was not there. 'Yes, I sent him away . . . Well, Kochnev, you look in at headquarters. Tell me if they are all there.'

Kochnev left the room. Fedor thought he looked like a professional athlete, he was so swift, light, supple and sinewy. He wore a short quilted jacket, with short sleeves, a very small cap pressed on the back of his head, boots and puttees. He could not have been thirty, but his forehead was already furrowed with wrinkles. His eyes were light grey and had a cunning twinkle in them; he had a way of tweaking his broad nose with his finger and assuming a mischievous air. He had the teeth of a wolf, white and very strong; and when he laughed he bared them ferociously as though he were going to tear people to shreds.

Then there was Chekov. He had extraordinary bushy red eyebrows, a formidable moustache, a powerful jaw and high mongolian cheek bones. His thick lower lip hung down like a blood-soaked leech, his jaw protruded like a square block of cast iron, and above it, sprouting fungus-like, was his pasty-coloured nose, covered with beads of sweat. From under his shaggy eyebrows his eyes glowed like live coals. His shoulders were square and broad, his hands heavy and strong like the paws of a bear. He must have been a little over forty years of age.

Ilya Tetkin, a Red Army man with a fine record of service, a house-painter by profession, was busying himself with kettles, cutting bread into big chunks, shouting wisecracks back and forth and laughing uproariously at his own jokes. He was very good-natured, noisy, popular with the other men, fond of songs and games, always performing all sorts of amusing antics. In years he must have been a little older than Petka – twenty-six or twenty-eight.

Next to Tetkin, silently and patiently waiting to get his share of bread, stood Vikhor, a daredevil cavalryman, the dashing commander of the mounted scouts. The little finger of his left hand was missing and this fact provided food for endless jokes.

'Give him a poke with your little finger, Vikhor, he's getting fresh!'

'Show us your little finger, mate, and I'll give you a cigar.'

'Hi, you with the nine hoofs!'

Vikhor was not easily roused; it was his nature to be calm, and he remained calm, even in battle. He was a living proof of the fact that great things can be done silently!

The one who threw his weight about most, and who swore and shouted the loudest, was Shmarin. He wore a tanned sheepskin coat, knee-high felt boots (he was a sick man and always suffered from the cold), had a croaking voice like Popov's, black eyes and black hair. He was about fifty, the oldest man there.

The young driver, Averka, had come in with the others. He stood leaning on his long-handled whip, eagerly watching the preparations for eating and tea-drinking. His face was purple, his nose the shape of an onion, his eyes watery from the cold, his lips cracked. A scarf, which he wore day and night, was wound around his neck.

Then there was Leksey, the orderly, an old acquaintance of Chapaev and a clever, resourceful fellow. When anything was wanted, it was always Leksey who was commissioned to get it, and he would never return empty-handed. When food was short, when a saddle strap or a linchpin was missing or when some home-made medicine was badly needed, everyone turned instinctively to Leksey for aid. He was the handy man of the company.

What a set!

Every face unique, worthy of an epic poem. No two fellows alike among the whole crowd, and yet they all dovetailed together perfectly, like a piece of masonry. Theirs was a rocklike unity. They formed one common family, and what a glorious family it was!

Kochnev entered.

'The brigade commander is at headquarters.'

All were astir. All eyes were riveted on Chapaev's face.

'Let's go!'

He gave a nod to Popov, crooked his finger in the direction of Shmarin and Vikhor. Spurs jingled, heavy boots with iron rimmed heels clattered on the floor. Fedor went out with the rest in a somewhat perplexed frame of mind. He thought that Chapaev was paying too little attention to him, putting him on a level with his 'following'. Somewhere, in the depths of his soul, lurked an unpleasant feeling. He remembered that there was a tale about Chapaev having horsewhipped a commissar. It was in 1918, in the heat of battle, when the enemy had surrounded our troops and the commissar was scared and did not know what to do. The memory of this incident rankled. Fedor tried to persuade himself that the story was exaggerated, perhaps even invented, but all the same, it might be true. Of course times were different then, and Chapaev himself was different, and perhaps the commissar was no good. Fedor was walking behind the others, and this fact made him feel slighted.

Chapaev greeted the brigade commander hastily and abruptly, looking away from him as he spoke; whereas the commander was all amiability; he clicked his spurs, and straightened himself up, as if reporting for duty. He had heard much about Chapaev and most of what he had heard was about his bad side, his reckless hooliganism; at best, he knew him as a crank, had not heard of his real feats of valour and did not believe the rumours of the steppe concerning his heroism.

All the doorways were crowded with curious onlookers. It reminded one of the old-time festivals in the house of a rich merchant when the shabbier members of the household would try to steal a glimpse of the honoured guests. Evidently it was not only the commander who had heard terrible rumours about Chapaev . . .

The apartment occupied by headquarters was unusually clean and tidy. The members of the staff were all sitting or standing in their places. Great preparations had been made; the staff did not want to make a bad show, and perhaps they were all a little apprehensive.

This fellow Chapaev had a violent temper; who could foretell how he might behave?

The brigade commander spread out a beautifully drawn plan of the forthcoming attack on the table. Chapaev picked it up, silently admired the fine drawing for an instant, and laid it down again. He drew up a stool and sat down. Some of those who had come with him followed his example.

'Give me a pair of compasses!'

A shabby, rusty pair was handed to him. He opened them and turned them over in his hand with evident distaste.

'Vikhor, go and fetch me my compasses from Averka's satchel!'

In two minutes Vikhor was back again with another pair, and Chapaev began taking measurements on the plan. First, he stuck to the plan, then he produced a map from his pocket and studied it closely. He kept enquiring about distances, the difficult parts of the road, about water, transport wagons, the morning twilight, about blizzards in the steppe.

All those around him kept silent. Only now and again the brigade commander edged in a word or answered a question. Chapaev's eye saw more on the map than was traced upon it; he saw snow-covered valleys, the ruins of burnt villages, columns of men marching in the dark, trundling baggage wagons – he heard the whine and whistle of the cold morning wind – he saw mounds and hillocks, wells, frozen streams, broken bridges, stunted bushes . . .

Chapaev was already leading the attack!

When he had finished taking measurements, he pointed out to the brigade commander the mistakes in the plan. Some distances that had to be covered were too great, some halts were ill-chosen, the men would leave some places too soon or reach others too late. And he would jot down each of his remarks while he was measuring. The brigade commander did not agree very willingly; sometimes he seemed secretly amused at all this, but he gave in, took notes, made alterations in the plan . . . In some cases Chapaev turned as if for sympathy and support now to Vikhor, now to Popov or Shmarin.

'What would you say? What do you think? Am I right?'

The men were not accustomed to air their opinions much in his presence, and moreover, there was little to add; he always weighed and foresaw everything down to the minutest detail. The proverb that 'two heads are better than one' had been changed by his followers into 'one head is better than two.'

There had been cases of old when he had followed the advice of others and he had always had occasion to regret it. He swore, burst into complaints, cursed himself for a fool. His men would always remember a 'conference' when in their excitement they had let themselves go and talked a lot of hot air. Chapaev had listened to them patiently, sometimes even encouraging them by throwing in a few words. 'Yes, yes . . . That's right . . . Very good . . . ' His followers had really imagined that he was in full agreement with them, and approved of all they were saying. But when they had finished: 'What we have to do,' he declared, 'is to forget all this nonsense you've been talking – get it right out of your heads. Now you listen to my commands.' And then he went on to give quite a different turn to the whole business, so that nothing was left of their suggestions.

Vikhor, Popov and Shmarin had all three attended that memorable conference, and now they were more diffident about putting themselves forward. They knew from experience when to speak and when to keep their mouths shut. 'Sometimes it may be wise to give advice, but sometimes a single word can spell disaster.'

They were silent now. Fedor, too, spoke but little. He was as yet ill-acquainted with military questions; it was only later on, after months of experience on the field of battle, that he came to have any insight into these matters. For the time being he was still a mere 'civilian', and what could one expect from him?

He stood by the table with his hands clasped behind his back and thoughtfully examined the map and the plan, frowning now and then or turning his head away to give a little cough, afraid to disturb so important a discussion. Outwardly he looked grave and self-possessed. An outsider might have thought that he was able to hold his own with the rest in the discussion.

Long before meeting Chapaev, Fedor had made up his mind to be particularly cautious and diplomatic in his dealings with him. At first he would avoid conversations on military topics, in order not to show that he was a mere layman in these matters. He would turn the conversation to politics, because then all the advantages would be on his side. He would gain Chapaev's confidence, encourage him to speak quite frankly on all subjects, including intimate, personal peculiarities and minor details. He, Fedor, would speak mostly about science, culture, general education – and here again Chapaev would be reduced to the role of listener. And later – later Fedor would reveal himself as a brave fighter. That he must do, the sooner the better, because that was the only way to win the respect of Chapaev and the Red Army men. Politics, science and personal qualities were of no avail without this. After having thus carefully approached Chapaev, and laid the foundations for more intimate relations, Fedor could get to know him more closely, but for the present he must be on his guard. The danger now was that Chapaev might think Fedor was playing up to him, behaving sycophantically towards a 'hero'. Chapaev, being so famous, having such enormous prestige, must know how ambitious countless people were of obtaining his friendship. Later on, when Chapaev was 'captivated' by him, began to listen to him, and perhaps to seek enlightenment from him, it would be all plain sailing. However, no riding the high horse! He must at once establish simple and cordial relations, with a touch of the necessary rudeness. It was imperative that Chapaev should not take him for a fastidious intellectual of the sort that was always treated at the front with suspicion and undisguised contempt.

This mental preparation was productive of results. It helped Fedor to find his way by the simplest, quickest and surest path into the environment in which he had to work, to merge with his surroundings, to become an organic part of them. He fully realised that Chapaev and his followers – this mass of semi-guerilla fighters – were rather bewildering folk, people with whom one had to watch one's step. Beside the good elements among them, there were others who required careful handling and had to be constantly watched.

What sort of a man was Chapaev? What was Klychkov's conception of Chapaev and why was he taking such elaborate pains to approach him in the proper way? Was it really worth while doing this?

When he had been working in the rear of the revolutionary army,

Klychkov had naturally heard and read a good deal about the 'popular heroes' who made a dazzling appearance on this or that sector of the Civil War front. He had noticed that they were mostly of peasant origin, only a few were townsmen and factory workers. The heroism of the worker was different from that of the peasant. Having grown up in a great industrial centre, Klychkov had witnessed the well-organised struggle of the weavers and he was therefore somewhat inclined to look askance at the semi-anarchic exploits of popular heroes of the Chapaev type. That did not prevent him from analysing and studying them very attentively and appreciating their acts of real courage. But in the depths of his soul he slightly distrusted them. Such was his attitude at the present moment.

'Chapaev is a hero,' Fedor thought to himself. 'He embodies in himself all the irrepressible and spontaneous feelings of rage and protest that have accumulated in the hearts of the peasants. But who can foresee what spontaneous protest will lead to? There are cases on record where such glorious chieftains as Chapaev have suddenly taken it into their heads to bump off their commissars! Not some contemptible, despicable, cowardly commissar, but first-rate revolutionaries! Or they have suddenly gone over to the Whites with their whole 'spontaneous' detachments at their heels . . .

'Workers are different. Never, under any circumstances, will they desert to the enemy's camp – at least those who have consciously joined the struggle will not. Of course, the workers include people who were peasants only yesterday; others are not fully class conscious, and others again have become too 'intellectual', and scorn hard work. But with workers it is easy to know what you are dealing with. Whereas there lurks an element of real danger in the devil-may-care attitude of Chapaev's reckless guerilla fighters.'

This feeling of mistrust made it all the more important for Fedor to strike the right note when mixing with this new crowd. He did not want to be submerged in it; his aim was, on the contrary, to gain a proper influence over it. And he would begin with the head, the chief, with Chapaev himself. He would focus all his attention upon him . . .

Petka – that was what everybody called Isayev – poked his tiny, birdlike head in at the door, beckoned to Popov with his little finger and gave him a chit on which was written in an illiterate hand: 'Tell Chapaev that the horses and everything are ready.'

Petka was aware that in some places and under some circumstances he was not allowed to butt in. In such cases he always wrote chits. His present message came at a very opportune moment, for all the orders had already been issued and signed, and would presently be sent to the regiments. Little or no time would be spent on formalities.

'I have come to take command,' Chapaev had declared, 'not to fuss around with papers. Clerks can do that.'

'Vassily Ivanovich,' Popov whispered to him, 'I see you have finished. Everything is ready, we can start.'

'Everything ready? Let's go!'

Chapaev sprang to his feet.

Everybody made way for him and he was the first to pass out of the room as he had been the first to enter it.

Outside, a crowd of Red Army men had gathered, having heard that Chapaev was in the house. Many of them had been his companions-in-arms in 1918; many knew him personally; all without a single exception knew him by repute. Craning their necks, their eyes lit up with enthusiasm and admiration, they grinned from ear to ear at the sight of Chapaev.

'Long live Chapaev!' yelled one of them as he appeared on the steps. 'Hurrah! Hurrah! . . . '

Red Army men came swarming from all sides, the townspeople following them. The crowd swelled rapidly.

'Comrades!' said Chapaev.

In an instant complete silence reigned.

'I have no time to speak now. I am going to the front. We'll meet there tomorrow, for we've prepared something for the Cossacks that they won't relish, and tomorrow we're going to shove it down their throats. We'll talk later on but for the present – goodbye to you all!'

A fresh burst of cheering followed his words. Chapaev seated himself in a sledge, with Popov at his side. Three mounted Red Army men were ready to escort them. Fedor was given a spirited black stallion to ride.

'Off we go!' shouted Chapaev.

The horses started off and the crowd opened before them, cheering vociferously. Chapaev's sledge sped away through an avenue of men that stretched to the very outskirts of the village.

The white expanse of bare steppe was monotonous and depressing. During the late thaw all the hillocks had become divested of snow till the bare ground was visible, but now the wind had buried them under snow again. The whole steppe was crisp with frost. The horses sped on lightly and merrily. Chapaev and Popov were sitting in the sledge almost back to back, making it look as if they had quarrelled. Each was pondering over tomorrow's difficult enterprise, and preparing himself for it. The sledge was followed at a small distance by the mounted escort, and that distance was never lengthened or shortened during the whole way. Fedor kept apart from the others. Sometimes he would loiter behind, let himself be outdistanced a whole verst, and then catch up with the party at the gallop. It was splendid to race over the steppe on a willing, spirited horse.

'Tomorrow,' he was thinking as he trotted along at an easy pace, 'tomorrow will usher in a new life for me, a life of real fighting . . . And this life of warfare will go on and on – for how long? Who can tell what the issue will be? Who can foretell the day of our victory? Day after day will rapidly fly past in campaigns, battles, dangers and anxieties . . . Will we survive, who are like puffs of down? Which of us will return to his native place and which will leave his bones here in some dark ravine or in the snowy waste of the steppe?'

Memories of everyday life and beloved, familiar faces arose before his mind's eye. He saw himself as a lifeless body, lying in the snow with his arms outspread, the blood oozing from a wound in his temple. He felt a twinge of self-pity. Some hours ago this feeling would have degenerated into melancholy, but now he shook himself free of it with a toss of his head and proceeded on his way, calm and serene, ready to laugh at the picture of his own death.

They had now been travelling for two hours and a half. Chapaev, evidently bored with sitting motionless so long, bade the driver stop and, getting out, told one of the mounted men to take his place in the sledge while he himself jumped on the man's horse. He rode up to Fedor.

from *Chapaev*

'So we two are going to be together, Comrade Commissar?'

'Yes, we'll be together,' said Fedor, and he noticed at a glance how firmly Chapaev was sitting his horse. Man and mount seemed moulded into one. Fedor himself feared he must look rather a bad horseman.

'With only a little more jolting and shaking I should lose my seat altogether,' he thought to himself ruefully. 'Chapaev, on the other hand, would never lose his seat.'

'Seen much fighting, comrade?'

Fedor thought he caught a smile on the man's face and sensed irony in his words. 'He knows well enough that I'm a newcomer to the front and is trying to make fun of me.'

'I am only a beginner . . . '

'But you've seen service in the rear, I suppose?'

There was a sting in the question.

One must bear in mind that to a born fighter like Chapaev 'the rear' was a place inhabited by a low contemptible species of being. Fedor had got some inkling of this before, and his recent conversation and trips with Red Army men and commanders had confirmed him in his suspicions.

'The rear?' he repeated, and added with feigned carelessness: 'I was working in Ivanovo-Voznesensk . . . '

'That's beyond Moscow, isn't it?'

'Yes, about three hundred versts beyond Moscow.'

'Well, how are things there?'

Fedor was pleased with the new turn the conversation was taking; he seized the opportunity to explain to Chapaev what a hard and hungry life the Ivanovo weavers were having. Why only the weavers? Were there no other inhabitants in the town save them? Yet somehow when he spoke of Ivanovo-Voznesensk, Klychkov could only picture to himself the serried ranks of the army of workers; he was proud of his nearness to this working-class army, and there was even a shade of pose in his mental attitude towards them.

'Seems as if they were having a hard time of it,' mused Chapaev in a serious tone. 'And all because of the famine. If it weren't for the famine, it'd be all right – things would be different then . . . Look at the stacks of food they gobble up, the sons of bitches, and they never think that . . . '

'Who gobbles up food?' asked Fedor, uncomprehendingly.

'The Cossacks. They don't give a damn . . . '

'Not all the Cossacks are like that . . . '

'Yes, they are, all of them,' cried Chapaev. 'You don't know, but I'll tell you they're all that way, every man jack of them.'

Chapaev chafed irritably in his saddle.

'That can't be,' Fedor protested. 'There must be some, at least, who side with us. Wait a bit,' he added in joyful excitement, 'what about the mounted scouts in our brigade, aren't they all Cossacks?'

'In our brigade?'

Chapaev looked thoughtful.

'Yes, here in our brigade.'

'Those must be town Cossacks. The ones here would never . . . '

Chapaev refused to let himself be convinced.

'I don't know whether they are town or steppe Cossacks, but that doesn't alter the fact that they are with us. You see, Comrade Chapaev, all the Cossacks can't be against us. It would be unthinkable, impossible . . . '

'Why do you say that? When you've been with us a bit longer . . . '

'However long I stay with you, I'll never change my mind.'

Fedor's voice was firm and stern.

'I'm not saying there aren't one or two,' said Chapaev, yielding a little. 'Of course, there are some – who says there aren't? But there are precious few of them.'

'No, not only a few. You're mistaken. They've sent us news from Turkestan that Cossack regiments there have established Soviet power over whole regions. And in the Ukraine, too, and on the Don. There are more than you think.'

'Don't you trust them! They'll soon show you, the sons of bitches . . . '

'I don't trust them over much,' explained Klychkov. 'I know that there is much truth in what you say. The Cossack is a black raven, it's true – nobody denies it. That's why the tsarist government went out of its way to gratify them . . . But look at the young Cossacks, they're not of the old breed. And it's the young ones that join us. Of course, it's more difficult for an old greybeard of a Cossack to accept the Soviet power. At least it's difficult for him now, when he hasn't come to understand what it means. All sorts of stories are told about us, and people believe them, too. How we convert churches into cowsheds, have common wives and common property and make everybody eat and drink together and sit at the same table. How can the Cossacks be expected to like this sort of thing, if they've been accustomed to go to church for generations and are fond of their rich, comfortable homes, of the free, wild life of the steppe, and of making other people work for them?'

'Ex-ploit-ers,' pronounced Chapaev painstakingly.

'Exactly,' said Fedor, repressing a smile. 'Exploitation is the very gist of the matter. Rich Cossacks do not merely exploit strangers and Kirghizians, they make no bones about exploiting their own people. And that brings discord. The old people, when they are oppressed, bow their heads and say that God has willed it so, but the youngsters have a simpler and bolder outlook, and that is why they are attracted to us. The old people can't be shaken in their convictions. It takes a bullet to get anything into their heads!'

'Yes, bullets, that's right,' said Chapaev with a toss of his head. 'But there's are things that make it hard for us at the front . . . '

Fedor could not see what Chapaev was driving at; nevertheless, he felt that much lay behind these words. He remained silent, and waited for Chapaev to go on.

'Our centres. They're no good,' dropped Chapaev vaguely.

Fedor's curiosity was aroused.

'What's wrong with the centres?' he asked.

'They've packed them with all kinds of bastards,' muttered Chapaev as if to himself, but quite audibly, obviously meaning Fedor to hear. 'He used to keep me standing in the frost for twenty-four hours at a stretch, the son of a bitch, and he gets treated with kid gloves. "Please be seated, general; there's a padded armchair for you, general. Sit down and issue orders. And be sure to please yourself, give us cartridges if you feel inclined to, or else let us fight with sticks!" '

That was Chapaev's sore spot – headquarters, with its generals, orders and disciplinary actions. Chapaev could not stomach it, and he was far from being the only Red Army chief who at that time loathed and hated headquarters.

'We can't manage without generals,' said Klychkov gruffly. 'You can't make war without generals!'

'We dam' well can!'

Chapaev gave an impatient tug at the bridle.

'No, we can't, Comrade Chapaev. Foolhardiness alone won't get us anywhere; we must have knowledge. And we haven't got it. Who, save the generals, can give us knowledge? They have studied and they must instruct us. In time we shall have teachers from among ourselves, but for the present we haven't. Admit that we haven't! You do? Very well then, we must learn from others.'

'Learn? Why, what the hell can they teach us?' Chapaev retorted hotly. 'Do you think they can tell you your business? Not on your life! I myself entered the Academy, knocked about the damned place for two months, felt like a fish out of water, and then left for good. Came back here. It's no place for people like me. One of the professors there – a fellow named Pechkin – as bald as an egg – started asking me questions at the exam. Do you know the River Rhine?' he asked me.

'I was all through the German war, and of course I knew about the Rhine. But why should I give him the answer he wanted?

' "No, I don't," I said, 'and you, do you know the River Solyanka?'

'His eyes nearly popped out of his head. He wasn't expecting such a question.

' "No, I don't know it," he said. "What about it?"

' "Don't ask questions then," I said. "I was wounded on the Solyanka, crossed it back and forth five times. To hell with your Rhine, I don't want it. I must know every hillock and bush and tree near the Solyanka because we're fighting the Cossacks on its banks!" '

Fedor burst out laughing and looked at Chapaev in amazement.

What a childish way of reasoning this popular hero had! Well, people have different tastes; some are attracted by knowledge, others repelled by it. This man had been at the Academy for two months and had understood nothing, found nothing good in it. And he was no ordinary man. Clever, beyond question, but raw and uncouth. He would not come round so soon.

'You didn't stay at the Academy long enough,' said Fedor. 'You couldn't learn much in two months. It's too difficult.'

'I might as well have not been there at all,' said Chapaev, with a contemptuous wave of his hand. 'I don't need to be taught, I know everything . . .'

'No, you must let yourself be taught,' retorted Fedor, 'there are always things you can learn.'

'There are, but not at the Academy,' exclaimed Chapaev excitedly. 'I know there are things to learn and I'm going to learn them. I'll tell you what, comrade . . . But what's your name?'

'Klychkov.'

'I want to tell you, Comrade Klychkov, that I am almost quite illiterate. I learned to read only four years ago, and I am thirty-five! I have spent half a lifetime in ignorance, you might say. But let that be, we'll speak about it another time . . . And, just look yonder, that must be Talovka.'

Chapaev spurred his horse. Fedor followed his example, and they rode up level with Popov. Ten minutes later they were entering Talovka.

Family Man

by Mikhail Sholokhov (translated by Valentina Brougher and Frank Miller, with Mark Lipovetsky)

The sun is sinking into the faint-green stubble of the undergrowth beyond the outskirts of a *stanitsa*.[22] I'm walking from the *stanitsa* to the Don, to the river crossing. The damp sand under my feet smells of decay like a tree that's rotten and swollen with water. The road zigzags like a rabbit's path and slips along the undergrowth.

---

22 *stanitsa*: a constellation of two or three Cossack villages, with 700 to 10,000 people, headed by a local military commander called an *ataman*

Lower now and turning crimson, the sun drops behind the village graveyard, and dusk wreathes the undergrowth behind me in blue.

The ferryboat is tied to a mooring line, and the violet water cackles under the boat's bottom; bobbing up and down and turning side to side, oars groan in their rowlocks.

As he bails out water, the ferryman scrapes a bucket along the moss-covered bottom. Raising his head, he gives me a sidelong glance with his yellowish, slit-like eyes and says gruffly, half-heartedly, 'Going to the other side? We'll go right now – untie the mooring line.'

'Are we both going to row?'

'We've got to. It's getting to be night and other people might show up or might not.'

Rolling up his wide Cossack trousers, he looked at me again and said, 'I can see you're not one of our folk, not from around here . . . Where in the world are you coming from?'

'I'm on my way home from the army.'

The ferryman threw off his cap, with a nod of his head tossed back his hair which looked like blackened filigree silver from the Caucasus, then winking at me, he grinned, revealing worn-down teeth.

'How're you going – got a pass, or on the sly?'

'Demobilised. They released my year.'

'Well, then, nothing to worry about . . . '

We sit down at the oars. The Don playfully pulls us towards the submerged young growth of the riverside forest. The water makes a dull sound as it beats against the rough bottom of the boat. The ferryman's bare legs, streaked with blue veins, swell with knots of muscle; the blue soles of his feet stick to the slippery cross plank as they press against it. His hands are long and bony, his fingers are gnarled. He's tall, narrow-shouldered; he rows awkwardly, all hunched over, but the oar comes down obediently on the crest of a wave and plunges deep in the water. I hear his even, uninterrupted breathing; his knitted wool shirt smells strongly of sweat, tobacco, and fresh water.

He let go of the oar and turned to face me. 'Looks like it's gonna send us crashing into the forest. A bad joke, but there's nothing we can do about it, my boy!'

The current was stronger in the middle. The boat rushed on, restively lurching in the rear and listing to one side, headed for the forest. In half an hour we were tossed against some flooded willows. The oars snapped. A splintered piece flapped about in the rowlock, as if offended. Water came sloshing in through a hole. We climbed a tree to spend the night. The ferryman, his legs wrapped around a branch, sat next to me, puffing away on his clay pipe, talking and listening to the whirring of the wings of geese cutting through the thick darkness above our heads.

'You're going home, to your family . . . Your mother's probably waiting for you. Her sonny boy the breadwinner is gonna come back and take care of her in her old age, but you probably don't take it to heart that she, your mother, pines for you during the day and weeps her eyes out at night . . . All you sonny boys are like that . . . Until you've got kids of your own, you don't really care about your parents' suffering. And how much each of them has to bear!

'A woman cuts open a fish and crushes its spleen. You eat the fish soup, but it's unbelievably bitter. And so here I am: I keep on living, but my lot in life is only to swallow bitterness . . . Sometimes you put up with it and put up with it, and then you say, "Life, oh life, when are you gonna get even worse?"

'You're not one of us, you're an outsider – go on, use your head. Which noose should I stick my head into?

'I've got a daughter, Natashka, this year she'll see her seventeenth spring. And she says to me, "It makes me sick, father, to eat at the same table with you. When I look at your hands, I remember right away that you killed my brothers with those hands – and it makes me want to throw up."

'But the little bitch doesn't understand why it turned out that way! It was all because of them, because of the children!'

'I married young. I got a fertile woman, she foaled me eight mouths to feed, and kicked the bucket with the ninth. She gave birth, but on the fifth day she ended up in a coffin because of a fever . . . I was left alone, like a woodcock in a marsh, but not one of the children did God take away, no matter how much I begged . . . The oldest was Ivan . . . He looked like me, dark-haired and good-looking. He was a handsome Cossack and an honest worker. I had another son, four years younger than Ivan. That one had his mother's looks from birth: short, plump, so fair-haired that he was almost white, brown eyes, and he was dearest to my heart, my most beloved. His name was Danila . . . The other seven mouths were little boys and girls. I married off Ivan to someone in our hamlet and soon they had a child. I was also about to try marrying off Danila, but then a time of troubles arrived. We had an uprising against Soviet power in our *stanitsa*! The next day Ivan comes running to me.

' "Father," he says "let's go over to the Reds. I beg you in the name of Christ the Lord! We have to support their side 'cause their government is extremely just."

'Danila also dug in his heels. They tried for a long time to lure me, but I said to them: I won't keep you against your will, you go ahead, but I'm not going anywhere. Besides you, I have seven more mouths to feed, with every mouth asking for some food!

'With that they disappeared from the hamlet, and our whole *stanitsa* armed itself with whatever it could, and me they packed off under White command to the front.

'I said at the gathering: "Dear village elders, you all know I'm a family man. I have seven little ones. So, if they knock me off, who's gonna watch out for my family then?

'I say this and that, but no . . . ! Showing no regard whatsoever, they grabbed me and sent me to the front.

'The front-line positions ran right below our hamlet. And so, it happened right before Easter, nine prisoners were herded into our hamlet and Danilushka – my favourite – was among them . . . They led them through the square to the regimental captain. The Cossacks poured into the street and raised a din.

' "Kill them, the bastards! As soon as they bring them out from interrogating them, leave them to us!"

'I'm standing among them, my knees are shaking, but I don't show I feel sorry for my son, for my Danilushka . . . I turn my eyes like this, to one side and the other, and see the Cossacks whispering and nodding their heads in my direction . . . The cavalry sergeant-major, Arkashka, comes up to me and asks, "Well, Mikishara, are you going to kill the commies?"

' "I am, those so-and-so scoundrels . . . !"

' "Here, take this bayonet and go stand on the porch." He gives me the bayonet and, grinning, says, "We're keeping an eye on you, Mikishara . . . Watch out – or you'll be sorry!"

'I stood on the porch steps, thinking, Most Holy Mother, am I really going to kill my own son?

'I heard the captain shouting. The prisoners were brought out, and my Danila was out in front . . . I looked at him and my blood ran cold . . . His head was swollen like a bucket, as though the skin had been ripped off . . . It was caked with dry blood, and wool mittens were on his head so that they wouldn't beat him on the bare spots . . . The gloves were soaked with blood and stuck to his hair . . . That's from the beating they got on the way to the hamlet . . . He's walking down the steps and staggering. He looks at me and reaches out his hands towards me . . . He wants to smile, but his eyes are bruised black and blue, and one is filled with blood.

'At this point I realised that if I didn't strike him, my fellow villagers would kill me, and my small children would be left poor orphans . . . He came alongside me.

' "Father dear," he says, "goodbye . . . !"

'Tears are washing the blood down his cheeks, and I . . . forced myself to raise my hand. It seemed to have become all numb . . . I've got the bayonet gripped in my fist. I struck him with the end that fits on the rifle. I struck him right here, above the ear . . . He cries out, "Oh!" and covers his face with his hands and falls down the steps . . . The Cossacks roar with laughter.

' "Make them soak in their own blood, Mikishara! It's obvious you're taking pity on him, on your Danilka! . . . Strike him again, or we'll make your blood flow!"

'The captain came out on the porch; he was swearing, but his eyes were laughing . . . When they began to slash them with their bayonets, my heart couldn't bear it. I started running down a small street, looked back and saw them rolling my Danilushka on the ground. The sergeant stuck his bayonet in his throat, but only "Khrrr" came out of him.'

Down below, the boards of the boat made cracking sounds from the pressure of the water; you could hear the water gushing in, and the willow quivered and made a drawn-out, creaking sound. With his foot Mikishara touched the back part of the boat sticking up and, knocking out a yellow snowstorm of sparks from his pipe, said, 'Our boat is sinking. Tomorrow we'll have to be on duty till noon on this willow. What a thing to happen!'

He was silent for a long time and then, lowering his voice, he said in a quiet, flat tone, 'For that there business they made me a senior non-commissioned officer . . .

'A lot of water has flowed down the Don since then, but even now at night I sometimes think I hear someone wheezing, choking . . . At that time, when I was running, I heard Danilushka wheezing . . . It's my conscience, and it's killing me . . .

'We held the front against the Reds till spring, then General Sekretyov joined forces with us and we drove the Reds beyond the Don, to the Saratov Province. I'm a family man, but they wouldn't give me a break, because my sons went over to the Bolsheviks. We reached the town of Balashov. There's neither hide nor hair of Ivan, my oldest son. Hell only knows how the Cossacks found out that Ivan had left the Reds and was now serving in the thirty-sixth Cossack battery. The villagers threatened, "If we come across Vanka, we'll beat him to death."

'We took this one village, and the thirty-sixth was there . . .

'They found my Ivan, tied his hands, and brought him to our company. Here the Cossacks gave him a brutal beating and said to me, "Take him to regimental headquarters!"

'The headquarters was about twenty versts from the village. The captain gives me a document and, without looking at me, says, "Here's a document for you, Mikishara. Get your son to headquarters. It's better if you do it – he won't run away from his father!"

'And at this point the Lord brought me to my senses. I figured they're making me the escort because they think I'll set him free, and then they'll catch him and kill me . . .

'I come to the hut where Ivan was being held under arrest and say to the guard, "Let me have the prisoner. I'm going to take him to headquarters."

' "Go on, take him, we don't care!"

'Ivan threw his greatcoat over his shoulders, but he twisted and twisted his cap in his hands and then threw it on a bench. He and I walked out of the village and up the knoll. He doesn't say anything, and I don't say anything. I look back from time to time – I want to see if they're keeping an eye on us. We went only halfway, passed a small chapel, and I couldn't see anyone behind us. At this point Ivan turned to me and said pitifully, "Father, they'll kill me at headquarters anyway. You're taking me to my death! Is your conscience really still asleep"

' "No, Vanya," I say, "my conscience isn't asleep!"

' "And don't you feel sorry for me?"

' "Yes, I do, my son, I'm so sick at heart I could die . . . "

' "And if you feel sorry for me, let me go . . . I haven't lived long enough in this world!"

'He fell to his knees in the middle of the road and bowed down to the ground three times before me. I say to him in response: When we reach the ravine, start running, and for appearance's sake I'll fire a couple of times after you . . .

'And just imagine, when he was a little boy, you couldn't get an affectionate word out of him at times, but now he threw himself at me and began kissing my hands . . . We walked about two versts. He doesn't say anything, and I don't say anything. We drew near the ravine and he stopped.

' "Well, dad, let's say goodbye! If I happen to stay alive, I'll take care of you for the rest of your life. You'll never hear a harsh word from me . . . "

'He embraces me, but my heart bleeds for him.

' "Run, my dear son!" I say to him.

'He started running towards the ravine, looking back and waving at me.

'I let him go about one hundred fifty feet, then took the rifle from my shoulder, got down on one knee so that my hand wouldn't falter, and I got him . . . in the back . . . '

Mikishara took a long time getting out his tobacco pouch, a long time striking the flint to get a spark, and then he began puffing on his pipe and smacking his lips. The tinder glowed in his cupped hand, the muscles on the ferryman's face twitched, and his squinting eyes looked out from under his swollen eyelids with a hard and unrepentant gaze.

'Well, there you are . . . Ivan jumped up, covered another sixty feet or so, running madly, grasped his stomach with both hands and turned to me, "Father, why?" He fell down and his legs began to jerk.

'I run to him, bend down, and his eyes have rolled back, and there are bubbles of blood on his lips. I thought he was dying, but right away he rose slightly and, touching my hand, said, "Father, I've got a wife and child . . . "

'His head dropped to the side and fell down again. He's pressing down on the wound with his fingers, but what's the use . . . Blood spurts out through his fingers . . . He begins groaning, lies flat on his back and looks at me very seriously, but his tongue is already stiffening . . . He wants to say something, but only "Fa-ther . . . fa . . . fa . . . ther" comes out. Tears came pouring down from my eyes and I said to him, "Vaniushka, accept a martyr's crown for me. You have a wife and child, but I've seven mouths to feed. If I had let you go, the Cossacks would kill me, and the children would go out into the world begging for their bread . . . "

'He lay there a bit longer and then died, but he held my hand in his . . . I took off his greatcoat and boots, covered his face with a piece of rag, and went back to the village.

'Well, now you be the judge, my good man! How much grief I've carried because of them, those children, how much grey hair I have. I keep bread on the table, I don't have any peace day or night, but they . . . take my daughter, Natasha, for example. She says, "It makes me sick, father, to eat at the same table with you."

'How can I possibly bear all this now?'

His head hanging down, Mikishara the ferryman looks at me with a heavy, fixed stare. A foggy dawn is curling behind him. On the right bank, in a black mass of shaggy poplars, the quacking of ducks blends with a hoarse and sleepy shout: 'Mi-ki-sha-ra-a! You de-e-vil! Hur-ry up, bring the ferry back!'

Somerset Maugham

The author of *Of Human Bondage* and *The Moon and Sixpence*, Somerset Maugham (1874–1965) was one of the most popular British authors of the twentieth century: he was also a British spy. In 1917, the British government was very keen to keep Russia in the war – this would help them defeat Germany. MI6 decided that Maugham who spoke Russian was the right man to be sent to Russia to persuade Kerensky, the leader of the Provisional Government. Supplied with $21,000 ($350,000 today), Maugham reached Petrograd in September 1917. On his arrival, Maugham re-established contact with the daughter of Peter Kropotkin, Sasha,[23] with whom Maugham had had an affair when the Kropotkins lived in London before the war. Maugham decided that the best way to win the trust of Kerensky was to entertain him and his ministers with the finest vodka and caviar at the best restaurant in Petrograd. Weeks before the October Revolution, Maugham was summoned by Kerensky and asked to take an urgent secret message to David Lloyd George, the British Prime Minister appealing for guns and ammunition. Without that help, Kerensky said, 'I don't see how we can go on. Of course, I don't say that to the people. I always say that we shall continue whatever happens, but unless I have something to tell my army it's impossible.' Maugham rushed back to convey this message to Lloyd George whose reply was: 'I can't do that. I'm afraid I must bring this conversation to an end. I have a cabinet meeting to go to.' After Kerensky was removed from power, Maugham was convinced that he could have had more success if he had been sent to Russia earlier. Maugham used his experiences as a spy to write *Ashenden: Or the British Agent*, a colletion of stories which includes 'Mr Harrington's Washing'. The book put

---

23 She appears as Anatasia Alexandrovna Leonidov in 'Mr Harrington's Washing'.

the spy novel on the map and influenced stars of the genre like Eric Ambler, Graham Greene, Ian Fleming and John Le Carré.

Mr Harrington's Washing

from *Ashenden: or The British Agent* by Somerset Maugham

Some years had passed since then and Ashenden had not seen Anastasia Alexandrovna again. He knew that on the outbreak of the Revolution in March she and Vladimir Semenovich had gone to Russia. It might be that they would be able to help him; in a way Vladimir Semenovich owed him his life, and he made up his mind to write to Anastasia Alexandrovna to ask if he might come to see her.

When Ashenden went down to lunch he felt somewhat rested. Mr Harrington was waiting for him and they sat down. They ate what was put before them.

'Ask the waiter to bring us some bread,' said Mr Harrington.

'Bread?' replied Ashenden. 'There's no bread.'

'I can't eat without bread,' said Mr Harrington.

'I'm afraid you'll have to. There's no bread, no butter, no sugar, no eggs, no potatoes. There's fish and meat and green vegetables, and that's all.'

Mr Harrington's jaw dropped.

'But this is war,' he said.

'It looks very much like it.'

Mr Harrington was for a moment speechless; then he said: 'I'll tell you what I'm going to do, I'm going to get through with my business as quick as I can and then I'm going to get out of this country. I'm sure Mrs Harrington wouldn't like me to go without sugar or butter. I've got a very delicate stomach. The firm would never have sent me here if they'd thought I wasn't going to have the best of everything.'

In a little while Dr Egan Orth came in and gave Ashenden an envelope. On it was written Anastasia Alexandrovna's address. Ashenden introduced him to Mr Harrington. It was soon clear that he was pleased with Dr Egan Orth and so without further to-do Ashenden suggested that here was the perfect interpreter for him.

'He talks Russian like a Russian. But he's an American citizen, so that he won't do you down. I've known him a considerable time and I can assure you that he's absolutely trustworthy.'

Mr Harrington was pleased with the notion and after luncheon Ashenden left them to settle the matter by themselves. He wrote a note to Anastasia Alexandrovna and presently received an answer to say that she was going to a meeting, but would look in at his hotel about seven. He awaited her with apprehension. Of course he knew now that he had not loved her, but Tolstoy and Dostoyevsky, Rimsky-Korsakov, Stravinsky and Bakst; but he was not quite sure if the point had occurred to her. When between eight and half-past she arrived he suggested that she should join Mr Harrington and him at dinner. The presence of a third party, he thought, would prevent any awkwardness their meeting might have; but he need not have had any anxiety, for five minutes after they had sat down to a plate of soup it was borne in upon him that the feelings of Anastasia Alexandrovna towards him were as cool as were his towards her. It gave him a momentary shock. It is very hard for a man, however modest, to grasp the possibility that a woman who has once loved him may love him no longer, and though of course he did not imagine that Anastasia Alexandrovna had languished for five years with a hopeless passion for him, he did think that by a heightening of colour, a flutter of the eyelashes or a quiver of the lips she would betray the fact that she had still a soft place in her heart for him. Not at all. She talked to him as though he were a friend she was very glad to see again after an absence of a few days, but whose intimacy with her was purely social. He asked after Vladimir Semenovich.

'He has been a disappointment to me,' she said. 'I never thought he was a clever man, but I thought he was an honest one. He's going to have a baby.'

Mr Harrington, who was about to put a piece of fish into his mouth, stopped, his fork in the air, and stared at Anastasia Alexandrovna with astonishment. In extenuation it must be explained that he had never read a Russian novel in his life. Ashenden, slightly perplexed too, gave her a questioning look.

'I'm not the mother,' she said with a laugh. 'I am not interested in that sort of thing. The mother is a friend of mine and a well-known writer on Political Economy. I do not think her views are sound, but I should be the last to deny that they deserve consideration. She has a good brain, quite a good brain.' She turned to Mr Harrington. 'Are you interested in Political Economy?'

For once in his life Mr Harrington was speechless. Anastasia Alexandrovna gave them her views on the subject and they began to speak on the situation in Russia. She seemed to be on intimate terms with the leaders of the various political parties and Ashenden made up his mind to sound her on the possibility of her working with him. His infatuation had not blinded him to the fact that she was an extremely intelligent woman. After dinner he told Mr Harrington that he wished to talk business with Anastasia Alexandrovna and took her to a retired corner of the lounge. He told her all he thought necessary and found her interested and anxious to help. She had a passion for intrigue and a desire for power. When he hinted that he had command of large sums of money she saw at once that through him she might acquire an influence in the affairs of Russia. It tickled her vanity. She was immensely patriotic, but like many patriots she had an impression that her own aggrandisement tended to the good of her country. When they parted they had come to a working agreement.

'That was a very remarkable woman,' said Mr Harrington next morning when they met at breakfast.

'Don't fall in love with her,' smiled Ashenden.

This, however, was not a matter on which Mr Harrington was prepared to jest.

'I have never looked at a woman since I married Mrs Harrington,' he said. 'That husband of hers must be a bad man.'

'I could do with a plate of scrambled eggs,' said Ashenden, irrelevantly, for their breakfast consisted of a cup of tea without milk and a little jam instead of sugar.

With Anastasia Alexandrovna to help him and Dr Orth in the background, Ashenden set to work. Things in Russia were going from bad to worse. Kerensky, the head of the Provisional Government, was devoured by vanity and dismissed any minister who gave evidence of a capacity that might endanger his own position. He made speeches. He made endless speeches. At one moment there was a possibility that the Germans would make a dash for Petrograd. Kerensky made speeches. The food shortage grew more serious, the winter was approaching and there was no fuel. Kerensky made speeches. In the background the Bolsheviks were active, Lenin was hiding in Petrograd, it was said that Kerensky knew where he was, but dared not arrest him. He made speeches.

It amused Ashenden to see the unconcern with which Mr Harrington wandered through this turmoil. History was in the making and Mr Harrington minded his own business. It was uphill work. He was made to pay bribes to secretaries and underlings under the pretence that the ear of great men would be granted to him. He was kept waiting for hours in antechambers and then sent away without ceremony. When at last he saw the great men he found they had nothing to give him but idle words. They made him promises and in a day or two he discovered that the promises meant nothing. Ashenden advised him to throw in his hand and return to America; but Mr Harrington would not hear of it; his firm had sent him to do a particular job, and, by gum, he was going to do it or perish in the attempt. Then Anastasia Alexandrovna took him in hand. A singular friendship had arisen between the pair. Mr Harrington thought her a very remarkable and deeply wronged woman; he told her all about his wife and his two sons, he told her all about the Constitution of the United States; she on her side told him all about Vladimir Semenovich, and she told him about Tolstoy, Turgenev and Dostoyevsky. They had great times together. He said he couldn't manage to call her Anastasia Alexandrovna, it was too much of a mouthful; so he called her Delilah. And now she placed her inexhaustible energy at his service and they went together to the persons who might be useful to him. But things were coming to a head. Riots broke out and the streets were growing dangerous. Now and then armoured cars filled with discontented reservists careered wildly along the Nevsky Prospekt and in order to show that they were not happy took pot-shots at the passers-by. On one occasion when Mr Harrington and Anastasia Alexandrovna were in a tram together shots peppered the windows and they had to lie down on the floor for safety. Mr Harrington was highly indignant.

'An old fat woman was lying right on top of me, and when I wriggled to get out, Delilah caught me a clip on the side of the head and said, "Stop still, you fool." I don't like your Russian ways, Delilah.'

'Anyhow you stopped still,' she giggled.

'What you want in this country is a little less art and a little more civilisation.'

'You are bourgeoisie, Mr Harrington, you are not a member of the intelligentsia.'

'You are the first person who's ever said that, Delilah. If I'm not a member of the intelligentsia I don't know who is,' retorted Mr Harrington with dignity.

Then one day when Ashenden was working in his room there was a knock at the door and Anastasia Alexandrovna stalked in followed somewhat sheepishly by Mr Harrington. Ashenden saw that she was excited.

'What's the matter?' he asked.

'Unless this man goes back to America he'll get killed. You really must talk to him. If I hadn't been there something very unpleasant might have happened to him.'

'Not at all, Delilah,' said Mr Harrington, with asperity. 'I'm perfectly capable of taking care of myself and I wasn't in the smallest danger.'

'What is it all about?' asked Ashenden.

'I'd taken Mr Harrington to the Lavra of Alexander Nevsky to see Dostoyevsky's grave,' said Anastasia Alexandrovna, 'and on our way back we saw a soldier being rather rough with an old woman.'

'Rather rough!' cried Mr Harrington. 'There was an old woman walking along the sidewalk with a basket of provisions on her arm. Two soldiers came up behind her and one of them snatched the basket from her and walked off with it. She burst out screaming and crying. I don't know what she was saying, but I can guess, and the other soldier took his gun and with the butt-end of it hit her over the head. Isn't that right, Delilah?'

'Yes,' she answered, unable to help smiling. 'And before I could prevent it Mr Harrington jumped out of the cab and ran up to the soldier who had the basket, wrenched it from him and began to abuse the pair of them like pickpockets. At first they were so taken aback they didn't know what to do and then they got in a rage. I ran after Mr Harrington and explained to them that he was a foreigner and drunk.'

'Drunk?' cried Mr Harrington.

'Yes, drunk. Of course a crowd collected. It looked as though it wasn't going to be very nice.'

Mr Harrington smiled with those large pale-blue eyes of his.

'It sounded to me as though you were giving them a piece of your mind, Delilah. It was as good as a play to watch you.'

'Don't be stupid, Mr Harrington,' cried Anastasia, in a sudden fury, stamping her foot. 'Don't you know that those soldiers might very easily have killed you and me too, and not one of the bystanders would have raised a finger to help us?'

'Me? I'm an American citizen, Delilah. They wouldn't dare touch a hair of my head.'

'They'd have difficulty in finding one,' said Anastasia Alexandrovna, who when she was in a temper had no manners. 'But if you think Russian soldiers are going to hesitate to kill you because you're an American citizen you'll get a big surprise one of these days.'

'Well, what happened to the old woman?' asked Ashenden.

'The soldiers went off after a little and we went back to her.'

'Still with the basket?'

'Yes. Mr Harrington clung on to that like grim death. She was lying on the ground with the blood pouring from her head. We got her into the cab and when she could speak enough to tell us where she lived we drove her home. She was bleeding dreadfully and we had some difficulty in staunching the blood.'

Anastasia Alexandrovna gave Mr Harrington an odd look and to his surprise Ashenden saw him turn scarlet.

'What's the matter now?'

'You see, we had nothing to bind her up with. Mr Harrington's handkerchief was soaked. There was only one thing about me that I could get off quickly and so I took off my – '

But before she could finish Mr Harrington interrupted her.

'You need not tell Mr Ashenden what you took off. I'm a married man and I know ladies wear them, but I see no need to refer to them in general society.'

Anastasia Alexandrovna giggled.

'Then you must kiss me, Mr Harrington. If you don't I shall say.'

Mr Harrington hesitated a moment, considering evidently the pros and cons of the matter, but he saw that Anastasia Alexandrovna was determined.

'Go on then, you may kiss me, Delilah, though I'm bound to say I don't see what pleasure it can be to you.'

She put her arms round his neck and kissed him on both cheeks, then without a word of warning burst into a flood of tears.

'You're a brave little man, Mr Harrington. You're absurd but magnificent,' she sobbed.

Mr Harrington was less surprised than Ashenden would have expected him to be. He looked at Anastasia with a thin, quizzical smile and gently patted her.

'Come, come, Delilah, pull yourself together. It gave you a nasty turn, didn't it? You're quite upset. I shall have terrible rheumatism in my shoulder if you go on weeping all over it.'

The scene was ridiculous and touching. Ashenden laughed, but he had the beginnings of a lump in his throat.

When Anastasia Alexandrovna had left them Mr Harrington sat in a brown study.

'They're very queer, these Russians. Do you know what Delilah did?' he said, suddenly. 'She stood up in the cab, in the middle of the street, with people passing on both sides, and took her pants off. She tore them in two and gave me one to hold while she made a bandage of the other. I was never so embarrassed in my life.'

'Tell me what gave you the idea of calling her Delilah?' smiled Ashenden.

Mr Harrington reddened a little.

'She's a very fascinating woman, Mr Ashenden. She's been deeply wronged by her husband and I naturally felt a great deal of sympathy for her. These Russians are very emotional people and I did not want her to mistake my sympathy for anything else. I told her I was very much attached to Mrs Harrington.'

'You're not under the impression that Delilah was Potiphar's wife?' asked Ashenden.

'I don't know what you mean by that, Mr Ashenden,' replied Mr Harrington. 'Mrs Harrington has always given me to understand that I'm very fascinating to women, and I thought if I called our little friend Delilah it would make my position quite clear.'

'I don't think Russia's any place for you, Mr Harrington,' said Ashenden smiling. 'If I were you I'd get out of it as quick as I could.'

'I can't go now. I've got them to agree to my terms at last and we're going to sign next week. Then I shall pack my grip and go.'

'I wonder if your signatures will be worth the paper they're written on,' said Ashenden.

He had at length devised a plan of campaign. It took him twenty-four hours' hard work to code a telegram in which he put his scheme before the persons who had sent him to Petrograd. It was accepted and he was promised all the money he needed. Ashenden knew he could do nothing unless the Provisional Government remained in power for another three months; but winter was at hand and food was getting scarcer every day. The army was mutinous. The people clamoured for peace. Every evening at the Europe, Ashenden drank a cup of chocolate with Professor Z— and discussed with him how best to make use of his devoted Czechs. Anastasia Alexandrovna had a flat in a retired spot and here he had meetings with all manner of persons. Plans were drawn up. Measures were taken. Ashenden argued, persuaded, promised. He had to overcome the vacillation of one and wrestle with the fatalism of another. He had to judge who was resolute and who was self-sufficient, who was honest and who was infirm of purpose. He had to curb his impatience with the Russian verbosity; he had to be good-tempered with people who were willing to talk of everything but the matter in hand; he had to listen sympathetically to ranting and rodomontade. He had to beware of treachery. He had to humour the vanity of fools and elude the greed of the ambitious. Time was pressing. The rumours grew hot as did many of the activities of the Bolsheviks. Kerensky ran hither and thither like a frightened hen.

Then the blow fell. On the night of the 7th of November 1917, the Bolsheviks rose, Kerensky's ministers were arrested and the Winter Palace was sacked by the mob; the reins of power were seized by Lenin and Trotsky.

Anastasia Alexandrovna came to Ashenden's room at the hotel early in the morning. Ashenden was coding a telegram. He had been up all night, first at the Smolny and then at the Winter Palace. He was tired out. Her face was white and her shining brown eyes were tragic.

'Have you heard?' she asked Ashenden.

He nodded.

'It's all over then. They say Kerensky has fled. They never even showed fight.' Rage seized her. 'The buffoon!' she screamed.

At that moment there was a knock at the door and Anastasia Alexandrovna looked at it with sudden apprehension.

'You know the Bolsheviks have got a list of people they've decided to execute. My name is on it, and it may be that yours is too.'

'If it's they and they want to come in they only have to turn the handle,' said Ashenden, smiling, but with ever so slightly odd a feeling at the pit of his stomach. 'Come in.'

The door was opened and Mr Harrington stepped into the room. He was as dapper as ever, in his short black coat and striped trousers, his shoes neatly polished and a derby on his bald head. He took it off when he saw Anastasia Alexandrovna.

'Oh, fancy finding you here so early. I looked in on my way out, I wanted to tell you my news. I tried to find you yesterday evening, but couldn't. You didn't come in to dinner.'

'No, I was at a meeting,' said Ashenden.

'You must both congratulate me, I got my signatures yesterday, and my business is done.'

Mr Harrington beamed on them, the picture of self-satisfaction, and he arched himself like a bantam-cock who has chased away all rivals. Anastasia Alexandrovna burst into a sudden shriek of hysterical laughter. He stared at her in perplexity.

'Why, Delilah, what is the matter?' he said.

Anastasia laughed till the tears ran from her eyes and then began to sob in earnest.

Ashenden explained. 'The Bolsheviks have overthrown the Government. Kerensky's ministers are in prison. The Bolsheviks are out to kill. Delilah says her name is on the list. Your minister signed your documents yesterday because he knew it did not matter what he did then. Your contracts are worth nothing. The Bolsheviks are going to make peace with Germany as soon as they can.'

Anastasia Alexandrovna had recovered her self-control as quickly as she had lost it.

'You had better get out of Russia as soon as you can, Mr Harrington. It's no place for a foreigner now and it may be that in a few days you won't be able to.'

Mr Harrington looked from one to the other.

'Oh my!' he said. 'Oh my!' It seemed inadequate. 'Are you going to tell me that that Russian minister was just making a fool of me?'

Ashenden shrugged his shoulders.

'How can one tell what he was thinking of? He may have a keen sense of humour and perhaps he thought it funny to sign a fifty-million-dollar contract yesterday when there was every chance of his being stood against the wall and shot today. Anastasia Alexandrovna's right, Mr Harrington, you'd better take the first train that'll get you to Sweden.'

'And what about you?'

'There's nothing for me to do here any more. I'm cabling for instructions and I shall go as soon as I get leave. The Bolsheviks have got in ahead of us and the people I was working with will have their work cut out to save their lives.'

'Boris Petrovich was shot this morning,' said Anastasia Alexandrovna with a frown.

They both looked at Mr Harrington and he stared at the floor. His pride in this achievement of his was shattered and he sagged like a pricked balloon. But in a minute he looked up. He gave Anastasia Alexandrovna a little smile and for the first time Ashenden noticed how attractive and kindly his smile was. There was something peculiarly disarming about it.

'If the Bolsheviks are after you, Delilah, don't you think you'd better come with me? I'll take care of you and if you like to come to

America I'm sure Mrs Harrington would be glad to do anything she could for you.'

'I can see Mrs Harrington's face if you arrived in Philadelphia with a Russian refugee,' laughed Anastasia Alexandrovna. 'I'm afraid it would need more explaining than you could ever manage. No, I shall stay here.'

'But if you're in danger?'

'I'm a Russian. My place is here. I will not leave my country when most my country needs me.'

'That is bunk, Delilah,' said Mr Harrington very quietly.

Anastasia Alexandrovna had spoken with deep emotion, but now with a little start she shot a sudden quizzical look at him.

'I know it is, Samson,' she answered. 'To tell you the truth I think we're all going to have a hell of a time. God knows what's going to happen, but I want to see; I wouldn't miss a minute of it for the world.'

Mr Harrington shook his head.

'Curiosity is the bane of your sex, Delilah,' he said.

'Go along and do your packing, Mr Harrington,' said Ashenden, smiling, 'and then we'll take you to the station. The train will be besieged.'

'Very well, I'll go. And I shan't be sorry either. I haven't had a decent meal since I came here and I've done a thing I never thought I should have to do in my life, I've drunk my coffee without sugar, and when I've been lucky enough to get a little piece of black bread, I've had to eat it without butter. Mrs Harrington will never believe me when I tell her what I've gone through. What this country wants is organisation.'

When he left them, Ashenden and Anastasia Alexandrovna talked over the situation. Ashenden was depressed because all his careful schemes had come to nothing, but Anastasia Alexandrovna was excited and she hazarded every sort of guess about the outcome of this new revolution. She pretended to be very serious, but in her heart she looked upon it all very much as a thrilling play. She wanted more and more things to happen. Then there was another knock at the door and before Ashenden could answer Mr Harrington burst in.

'Really the service at this hotel is a scandal,' he cried heatedly. 'I've been ringing my bell for fifteen minutes and I can't get anyone to pay the smallest attention to me.'

'Service?' exclaimed Anastasia Alexandrovna. 'There is not a servant left in the hotel.'

'But I want my washing. They promised to let me have it back last night.'

'I'm afraid you haven't got much chance of getting it now,' said Ashenden.

'I'm not going to leave without my washing. Four shirts, two union suits, a pair of pyjamas and four collars. I wash my handkerchiefs and socks in my room. I want my washing and I'm not going to leave this hotel without it.'

'Don't be a fool,' cried Ashenden. 'What you've got to do is to get out of here while the going's good. If there are no servants to get it you'll just have to leave your washing behind you.'

'Pardon me, sir, I shall do nothing of the kind. I'll go and fetch it myself. I've suffered enough at the hands of this country and I'm not going to leave four perfectly good shirts to be worn by a lot of dirty Bolsheviks. No, sir. I do not leave Russia till I have my washing.'

Anastasia Alexandrovna stared at the floor for a moment; then with a little smile looked up. It seemed to Ashenden that there was something in her that responded to Mr Harrington's futile obstinacy. In her Russian way she understood that Mr Harrington could not leave Petrograd without his washing. His insistence had given it the value of a symbol.

'I'll go downstairs and see if I can find anybody about who knows where the laundry is, and if I can I'll go with you and you can bring your washing away with you.'

Mr Harrington unbent. He answered with that sweet and disarming smile of his.

'That's terribly kind of you, Delilah. I don't mind if it's ready or not, I'll take it just as it is.'

Anastasia Alexandrovna left them.

'Well, what do you think of Russia and the Russians now?' Mr Harrington asked Ashenden.

'I'm fed up with them. I'm fed up with Tolstoy, I'm fed up with Turgenev and Dostoyevsky, I'm fed up with Chekov. I'm fed up with the Intelligentsia. I hanker after people who know their mind from one minute to another, who mean what they say an hour after they've said it, whose word you can rely on; I'm sick of fine phrases and oratory and attitudinising.'

Ashenden, bitten by the prevailing ill, was about to make a speech when he was interrupted by a rattle as of peas on a drum. In the city, so strangely silent, it sounded abrupt and odd.

'What's that?' asked Mr Harrington.

'Rifle firing. On the other side of the river, I should think.'

Mr Harrington gave a funny little look. He laughed, but his face was a trifle pale; he did not like it, and Ashenden did not blame him.

'I think it's high time I got out. I shouldn't so much mind for myself, but I've got a wife and children to think of. I haven't had a letter from Mrs Harrington for so long I'm a bit worried.' He paused an instant. 'I'd like you to know Mrs Harrington, she's a very wonderful woman. She's the best wife a man ever had. Until I came here I'd not been separated from her for more than three days since we were married.'

Anastasia Alexandrovna came back and told them that she had found the address.

'It's about forty minutes' walk from here and if you'll come now I'll go with you,' she said.

'I'm ready.'

'You'd better look out,' said Ashenden. 'I don't believe the streets are very healthy today.'

Anastasia Alexandrovna looked at Mr Harrington.

'I must have my washing, Delilah,' he said. 'I should never rest in peace if I left it behind me and Mrs Harrington would never let me hear the last of it.'

'Come on then.'

They set out and Ashenden went on with the dreary business of translating into a very complicated code the shattering news he had to give. It was a long message, and then he had to ask for instructions upon his own movements. It was a mechanical job and yet it was one in which you could not allow your attention to wander. The mistake of a single figure might make a whole sentence incomprehensible.

Suddenly his door was burst open and Anastasia Alexandrovna flung into the room. She had lost her hat and was dishevelled. She was panting. Her eyes were starting out of her head and she was obviously in a state of great excitement.

'Where's Mr Harrington?' she cried. 'Isn't he here?'

'No.'

'Is he in his bedroom?'

'I don't know. Why, what's the matter? We'll go and look if you like. Why didn't you bring him along with you?'

They walked down the passage and knocked at Mr Harrington's door; there was no answer; they tried the handle; the door was locked.

'He's not there.'

They went back to Ashenden's room. Anastasia Alexandrovna sank into a chair.

'Give me a glass of water, will you? I'm out of breath. I've been running.'

She drank the water Ashenden poured out for her. She gave a sudden sob.

'I hope he's all right. I should never forgive myself if he was hurt. I was hoping he would have got here before me. He got his washing all right. We found the place. There was only an old woman there and they didn't want to let us take it, but we insisted. Mr Harrington was furious because it hadn't been touched. It was exactly as he had sent it. They'd promised it last night and it was still in the bundle that Mr Harrington had made himself. I said that was Russia and Mr Harrington said he preferred coloured people. I'd led him by side streets because I thought it was better, and we started to come back again. We passed at the top of a street and at the bottom of it I saw a little crowd. There was a man addressing them.

' "Let's go and hear what he's saying," I said.

'I could see they were arguing. It looked exciting. I wanted to know what was happening.

' "Come along, Delilah," he said. "Let us mind our own business."

' "You go back to the hotel and do your packing. I'm going to see the fun," I said.

'I ran down the street and he followed me. There were about two or three hundred people there and a student was addressing them. There were some working men and they were shouting at him. I love a row and I edged my way into the crowd. Suddenly we heard the sound of shots and before you could realise what was happening two armoured cars came dashing down the street. There were soldiers in them and they were firing as they went. I don't know why. For fun, I suppose, or because they were drunk. We all scattered like a lot of rabbits. We just ran for our lives. I lost Mr Harrington. I can't make out why he isn't here. Do you think something has happened to him?'

Ashenden was silent for a while.

'We'd better go out and look for him,' he said. 'I don't know why the devil he couldn't leave his washing.'

'I understand, I understand so well.'

'That's a comfort,' said Ashenden irritably. 'Let's go.'

He put on his hat and coat, and they walked downstairs. The hotel seemed strangely empty. They went out into the street. There was hardly anyone to be seen. They walked along. The trams were not running and the silence in the great city was uncanny. The shops were closed. It was quite startling when a motor car dashed by at breakneck speed. The people they passed looked frightened and downcast. When they had to go through a main thoroughfare they hastened their steps. A lot of people were there and they stood about irresolutely as though they did not know what to do next. Reservists in their shabby grey were walking down the middle of the roadway in little bunches. They did not speak. They looked like sheep looking for their shepherd. Then they came to the street down which Anastasia Alexandrovna had run, but they entered it from the opposite end. A number of windows had been broken by the wild shooting. It was quite empty. You could see where the people had scattered for strewn about were articles they had dropped in their haste, books, a man's hat, a lady's bag and a basket. Anastasia Alexandrovna touched Ashenden's arm to draw his attention: sitting on the pavement, her head bent right down to her lap, was a woman and she was dead. A little way on two men had fallen together. They were dead too. The wounded, one supposed, had managed to drag themselves away or their friends had carried them. Then they found Mr Harrington. His derby had rolled in the gutter. He lay on his face, in a pool of blood, his bald head, with its prominent bones, very white; his neat black coat smeared and muddy. But his hand was clenched tight on the parcel that contained four shirts, two union suits, a pair of pyjamas and four collars. Mr Harrington had not let his washing go.

Teffi

Teffi (1872–1952) was the pseudonym of Nadezhda Alexandrovna Lokhvitskaya, a brilliant chronicler of Russian life both in the Soviet Union and as an émigré. She lived in Paris from 1920 until her death in 1952. Like many other Russian intellectuals, Teffi was initially a sympathiser with the Bolsheviks. In 1905, she was, with Maxim Gorky, Zinaida Gippius and Maxim Litvinov, on the editorial board of the (first legal) Bolshevik newspaper *Novaia Zhizn* (New Life): a newspaper to which she frequently contributed. When Lenin returned from exile in November 1905, he established the party line over literature and culture: 'Nowadays we don't need theatre. Nor do we need music. We don't need articles about art or culture of any sort.' Out of a job, Teffi resigned with the rest of the editorial board.[24] This collision of ideas led to her lifelong contempt for Lenin and distrust of the Bolsheviks. She had no time for a political movement without culture and a sense of humour. However, Teffi kept her faith in socialism even when she had lost faith in its agents: 'Leninists, Bolsheviks, anarchists and communists, thugs, registered

---

24 She wrote:

> A piece of literary criticism by 'Anton the Extreme' (Zinaida Gippius) was not published. And a review of a new play failed to appear.
> Why?
> 'Lenin says it's of no interest to the working-class reader,' we were told. 'The working-class reader has no interest in literature and does not go to the theatre.'
> I asked Lenin about this.
> 'Yes,' he said. 'That's right. Now is not the time.'
> 'But workers aren't the only readers of our paper.'
> 'Maybe so, but they're the only readers we're interested in.'
>
> from 'New Life' in *Rasputin and Other Ironies*, page 102–3, London, 2016

housebreakers – what a muddle! What a Satanic vinaigrette! What immense work – to raise once more and cleanse from all this garbage the great idea of socialism!' (from Teffi's essay 'A Few Words about Lenin').

Whether she is writing about Rasputin, about the fight for survival in post-revolutionary Russia or scrubbing a ship's deck wearing silver shoes, Teffi writes in a comic register – she leaves to others the tragic. But this contrast is far from clear cut. For Teffi: 'A joke is not funny when you are living inside it. It begins to seem more like a tragedy.' Scintillating translations have, recently, made available to English-language readers a wonderful writer whose self-deprecation should not be taken at face value.

Rasputin

from *Rasputin and Other Ironies* by Teffi
(translated by Anne Marie Jackson)

Sometime after ten o'clock I arrived at Filippov's.

Our host greeted me in the hall. After saying in a friendly way that we'd already met once before, he showed me into his study.

'Your friends arrived some time ago.'

In the small, smoke-filled room were some half a dozen people.

Rozanov was looking bored and disgruntled. Izmailov appeared strained, as if trying to make out that everything was going fine when really it wasn't.

Manuilov was standing close to the doorway, looking as if he felt entirely at home. Two or three people I didn't know were sitting silently on the divan. And then there was Rasputin. Dressed in a black woollen Russian kaftan and tall patent-leather boots, he was fidgeting anxiously, squirming about in his chair. One of his shoulders kept twitching.

Lean and wiry and rather tall, he had a straggly beard and a thin face that appeared to have been gathered up into a long fleshy nose. His close-set, prickly, glittering little eyes were peering out furtively from under strands of greasy hair. I think these eyes were grey. The way they glittered, it was hard to be sure. Restless eyes. Whenever he said something, he would look round the whole group, his eyes pricking each person in turn, as if to say, 'Have I given you something to think about? Are you satisfied? Have I surprised you?'

I felt at once that he was rather preoccupied, confused, even embarrassed. He was posturing.

'Yes, yes,' he was saying. 'I wish to go back as soon as possible, to Tobolsk. I wish to pray. My little village is a good place to pray. God hears people's prayers there.'

And then he studied each of us in turn, his eyes keenly pricking each one of us from under his greasy locks.

'But here in your city nothing's right. It's not possible to pray in this city. It's very hard when you can't pray. Very hard.'

And again he looked round anxiously, right into everyone's faces, right into their eyes.

We were introduced. As had been agreed, my fellow scribes did not let on who I really was.

He studied me, as if thinking, 'Who is this woman?'

There was a general sense of both tedium and tension – not what we wanted at all. Something in Rasputin's manner – maybe his general unease, maybe his concern about the impression his words were making – suggested that somehow he knew who we were. It seemed we might have been given away. Imagining himself to be surrounded by 'enemies from the press', Rasputin had assumed the posture of a man of prayer.

They say he really did have a great deal to put up with from journalists. The papers were always full of sly insinuations of every kind. After a few drinks with his cronies, Rasputin was supposed to have divulged interesting details about the personal lives of people in the very highest places. Whether this was true or just newspaper sensationalism, I don't know. But I do know that there were two levels of security around Rasputin: one set of guards whom he knew about and who protected him from attempts on his life; another set whom he was supposed not to know about and who kept track of whom he was talking to and whether or not he was saying anything he shouldn't. Just who was responsible for this second set of guards I can't say for certain, but I suspect it was someone who wanted to undermine Rasputin's credibility at court.

He had keen senses, and some animal instinct told him he was surrounded. Not knowing where the enemy lay, he was on the alert, his eyes quietly darting everywhere.

I was infected by my friends' discomfort. It felt tedious and rather awkward to be sitting in the house of a stranger and listening to Rasputin straining to come out with spiritually edifying pronouncements that interested none of us. It was as if he were being tested and was afraid of failing.

I wanted to go home.

Rozanov got to his feet. He took me aside and whispered, 'We're banking on dinner. There's still a chance of him opening up. Filippov and I have agreed that you must sit beside him. And we'll be close by. You'll get him talking. He's not going to talk freely to us – he's a ladies' man. Get him to speak about the erotic. This could be really something – it's a chance we must make the most of. We could end up having a most interesting conversation.'

Rozanov would happily discuss erotic matters with anyone under the sun, so it was hardly a surprise that he should be so eager to discuss them with Rasputin. After all, what didn't they say about Rasputin? He was a hypnotist and a mesmerist, at once a flagellant and a lustful satyr, both a saint and a man possessed by demons.

'All right,' I said. 'I'll do what I can.'

Turning around, I encountered two eyes as sharp as needles. Our surreptitious conversation had obviously disturbed Rasputin.

With a twitch of the shoulder, he turned away.

We were invited to the table.

I was seated at one corner. To my left sat Rozanov and Izmailov. To my right, at the end of the table, Rasputin.

There turned out to be around a dozen other guests: an elderly lady with a self-important air ('She's the one who goes everywhere with him,' someone whispered to me); a harassed-looking gentleman, who hurriedly got a beautiful young lady to sit on Rasputin's right (this young lady was dressed to the nines – certainly more than 'a bit glamorous' – but the look on her face was crushed and hopeless, quite out of keeping with her attire); and at the other end of the table were some strange-looking musicians, with a guitar, an accordion and a tambourine – as if this were a village wedding.

Filippov came over to us, pouring out wine and handing round hors d'oeuvres. In a low voice I asked about the beautiful lady and the musicians.

The musicians, it turned out, were a requirement – Grisha sometimes liked to get up and dance, and only what they played would do. They also played at the Yusupovs'.

'They're very good. Quite unique. In a moment you'll hear for yourself.' As for the beautiful lady, Filippov explained that her husband (the harassed-looking gentleman) was having a difficult time at work. It was an unpleasant and complicated situation that could only be sorted out with the help of the elder. And so this gentleman was seizing every possible opportunity to meet Rasputin, taking his wife along with him and seating her beside Rasputin in the hope that sooner or later he would take notice of her.

'He's been trying for two months now, but Grisha acts as if he doesn't even see them. He can be strange and obstinate.'

Rasputin was drinking a great deal and very quickly. Suddenly he leant towards me and whispered, 'Why aren't you drinking, eh? Drink. God will forgive you. Drink.'

'I don't care for wine, that's why I'm not drinking.'

He looked at me mistrustfully.

'Nonsense! Drink. I'm telling you: God will forgive you. He will forgive you. God will forgive you many things. Drink!'

'But I'm telling you I'd rather not. You don't want me to force myself to drink, do you?'

'What's he saying?' whispered Rozanov on my left. 'Make him talk louder. Ask him again, to make him talk louder. Otherwise I can't hear.'

'But it's nothing interesting. He's just trying to get me to drink.'

'Get him to talk about matters erotic. God Almighty! Do you really not know how to get a man to talk?'

This was beginning to seem funny.

'Stop going on at me! What am I? An agent provocateur? Anyway, why should I go to all this trouble for you?'

I turned away from Rozanov. Rasputin's sharp, watchful eyes pricked into me.

'So you don't want to drink? You are a stubborn one! I'm telling you to drink – and you won't.'

And with a quick and obviously practised movement he quietly reached up and touched my shoulder. Like a hypnotist using touch to direct the current of his will. It was as deliberate as that.

From his intent look I could see he knew exactly what he was doing. And I remembered the lady-in-waiting and her hysterical babbling: '*And then he put his hand on my shoulder and said so commandingly, with such authority . . .*'

So it was like that, was it? Evidently Grisha had a set routine. Raising my eyebrows in surprise, I glanced at him and smiled coolly.

A spasm went through his shoulder and he let out a quiet moan. Quickly and angrily he turned away from me, as if once and for all. But a moment later he was leaning towards me again.

'You may be laughing,' he said, 'but do you know what your eyes are saying? Your eyes are sad. Go on, you can tell me – is he making you suffer badly? Why don't you say anything? Don't you know we all love sweet tears, a woman's sweet tears. Do you understand? I know everything.'

I was delighted for Rozanov. The conversation was evidently turning to matters erotic.

'What is it you know?' I asked loudly, on purpose, so that Rasputin, too, would raise his voice, as people often unwittingly do.

Once again, though, he spoke very softly. 'I know how love can make one person force another to suffer. And I know how necessary it can be to make someone suffer. But I don't want *you* to suffer. Understand?'

'I can't hear a thing!' came Rozanov's cross voice, from my left.

'Be patient!' I whispered.

Rasputin went on.

'What's that ring on your hand? What stone is it?'

'It's an amethyst.'

'Well, that'll do. Hold your hand out to me under the table so no one can see. Then I'll breathe on the ring and warm it . . . The breath of my soul will make you feel better.'

I passed him the ring.

'Oh, why did you have to take it off? That was for me to do. You don't understand . . . '

But I had understood only too well. Which was why I'd taken it off myself.

Covering his mouth with his napkin, he breathed on to the ring and quietly slid it on to my finger.

'There. When you come and see me, I'll tell you many things you don't know.'

'But what if I don't come?' I asked, once again remembering the hysterical lady-in-waiting.

Here he was, Rasputin in his element. The mysterious voice, the intense expression, the commanding words – all this was a tried and tested method. But if so, then it was all rather naïve and straightforward. Or, perhaps, his fame as a sorcerer, soothsayer and favourite of the Tsar really did kindle within people a particular blend of curiosity and fear, a keen desire to participate in this weird mystery. It was like looking through a microscope at some species of beetle. I could see the monstrous hairy legs, the giant maw – but I knew it was really just a little insect.

'Not come to me? No, you shall come. You shall come to me.'

And again he quickly reached up and quietly touched my shoulder. I calmly moved aside and said, 'No, I shan't.'

And again a spasm went through his shoulder and he let out a low moan. Each time he sensed that his power, the current of his will, was not penetrating me and was meeting resistance, he experienced physical pain. (This was my impression at the time – and it was confirmed later.) And in this there was no pretence, as he was evidently trying to conceal both the spasms in his shoulder and his strange, low groan.

No, this was not a straightforward business at all. Howling inside him was a black beast . . . There was much we did not know.

'Ask him about Vyrubova,' whispered Rozanov. 'Ask him about everyone. Get him to tell you everything. And *please* get him to speak up.'

Rasputin gave Rozanov a sideways look from under his greasy locks. 'What's that fellow whispering about?'

Rozanov held his glass out towards Rasputin and said, 'I was wanting to clink glasses.'

Izmailov held his glass out, too.

Rasputin looked at them both warily, looked away, then looked back again.

Suddenly Izmailov asked, 'Tell me, have you ever tried your hand at writing?'

Who, apart from a writer, would think to ask such a question?

'Now and again,' replied Rasputin without the least surprise. 'Even quite a few times.'

And he beckoned to a young man sitting at the other end of the table.

'Dearie! Bring me the pages with my poems that you just tapped out on that little typing machine.'

'Dearie' darted off and came back with the pages.

Rasputin handed them around. Everyone reached out. There were a lot of these typed pages, enough for all of us. We began to read.

It turned out to be a prose poem, in the style of the 'Song of Songs' and obscurely amorous. I can still remember the lines: 'Fine and high are the mountains. But my love is higher and finer yet, because love is God.'

But that seems to have been the only passage that made any sense. Everything else was just a jumble of words.

As I was reading, the author kept looking around restlessly, trying to see what impression his work was making.

'Very good,' I said.

He brightened.

'Dearie! Give us a clean sheet, I'll write something for her myself.'

'What's your name?' he asked.

I said.

He chewed for a long time on his pencil. Then, in a barely decipherable peasant scrawl, he wrote:

To Nadezhda.
God is lov. Now lov. God wil forgiv yu.
Grigory'

The basic pattern of Rasputin's magic charms was clear enough: love, and God will forgive you.

But why should such an inoffensive maxim as this cause his ladies to collapse in fits of ecstasy? Why had that lady-in-waiting got into such a state?

This was no simple matter.

I studied the awkwardly scrawled letters and the signature below: 'Grigory'.

What power this signature held. I knew of a case where this scrawl of seven letters had recalled a man who had been sentenced to forced labour and was already on his way to Siberia.

And it seemed likely that this same signature could, just as easily, transport a man there . . .

'You should hang on to that autograph,' said Rozanov. 'It's quite something.'

It did in fact stay in my possession for a long time. In Paris, some six years ago, I found it in an old briefcase and gave it to J. W. Bienstock, the author of a book about Rasputin in French.

Rasputin really was only semi-literate; writing even a few words was hard work for him. This made me think of the forest-warden in our home village – the man whose job had been to catch poachers and supervise the spring floating of timber. I remembered the little bills he used to write: 'Tren to dacha and bak fife ru' (five roubles).

Rasputin was also strikingly like this man in physical appearance. Perhaps that's why his words and general presence failed to excite the least mystical awe in me. 'God is love, you *shall* come' and so on. That 'fife ru', which I couldn't get out of my head, was constantly in the way . . .

Suddenly our host came up, looking very concerned.

'The palace is on the line.'

Rasputin left the room.

The palace evidently knew exactly where Rasputin was to be found. Probably, they always did.

Taking advantage of Rasputin's absence, Rozanov began lecturing me, advising me how best to steer the conversation on to all kinds of interesting topics.

'And do please get him to talk about the Khlysts and their rites. Find out whether it's all true, and if so, how it's all organised and whether it's possible, say, to attend?

'Get him to invite you, and then you can bring us along, too.'

I agreed willingly. This truly would be interesting.

But Rasputin didn't come back. Our host said he had been summoned urgently to Tsarskoye Selo – even though it was past midnight – but that, as he was leaving, Rasputin had asked him to tell me he would definitely be coming back.

' "Don't let her go," said Filippov, repeating Rasputin's words. "Have her wait for me. I'll be back."

Needless to say no one waited. Our group, at least, left as soon as we had finished eating.

They Got Her to Scrub the Deck

from *Memories: From Moscow to the Black Sea by Teffi*
(translated by Robert Chandler and Irina Steinberg)

That morning Smolyaninov came to see me. He was in charge of various administrative tasks on our ship. In his previous life he may have worked for *The New Age*,[25] though I don't know for sure.

'I have to tell you,' he said, 'that some of the passengers are unhappy that you didn't join in yesterday when they were gutting fish. They're saying you're work-shy and that you're being granted unfair privileges. You must find a way to show that you are willing to work.'

'All right, I'm quite willing to show my willingness.'

'But I really don't know what to suggest. I can hardly make you scrub the deck.'

Ah! Scrubbing the deck! My childhood dream!

As a child I had once seen a sailor hosing the deck with a large hose while another sailor scrubbed away with a stiff, long-handled brush with bristles cut at an angle. I had thought at the time that nothing in the world could be jollier. Since then, I've learned about many things that are jollier, but that stiff, oddly-shaped brush, those rapid, powerful splashes as the water hit the white planks, and the sailors' brisk efficiency (the one doing the scrubbing kept repeating 'Hup! Hup!') had all stayed in my memory – a wonderful, joyous picture.

There I had stood, a little girl with blue eyes and blonde pigtails, watching this sailors' game with reverence and envy, upset that fate would never allow me this joy.

But kind fate had taken pity on that poor little girl. It had tormented her for a long time, but it never forgot her wish. It staged a war and a revolution. It turned the whole world upside down, and now, at last, it

25 *Novoe Vremya*, a Petersburg daily newspaper. Under its last editor, A. S. Suvorin, it was considered reactionary; the Bolsheviks closed it down the day after the October Revolution.

had found an opportunity to thrust a long-handled brush into the girl's hands and send her up on deck.

At last! Thank you, dear fate!

'Tell me,' I said to Smolyaninov. 'Do they have a brush with angled bristles? And will they be using a hose?'

'What!' said Smolyaninov. 'Do you mean it? You're really willing to scrub the deck?'

'Of course I mean it! Only don't, for heaven's sake, change your mind. Come on, let's go . . . '

'You must at least change your clothes!'

But I had nothing to change into.

For the main part, the *Shilka's* passengers wore whatever they could most easily do without. We all knew that it would be impossible to buy anything when we next went ashore, so we were saving our everyday clothes for later. We were wearing only items for which we foresaw no immediate need: colourful shawls, ball gowns, satin slippers . . .

I was wearing a pair of silver shoes. Certainly not the kind of shoes I'd be wearing next time I had to wander about searching for a room.

We went up on deck.

Smolyaninov went off for a moment. A cadet came over with a brush and a hose. Jolly streams of water splashed on to my silver shoes.

'Just for a few minutes,' whispered Smolyaninov. 'For appearances' sake.'

'Hup! Hup!' I repeated.

The cadet looked at me with fear and compassion. 'Please allow me to relieve you!'

'Hup-hup!' I replied. 'We must all do our share. I imagine you've been humping coal; now I must scrub the deck. Yes, sir. We must all do our share, young man. I'm working and I'm proud of the contribution I'm making.'

'But you'll wear yourself out!' said somebody else. 'Please allow me!'

'They're jealous, the sly devils!' I thought, remembering my childhood dream. 'They want to have a go too! Well, why wouldn't they?'

'Nadezhda Alexandrovna! You truly have worn yourself out,' said Smolyaninov. 'The next shift will now take over.'

He then added, under his breath, 'Your scrubbing is abominable.'

Abominable? And there I was, thinking I was just like that sailor from my distant childhood.

'And also, you look far too happy,' Smolyaninov went on. 'People might think this is some kind of game.'

I had no choice but to relinquish my brush.

Offended, I set off down below. As I passed three ladies I didn't know, I heard one of them say my name.

'Yes, I've heard she's here on our boat.'

'You don't say!'

'I'm telling you, she's here on this boat. Not like the rest of us, of course. She's got a cabin to herself, a separate table, and she doesn't want to do any work.'

I shook my head sadly.

'You're being terribly unfair!' I said reproachfully. 'She's just been scrubbing the deck. I saw her with my own eyes.'

'They got her to scrub the deck!' exclaimed one of the ladies. 'That's going too far!'

'And you saw her?'

'Yes, I did.'

'Well? What's she like?'

'Long and lanky. A bit like a gypsy. In red boots.'

'Goodness me!'

'And nobody's breathed a word to us!'

'That must be very hard work, mustn't it?'

'Yes,' I said. 'A lot harder than just stroking a fish with a knife.'

'So why's she doing it?'

'She wants to set an example.'

'And to think that nobody's breathed a word to us!'

'Do you know when she'll be scrubbing next? We'd like to watch.'

'I'm not sure. I've heard she's put her name down to work in the boiler room tomorrow, but that may just be a rumour.'

'Now that really is going too far!' said one of the ladies, with concern. 'It's all right,' said one of her companions reassuringly. 'A writer needs to experience many things. It's not for nothing that Maxim Gorky worked as a baker when he was young.'

'But that,' said the other lady, 'was before he became a writer.'

'Well, he must have known he'd become a writer. Why else would he have gone to work in a bakery?'

Late that evening, when I was sitting alone in our bathroom-cabin, there was a quiet knock at the door.

'May I?'

'You may.'

In came a man in uniform. I had never seen him before. He looked around the cabin.

'You're alone? Perfect.'

And, turning round, he called out, 'Come in, gentlemen, we'll be on our own.'

In came a few other men. Among them was O, the engineer.

'Well?' asked O. 'What is it we've come here to discuss?'

'A very serious matter indeed,' whispered the man in uniform. 'We're being deceived. They say we're going to Sebastopol, but really we're heading for Romania, where the captain will hand us over to the Bolsheviks.'

'Why on earth would there be Bolsheviks in Romania? You're talking nonsense.'

'By the time you know for sure that I'm not, it will be too late. I can only tell you that the *Shilka* is at this very moment heading towards Romania. There's only one thing we can do: go to the captain tonight and confront him. Then we must hand over the command to Lieutenant F—. He's a man we can trust. I know him well, and what's more, he's related to a very well-known public figure. So, we must act straightaway. Please make your decision.'

Everyone fell silent.

'Gentlemen,' I began, 'none of this is substantiated and it is all extremely unclear. Why don't we just wait till tomorrow? We could simply go to the captain and ask him why we're no longer heading for Sebastopol. Confronting him in his cabin at night would be outright mutiny.'

'So that's where you stand, is it?' said the ringleader – and fell ominously silent.

There we were in the half-dark little cabin, whispering together like inveterate conspirators. Clattering above our heads was the tiller chain – our traitorous little captain steering the boat towards Romania. All straight out of an adventure novel.

'You're right,' said O the engineer. 'Best to wait till tomorrow.'

And the ringleader unexpectedly agreed: 'Yes, maybe. Perhaps that will be best of all.'

In the morning O told me that he had been to see the captain. And the captain had gladly given him a very simple explanation: He had changed course in order to avoid some minefields.

How surprised the poor man would have been had we burst into his cabin in the middle of the night, clenching daggers between our teeth.

Later I saw Lieutenant F—. A tall, melancholy neurotic, he seemed not to have known about the plan to proclaim him the ship's dictator. Or maybe he *had* known . . . When we reached Sebastopol, he left the ship.

Isaac Babel

Isaac Babel (1894–1940) was a Jewish-Russian writer best known for his extraordinary short stories, especially those included in *Red Cavalry*, a collection of tales about Babel's Cossack division. The subject of *Diary: 1920* is the Soviet-Polish War which began in February 1919. Outfought in the beginning by the Polish, the Russians brought to the front the pro-Soviet First Cavalry Army, made up of sixteen thousand Cossacks, commanded by Marshal Budyonny. Babel joined the Cavalry Army as a journalist for its daily newspaper, the *Red Cavalryman*. The themes that are central to the stories of *Red Cavalry* are also central to *Diary: 1920* – how being Jewish affects the narrator's commitment to the Bolshevik Revolution and his support for the Cossacks, in view of the fate of civilians, many of whom are Jewish, caught up in the war. Babel was well aware of the savagery towards the Jews of the Whites in the Civil War and the Poles in the Soviet-Polish War, but he was also confronted with the manifold acts of 'bestial cruelty' of the Cossacks on the Bolshevik side. So unflattering was Babel's portrayal of the Cossacks that Marshal Budyonny demanded his execution. Saved by Gorky's protection, Babel followed *Red Cavalry* with the *Odessa Tales* that describe the life of Jewish gangsters in the Odessa ghetto before and after the Revolution. In the 1930s, Babel found it harder to maintain a position of critical support for the government. As the situation in the country deteriorated, it was more and more difficult for him to get his work past the censors – he continued to write but after a few attempts no longer tried to get his work published. As he ironically noted at the first Congress of the Union of Soviet Writers, he was becoming 'the master of a new literary genre, the genre of silence'. Arrested by the NKVD in May 1939, Babel's interrogation is surreal even by Soviet standards:

> Q   You have been arrested for treacherous anti-Soviet activities. Do you acknowledge your guilt?

A No, I do not.

Q How can you reconcile that declaration of innocence with the fact of your arrest?

A I consider my arrest the result of a fateful coincidence and of my own inability to write. During the last few years, I have not published a single major work and this might be considered sabotage and an unwillingness to write under Soviet conditions.

Q You wish to say you have been arrested as a writer? Does that not strike you as an excessively naïve explanation for your arrest?

A You are right, of course. Authors are not arrested because they can no longer write.

Q So what was the real reason for your arrest?

A I often went abroad and have been friendly with leading Trotskyists . . . [26]

This bizarre procedure whereby the accused was asked to prove his own guilt was an innovation of Soviet jurisprudence. Babel was executed on the 27 January 1940. In 1948, the NKVD was still writing to his widow: 'He is alive, well and being held in the camps.'

Isaac Babel's *Diary: 1920*

(translated by Nicholas Stroud)

Zhitomir. 3 June 1920

At daybreak on the train, got my service blouse and boots. I sleep with Shukov, Topolnik. It's filthy, the burning morning sun, muck in the railroad car. The tall Shukov, the greedy Topolnik, the entire editorial staff – unbelievably disgusting people. Wretched tea in hidden kettles, letters to home, packages to Yugrosta, an interview with a Pole, operation assault on Novograd, the broken-down discipline in the Polish Army, Polish 'White Guard' literature, booklets out of cigarette

26 This is taken from 'I Beg You to Hear Me': the file on Isaac Babel in Vitaly Shentalinsky's *The KGB's Literary Archive*: an extraordinary record.

from *Diary:1920*

paper . . . Ukrainian Jews, commissars; they're all stupid, enraged, powerless, incompetent and remarkably unconvincing. Mikhailov's excerpts from Polish newspapers. The kitchen on the train, red-faced, fat soldiers, gutted pigs, stifling heat in the kitchen, mush-porridge, midday, sweat, laundresses with stout legs, apathetic women . . . To describe the soldiers, the fat, satiated, lethargic women. Love in the kitchen. In the afternoon off to Zhitomir. A clean city, not a sleepy, but a subdued, tamed city. I search for traces of Polish culture. Well-dressed women, white stockings. A church. Near Nushka I bathe in the Teterev, a detestable stream, there bathe old Jews with long skinny grey-haired legs. The young Jews. Women rinse clothes in the Teterev. One family, a beautiful wife, the husband carries the child. The open bazaar in Zhitomir, an old cobbler, bluing, chalk, twine. The synagogues, old architecture, how deeply all that touches me. An hourglass 1200 rubles. The market. A small Jew-philosopher. Incredible shops – Dickens, brooms and golden slippers. His philosophy – everyone says they fight for the truth and yet everybody steals. If there were only a good government at least. Beautiful words, a little beard, we enjoy ourselves, tea and three pieces of apple cake – 750 rubles. An interesting old woman, mean, enterprising, how avaricious they all are. To describe the bazaar, baskets full of cherries, the inside of an inn. Conversation with a Russian woman, who comes to borrow a washtub. Then weak tea. I eat, I'm alive, farewell, you dead ones. Brother-in-law Podolski, a degenerate intellect, something about trade unions, something about serving Budyonny. I am, of course, a Russian, his mother is a Jew, why? A pogrom in Zhitomir, plotted by the Poles, naturally afterwards also by the Cossacks. When our advance units appeared, the Poles occupied the city for three days, a pogrom, they cut beards off, that's only common. They apprehended forty-five Jews at the market, drove them to the slaughterhouse, tongues were cut out, groaning throughout the entire place. Six houses were set afire, Konyukhovski's home on the cathedral square – I watched it, I wonder who saved it from being chopped up by the machine guns, it was entrusted to the caretaker, to whom the mother threw the infant child from the burning window. They were detained, the priest rested a ladder against the rear of the house, thus enabling them to escape.

The Sabbath is approaching, we are going from father-in-law to the Tsaddik's. The name I never did understand. A most unusual sight for me, although death and complete ruin are unmistakable. The Tsaddik's narrow-shouldered, haggard, petite figure. The son – a well-bred young boy in a small tallis, we look into the petit-bourgeois but spacious rooms. Everything's neat. The wife is an average Jew, has a tendency to be somewhat modern. The faces of the old Jews. Discussions about famine in the corner of the room. I'm lost in the prayer book. Podolski helps. A pine torch is used in place of candles. I'm happy – huge faces, aquiline noses, black beards shot with grey, I think about many things, farewell, you dead, Tsaddik's face, a real penny-pincher, where do you come from, young man? From Odessa. How are things there? One lives. Here things are dreadful. A short conversation. I leave stunned. Podolski, pale and sad, gives me his address, a wonderful evening. I walk, think about the quiet, unknown streets. Kondratev with a black-haired Jewess. The poor commander, with Papashka, he's got no luck. Then night, the train, the painted cries of communism (in contrast to what I saw at the old Jew's), machine-gun fire, their own electric power station, their own newspaper, the movie's on, the train flashes, roars, big-lipped soldiers stand in line for the laundresses (2 days).

Zhitomir. 4 June 1920

In the morning – letters to Yugrosta, information about the pogrom in Zhitomir, to home, to Oreshchnikov, to Narbut. I'm reading Hamsun. Sobelman tells me about the subject of his novel: Hiob's new manuscript, the old man who's been living for centuries, the students stole it in order to sham a resurrection, a gorged foreigner, the Russian revolution. Schulz, the most important thing, lust, communism is whenever we pilfer apples from our masters, Schulz tells me, his bald head, apples stuffed in his shirt, communism, a Dostoyevsky-like character, there's something to it, you just have to think about it some more, this insatiable lust, Schulz on the streets of Berdichev. Khelemskaia, who had pleurisy, diarrhoea, looks yellow, a dirty hood, apple sauce, why are you here, Khelemskaia? You should have married, a man – accountant, engineer, abortion, or the first child, that was your life, your mother, you bathed twice a week, your novel, Khelemskaia – this is how you must live and adapt yourself to the revolution. The opening of the communist club in the editor's office. There it is – the proletariat – these unbelievably emaciated Jews, who crawled forth out of illegitimacy. Miserable, powerful race – onwards! Then to describe the concert, the women sing Little Russian songs. Bathing in the Teterev.

Belev. 11 July 1920

Night, the staff works in Belev. What does Zolnarkevich mean? A Pole? His feelings? Touching friendship between two brothers. Konstantin and Mikhailo.

Z— a war horse, exactly, works feverishly without growing tired, full of energy without being loud, a Polish moustache, thin Polish legs. The staff – there's Zolnarkevich, then three clerks who wear themselves out at night.

Lodging for the brigrade's an immense problem, there are no provisions. Most importantly – the manoeuvre – goes unnoticed. The orderlies sleep at the headquarters on the ground. Thin candles burn, the commander of the divisional staff, with cap on, rubs his brow and dictates, dictates incessantly – operational reports, commands to the artillery division, we are going to march on Lutsk.

Night, I'm sleeping next to Lepin, the Latvian, in the hay, horses that have freed themselves roam about, eat away the hay from beneath our heads.

I spent the night in the hay with soldiers from the staff squadron. Slept badly, think of my manuscripts, depression, my energy weakens, I know that I'll make it, but when? Klevan, its ways, streets, peasants and communism – how far apart they are from one another.

Belev. 12 July 1920

At dawn the journal of hostile actions was begun – I'm analysing the official army communiqués.

A mill – naturally not quite up to date. The Czech has heaps of receipts. A note to the district commissariat in Rovno that four horses have been seized, in place of a confiscated cabriolet – a broken-down machine-gun wagon, three receipts for four and oats. A brigade arrives, red flags, a powerful, welded-together body, self-assured commanders, skilled, peaceful, Cossack eyes, dust, stillness, order, an orchestra, everything is to be sucked up by the barracks, the brigade commander calls to me, nothing is to be requisitioned, this is our territory.

Belev. 13 July 1920

My birthday. I'm twenty-six. I think of home, of my work, my life is just flying by. No manuscripts. Dismal melancholy, I'm going to make it. I keep up with my diary – that will be interesting.

I'm going to Yasienevishchi to exchange my touring car for a machine-gun wagon and horses. Unbelievable dust, heat. We're driving through Peresopnitsa, what a joy to gaze at the fields, my twenty-seventh year, I believe the rye is ripe, the barley is growing quite well here and there, oats, the poppies are ready to bloom, no cherries, apples still green, much hemp, buckwheat, many trampled fields, hops. A rich land, rich with limitations.

The clerks – handsome, young. The young Russian field officers sing operatic melodies, everybody has been slightly spoiled by the field work. To characterise the orderlies – gossips, parasites, flatterers, gluttons, idlers, inheritors of the old system, they know their masters well.

Work of the staff in Belev. Well-coordinated machines, the wonderful staff commander, both a mechanical worker and a lively man. A disclosure – a Pole was set free, brought back under the order of the divisional commander, something that he can readily sense. He's not a Communist – a Pole, and serves loyally, like a watchdog, that one truly has to understand. The commander of the cavalry reserve Diakov – a fantastic sight. Red pants with silver stripes, belt with a golden embellishment, comes from Stavropol, built like Apollo, short, grey moustache, forty-five years old, has a son and nephews, excessive cursing . . . Diakov, his soldiers love him, a devil of a fellow, our commander, was an athlete, almost illiterate . . . General Diakov is a Communist, an experienced, brave Budyonny fighter. He once met a millionaire with a lady on his arm: Mr Diakov, don't we know each other from the club? Was in eight states, wherever I appear all I have to do is snap my fingers – dancer, harmonica player, sly fox, boaster, extremely picturesque character. Barely decodes the commands, loses them constantly, this office junk, I'll just give up completely, what would they do without me, curses, conversations with peasants, they gape in awe. Machine-gun wagons and a pair of emaciated horses.

Belev. 14 July 1920

A shot-down American pilot, oh how that smelled of Europe, like a coffee-house, civilisation, power, old culture, I ponder and observe, I see it all, barefoot, but elegant, his neck like a pillar, dazzling white teeth, suit covered with oil and dirt. Asks me fearfully whether it is a crime to fight against Soviet Russia. We have a strong cause . . . A letter from Major Font-le-Roy – things are bad in Poland, no existing system of government, the Bolsheviks are strong, the socialists in the centre of interest, however not in power.

We study the new conduct of the war. What are the soldiers in Western Europe told? Russian imperialism, they want to destroy nations, to abolish customs, that's their main goal, they want to conquer all the Slavic lands – the same old nonsense. Endless conversation with Mosher, I'm engrossed in the old man, we'll bring you back to your senses, Mosher, ah, Conan Doyle, letters to New York. Whether Mosher pretends it or not, he's frantically trying to figure out what Bolshevism is. An impression – sad, but sweet. I'm familiarising myself with the staff, I have a driver, Grishchuk, thirty-nine. Spent six years in a German prison, it's fifty versts to his home (he comes from the Krements District), he's not allowed to go there, he's silent. Divisional commander Timoshchenko on the staff. Colourful character. A colossal man, red leathery pants, red cap, slender, corporal, machine-gunner, was a cadet in the artillery. Legendary stories.
Budyonny's riders bring Communism, a woman cries.

Belev. 15 July 1920

Life is dull here. Where is the Ukrainian gaiety? Harvest begins.

Pilsudski's call intercepted: soldiers of the Rzeczpospolita, sentimental, sad, but without the ironclad arguments of Bolshevism . . . A hearing about deserters. We present our flyers. Immense effect, the leaflet helps the Cossacks.

Novoselki. 16 July 1920

I'm riding with the divisional commander and the staff squadron, we're chasing the horses, forests, horses, the red cap of the divisional commander, his strong stature, trumpeter, it's grand, the new army, the divisional commander and squadron – one body . . . To describe the ride with the divisional commander, the small staff squadron, the divisional commander's convoy. Bakhturov, the old Budyonny fighters, while decamping – a march.

Novoselki. Mal. Dorogostai. 18 July 1920

Command from the southwestern front concerning movement into Galicia, for the first time Soviet troops cross the border. They treated the inhabitants well. We are not coming into a conquered land. The land belongs to the Galician workers and peasants and only to them, we are only coming to help them, to establish Soviet power. An important and shrewd command; are the boasters going to execute it? No.

We ride on dirt roads with two staff squadrons, the constant companions of the divisional commander. Special troops. To describe the cavalry equipment, swords in red velvet, scimitars, Cossack waistcoats, blankets on the saddles, poorly dressed, even though each one owns ten jackets, that most certainly is a part of the fashion.

Their grand comradeship, determination, love for horses, the horse alone takes up a fourth of the day, never-ending haggling, conversations. The role and life of the horse. The most unusual relation to authority – almost on a first-name basis.

At the priest's I ate my fill for the whole year. It's over for him, they say, he's trying to find a position, do you also have a regimental chaplain?

M. Dorogostai. Smordva-Beregi. 19 July 1920

The wounded are arriving, units, bare bellies, patience, unbearable heat, constant bombardment from both sides, you can't recover your senses. Budyonny and Voroshilov on the small stairs.

Battle scene, the cavalrymen returning, covered with dust, soaked with perspiration, bloody, not a trace of excitement, war horses, professionals, everything proceeds in the greatest peace – that's the extraordinary thing, self-confidence, the difficult work, the nurses rush over to their horses, the glowing tank.

21 July 1920

Dubno's taken. Resistance was minimal, why? The prisoners say, and it's quite obvious – a small people's revolution. There would be a lot to say about that, the beauty of the pointed Polish gable-ends, touching the countess. Fate, honour, Jews, Count Ledóchowski? A proletarian revolution? How I inhale the fragrance of Europe, which emanates from there. And what about the Cossack? Traits: tale-bearing, boldness, professionalism, revolutionary spirit, bestial cruelty.

22 July 1920

In two hours I'll be riding to Khotin. Woodland path, restlessness. Grishchuk is apathetic and horrible. I'm riding Sikolov's difficult horse. I'm alone on the road. It's bright, clear, not hot, pleasantly warm. In front a small wagon, five men, look like Poles. A game, we ride, stop, where to? Fear and anxiety on both sides. At Khotin we discover our troops, we ride into it, haphazard fighting. A wild fight back, I pull the horse by the reins. The bullets zoom by, they whistle. Artillery fire, Grishchuk takes off at times, crazily, sullen, without saying a word, in dangerous moments he's sometimes incomprehensible, careless, morose, his hairy chin. Grishchuk grabs the torn reins and calls out in his unexpected clear and small tenor – we're lost, the Pole overtakes us.

23 July 1920

Then on to Dubno. I'm travelling with Prishchepa, a new acquaintance, coachman's coat, white hood, illiterate, Communist. The synagogues of Dubno. Everything demolished. Two small entrances have remained standing, centuries, two small rooms, full of remembrances, four synagogues, next to each other, and then pasture, fields, the sunset.

Synagogues – obscure, old, little green and blue buildings. Hasidic, inside not a bit of architecture. I enter one of the Hasidic synagogues. It's Friday. What deformed small figures, what emaciated faces, everything that existed three hundred years ago has risen from the dead for me, the aged run through the synagogue – no lamenting, for some reason they run from one corner to the other, a completely informal prayer. The ugliest Jews of Dubno have probably gathered here. I pray, I pray quickly and think of Hershele, in this way one should have to describe him. One quiet evening in the synagogue – that always has an unexplainable effect on me – four synagogues next to each other.

Here Grishchuk is fifty versts away from home. He doesn't escape.

24 July 1920

From Krivye I head towards Leszniów with Prishchepa, then farther on to Demidovka. Prishchepa's mind – illiterate, just a lad, Communist, the cadets slew his parents, he tells me how he gathered up his things in the village. Decorative, hood, simple, like a blade of grass, one day he will become a boaster, despises Grishchuk, because he doesn't love horses and doesn't understand. We drive through Khorupan and Smordva towards Demidovka. To note the scene – baggage train, riders, half-destroyed villages, fields and forests, oaks, wounded here and there and my wagon. Towards evening we arrive in Demidovka. It's a Jewish place. I have to be on my guard. The Jews are exiled, everything's destroyed. We are in a house with many women. Liakhetsky, Shvekhvel, but no, that's not Odessa. The dentist Dora Antonovna reads Artsybashev, surrounded by Cossacks she is proud, bitter, tells of how the Poles wounded her honour, despises the Communists because they're too plebeian for her, a number of daughters, the main worry – today is Sabbath. Prishchepa orders potatoes to be cooked, and I am silent, because I'm a Russian, and tomorrow is a time of fasting, the ninth of Av . . . The dentist, pallid from pride and dignity, announces potatoes will not be pulled out, it is a day of rest. Prishchepa, restrained long enough by me, breaks into a rage, Jews, lets out his complete arsenal of curses, they all hate us and me, how dare they not cook potatoes, do they fear in a strange garden, will they trip over crosses? Prishchepa has flown into a fit of rage. Everything's just distressing – Artsybashev and the secondary-school girl, an orphan from Rovno, and Prishchepa in his hood. The mother wrings her hands – a quarrel on Sabbath, curses left and right. Budyonny was here and is gone again. An argument between a young Jewish boy and Prishchepa. The young boy with glasses, black hair, nervous, flushed with excitement, broken Russian. He believes in God, God is an ideal that we carry in our hearts, every man carries his own God in his heart – if you sin, God grieves for you, ecstatically and full of grief he tells us this nonsense. Prishchepa is embarrassingly dumb, he tells something about religion in antiquity, mixes up Christianity and paganism, the main point is – at that time there were the Bolshies, complete rubbish, naturally. They have absolutely no education at all – and the Jew, with six classes in the secondary school in Rovno, speaks like Plato – sentimental and comical – birth, the ancients, Perun, paganism.

We devour the cooked potatoes like wolves, and each one has five glasses of coffee . . . the ninth of Av. The old woman howls, sitting on the floor, her son who idolises his mother and says that he believes in God, in order to do something pleasant for her – sings in a pleasant small tenor and tells the story of the destruction of the temple: the frightful words of the prophet – they eat manure, the girls are raped, the men slain, Israel destroyed, angry, wailing words. The lamp smokes, the old woman howls, outside is Demidovka, Cossacks, everything like the time when the temple fell . . .

25 July 1920

At morning departure from Demidovka. An agonising two hours, the Jewish women were awakened at four o'clock in the morning and had to cook Russian meat, and that of all things on the ninth of Av. The girls run half-naked and sluggishly through the damp gardens. Prishchepa, lustful, assails the bride of the dishonest old man's son, in the meantime the wagon was ready, atrocious swearing, the soldiers eat meat out of the kettles, she – I shout, her face, he's squeezing her against the wall, sickening scene; she's frantically defending the wagon, he was hidden on the ground, she'll become a good Jewish woman someday. There's an argument with the commissioner, who maintains that the Jews didn't want to help the Red Army.

26 July 1920
The Galicians on the streets, Austrian uniforms, barefoot, tobacco-pipes in their mouths, the secret of lowliness, the triteness of obedience.

That remains to be thought through – Galicia, the world war, one's own fate.

Khotin. 27 July 1920
They live poorly, primitively, a tiny room with a myriad of flies, abominable grub, and they don't need anything better – greed and the unaltered ghastly living conditions.

29 July 1920
The situation in Galicia is intolerably hopeless, destroyed churches and crucifixes, ominous sky . . . After a depressing and monotonous day – a rainy night, mud – I'm wearing half-shoes. Now it's really pouring, the majestic rain, the one and only victor. We wade through bog, penetrating, fine rain.

A new driver – the Pole, Gowinski, tall, skilful, talkative, restless and naturally, audacious.

Brody. 30 July 1920
The city is destroyed, plundered. A very interesting city. Polish culture. An ancient, rich Jewish colony. These frightening bazaars, dwarfs in hooded coats, hoods and side-locks, the aged, a school street, ninety-six synagogues, all half-destroyed, and stories – American soldiers were here, oranges, cloth, thoroughfare, wire, deforestation and wasteland, endless barren land. Nothing to eat, no hope, war, everyone is equally bad, equally foreign, hostile, inhuman, before life was traditionally peaceful.

Brody, Leszniów, 31 July 1920
At morning, before departing, my wagon stood on Zolotaya Street, one hour I was in the bookstore, a German store. All the beautiful books, film strips, the West, there it is, the West and Poland during

the age of chivalry, anthologies, the story about all the Boleslaws, and I don't know why, it seems so nice to me, Poles, the old body clad with brilliant clothes. I act as if I were totally insane, run to and from, it's dark, the plunderings are in full speed, stationery is stolen, disgusting young boys of decidedly military manner from the requisitions commission. In desperation I tear myself away from the store.

2 August 1920

I'm getting the second squadron's first-aid wagon, we drive to the forest, there I remain with my driver Ivan. Budyonny comes, Voroshilov, the deciding battle, not a single step back. Then the brigades break open, I speak with the staff commander. The atmosphere at the beginning of the battle – a giant field, aeroplanes, the cavalry attacks, our horsemen, explosions in the distance, the battle has begun, machine guns, sun, somewhere they are uniting themselves, a subdued hurrah, Ivan and I drive back, imminent danger, what I feel is not fear but passivity, he is obviously afraid to decide a course of direction, Koroshchaev's group retreats to the right, we to the left. The battle's raging, horses retrieve us – the wounded, one is deathly pale: brothers, take me along – his pants overflowing with blood, he threatens to shoot if we don't take him along, we lift him up, horrid sight, blood flows down Ivan's coat, Cossack, stop! I tie him up, he is only slightly wounded, stomach gunshot wound, right through the bones, we go for still another one, whose horse is dead. A long while we can't find our way (to describe the wounded) across the fields under fire, can't see anything. These indifferent roads and blades of grass, we dispatch messengers, who ride towards the thoroughfare – which way, to Radziwiłłów or Brody.

The administrative staff and the entire baggage train should be in Radziwiłłów, in my opinion it's more interesting to drive to Brody. Brody is being fought for. Ivan's opinion prevails. Some say the Poles are in Brody; the baggage train is fleeing, the staff is already gone. We drive back towards Radziwiłłów. We're there at night. The whole time ate carrots and peas – raw, biting hunger, covered with dirt, not having slept, I seize a cottage on the outskirts of Radziwiłłów.

An old man, a girl. The sour milk is great, we ate it up, then tea with milk. Ivan goes to get sugar. Shooting, uproar, we run out, the horse is lame, we flee in panic, hurry, they're shooting after us, everything's totally unexplainable, soon they'll catch up with us, we race towards a bridge. Collision, we stick in mud, wild panic, a corpse, deserted carts, grenades, machine-gun wagons. Stoppage, night, fear, the endless line of baggage-train cars, we make off to an open field, stop, sleep, stars. What I regret most from this whole episode is the tea we had to leave behind, in fact so much so that just the sound of the word is wonderful. I spend the whole night thinking about it and hate the war. What an unstable life.

3 August 1920

The battlefield. I meet the divisional commander, where is the staff? We lost Zolnarkievich. The battle begins, the artillery covers, grenade impacts close by, a frightful hour, the deciding battle – will we stop the Polish charge or not? Budyonny to Kolesnikov or Grishchin – I'm going to shoot you dead, they leave him looking pale.

Before that – a terrible field, dotted with maimed bodies, inhuman cruelty, monstrous injuries, caved in skulls, young, white naked bodies glistening in the sun, scattered notebooks, loose pages, paybooks, Bibles, bodies in the corn. I'm trying to rationalise my impressions. The battle begins, I'm given a horse. I see how the columns are forming, advancing in line, I feel sorry for these unlucky souls, not human beings but columns, the firing is at its peak, silence whenever the swords are at work. I ride forward, rumours about the recall of the divisional commander.

The beginning of my adventures. I ride with the baggage train to the highway, the battle is expanding, I found the supply centre. Firing on the highway, the whistling of bullets, impacts twenty paces away, a feeling of hopelessness, the baggage-train horses run away, I went over to the 20th regiment of the 4th division. To describe above all else on this day – the Red Army soldiers and the air.

Khotin. 6 August 1920

From time to time Apanassenko emerges, he's different from the reticent Timoshchenko, he belongs to us – he's father, commander. In the morning Bakhturov rides, his entourage after him, I observe the work of the war commissioner, a dull, but proven Muscovite worker, therein lies his strength, he's a robot, but great goals, the three war commissioners.

Berestechko. 7 August 1920

A memorable day. Morning from Sotin to Berestechko . . . Corpse of a slain Pole, horrible corpse, bloated and naked, ugly, Berestechko has seen several different occupants. The historical sites near Berestechko, Cossack graves. And above all, everything repeats itself – Cossacks against Poles, servant against master. I'll never forget this place, spread out, long, narrow, stinking yards. Everything's between one and two hundred years old, the population hardier here than in other places, most importantly – the architecture, white, water-blue houses, lanes, synagogues, peasant women. Life gradually returns to normal. It was good to live here – an honourable Jewry, rich Ukrainians, Sunday markets, a special class of Russian petite bourgeoisie – furriers, leather trade with Austria, smuggling. The Jews are less fanatic here, more elegant, more powerful, almost happier, aged old men, hoods, little old women, everything is redolent of the old times, of tradition, the place is enriched with the bloody history of European–Polish ghettos . . . The old church, graves of Polish officers at the church wall, fresh piles of dirt, ten days old, white birchwood crosses, everything's horrible, the priest's house destroyed, I find old books, valuable Latin manuscripts. Father Tuzinkiewicz – I find his apartment – plump and short, he has worked here forty-five years, lived at one place, scholastic, books, much Latin, editions from 1860, an old spacious room, darkened pictures, photos from the conferences of the priests in Zhitomir, portraits of Pius X, an honest face, a beautiful picture of Sienkiewicz – there he is, the essence of the nation.

The plundering of the church was an awful event, the official robes torn to shreds, precious, brilliant material destroyed, on the floor a nurse drags away three bundles, lining torn out, the candles have disappeared, trunks forced open, papal bulls strewn about, money stolen, a wonderful church – two hundred years old – what hasn't it seen (Tuzinkiewicz's manuscripts), how many counts and peasants, beautiful, grand Italian painting, rosy-cheeked fathers, who rock the

Christ child, a wonderfully mysterious Christ, Rembrandt, a Murillo-like Madonna, why not really Murillo, but most important are these well-fed, holy Jesuits, behind a veil of fearsome petite Chinese figure in a raspberry coloured kontush, a bearded Jew, a reliquary broken into, a sculpture of St Valentine.

Evening in this place. The church is closed. Towards evening I go to the castle of Count Raciborski. A seventy-year-old bachelor and his mother, ninety. They were alone, went mad, it was rumoured. To describe the couple. The old Polish count's house, certainly over a hundred years old, antlers, antique, brilliant painted ceilings, antler remains, the small servants' rooms upstairs, tiles, passages, excrement on the floor, young Jewish boys, a Steinway grand piano, sofas slit open to the feathers, not to be forgotten: the white, light, oaken doors, French letters from 1820 . . . My God, who wrote them, when, the trampled down letters, I took the relics with me, a century, the mother countess. Steinway grand piano, park, pond.

I can't get away from it – think about the captain, Elga. Meeting in the castle park, the Jews of Berestechko, the gloomy Vinokurov, children running around, a revolutionary committee is chosen, the Jews curl their beards, the Jewish women eavesdrop on talks about the Russian paradise, about the international situation, about the rebellion in India.

Berestechko. 8 August 1920
One has to look closely at Apanassenko. An ataman.

Laszków. 9 August 1920
From Berestechko to Laszków, Galicia. The divisional commander's wagon, his orderly Lyovka – who loiters around and is crazy about horses. How he abused his neighbour Stepan, who was Denikin's watchman, insulted the people, and then returned to the village. They weren't allowed to cut his throat, therefore they threw him into prison, whipped him till his back bled, sprang all over him, danced, epic dialogue: pleasant, Stepan? Bad. And those whom you've insulted – what became of them? Things went badly for them. And did you ever

think that it could be bad for you? No. But you should have thought of that, Stepan, we believe, if we were arrested you would have cut our throats . . . but now, Stepan, we're going to kill you. They let him be only when he was almost cold dead.

We are hurrying, the first squadron is in my yard. Night, a lamp stands on my table, the horses are quietly snorting, everybody here is from the Kuban, we eat, sleep, cook together, it's a reserved community. Everyone is rustic, evenings they sing their songs in a full voice, they resemble church songs, devotion to the horses, small little heaps – saddles, bridles, adorned swords, coats. I sleep surrounded by them. Days I sleep outside. No operations, what a splendid and essential thing. Repose for the cavalry, horses rest from this inhuman work, men rest from the cruelty of war, they live together, sing softly, chat with each other.

Laszków. 11 August 1920

About the Kuban Cossacks. A community, always together, outside the window horses snort day and night, the wonderful odour of manure, sun, sleeping Cossacks; twice a day they cook a giant cauldron of soup and meat. Nights they're guests somewhere. Continuous rain, they dry off and eat in my room.

Interview with Apanassenko. Very interesting. That I must bear in mind.

Apanassenko – thirsting for glory, that's it – the new class.

In spite of all operational duties, he frees himself and returns again and again, organised units, simply against the officers, four St George's crosses, goes on duty, corporal, cadet under Kerensky, chairman of the regimental committee, tore off the soldiers' shoulder boards, long months in the steppe near Astrakhan, indisputable authority, professional soldier. About the atamans, there were many of them, they obtained machine guns, fought against Shukuro and Mamontov, merged with the Red Army, heroic epopee. That is not a Marxist revolution, but rather a Cossack rebellion, which would like to gain everything and lose nothing. Apanassenko's hate for the rich, the intellectuals, an undying hate.

12 August 1920

A free day, a good thing – correspondence, if one only didn't have to neglect it. I also have to prepare Apanassenko's biography for the newspaper. I'm still writing about tobacco-pipes, long since forgotten things.

13 August 1920

The whole day on horseback with the divisional commander. Khutor Porady. In the forest, four enemy aeroplanes, volleys. Three brigade commanders – Kolesnikov, Korochaev, Kniga.

[On 13 August Babel wrote a letter. It remained between the pages of the diary.]

Today my letterhead must read: at the edge of the forest, northwest of Starie Maidany. Since this morning both the staff squadron and the divisional staff are here. All day long we drive from brigade to brigade, pursuing battles, writing reports, we spend the night . . . in the forests, flee from the aeroplanes that bombard us. Above us an enchanting sky, a warm sun, the fragrance of firs all around us, hundreds of steppe horses snort – here one should live, however, our thoughts are occupied by the dead. This may sound silly, but war is, although in fact sometimes beautiful, in every respect destructive.

I have two weeks of total confusion behind me, it resulted from the raging cruelty which ceases not a single minute here, and from all of this I've clearly understood how unfit I am for the work of destruction, how difficult it will be for me to free myself from my old ways – from that which is perhaps bad, but which smells like poetry to me, as the beehive smells of honey, now I'm coming back to myself, what's there to worry about, some are going to cause revolution, and I am going to sing of that which is off to the side, which lies deeper, I have the feeling that I can do that and that there will be a time and a place for that . . . I recovered my senses, there's a storm raging in my breast, one hundred horsepower strong, again I continue with my thoughts, and the two demons, i.e., bombs, that exploded half an hour ago a hundred paces from us, even they are unable to keep me from them.

from *Diary:1920*

18 August 1920

In a night attack the second brigade took Toporov. Apanassenko's beaming. The second brigade rides by. Tufts of hair, uniforms out of carpets, red tobacco pouches, short carbines, the commanders on beautiful horses, Budyonny's brigade. Parade, orchestra, good day, sons of Revolution, Apanassenko's beaming.

The epopee with the nurse – and above all, much is spoken about her and everybody despises her, her own driver doesn't speak to her, her shoes, her aprons, she gives away Bebel's *Woman and Socialism*. One could write an entire book about women in the cavalry. The squadrons march into battle, dust, noise, drawn swords, atrocious swearing, with gathered up skirts they ride along from the very start, covered with dust, huge breasts, all whores, but comrades, and whores because they're comrades, that's most important; they help with every- thing, in any way they can, heroes, even though despised, they water the horses, fetch hay, clean the horses' bridles, steal in the churches and from the population. What's so special about the Galician cities? The mixture of the sordid and heavy flavour of the East with the German beer of the West.

Adamy. 21 August 1920

Two from Odessa – Manuilov and Boguslavsky, district war commander of the air force, Paris, London, a handsome Jew, talks a lot, article in a Jewish newspaper, the Jews in the cavalry, I scout them. In waisted uniform – the extravagance of the Odessa bourgeoisie, bad news from Odessa. They were tormented. How are you, father? Are they really going to take everything away from him. I must think of home.

26 August 1920

A synagogue – like it was two hundred years ago, the same figures in loose robes, they pace up and down, gesticulate. That is the orthodox faction, they're for the rabbi from Belz, the famous one, who has fled to Vienna. The moderate ones are for the rabbi from Husiatin. It's their synagogue, a beautiful ark, carved by an artisan, brilliant green chandeliers, bruised tables. The synagogues of Belz – a vision of the past. The Jewish neighbourhood, indescribable poverty, filth, isolation, ghetto . . . In Sokal – masters and workmen, Communism, they tell me, they'll barely get accustomed to. Such ragged, tortured people.

Komarov. 28 August 1920

We ride on. Kulaczkowski's pillaged property near Labunie. White columns. Lordly furnishings, but very tasteful. Unbelievable destruction. The authentic Poland – administrators, old women, blonde children, rich, almost European-like villages with a village elder, all Catholics, beautiful women. They steal oats from the property, horses in the drawing room, black horses, what else can you expect – protection from the rain. The most valuable books in a suitcase, it would have been too late – a constitution from the beginning of the eighteenth century confirmed by the Seim, antique folio volumes from the time of Nicholas I, a Polish code of laws, valuable book bindings, Polish manuscripts from the sixteenth century, sketches by monks, old French novels.

Nothing has been destroyed upstairs, but everything has been searched thoroughly, all the chairs, walls, sofas are slit open, the floor torn up, nothing was destroyed here, it was searched. Exquisite crystal, bedrooms, oaken beds, a powder box, French novels on the tables, many French and Polish books about infant care, intimate women's apparel – everything shattered, bits of butter in a butter dish, were they young marrieds?

We're approaching Zamość. A terrible day. The rain is victor, it doesn't let up for a single minute. The horses barely make it. To describe this unbearable rain. We toil till late into the night. Thoroughly drenched, dead tired. Apanassenko's red bashchuk. We circle Zamość at a distance of three to four versts. We don't approach, armoured trains beleaguer us with artillery fire. We stop in an open field, wait for messages – it's pouring in torrents. The brigade commander dictates a report in a tent. Commander! We aren't able to do anything against the armoured trains. It turned out that we didn't know there was a railway line here, it wasn't on the map, that's how our reconnaissance works.

from *Diary:1920*

Chesniki. 31 August 1920

A fruit garden, an apiary, the destruction of the beehives, it disgusts me, they buzz desperately, they're blowing up the hives with powder, they wrap themselves up in coats and go to attack the hives, a bacchanalia, the frame removed with the swords, honey flows out on to the earth, the bees sting, they're smoked out with tar rags. Circassian style. In the apiary – chaos and complete destruction, the ruins smoke. I write in the garden, a meadow, flowers, it pains me . . .

The story of a nurse – there are nurses who are strongly inclined to flirt, but we help the soldier, we endure everything together, I would shoot them if I could, but with what . . . we don't even have that much.

Budiatichi. 7 September 1920

For two weeks now the report that the army has to catch its breath has become more and more emphatic.

V. Volynski. 9 September 1920

The city is miserable, filthy, starved out, one doesn't get anything for his money any more, one piece of candy is twenty rubles, cigarettes. Grief, army's staff, trade-union council, young Jewish men. The way through the political-economy councils and trade-union commissions, sorrow, military tribunals; they kick over all traces. Impoverished young Jews.

A sumptuous repast – meat, groats.

One consolation – food.

The new war commissioner, of apelike appearance. The innkeeper and his wife want to make an exchange for my shawl. I don't give in.

My driver – barefoot and bleary-eyed.

Synagogue – I pray, bare walls, a soldier collects incandescent lamps. A bath. Damned life of a soldier, damned war. Conglomeration of young, plagued, primitive young people.

The life of my innkeepers, they make some kind of a profit, tomorrow is Friday, everything is being made ready, a good old woman, the husband's sly, they only act as if they're poor; but they say: better to starve under the Bolsheviks than to eat white bread under the Poles.

H. G. Wells

H. G. Wells (1866–1946), best known for the novel, *The War of the Worlds*, made three trips to Russia: the first in 1914 to visit Maxim Gorky, the second in 1920, the third in 1934; the last included an interview with Stalin. Wells's account of the 1920 trip was first published as articles in the *Sunday Express* then as the book, *Russia in the Shadows*. His views on the Bolsheviks were balanced. On the one hand he deplored the lack of democracy in the country, on the other he realised that there were strict limits to what the Bolsheviks could do having seized power in so underdeveloped a country. Many of the leading Bolsheviks that Wells met repeated to him their expectations of revolutions in the West – expectations that Wells saw as complete fantasies. Wells was quite clear that the appeal of Marxism to many was not an intellectual one but rather one born out of their own living conditions:

> There would have been Marxists if Marx had never lived. When I was a boy of fourteen I was a complete Marxist long before I had heard the name of Marx. I had been cut off abruptly from education, caught in a detestable shop, and I was being broken into a life of mean and dreary toil. I was worked too hard and for such long hours that all thoughts of self-improvement seemed hopeless. I would have set fire to the place if I had not been convinced it was over-insured.

Russia in the Shadows sold well on publication but was denounced by left and right: the Communists objected to its critique of Marx and the Conservatives were critical of its open-mindedness towards the Russian Revolution and its admiration of the Bolshevik leaders. And they obviously could not accept his analysis of who was to blame for Russia's state of collapse:

> It was not Communism that plunged this huge, creaking, bankrupt empire into six years of exhausting war. It was European

imperialism. Nor is it Communism that has pestered this suffering and perhaps dying Russia with a series of subsidised raids, invasions and insurrections, and inflicted upon it an atrocious blockade. The vindictive French creditor, the journalistic British oaf are far more responsible for these deathbed miseries than any Communist.

The Shaving of Karl Marx

from *Russia in the Shadows* by H. G. Wells

It will be best if I write about Marx without any hypocritical deference. I have always regarded him as a Bore of the extremist sort. His vast unfinished work, *Das Kapital*, a cadence of wearisome volumes about such phantom unrealities as the *bourgeoisie* and the *proletariat*, a book for ever maundering away into tedious secondary discussions, impresses me as a monument of pretentious pedantry. But before I went to Russia on this last occasion I had no active hostility to Marx. I avoided his works, and when I encountered Marxists I disposed of them by asking them to tell me exactly what people constituted the proletariat. None of them knew. No Marxist knows. In Gorki's flat I listened with attention while Bokaiev discussed with Shalyapin the fine question of whether in Russia there was a proletariat at all, distinguishable from the peasants. As Bokaiev has been head of the Extraordinary Commission of the Dictatorship of the Proletariat in Petersburg, it was interesting to note the fine difficulties of the argument. The 'proletarian' in the Marxist jargon is like the 'producer' in the jargon of some political economists, who is supposed to be a creature absolutely distinct and different from the 'consumer'. So the proletarian is a figure put into flat opposition to something called capital. I find in large type outside the current number of the *Plebs*, 'The working class and the employing class have nothing in common.' Apply this to a works foreman who is being taken in a train by an engine-driver to see how the house he is having built for him by a building society is getting on. To which of these immiscibles does he belong, employer or employed? The stuff is sheer nonsense.

In Russia I must confess my passive objection to Marx has changed to a very active hostility. Wherever we went we encountered busts, portraits and statues of Marx. About two-thirds of the face of Marx is beard, a vast solemn woolly uneventful beard that must have made all normal exercise impossible. It is not the sort of beard that happens to a man, it is a beard cultivated, cherished, and thrust patriarchally upon the world. It is exactly like *Das Kapital* in its inane abundance, and the human part of the face looks over it owlishly as if it looked to see how the growth impressed mankind. I found the omnipresent images of that beard more and more irritating. A gnawing desire grew upon me to see Karl Marx shaved. Some day, if I am spared, I will take up shears and a razor against *Das Kapital*; I will write *The Shaving of Karl Marx*.

But Marx is for the Marxists merely an image and a symbol, and it is with the Marxist and not with Marx that we are now dealing. Few Marxists have read much of *Das Kapital*. The Marxist is very much the same sort of person in all modern communities, and I will confess that by my temperament and circumstances I have the very warmest sympathy for him. He adopts Marx as his prophet simply because he believes that Marx wrote of the class war, an implacable war of the employed against the employer, and that he prophesied a triumph for the employed person, a dictatorship of the world by the leaders of these liberated employed persons (dictatorship of the proletariat), and a Communist millennium arising out of that dictatorship. Now this doctrine and this prophecy have appealed in every country with extraordinary power to young persons, and particularly to young men of energy and imagination who have found themselves at the outset of life imperfectly educated, ill-equipped and caught into hopeless wages slavery in our existing economic system. They realise in their own persons the social injustice, the stupid negligence, the colossal incivility of our system; they realise that they are insulted and sacrificed by it; and they devote themselves to break it and emancipate themselves from it. No insidious propaganda is needed to make such rebels; it is the faults of a system that half-educates and then enslaves them which have created the Communist movement wherever industrialism has developed. There would have been Marxists if Marx had never lived. When I was a boy of fourteen I was a complete Marxist, long before I had heard the name of Marx. I had been cut off abruptly from education, caught in a detestable shop, and I was being broken into a life of mean and dreary toil. I was worked too hard and for such long hours that all thoughts of self-improvement seemed hopeless. I would have set fire to that place if I had not been convinced it was over-insured. I revived the spirit of those bitter days in a conversation I had with Zorin, one of the leaders of the Commune of the North. He is a young man who has come back from unskilled work in America, a very likeable human being and a humorous and very popular speaker in the Petersburg Soviet. He and I exchanged experiences, and I found that the thing that rankled most in his mind about America was the brutal incivility he had encountered when applying for a job as packer in a big dry goods store in New York. We told each other stories of the way our social system wastes and breaks and maddens decent and willing men. Between us was the freemasonry of a common indignation.

It is that indignation of youth and energy, thwarted and misused, it is that and no mere economic theorising, which is the living and linking inspiration of the Marxist movement throughout the world. It is not that Marx was profoundly wise, but that our economic system has been stupid, selfish, wasteful and anarchistic. The Communistic organisation has provided for this angry recalcitrance certain shibboleths and passwords: 'Workers of the World unite', and so forth. It has suggested to them an idea of a great conspiracy against human happiness concocted by a mysterious body of wicked men called capitalists. For in this mentally enfeebled world in which we live today conspiracy mania on one side finds its echo on the other, and it is hard to persuade a Marxist that capitalists are in their totality no more than a scrambling disorder of mean-spirited and short-sighted men. And the Communist propaganda has knitted all these angry and disinherited spirits together into a worldwide organisation of revolt – and hope – formless though that hope proves to be on examination. It has chosen Marx for its prophet and red for its colour . . .

Institutionalising the Town Children

from *Russia in the Shadows* by H. G. Wells

The common practice of coeducating youngsters up to fifteen or sixteen, in a country as demoralised as Russia is now, has brought peculiar evils in its train. My attention was called to this by the visit of Bokaiev, the former head of the Petersburg Extraordinary Commission, and his colleague Zalutsky to Gorky to consult him in the matter. They discussed their business in front of me quite frankly, and the whole conversation was translated to me as it went on. The Bolshevik authorities have collected and published very startling, very shocking figures of the moral condition of young people in Petersburg, which I have seen. How far they would compare with the British figures – if there are any British figures – of such bad districts for the young as are some parts of East London or such towns of low-type employment as Reading I do not know. (The reader should compare the Fabian Society's report on prostitution, *Downward Paths*, upon this question.) Nor do I know how they would show in comparison with preceding Tsarist conditions. Nor can I speculate how far these phenomena in Russia are the mechanical consequence of privation and overcrowding in a home atmosphere bordering on despair. But there can be no doubt that in the Russian towns, concurrently with increased educational effort and an enhanced intellectual stimulation of the young, there is also an increased lawlessness on their part, especially in sexual matters, and that this is going on in a phase of unexampled sobriety and harsh puritanical decorum so far as adult life is concerned. This hectic moral fever of the young is the dark side of the educational spectacle in Russia. I think it is to be regarded mainly as an aspect of the general social collapse; every European country has noted a parallel moral relaxation of the young under the war strain; but the Revolution itself, in sweeping a number of the old experienced teachers out of the schools and in making every moral standard a subject of debate, has no doubt contributed also to an as yet incalculable amount in the excessive disorder of these matters in present-day Russia.

Faced with this problem of starving and shattered homes and a social chaos, the Bolshevik organisers are *institutionalising* the town children of Russia. They are making their schools residential. The children of the Russian urban population are going, like the children of the British upper class, into boarding schools. Close to this second school I visited stood two big buildings which are the living places of the boys and of the girls respectively. In these places they can be kept under some sort of hygienic and moral discipline. This again happens to be not only in accordance with Communist doctrine, but with the special necessities of the Russian crisis. Entire towns are sinking down towards slum conditions, and the Bolshevik government has had to play the part of a gigantic Dr Barnardo.

We went over the organisation of a sort of reception home to which children are brought by their parents who find it impossible to keep them clean and decent and nourished under the terrible conditions outside. This reception home is the old Hotel de l'Europe, the scene of countless pleasant little dinner-parties under the old *régime*. On the roof there is still the summertime roof garden, where the string quartet used to play, and on the staircase we passed a frosted-glass window still bearing in gold letters the words *Coiffure des Dames*.

Slender gilded pointing hands directed us to the 'Restaurant', long vanished from the grim Petersburg scheme of things. Into this place the children come; they pass into a special quarantine section for infectious diseases and for personal cleanliness – nine-tenths of the newcomers harbour unpleasant parasites – and then into another section, the moral quarantine, where for a time they are watched for bad habits and undesirable tendencies. From this section some individuals may need to be weeded out and sent to special schools for defectives. The rest pass on into the general body of institutionalised children, and so on to the boarding schools.

Here certainly we have the 'break-up of the family' in full progress, and the Bolshevik net is sweeping wide and taking in children of the most miscellaneous origins. The parents have reasonably free access to their children in the daytime, but little or no control over their education, clothing, or the like. We went among the children in the various stages of this educational process, and they seemed to us to be quite healthy, happy and contented children. But they get very good people to look after them. Many men and women, politically suspects or openly discontented with the existing political conditions, and yet with a desire to serve Russia, have found in these places work that they can do with a good heart and conscience. My interpreter and the lady who took us round this place had often dined and supped in the Hotel de l'Europe in its brilliant days, and they knew each other well. This lady was now plainly clad, with short-cut hair and a grave manner; her husband was a White and serving with the Poles; she had two children of her own in the institution, and she was mothering some scores of little creatures. But she was evidently keenly proud of the work of her organisation, and she said that she found life – in this city of want, under the shadow of a coming famine – more interesting and satisfying than it had ever been in the old days.

I have no space to tell of other educational work we saw going on in Russia. I can give but a word or so to the Home of Rest for Workmen in the Kamenni Ostrof. I thought that at once rather fine and not a little absurd. To this place workers are sent to live a life of refined ease for two or three weeks. It is a very beautiful country house with big gardens, an orangery and subordinate buildings. The meals are served on white cloths with flowers upon the table and so forth. And the worker has to live up to these elegant surroundings. It is a part of his education. If in a forgetful moment he clears his throat in the good old resonant peasant manner and spits upon the floor, an attendant, I was told, chalks a circle about his defilement and obliges him to clean the offended parquetry. The avenue approaching this place has been adorned with decoration in the futurist style, and there is a vast figure of a 'worker' at the gates resting on his hammer, done in gypsum, which was obtained from the surgical reserves of the Petersburg hospitals . . . But after all, the idea of civilising your work people by dipping them into pleasant surroundings is, in itself, rather a good one . . .

I find it difficult to hold the scales of justice upon many of these efforts of Bolshevism. Here are these creative and educational things going on, varying between the admirable and the ridiculous, islands at least of cleanly work and, I think, of hope, amidst the vast spectacle of grisly want and wide decay. Who can weigh the power and possibility of their thrust against the huge gravitation of this sinking system? Who can guess what encouragement and enhancement they may get if Russia can win through to a respite from civil and foreign warfare and from famine and want? It was of this recreated Russia, this Russia that may be, that I was most desirous of talking when I went to the Kremlin to meet Lenin.

Bertrand Russell

Like H. G. Wells, the British philosopher and pacifist **Bertrand Russell** (1872–1970) went to Russia in 1920. He went as a supporter of Communism as a system he hoped would replace Capitalism – his trip led him to take a much more critical view of the Bolshevik Revolution. Russell was fully aware of the difficulties that the Bolshevik government faced in the years after the October Revolution, including the need to wage a Civil War against enemies supported by the most powerful capitalist empires. He also acknowledged the economic and political discipline necessary to industrialise and develop an economy that before the Revolution was overwhelmingly rural. But he came to believe that the methods used by the Bolsheviks would take them further and further from their democratic aims. Russell's views on the Bolshevik Revolution were published in his lucid 1920 book *The Practice and Theory of Bolshevism*. They were a hostile assessment of the Revolution: 'I am compelled to reject Bolshevism for two reasons: First, because the price mankind must pay to achieve Communism by Bolshevik methods is too terrible; and, secondly, because even after paying the price, I do not believe the result would be what the Bolsheviks profess to desire' (*The Practice and Theory of Bolshevism*, London, 1920, page 89).

From his letters reprinted here it is clear that Russell wondered whether his own position of privilege did not influence his views:

When the body of a new society has been built, there will be time enough to think about giving it a soul – at least so I am assured. 'We have no time for a new art or a new religion,' they tell me with a certain impatience. I wonder whether it is possible to build a body first, and then afterwards inject the requisite amount of soul. Perhaps – but I doubt it [. . .] I cannot give that importance to man's merely animal needs that is given here by those in power. No doubt that is because I have not spent half my life in hunger and want, as many of them have.   [Petrograd, 13 May 1920]

In his letters from Russia, Russell shows us the painful and far from straightforward process of how he reached the conclusions he did. They remain remarkably relevant today as we assess the Russian Revolution with the benefit of a century's hindsight.

Letters from Russia [*1920*]

from *Uncertain Paths to Freedom: Russia and China 1919–22* by Bertram Russell

London, 24 April 1920

MY DEAR – The day of my departure comes near, I have a thousand things to do, yet I sit here idle, thinking useless thoughts, the irrelevant, rebellious thoughts that well-regulated people never think, the thoughts that one hopes to banish by work, but that themselves banish work instead. How I envy those who *always* believe what they believe, who are not troubled by deadness and indifference to all that makes the framework of their lives. I have had the ambition to be of some use in the world, to achieve something notable, to give mankind new hopes. And now that the opportunity is near, it all seems dust and ashes. As I look into the future, my disillusioned gaze sees only strife and still more strife, rasping cruelty, tyranny, terror and slavish submission. The men of my dreams, erect, fearless and generous, will they ever exist on earth? Or will men go on fighting, killing and torturing to the end of time, till the earth grows cold and the dying sun can no longer quicken their futile frenzy? I cannot tell. But I do know the despair in my soul. I know the great loneliness, as I wander through the world like a ghost, speaking in tones that are not heard, lost as if I had fallen from some other planet.

The old struggle goes on, the struggle between little pleasures and the great pain. I know that the little pleasures are death and yet – I am so tired, so very tired. Reason and emotion fight a deadly war within me, and leave me no energy for outward action. I know that no good thing is achieved without fighting, without ruthlessness and organisation and discipline. I know that for collective action the individual must be turned into a machine. But in these things, though my reason may force me to believe them, I can find no inspiration. It is the individual human soul that I love – in its loneliness, its hopes and fears, its quick impulses and sudden devotions. It is such a long journey from this to armies and States and Officials; and yet it is only by making this long journey that one can avoid a useless sentimentalism.

All through the rugged years of the war, I dreamed of a happy day after its end, when I should sit with you in a sunny garden by the Mediterranean, filled with the scent of heliotrope, surrounded by cypresses and sacred groves of ilex – and there, at last, I should be able to tell you of my love, and to touch the joy that is as real as pain. The time is come, but I have other tasks, and you have other desires; and to me, as I sit brooding, all tasks seem vain and all desires foolish.

Yet it is not upon these thoughts that I shall act.

Petrograd, 12 May 1920

I am here at last, in this city which has filled the world with history, which has inspired the most deadly hatreds and the most poignant hopes. Will it yield me up its secret? Shall I learn to know its inmost soul? Or shall I acquire only statistics and official facts? Shall I understand what I see, or will it remain an external bewildering show? In the dead of night we reached the empty station, and our noisy motors panted through the sleeping streets. From my window, when I arrived, I looked out across the Neva to the fortress of Peter and Paul. The river gleamed in the early northern dawn; the scene was beautiful beyond all words, magical, eternal, suggestive of ancient wisdom. 'It is wonderful,' I said to the Bolshevik who stood beside me. 'Yes,' he replied, 'Peter and Paul is now not a prison, but the Army Headquarters.'

I shook myself. 'Come, my friend,' I thought, 'you are not here as a tourist, to sentimentalise over sunrises and sunsets and buildings starred by Baedeker; you are here as a social investigator, to study economic and political facts. Come out of your dream, forget the eternal things. The men you have come among would tell you they are only the fancies of a bourgeois with too much leisure, and can you be sure they are anything more?' So I came back into the conversation, and tried to learn the mechanism for buying an umbrella at the Soviet Stores, which proved as difficult as fathoming the ultimate mysteries.

The twelve hours that I have so far spent on Russian soil have chiefly afforded material for the imp of irony. I came prepared for physical hardship, discomfort, dirt and hunger, to be made bearable by an atmosphere of splendid hope for mankind. Our communist comrades, no doubt rightly, have not judged us worthy of such treatment. Since crossing the frontier yesterday afternoon, I have had two feasts and a good breakfast, several first-class cigars, and a night in a sumptuous bedroom of a palace where all the luxury of the *ancien regime* has been preserved. At the stations on the way, regiments of soldiers filled the platform, and the *plebs* was kept carefully out of sight. It seems I am to live amid the pomp surrounding the government of a great military empire. So I must readjust my mood. Cynicism is called for, but I am strongly moved, and find cynicism difficult. I come back eternally to the same question: What is the secret of this passionate country? Do the Bolsheviks know its secret? Do they even suspect that it has a secret? I wonder.

Petrograd, 13 May 1920

MY DEAR – This is a strange world into which I have come, a world of dying beauty and harsh life. I am troubled at every moment by fundamental questions, the terrible insoluble questions that wise men never ask. Empty palaces and full eating-houses, ancient splendours destroyed, or mummified in museums, while the sprawling self-confidence of returned Americanised refugees spreads throughout the city. Everything is to be systematic: there is to be organisation and distributive justice. The same education for all, the same clothes for all, the same kind of houses for all, the same books for all, and the same creed for all – it is very just, and leaves no room for envy, except of the fortunate victims of injustice in other countries.

And then I begin upon the other side of the argument. I remember Dostoyevskiy's *Crime and Punishment*, Gorki's *In the World*, Tolstoy's

Resurrection. I reflect upon the destruction and cruelty upon which the ancient splendour was built: the poverty, drunkenness, prostitution, in which life and health were uselessly wasted; I think of all the lovers of freedom who suffered in Peter and Paul; I remember the knoutings and pogroms and massacres. By hatred of the old, I become tolerant of the new; but I cannot like the new on its own account.

Yet I reproach myself for not liking it. It has all the characteristics of vigorous beginnings. It is ugly and brutal, but full of constructive energy and faith in the value of what it is creating. In creating a new machinery for social life, it has no time to think of anything beyond machinery. When the body of the new society has been built, there will be time enough to think about giving it a soul – at least so I am assured. 'We have no time for a new art or a new religion,' they tell me with a certain impatience. I wonder whether it is possible to build a body first, and then afterwards inject the requisite amount of soul. Perhaps – but I doubt it.

I do not find any theoretical answer to these questions, but my feelings answer with terrible insistence. I am infinitely unhappy in this atmosphere – stifled by its utilitarianism, its indifference to love and beauty and the life of impulse. I cannot give that importance to man's merely animal needs that is given here by those in power. No doubt that is because I have not spent half my life in hunger and want, as many of them have. But do hunger and want necessarily bring wisdom? Do they make men more or less capable of conceiving the ideal society that should be the inspiration of every reformer? I cannot avoid the belief that they narrow the horizon more than they enlarge it. But an uneasy doubt remains, and I am torn in two . . .

On the Volga, 2 June 1920

Our boat travels on, day after day, through an unknown and mysterious land. Our company are noisy, gay, quarrelsome, full of facile theories, with glib explanations of everything, persuaded that there is nothing they cannot understand and no human destiny outside the purview of their system. One of us lies at death's door, fighting a grim battle with weakness and terror and the indifference of the strong, assailed day and night by the sounds of loud-voiced love-making and trivial laughter. And all around us lies a great silence, strong as Death, unfathomable as the heavens. It seems that none have leisure to hear the silence, yet it calls to me so insistently that I grow deaf to the harangues of propagandists and the endless information of the well-informed.

Last night, very late, our boat stopped in a desolate spot where there were no houses, but only a great sandbank, and beyond it a row of poplars with the rising moon behind them. In silence I went ashore, and found on the sand a strange assemblage of human beings, half-nomads, wandering from some remote region of famine, each family huddled together surrounded by all its belongings, some sleeping, others silently making small fires of twigs. The flickering flames lighted up gnarled bearded faces of wild men, strong patient primitive women, and children as sedate and slow as their parents. Human beings they undoubtedly were, and yet it would have been far easier for me to grow intimate with a dog or a cat or a horse than with one of them. I knew that they would wait there day after day, perhaps for weeks, until a boat came in which they could go to some distant place where they had heard – falsely perhaps – that the earth was more generous than in the country they had left. Some would die by the way, all would suffer hunger and thirst and the scorching midday sun, but their sufferings would be dumb. To me they seemed to typify the very soul of Russia, unexpressive, inactive from despair, unheeded by the little set of westernisers who make up all the parties of progress or reaction. Russia is so vast that the articulate few are lost in it as man and his planet are lost in interstellar space. It is possible, I thought, that the theorists may increase the misery of the many by trying to force them into actions contrary to their primeval instincts, but I could not believe that happiness was to be brought to them by a gospel of industrialism and forced labour.

Nevertheless, when morning came, I resumed the interminable discussions of the materialistic conception of history and the merits of a truly popular government. Those with whom I discussed had not seen the sleeping wanderers, and would not have been interested if they had seen them, since they were not material for propaganda. But something of that patient silence had communicated itself to me, something lonely and unspoken remained in my heart through all the comfortable familiar intellectual talk. And at last I began to feel that all politics are inspired by a grinning devil, teaching the energetic and quick-witted to torture submissive populations for the profit of pocket or power or theory. As we journeyed on, fed by food extracted from the peasants, protected by an army recruited from among their sons, I wondered what we had to give them in return. But I found no answer. From time to time I heard their sad songs or the haunting music of the balalaika; but the sound mingled with the great silence of the steppes, and left me with a terrible questioning pain in which occidental hopefulness grew pale.

Lev Lunts, Mikhail Zoshchenko
& Marietta Shaginian

In early 1921, the group that was to become the Serapion Brothers started to meet. A very informal group, its members were brought together by friendship and a desire to make literature that was sympathetic to the aims of the Revolution but free from interference by the Communist Party. The group took its name and inspiration from the writings of E. T. A. Hoffman who in his collection of stories *The Stories of the Serapion Brothers* describes the meeting of old friends who dispense with all literary rules and regulations and gather to read one another their works.[27] The theorist of the Serapion Brothers was Lev Lunts and its most popular writer Mikhail Zoshchenko.

The son of Jewish parents, **Lev Lunts** (1901–24) spent his whole life trying to reconcile his Russian and his Jewish roots, his feeling of being stranded somewhere between Eastern and Western literature. In August 1922, he published the Serapion Brothers manifesto 'Why We Are the Serapion Brothers'. At a time when the state wanted literature to be utilitarian, Lunts argued that:

> We are not promoting new slogans, not publishing manifestos and programmes. But for us the old truth contains a great practical significance which has been misunderstood or forgotten, especially here in Russia.
>
> We consider the Russian literature of today to be remarkably sedate, stuffy and monotonous. We are permitted to write stories, novels and tedious dramas in either the old style or the new, but they must without fail be about everyday life and without fail

---

27 For this and other relevant information, see the introduction to *The Serapion Brothers: A Critical Anthology*, edited by Gary Kern and Christopher Collins, Ardis, Ann Arbor, 1975.

contain contemporary themes . . . A work of literature may reflect the epoch, but also may not reflect it and be none the worse for it.[28]

Incendiary stuff at a time when the Russian Association of Proletarian Writers (RAPP) had been formed to 'scourge and chastise' in the name of the Party – to encourage the censorship of literature on ideological grounds. *The Outgoing Letter N37* was written by Lunts in 1921. In this satirical fable, a bureaucrat finds a solution to the lack of transport, the lack of paper and military logistics – hypnosis! *N37* does not attack the Revolution but on the contrary warns against the return of a reactionary system and values brought on by a total denial of reality for which the bureaucrat's solution is a powerful metaphor.

After his brilliant play *Outside the Law*, which was performed throughout Europe in the 1920s and praised by Pirandello, was banned in 1923 in the Soviet Union, Lunts moved to Germany to be with his parents who had emigrated there in 1921. He died in 1924 in Hamburg.

Mikhail Zoshchenko (1894–1958) was one of the most popular Soviet writers of the 1920s; his books sold in the millions. His success lay is his ability to write about the daily experiences of the common people in a way that did not put his subjects down and made them laugh. Like Gogol before him, Zoshchenko was the chronicler of the hazards of everyday life. In the satirical magazines Zoshchenko and others wrote for, there was a dialogue with readers. Many of whom wrote in telling of everyday absurdities and Zoshchenko took the bare bones of these letters and spun them into what are known as *skaz* tales. The narrator appears (and is) a dimwit who fails to understand what is happening to him, but in exposing his lack of understanding he reveals all. When the satirical press was closed down, to earn a living, Zoshchenko was forced to write stories for children, including a series on Lenin. One of his children's stories, 'The Adventures of a Monkey', features a monkey who escapes from the zoo, spends a day observing Soviet life and willingly returns to its cage. To Andrey Zhdanov, the party spokesman of cultural affairs, the story suggested

28 Lunts's 'Why We Are the Serapion Brothers', in Kern and Collins, op. cit., p. 134

that life in a cage was preferable to life in the Soviet Union. In 1946, Zoshchenko, the poet Akhmatova and, later, in 1948, the composers Prokofiev and Shostakovich, were charged with 'formalism'. Zoshchenko died in poverty, ostracised and deprived of work and his worker's ration card

– the only way to get food. Now, his stories are widely read in Russia; their gallows humour much appreciated.

Also a Serapion was **Marietta Shaginian** (1888–1982), the daughter of an Armenian physician, who enthusiastically welcomed the October Revolution. In the mid-1920s, the Bolshevik leaders became worried about the anti-Soviet attitudes of many young people and saw the need for a literature to win over these 'hooligans' – this led to Bukharin's appeal for writers to produce 'red Pinkertons' – crime novels that used the Western crime-fiction formula to write novels that promoted Soviet values while appealing to young and/or proletarian readers. This cultural policy produced 'red Pinkerton' novels[29] – the most famous of which were those of Shaginian. Under the pen name Jim Dollar, she wrote a series with the collective title *Mess-Mend*; best sellers at the time, they were translated all over the world and filmed in 1926. In the novels, Mess-Mend, an international proletarian fraternity, is led by Mick Thingmaster. His dastardly enemy is the capitalist billionaire Jack Kressling, sent to sabotage the Revolution, reinstate the monarchy and grab Russia's mineral wealth. No prizes for guessing who wins this heroic struggle! With Bukharin's defeat in his power struggle with Stalin, Shaginian lost his protection. In the 1930s, she put her writing at the service of economic development and wrote the socialist-realist novel *Hydrocentral*, which deals with the relationship between socialist construction and new human relationships. In a later essay 'Journey Through Soviet Armenia', Shaginian drew on her Armenian roots to explain changes in the country to a Soviet readership. The last years of her life were spent writing a series of historical novels on Lenin for which she was awarded the Lenin Prize.

29 An excellent guide to the red Pinkerton phenomenon is *Western Crime Fiction Goes East: The Russian Pinkerton Craze 1907-1934*, by Boris Dralyuk, Brill, Leiden/Boston, 2012.

The Outgoing Letter N37

by Lev Lunts
(translated by Grigori Gerenstein)

3 January 1921. At night.
. . . I consider today a great day, for today I conceived an idea which is
bound to bring me fame and earn me eternal gratitude on the part of
grateful posterity.

I got up at eight o'clock in the morning. Here I must allow myself a
short digression in order to put it on record that I didn't sleep well last
night as I had been considerably stirred by the director's passionate
speech and spent the night thinking about the new reforms.

I entered the office at ten o'clock precisely. To my extreme indignation I discovered that none of my subordinates was at his place
of work. In order to ascertain the rightfulness of my indignation, I
perused once more the order of the Head of the Ministry of Political
Education of 7 September, which states that work at the Ministry will
be organised on new principles (not the new principles that were put
forward yesterday but the old new principles), and that therefore
every employee is to present himself at the office at ten o'clock
precisely. Those who are late are to be sent to the Palace of Labour as
deserters from the Ministry's work. As a departmental head I had
considered it my duty to read the order to each late-comer personally,
to which they had replied unanimously that they knew the order by
heart. If they know it by heart, why are they late?

The day was fraught with trouble. For instance, I discovered that a
woman journalist registered her papers under forty-two headings
instead of forty-three. But the main unpleasantness occurred at three-
twenty-five, namely: the club instructor Barinov entered the office
without urgent business in spite of the fact that the door is equipped
with a notice, 'Do not enter unless on urgent business.' Having entered
without urgent business he proceeded to converse with the typist,
thereby obstructing her work. When I attempted to point out to him
that such behaviour was unworthy of a communist, he told me to go to

hell and that he knew a communist's duty better than I, as I was an office rat. To this I replied that I was an honest proletarian worker. To this his reply was, 'The hell you are a proletarian worker. Don't think I don't know that you worked for twenty years as a chief clerk at the Tsarist Senate.' Then I retreated to my desk and commenced to write a report to the Head of the Ministry of Political Education.

It was then that the great idea struck me. Namely: we propose to undertake a fundamental reconstruction of our Ministry of Political Education. But how are we to reconstruct it if the organisation consists entirely of politically unsound employees? Because of this reconstruction is impossible. But we have to reconstruct, for such is the logic of revolutionary life. Consequently it is the employees who should be reconstructed on new principles, in other words, the citizens.

That was the remarkable conclusion at which I arrived on the train of my thought. The significance of my discovery became immediately clear to me. In great excitement I put aside my report and attempted to direct my attention to current work, but I couldn't.

4 January. In the morning
Didn't sleep well last night. I have decided to submit a memorandum to the Soviet of People's Commissars as I am convinced that the reconstruction of citizens on new principles should be carried out on a national scale.

5 January. In the morning
Didn't sleep well last night. I have decided that the reconstruction should be carried out on a universal or, in other words, cosmic scale.

The same date. In the evening
The moment I got home I sat down at my desk to work on my memorandum. However, when I came to practical suggestions I was compelled to discontinue my composition as the train of my thought had come to an obstacle. Namely: I didn't know how and into what substance the citizens should be turned.

Just as I came to this point in my deliberations my wife entered the premises in a state of great agitation. Her cheeks were flushed and her bosom heaved. She informed me that a hypnotist had moved into our apartment building and that at that very moment he was demonstrating miracles in the office of the house committee. I objected that according to the appropriate decrees miracles were not possible.

On entering the office of the house committee I witnessed the following scene. The room was crowded with people. An individual of suspicious appearance stood in a corner and, waving his arms over the head of a sleeping man, demanded that he do this and that. I stepped forward and delivered a speech on the current political situation. Those present abused me with words which I am reluctant to mention in writing. The hypnotist fixed his eyes on me, which made me feel sleepy. At this point in the proceedings my memory failed me. When I regained consciousness I discovered that the audience was in a paroxysm of mirth while the hypnotist was smiling triumphantly. It transpired that he had put me to sleep and turned me into a donkey. Apparently I had brayed like a donkey and, when given straw, had eaten it with considerable appetite. Outraged by such an insult, I declared that I would report the hypnotist to the Cheka, to which he replied that he was not afraid of me as he had a paper from the People's Commissar of Health. Then I retreated accompanied by a sobbing wife.

The same date. At night
This evening was a great evening for I found the missing link in my theory.

A donkey, I thought, is a useless animal. However, if it were possible to turn a citizen into a cow, the milk crisis would be resolved. Or, say, those sentenced to compulsory labour could be turned into horses and sent to the state transport agency.

All this was good enough for the politically unsound element, for the bourgeoisie and its flunkeys, because a cow, a donkey and a horse are inferior creatures. But what should we turn the honest workers into?

Here my train of thought was interrupted by the following consideration: do I have a right to resort to the assistance of a hypnotist and will his utilisation contradict the established philosophy? Then I recalled that the hypnotist had a paper from the People's Commissar of Health and my doubts were put to rest. New perspectives opened before my inner eye: the Ministry of Health introduces compulsory registration of all hypnotists, gives short courses in hypnosis and produces crack hypnotists who are put at the disposal of the highest authorities.

6 January. After work

At two o'clock the Head of the Ministry of Political Education summoned us, responsible executives, to his office in order to familiarise us with his Project of Reconstruction of the Ministry on New Principles.

The essence of the Project was as follows. It was based on the initiative of the masses, which was to be stimulated by the abolition of the Institute of Executives. The Head of the Ministry would remain while all the heads of departments, sub-departments, sections and sub-sections were to be renamed Senior Instructors. Thus the Ministry would achieve a closer contact with the masses, who mistrusted the Executives. The Project was met with great enthusiasm. Furthermore, there was to be a reform of the filing system, which would involve a forty-per-cent increase in the number of files. The number of forms to be filled in by every employee was to be increased from ten to sixteen. Furthermore, all conferences between the employees were to be abolished and all communication between them was to be carried out in the form of written reports which were to be filed under special numbers.

The meeting received all these suggestions with great delight. Only the club instructor Barinov objected that the new principles would result in nothing but a new load of paperwork. Then, despite the indignation that was choking me, I took the floor and in curt and powerful expressions accused the club instructor Barinov of harbouring a bourgeois philosophy, as correct filing based on correct paperwork is the basis of Socialist construction, therefore paper is . . . but here my voice faltered and I lost my faculty of speech because at that moment a great thought occurred to me.

The superior substance into which the citizens should be transformed is paper. I immediately entered this idea in my memorandum, supporting it with the following arguments: first – paper is a superior substance; secondly – it lends itself to easy registration; thirdly – paper is a substance, therefore it is useful to Soviet Russia in its present state of economic crisis.

I went on to expound my practical suggestions. My enthusiasm grew, words sang under my pen and fused into marvellous harmony. I was becoming a poet. A multitude of advantages on a cosmic scale presented themselves to my inspired imagination.

First of all: the struggle at the front would be considerably facilitated. For instance, the commander of a regiment or even of a whole army could turn his Red soldiers into pieces of paper and pack them into a suitcase. Having smuggled the suitcase behind the White bandits' lines, he could turn the pieces of paper back into soldiers and strike at the enemy from behind.

Secondly: the food and fuel crisis would be resolved since paper has none of the requirements peculiar to man. Under the same heading one could enter our struggle against criminals and women who are not involved in honest labour.

Finally: the paper crisis would be resolved as citizens could be utilised as paper in the true sense of the word.

This was the general drift of my deliberations. Completing my memorandum I went home. My wife asked me why I was so pale but I didn't answer her as, although a supporter of the equality of women, I consider their substance inferior to men's and propose to turn them into a paper of inferior quality.

7 January
I suspect that the club instructor Barinov suspects something. I must be careful.

8 January
Didn't sleep well last night, thinking what to do next. No solution presented itself.

9 January. In the evening
Today during office hours I had an idea. What if I hypnotise myself

and turn myself into paper? In extreme agitation I hastened after work to see the hypnotist with a view to receiving the necessary instructions, which he supplied with readiness. It transpired that in order to turn into some substance you had to spend a long time thinking that you were that substance. The experiment required continuous practise, silence and solitude. You had to think for three or four hours at a stretch.

10 January. In the morning

I have encountered an unforeseen and fundamental obstacle. Namely: the transformation requires three or four hours of complete silence. My wife, being of an inferior substance, is unable to keep silent for more than three or four minutes at a time. I hoped that at night while she was asleep I would make my first attempt, but my wife, even in her deepest sleep, obstructed the experiment by snoring. I waited until four o'clock in the morning hoping that she would subside, but, being worn out by the excitements of the previous day, I fell asleep myself without noticing it.

The same day. In the evening

On coming home after work, I sent my wife to see her mother with the intention of continuing my efforts in her absence. As soon as she left I began to think that I was paper. However, paper is a rather vague notion embracing a variety of images, some of them quite indecent, and thinking of paper in general is an uncomfortable activity. Therefore I decided to concentrate on a specific article of paper production. After serious thought I chose an ingoing or an outgoing letter because they are the most subtle, the most ethereal phenomena. Some time passed and suddenly I felt rustling in my left leg. This affected me to such an extent that I jumped up, thereby ruining the experiment. But it was a beginning. I need more self-control.

11 January. In the evening

Today I achieved further success. There was rustling in both my legs and in the left side of my abdomen. The rustling spread into my fingers, but my wife came home and spoiled everything. I don't know what to do.

12 January. In the morning

Didn't sleep well, thinking what to do. Then I had a brilliant idea. Tonight I am on duty at the Ministry where I shall turn into paper, as turning into paper at home is too troublesome. First: my wife never leaves home for more than three hours at a time. Secondly: even if I did turn into paper at home, what would I do then? The appearance of an outgoing document in our conjugal bed may arouse my wife's suspicions. Both these complications are removed if the experiment is carried out at the Ministry of Political Education.

12 January. Ministry of Political Education. At night

My hand trembles as I write these words. I am about to commence the final experiment. I am alone in the building. The wind howls outside and the fire crackles in the fireplace. My soul is full of heavenly visions, my heart beats like a clock and my chest is constricted.

I have decided to lie down on my superior's desk so, when I have turned into an outgoing letter, I will be where an outgoing letter is supposed to be. I cannot stand disorder.

I will not turn into an outgoing letter itself but into its file-copy. An outgoing letter is bound to leave the Ministry, which eventuality I consider undesirable.

13 January. At dawn

The great event has taken place. I have become a sheet of paper. The sun floods the room with the rays of sunrise, the birds chirp outside and my paper soul is full of joy.

I have a feeling there is something written on me. After a few attempts, overcoming all the attendant difficulties, I manage to read myself, thereby solving a great riddle posed by a foreign philosopher; 'Peruse yourself and you will know who you are.'

FILE-COPY

Russian Soviet Federal Socialist Republic. Ministry of Political Education.

13 January. N37

Petrograd Commune. Distribution Department.

The Ministry of Political Education hereby notifies you that the 2·268 pounds of potatoes sent by you, for distribution to the employees of the Ministry of Political Education in accordance with the home-front ration, have arrived in the most inedible condition.

Head of the Ministry of Political Education (signature)

Secretary (signature)

On perusing the above document I broke out in a cold sweat for the following reason: if I was the file-copy of an outgoing letter, why was I lying on the desk of the head of the Ministry when a file-copy was supposed to be in a special file? It goes without saying that had I been in a human shape or, in other words, in the shape of a departmental head, I should have restored order immediately. Now I feared that the file-copy might be mislaid.

I could hear the cleaning ladies behind the wall. The office hours were about to begin.

The same date. In the evening

I am writing this while lying on the floor, in which position I find myself for the following reason.

At three o'clock the head of the Ministry held a general meeting of the employees to discuss matters concerning trade unions. When the comrades began to leave the office a great misfortune befell me. The club instructor Barinov brushed me off the desk with his sleeve and, when I fell to the floor, stepped on me, thereby causing me severe pain. However, this severe pain was drowned by a still more severe anxiety regarding the fate of the file-copy N37 as, lying on the floor, it was in danger of being thrown into the wastepaper basket. Moreover, I recalled that it was the club instructor Barinov's turn to do night duty at the Ministry. What if he suspected that the file-copy N37 was the head of his department? Hating me the way he does, he could cause me considerable discomfort.

In view of the above considerations I decided to turn back into a human shape and began to think that I was a human being. But soon I was struck by a thought which caused me to break out in a cold sweat.

Namely: if I turned back into a human being the file-copy N37 would disappear. As a departmental head I could not allow such disorder. Therefore I decided to postpone a reverse transformation.

The same date. At night

It is dark. Silence. A clock is ticking on the wall. The club instructor Barinov has gone. He must have left his post. I will report this to the head of the Ministry.

My soul is full of light and joy. Now there can be no doubt as to the validity of my discovery. I have been a paper for almost an entire day and I have not felt hunger or thirst or any other need peculiar to a human being in a human shape.

A chain of noble thoughts passes before my radiant inner eye.

All people are equal or, in other words, all people are papers. Man's ideal has been attained.

Just as my thoughts reach this exalted point I see someone bending over me. It is the club instructor Barinov. He is looking for something.

'Ah, here we are!'

He takes me by the head or, in other words, by the corner of the paper, and fingers me.

'Soft paper. It'll do.'

With these words he picks me up and . . .

Here, for an unknown reason, ends the diary of the departmental head. The latter disappeared without a trace. All efforts to find him were unsuccessful.

Electrification

by Mikhail Zoshchenko (translated by Jeremy Hicks)

What's the most fashionable word these days, eh comrades?

The most fashionable word you could possibly find these days is, of course, electrification.

It's a matter of immense importance, the illumination of Soviet Russia, I'm not arguing with that. But even this, for the moment, has its not so good sides.

I'm not saying, comrades, that it's expensive. It's not expensive. It's worth every kopeck. I'm not talking about that, I'm not making all this fuss over that and not wasting ink over that.

But there was this case, listen.

We were living in this building. The building was big and all the lighting was kerosine. Some people had basic oil lamps, others had bigger ones, others didn't have anything at all – they used church candles for their lighting. It was a right mess.

And then they started to install lighting.

Our official representative was the first to have it installed. Yes, he went and installed it. He's a quiet man, doesn't make a song and dance about things. All the same, he walks in a strange way and is constantly blowing his nose in a thoughtful manner.

But he hasn't made a song and dance about it.

Then our beloved landlady, Yelizaveta Ignatyevna Prokhorov, came along one day and suggested we got lighting installed in the apartments.

'Everyone's getting it installed,' she said. 'Even the official representative himself has had it installed.'

So what could we do! We got it installed too.

They installed it, lit us up. My God! Everything was rotten and revolting.

Before, you'd go off to work in the morning, come home in the evening, drink some tea and go to bed. And with kerosine lighting you didn't notice anything much.

But now, we switched the light on and looked around: there was someone's torn slipper lying on the floor, the wallpaper was peeling away and dangling, there was a bedbug galloping off – to get away from the light, some unidentified rag lying there, a gob of spit, a dog-end, a flea bouncing about.

My God! It was enough to make you scream out loud. Just looking at the spectacle made you sick.

There was a sofa that stood in our room. I thought it was pretty good. I even used to sit on it in the evenings. But now, you switch on the light: my God! What a mess! Some sofa! Bits sticking out, hanging off, all its insides falling out. I can't sit on a sofa like that. And that's that.

'Well,' I thought, 'I don't exactly live in luxury. Makes you feel like just getting away from it all. You can't bear to look at it. You can't concentrate.'

I saw my landlady Yelizaveta Ignatyevna walking around looking sad, pottering about in her part of the kitchen, tidying up.

'What,' I said, 'are you so down about?'

She gave a despairing shrug.

'Semyon Yegorovich,' she said, 'I never thought that we lived in such poverty.'

I glanced over at the landlady's stuff: it was true, I thought, this was no palace: rotten, revolting, all kinds of rags. And all this was flooded with bright light, and you couldn't avoid seeing it.

I started to come home feeling depressed. I'd come home and head straight for bed without switching on the light.

Then I thought better of it, and after pay day, I bought some whitewash, mixed it up and got to work. Tore off the wallpaper, got rid of the cobwebs, cleared out the sofa, painted everything: it gave me a great feeling inside.

But though everything was better, it wasn't really. I'd wasted my money: the landlady had the electricity cut off.

'All that light,' she said, 'makes everything look too squalid. Why bring poverty to light so glaringly?' she said.

I pleaded with her and presented the arguments, but it was no use.

'You can move out if you want,' she said. 'But I don't want to live under all that light. I haven't got the money to be redecorating the decor.'

But it's not exactly easy to move out, comrades, when you've splashed out on redecorating. So I gave in.

So you see, comrades, light's good, but even light has its problems. We've got to change every aspect of our lives. There must be cleanliness and order. We must decisively sweep away all that is rotten and revolting. What's good in the dark is bad in the light! Wouldn't you agree, comrades?

Domestic Bliss

by Mikhail Zoshchenko (translated by Jeremy Hicks

The other day I dropped in on someone I know, Yegorov. He's the timekeeper in our factory.

I arrived at his apartment.

He was sitting at the table looking very pleased with himself, reading the paper. His wife was sitting beside him doing some sewing.

My host's eyes lit up when he saw me.

'Ah,' he said, 'come on in my friend . . . Aren't you going to congratulate us then?'

'Congratulate you on what, Mitrofan Semyonych?' I asked.

'You mean you don't know?' he said. 'On our new life, on the changes we've made: we've built the new family.'

'How do you mean?' I said. 'You're not expecting an addition to the family are you?'

'Nope,' Yegorov laughed. 'That's not it. Missed by a mile . . . You can ask the wife yourself. It concerns her more . . . Look how happy she is sitting there sewing . . . Just like an angel . . . Let her tell you about her domestic bliss herself.'

I looked at Mitrofan Semyonych's spouse. But she gave a bit of a wry smile and said: 'Yes,' she said, 'you see, we don't cook at home any more . . . We're doing without a cooker. We go to the canteen now.'

'That's right!' exclaimed her husband, pleased with himself. 'We've had enough! We've started a new life. Out the window with the lot of it: the cooker, the saucepans, the washtub . . . Let the woman know freedom . . . She's got the same rights as me.'

My host talked about the unquestionable advantages of communal eating and then started to laugh.

'You can't imagine how much better off we are for this change. It's brought nothing but advantages, clear profit! When guests come, say. They sit there and wait. Constantly wondering if you're going to lay the table. But you announce to them, the free-loading bastards: "By the way," you say, "I'm afraid we dine in the canteen. You can come too if you like, but you don't have to, we're not forcing you." '

The husband started chuckling and glanced at his wife.

'Yes,' he said. 'It's a win-win situation. Time, for example. We've got so much free time on our hands! All the time in the world . . . The way things used to be, the wife would get home from work and rush about, bang, crash, light the cooker . . . Think of the waste of matches alone! But now when she comes home, the stupid woman's got nothing to do. She can sew all day long if she wants. Let her enjoy her freedom.'

'Cooking,' I agreed, 'certainly does take up a lot of time.'

'You're not joking!' exclaimed my host with renewed enthusiasm. 'Now at least she comes home and she can sew, and when she's finished sewing, she can do some laundry. If there's no laundry to do, then she can knit some socks . . . She could even start taking orders for sewing, because she's got more free time than she knows what to do with.'

The husband fell silent, then continued, struck by the thought: 'That's a point. Why don't you start taking orders, Motya? You know, for sewing . . . The odd shirt, blouses, smocks . . . '

'Yes, all right,' said his wife, 'I suppose I could take some orders. I don't see why not . . . '

Clearly, the husband was upset by such a lukewarm response.

' "I suppose I could," ' he mimicked his wife. 'You, Motya, there's no pleasing you. Another woman in your place would be jumping for joy that she'd been emancipated, but you go round sulking like a mouse with a migraine, and don't say a word . . . Aren't you pleased you're not stuck in the kitchen all day? Come on, our guest is waiting for an answer!'

'Don't say that, of course I am,' the wife agreed in a despondent tone.

'As if you wouldn't be pleased! You used to slave over a hot stove all day long . . . The smoke, fumes, steam, flames, the smell . . . Yuch! Now you can sew to your heart's content, Motya. Enjoy your free time. Even you deserve a life.'

I looked at the husband. He was serious.

'Listen,' I said, 'a stone's no softer than a rock.'

'What do you mean?' Mitrofan Semyonych exclaimed in astonishment.

'I said: a stone's no softer than a rock. Cooking, sewing, what's the difference? Maybe your wife would like to read that paper of yours? Maybe she doesn't feel like sewing?'

'You what?' The husband took offence. 'What do you mean not sew? She's a woman.'

I stood up, said goodbye to my host and left. But as I was going, I heard the husband say to his wife: 'The bastard didn't like that. We didn't feed him, so he starts moaning and taking it out on other people . . . If he wants some dinner, he'd better go to the canteen and not hang around other people's houses . . . Come on, sew Motya, sew, pay attention to what you're doing.'

Crisis

by Mikhail Zoshchenko (translated by Jeremy Hicks)

The other day, citizens, I saw a cartload of bricks going down the road. I'm not joking!

You know, my heart palpitated with joy. It must mean we're building something, citizens. They don't just transport bricks for no reason at all. They must be building a nice little house somewhere. They've started, touch wood.

In maybe twenty years' time, and who knows, even less, every citizen will probably have a whole room to themselves. And if the population doesn't grow too quickly and they allow everyone to have abortions, then two rooms. Or it might even be three. With a bathroom.

What a life we'll lead then, eh citizens! In one room we'll sleep, say, in another receive guests, and in a third something else . . . Who knows? With all that freedom, we'll find something to be getting on with.

But just now things are a bit difficult with floor space. There's not a lot of it about on account of the housing crisis.

I was living in Moscow, comrades. I've only just returned from there. I myself have undergone this crisis.

So I arrived in Moscow, you see. I was walking around the streets with my stuff. And there was nowhere. Not just nowhere to stay, but nowhere even to put my stuff.

Can you imagine, two weeks I was walking around the streets with my stuff. I grew a beard and gradually lost my stuff. So there I was, you see, walking around light, without any stuff. Hunting for accommodation.

Finally, in one building, some man came down the stairs.

'For thirty roubles,' he said, 'I can fix you up in the bathroom. The apartment,' he said, 'is fit for royalty . . . Three toilets . . . A bath . . . You can live there in the bathroom to your heart's content,' he said. 'There's no windows, I'll grant you that, but there is a door. And running water's freely available. If you want,' he said, 'you can run yourself a bath full of water and dive around all day long.'

I said: 'Esteemed comrade, I'm not a fish,' I said. 'I don't require diving facilities. I'd rather,' I said, 'live on dry land. Knock a bit off,' I said, 'for the damp.'

He said: 'I can't comrade. I'd love to, but I can't. It doesn't depend on me alone. It's a communal apartment. And there's been a fixed price agreed for the bathroom.'

'What choice do I have then?' I said. 'All right. Extract,' I said, 'thirty from me then and let me get in there straight away,' I said. 'I've been walking the pavements for three weeks,' I said, 'and I might get tired otherwise.'

All right then. They let me in. I began living there.

And the bath really was fit for royalty. All over the place, wherever you put your foot, there was the marble bath, boiler and taps. Mind you, there was nowhere to sit. You could just about sit on the side of the bath, but you kept falling down, straight into the marble bath.

So I put down some planks as floorboards, and went on living there.

After a month, though, I got married.

I met a young, kind-hearted wife. You know. Without a room of her own.

I thought she'd reject me on account of the bath, and I'd never know conjugal bliss and comfort, but not her, she didn't reject me. Just gave a little frown and answered: 'So what,' she said, 'living in a bath doesn't make you a bad person. If it comes to it,' she said, 'we can always put up a partition. Here, for example,' she said, 'we could have my boudoir, and over there we'd have the dining room . . .'

I said: 'We could put up a partition, citizen. The only thing is the tenants,' I said, 'the bastards won't let us. That's what they keep on saying: no alterations.'

All right then. So we carried on living there as before.

In less than a year me and the wife had a tiny baby.

We called him Volodya and carried on with life. We could always give him a bath, and carry on living.

You know, it was even working out pretty well. The baby, you see, was getting a bath every day and never once caught a cold.

The only inconvenient thing was in the evenings the tenants of the communal apartment kept on barging into the bathroom to take baths.

While this went on the whole family had to be moved out into the corridor.

So I asked the tenants: 'Citizens,' I said, 'take your baths on a Saturday. Come on,' I said, 'you can't have a bath every day. When are we going to have a life?' I said. 'You've got to see it from our point of view.'

But the bastards – there were thirty-two of them, all swearing. And they threatened to smash my face in if I started making trouble.

Well, what can you do? You can't do anything. We carried on living there as before.

After a while, my wife's mum turned up in our bath from the provinces. She settled in behind the boiler.

'I've been dreaming for so long' she said, 'of cradling my grandson in my arms. You can't,' she said, 'deny me that entertainment.'

I said: 'I'm not denying it. Go on, granny,' I said, 'cradle away. You can even,' I said, 'fill up the bath and dive in with your grandson.'

Then I said to my wife: 'Look citizen, if you've got any more relatives coming to stay with you, then tell me now, and put me out of my misery.'

She said: 'No, only my brother for Christmas . . . '

I left Moscow without waiting for her brother. I send my family money by post.

Nervous People

by Mikhail Zoshchenko (translated by Jeremy Hicks)

The other day there was a fight in our communal apartment. Not so much a fight as a full-scale battle. On the corner of Glazovaya and Borovaya.

Of course, they were really putting everything into the fight. Gavrilov, the invalid, nearly got his head – all he had left – chopped off.

The main reason for it all is that people are very nervous. They get upset about minor trivialities. Tempers flare. And that makes them lash out like blind things.

Of course, they say that nerves are always shaken after a civil war. Maybe that's true, but all the same, this ideology won't make the invalid Gavrilov's head heal up any sooner.

So one of the tenants, Marya Vasilyevna Shchiptsova, went into the kitchen at nine o'clock in the evening and lit the primus. She always, you see, lights the primus around this time. She drinks tea and applies a compress.

So she went into the kitchen. Stood the primus in front of her and lit it. But it wouldn't light, the stupid damned thing.

She thought: 'Why the hell's it not lighting? The stupid damned thing's not gone and got clogged up with soot has it?'

So she took a scourer in her left hand and was about to clean it.

She was about to clean it and took the scourer in her left hand, but another tenant, Darya Petrovna Kobylina, whose scourer it was, saw what had been taken and answered: 'By the way, most esteemed Marya Vasilyevna, would you mind putting that scourer back.'

Shchiptsova, of course, lost her temper at these words and answered: 'There you are Darya Petrovna, go and choke on your scourer. I can't even bear to touch it,' she said, 'let alone pick it up.'

So then of course, Darya Petrovna Kobylina lost her temper at these words. They started conversing. Then the noise began: crashing and banging.

The husband, Ivan Stepanych Kobylin, whose scourer it was appeared on hearing all this noise. A healthy sort of man, even got a big paunch, but he too suffers from nerves.

So Ivan Stepanych appeared and said: 'I,' he said, 'work like an elephant for thirty-two roubles and a few kopecks in a co-operative. I smile to the customers,' he said, 'and weigh out their sausage for them, and out of this,' he said, 'with my hard-earned kopecks, I buy myself scourers, and there's no way I'm going to allow some passing personnel I hardly know to make use of these scourers.'

Then noise and discussions started up again on the subject of the scourer. So of course all the tenants came barging into the kitchen. Making a fuss. Even the invalid Gavrilov appeared.

'What's all the noise for,' they said, 'and where's the fight?'

Then straight after these words the fight was realised. It started.

But our kitchen's narrow, you see. Not suited to fighting. No room. Saucepans and primuses all over the place. Not even space to turn round. And now there were twelve people who'd shoved their way in. You want to smash some bastard in the face, say, and get three instead. And of course you bump into everything and fall over. An invalid with no legs hasn't a chance, even with three legs you haven't a hope in hell of staying standing.

But this invalid, the bloody dodderer, despite this pushed his way right into the thick of it. Ivan Stepanych, whose scourer it was, shouted at him: 'Get out of the way, Gavrilov. Look out or your other leg will get torn off.'

Gavrilov said: 'Then my leg's had it,' he said. 'But I can't get out now. My facial ambition's been beaten to a pulp,' he said.

And that moment someone really did give him one in the mouth. So he didn't get out, but kept on throwing himself about. Then someone hit the invalid across the skull with a saucepan.

The invalid just flopped on to the floor and lay there. Looking depressed.

Then some parasite ran off to get the militia.

The copper appeared. He shouted: 'Get the coffins ready you bastards, I'm going to shoot!'

Only after these fateful words did people come to a bit. They ran off to their rooms.

'Well, that's a strange thing,' they thought, 'however did we get into a fight, esteemed comrades?'

People ran off to their rooms, only Gavrilov the invalid didn't run off. He just lay there, looking depressed. And blood was trickling from his crown.

Two weeks after this incident the trial took place.

The People's Judge was a nervous sort of man too: he booked everyone.

An Incident on the Volga

by Mikhail Zoshchenko (translated by Jeremy Hicks)

To start with, we wanted to tell you about an amusing little piece of bad luck.

The precise nature of this bad luck was that a group of holiday-makers received a profound shock on account of a misunderstanding.

This is how it happened. It's a true story.

In the first years after the Revolution, when life was settling down and wonderful ships offering first-class cabins and serving passengers hot meals started sailing down the Volga again, a group of holiday-makers – six office-workers, including myself – went to have a holiday on the Volga.

Everyone had been advising us to take a trip down the Volga. Because you can have a really wonderful holiday there. The nature. The shores. The water, the food and the cabins.

So the group of office-workers, having got tired, so to speak, of the thunder of Revolution, went off to revive themselves.

We got a wonderful first-class steamer, *Comrade Penkin* was her name.

We wondered who this Penkin was, and were told that apparently he worked in water-borne transportation.

We couldn't care less really and, regardless, we took a trip on this unknown comrade.

We arrived at Samara.

We got out in our group and went to look round the town. We looked round. Suddenly we heard a whistle.

People said: 'The timetable's unreliable these days. Our *Penkin* could suddenly decide to leave. Let's go back.'

And so, having just about managed to look round the town, back we went.

As we approached the jetty we could see that our steamer wasn't there any more. She had gone.

People started shouting and wailing.

One of our group shouted: 'I left my documents there in my trousers.'

Others shouted: 'And we've left our luggage and our money. What are we going to do now? . . . This is terrible!'

I said: 'Let's get on this steamer that's going the other way and go home.'

We saw that there really was a Volga steamer at the jetty, named *Thunderstorm*.

We asked people in mournful tones whether the *Penkin* had left long ago. Maybe we could catch up with her by land.

People said: 'What do you want to catch up with her for? That's the *Penkin* over there. It's just that she's now *Thunderstorm*. It's the former *Penkin*. They've painted over the name.'

We were extremely pleased to hear this. We all made for our steamer and didn't get off until we'd travelled all the way to Saratov. We were afraid to.

We asked the captain, by the way, what was the reason for this amusing incident and for the hurry.

The captain said: 'You see, we gave this steamer that name by a sort of mistake. Penkin does work in water-borne transport, only he was sort of not quite up to the job. At the moment he's being prosecuted for exceeding his authority. So we received a telegram telling us to get rid of his name. And we renamed her *Thunderstorm*.'

Then we said: 'Ah, so that's why!' and laughed hollowly.

We arrived at Saratov. We got out in our group and went to look round the town.

We didn't exactly hang around there for long either. But we went to a stall and bought some cigarettes. And looked at a couple of buildings.

We returned, and again we saw that our steamer had gone. We saw another steamer standing there in her place.

We weren't as scared as we had been in Samara, of course. We thought we might have a chance. Maybe they'd painted over the name again. But all the same, some of us got very frightened again.

We ran up to the bank. We asked people: 'Where's *Thunderstorm*?'

The people said: 'That's *Thunderstorm* over there. Formerly *Penkin*. Now, starting from Saratov, they're calling her *Korolenko*.'

We said: 'Why are they doing all this repainting?'

The people said: 'We don't know. Ask the boatswain.'

The boatswain said: 'These names are a real pain. They called us *Penkin* by mistake. And as for *Thunderstorm*, that was an irrelevant name. It sort of lacked a principled position. It's a natural phenomenon. It's no benefit to heart or brain. And so the captain got it in the neck. So that's why we did the repainting.'

We all cheered up then and said: 'Oh, so that's it!' We got on this *Korolenko* and off we went.

Then the boatswain said: 'Remember, at Astrakhan don't be afraid if you come back to find another name.'

But we said: 'Well, that's hardly likely, since this Korolenko is a famous writer.'

Anyway, we got to Astrakhan. And from there we set off on dry land.

So we don't know the subsequent fate of the steamer.

But you can rest assured that she kept this last name. For ever and ever. Especially since Korolenko's dead. Penkin was alive, you see, and that was his main stroke of bad luck, which led to the steamer being renamed.

So bad luck most probably consists in the simple fact that people are sometimes alive then, does it? No, I'm sorry, I really can't understand what the essence of misfortune is. On the one hand, sometimes it seems we're better off dead. But on the other, as they say, thanks all the same. A funny kind of good fortune. I'd rather not. At the same time, being alive is in that respect a sort of relative misfortune.

So, you could say, unpleasant things are coming at people from two directions at once.

And that is why we have put this little piece of nonsense about a kind of misunderstanding with our stories about misfortune.

Pelageya

by Mikhail Zoshchenko (translated by Robert Chandler)

Pelageya was illiterate. She didn't even know how to sign her name.

But Pelageya's husband was a Soviet worker in a position of responsibility. And though he was a simple lad from a village, five years in the city had taught him a lot. Not only how to sign his name. Goodness knows if there was anything he hadn't learned.

And he was very ashamed of having an illiterate wife.

'You could at least, Pelageya, learn how to sign your name,' he would say to his wife. 'My surname's so easy. Two syllables – *Kuchkin*. But you can't even do that. It's embarrassing.'

But Pelageya just shrugged her shoulders and said, 'Why, Ivan Nikolayevich? The years are going by for me. My fingers don't bend so well any more. What good will it do me to study and copy out letters? Study's for Young Pioneers – I can't change myself now. I'll stay this way till the end of my days.'

Pelageya's husband was a very busy man and he couldn't afford to spend a lot of time on his wife. He would just shake his head. 'Ah, Pelageya, Pelageya . . . ' And say no more.

But then one day Ivan Nikolayevich came home with a special little book.

'Pelageya,' he said, 'here is the very newest self-teaching ABC, compiled according to the latest methods. I'll show it to you myself.'

Pelageya smiled quietly, took the ABC from him, turned it this way and that way and hid it in the chest of drawers. 'Maybe future generations will need it,' she thought. 'Maybe it'll come in useful.'

But then one day Pelageya sat down to do some work. Ivan Nikolayevich's jacket needed mending – the sleeve was worn through.

Pelageya sat down at the table. She took a needle. She put one hand under the jacket. Something rustled.

'Money?' she thought.

It was a letter. A clean, neat little envelope, with fine little writing on it. And the paper, she thought, smelled of perfume or eau de Cologne. Pelageya's heart missed a beat.

'No,' she thought. 'Don't say Ivan Nikolayevich is deceiving me. Don't say he's having intimate correspondence with ladies of importance and laughing at his illiterate fool of a wife!'

Pelageya looked at the envelope, took out the letter and unfolded it – but she couldn't make out a thing; she was illiterate.

For the first time in her life Pelageya was sorry she couldn't read.

'It may not be addressed to me,' she thought, 'but I need to know what it says. My whole life may be about to change. Maybe I should go back to the country and work in the fields.'

Pelageya began to cry. She thought how Ivan Nikolayevich seemed to have changed recently. Yes, he was fussing about his moustache more often. Washing his hands more often.

Pelageya sits there. She looks at the letter and howls. She can't read the letter. And how can she show it to anyone else?

Then Pelageya hid the letter in the chest of drawers, darned the jacket and began to wait for Ivan Nikolayevich. And when he arrived Pelageya didn't let anything show. On the contrary, she talked calmly and quietly and even hinted she wouldn't mind doing a little study. Really she had had enough of being a dark and illiterate peasant.

Ivan Nikolayevich was delighted. 'Splendid,' he said. 'I'll teach you the letters myself.'

'All right then,' said Paelageya.

And she looked very intently at Ivan Nikolayevich's neatly trimmed little moustache.

Day after day, for two months on end, Pelageya taught herself letters. Patiently, syllable by syllable, she formed words. She copied letters of the alphabet and learned sentences off by heart. And every evening she took the forbidden letter out of the chest and tried to divine its mysterious meaning.

This, however, wasn't at all easy.

Only during the third month did Pelageya fully master learning.

One morning, when Ivan Nikolayevich went off to work, Pelageya took out the letter and began to read it.

The fine handwriting was hard to decipher. Only the faint hint of perfume kept Pelageya going.

The letter was addressed to Ivan Nikolayevich.

Pelageya began to read.

DEAR COMRADE KUCHKIN – I'm sending you the promised ABC. I think within two or three months your wife will be able to master learning completely. Promise, my dear, to make sure she does this. Explain things to her. Impress on her how awful it is, really, to be an illiterate peasant.

At this moment, for the coming anniversary, we are using every means to eliminate illiteracy from the whole of our Republic, but we forget, for some reason, about those who are near and dear to us.

Do this without fail, Ivan Nikolayevich.

With Communist greetings

Mariya Blokhina

Pelageya read this letter twice and, sorrowfully pursing her lips and feeling some kind of secret hurt, began to cry.

The Hat

by Mikhail Zoshchenko (translated by Robert Chandler)

Only now can one totally understand and grasp the great strides with which, in the last ten years, we have moved forward.

Take any aspect of our life – nothing to be seen but total development and happy success.

And I, my brothers, as a former transport worker, can see very evidently what, for instance, has been achieved on this really rather important front.

Trains run backwards and forwards. Rotten sleepers are removed. Signals are repaired. Whistles give the right whistles. Travelling has become truly pleasant and satisfactory.

Whereas in the past! Back in 1918! You travelled, you travelled and then – total standstill. And the engine driver, up at the head of the train, is shouting: 'Brothers! Come here!'

So the passengers gather.

And the driver says to them: 'I am afraid I can't, brothers, for reasons of fuel, keep going. Those of you with an interest in further travel,' he says, 'should jump down from your carriages. And run along into the forest to collect firewood.'

Well, the passengers aren't too happy. They fuss and grumble about this kind of innovation, but soon enough they're deep in the forest. Chopping and sawing.

They saw up a yard of firewood and move off. The wood, needless to say, is green. Hisses like hell and our progress is halting.

And I remember another incident. In 1919. We were moving modestly along towards Leningrad . . . We stop in the middle of nowhere. Then – reverse drive. And we come to standstill.

The passengers ask: 'Why have we stopped? And why all that way in reverse? Do we, dear God, need firewood? Is the driver looking for birch trees? Is it an upsurge in banditry?'

The fireman explains: 'There's been an unfortunate incident. The driver's hat's blown off. He's gone to look for it.

'The Hat'

The passengers got off the train. Settled down on the embankment.

Suddenly they see the driver coming out of the forest. Downcast. Pale. Shrugging his shoulders.

'No,' he says. 'I can't find it. The devil knows where it has blown.'

They move the train back another five hundred yards. The passengers are divided into search parties.

About twenty minutes later some man with a sack shouts out: 'Here it is, you devils! Look!'

And there it is. The engine driver's hat. Hanging up on a bush.

The driver put his hat on, tied it with a string to one of his buttons so it wouldn't blow off again, and began getting up steam.

And half an hour later we were safely on our way.

Yes. Transport was in a totally bad state.

But today, even if a passenger – let alone a mere hat – were blown off, we wouldn't stop for more than a minute.

Because time is precious. We must keep moving.

The Secret of the Cheka

from *Mess-Mend: The Yankees in Petrograd*
by Marietta Shaginian (translated by Samuel Cioran)

In America Arthur Morlender had heard quite a bit about the terrifying Cheka of the Bolsheviks. The newspapers had printed sensational confessions by White Russian émigrés about how they had been tortured by incredible instruments that had not even been known in the Middle Ages. Some refugee landowner had serialised an entire novel by the title of *The Secret of the Cheka* in one issue after the other of the *Chicago Sunday* and then had admitted to his friends whenever they got drunk that 'if it hadn't been for that dear old Cheka – God bless it – I'd have absolutely nothing for grub'. And so now Arthur was sitting in that same Cheka, in a comfortable chair, in front of a table on which stood a glass of tea and two ham sandwiches which had been pushed towards him by a handsome, dark-skinned investigator in a military uniform and with a dozen medals on his chest.

'And so you're the son of the famous inventor, Morlender,' he said thoughtfully, tapping the tip of his pencil on the table in front of him. 'But why didn't you come here under your own name? You would have been afforded the most generous hospitality. What purpose did this masquerade serve? And where is the real Vasilov? Answer these questions in order, please.'

'I am the son of the famous inventor, Arthur Morlender,' the arrested man said with a heavy sigh. 'My father was killed in Russia by the Bolsheviks, or so I was told by the head of the organisation that my father worked for, Jack Kressling the billionaire. I swore to have revenge on my father's murderers. Jack Kressling and his friends arranged this masquerade, equipped me with money, weapons, poison, bombs and sent me here under the name of Vasilov. Where the real Vasilov is, I don't know. A woman came with me who pretends to be the wife of Vasilov. Who she is, I also don't know. That's everything. No, that's not everything, actually. When I saw your country and your people, from the first day I began to doubt the fact that my father was killed by your people. And the desire to avenge him was extinguished in me.'

'You are right. Morlender left here alive and well.' The investigator rang, a youngish Red Army man entered. 'Sidorov, a copy from the ship's log of the *Torpedo*!'

When the copy was delivered, the investigator leafed through it until he had hunted down the page.

'Read it, there's the entry: "A cabin reserved to New York on 6 July . . . " But what's this?' The investigator suddenly turned red as he read the concluding lines: " . . . remained unoccupied." ' Once more, more forcefully than before, he pressed the button. 'Sidorov, find out immediately where, when and by what means the engineer Jeremy Morlender, who was a guest in the Soviet Union for about a month, left our country!'

While Sidorov disappeared soundlessly to fulfil the order, the investigator gazed sympathetically at Arthur.

'To tell the truth, we did not attribute any significance to the newspaper furore surrounding this phoney murder. After all the things they write about over there! And where do they get them from? But didn't this whole affair seem strange to you? Tell me, what about your father's estate, his famous invention that has provoked rumours in both hemispheres, a new form of some kind of energy? Are you yourself working on it?'

Arthur had already begun to get accustomed to the investigator's manner of asking not one but an entire series of questions. He understood that with a group of several questions posed all at once, the investigator was helping him to see the connection between various things that had eluded him earlier. And, bearing this connection in mind, he replied: 'My father's invention was not bequeathed to me. Father wrote a new will in Russia. According to this new will, the invention was supposed to be used for the struggle against the communists. But now, it all seems strange to me. I was his only son. For some reason or other, father deprived me of all of his fortune. Everything was awarded to his new wife, whose existence I had not even suspected.'

'And who is this new wife?'

'The former secretary of Jack Kressling.'

As he answered, Arthur Morlender himself saw how his answers became linked into a circle and how all of them pointed to a single person. Listening to him, the investigator nodded his head in understanding. He had managed, in the course of those moments, to contact someone on the telephone; he listened to them, gave brief replies into the mouthpiece and continued to watch Morlender. And when he put the telephone down, he turned to face Morlender full on.

'There's no need to wait for Sidorov. I was just speaking with the person who had the responsibility of guiding your father around our country and who was present when he departed. This person has informed me of some curious things. They'll be here in a moment.'

All this time, Rebrov had been sitting by the window and smoking his pipe. He had not intruded with a single word into the conversation. But when the investigator fell silent, and Morlender, his chin on his chest, was mentally resurrecting in his mind everything that had happened to him in New York, Rebrov said quietly: 'The engineer Jeremy Morlender was at our place as well, at the experimental division. He acted very friendly. It doesn't seem likely that he would have bequeathed this new discovery you were telling us about to the struggle against communism.'

He did not manage to finish before the door was softly opened, and on the threshold appeared the 'person' about whom the investigator had been talking. This person – an attractive and stern young lady with curly hair and gold pince-nez on her aquiline nose, wearing Swedish suede shoes, a Finnish jumper and a Parisian blouse – took them all in with a questioning look in her eyes.

'Here, let me introduce you,' the investigator smiled broadly, 'this is our well-known interpreter, a worker in the commissariat of foreign affairs, a trusted person, you can rely on her every word. Sit down, Comrade Serezhkina. Repeat for those present what you just told me.'

Comrade Serezhkina pulled a fine Estonian notebook out of her Italian purse with a view of Mount Vesuvius, opened it up and, peering into it, rapped out: 'Mr Jeremy Morlender visited four of our Republics, eight regional centres, Moscow, Petrograd, twelve factories, had conversations and meetings with academicians, professors, workers, planners, spent three days at the Central Aero-Electric Station, was received by the leaders of our government, stepped before the microphone with words of gratitude and great satisfaction, spoke in favour of closer contact between the sciences here and abroad. According to his wish, a ticket was reserved for him on the steamship *Torpedo* departing for New York on 6 July. But Mr Jeremy did not depart on this steamship.'

'Did not depart!' Arthur whispered. 'Why not?'

'For the reason that on the morning of the 4th a private American aeroplane for the exclusive use of the capitalist Jack Kressling landed at the Petrograd airport. Information was given by the pilot to the effect that he had to find Mr Jeremy that same day and offer to fly him back immediately for some unavoidable reason. I personally accompanied Mr Morlender at six o'clock in the morning and was a witness to his departure by air. Mr Morlender did not have time to request the money back for the cabin on the *Torpedo*.'

'But his coffin arrived on the *Torpedo*,' Arthur let drop in a hoarse voice. 'What nasty business is lurking behind all of this?'

'You figure it out!' the investigator said curtly and amiably. 'Comrade Serezhkina, you may go. And now I am going to ask you to inform us what specifically the organisers of your disguise wanted from you, the same organisers who in all probability murdered the unfortunate Vasilov. Be very precise in your answers. This time I'm going to record them!'

Arthur Morlender stuck his hand in his pockets and subsequently pulled out and distributed in front of the investigator everything that he had received from Kressling's gang. One item after the another, the investigator picked up the 'material evidence'. He held the ampoule up to the light and carefully looked at its contents, counted the little blue capsules in the box, weighed in the palm of his hand the loaded automatic pistol of the latest design. He thumbed the thick packet of new Soviet bills as though it were a deck of cards. Then he pushed everything off to the side, pronounced ' . . . good' and again selected the ampoule out of the pile.

'Rebrov, take that for your laboratory. Well, now, I'm listening to you, Morlender!'

'In addition to all the sabotage which I was to carry out at my discretion, I am supposed to present a gift – an explosive contrivance – which will be sent to me from America. For the time being I don't know the specific time, the operation or the nature of this gift.'

The investigator recorded the last word, stuck the pen back into the inkwell, handed to Arthur what he had written and gave him the pen to sign.

Morlender read it through and signed. He felt immeasurably exhausted. He sat and waited for them to send him off to jail. But Rebrov suddenly stood up, went up to him as though nothing were amiss, took him by the arm and pulled him after himself towards the door. The investigator shouted after them: 'Don't forget to go on playing your part! And don't be afraid of anything – we'll take measures. Under no circumstances should you have anything further to do with us, otherwise they might get suspicious and kill you before we can get to the bottom of this business. Goodbye and good luck!'

To Morlender's great amazement, he now understood that they believed him, that he was free, and, the main thing, that from now on he was not alone in the world.

Alexandra Kollontai
&
Vera Inber

There is no doubt that the position of women in Russia improved in the period immediately after the 1917 Revolution. The Provisional Government had given women the right to vote and in 1918 Bolshevik decrees on labour, marriage and the family, and the political system recognised women's right to equality within marriage and to equal pay. In 1920 abortion was legalised. For the Bolsheviks, these changes came from their equating liberation with productive as opposed to domestic labour – women would become liberated by becoming waged workers. Sexual liberation was not on the Bolshevik agenda – in fact, Lenin made it clear that for him the demand for free love to which he was fiercely opposed was bourgeois and not proletarian.[30] **Alexandra Kollontai** (1872–1952) was one of the few women who rose to a prominent position in the Bolshevik Party. Strongly opposed to the First World War, Kollontai went first to Germany, then to Denmark and finally to Norway in search of a community of like-minded radicals who opposed the war. In 1917, on receiving news of the Tsar's abdication, she left for Russia to be involved in the revolutionary process. Kollontai had joined the Bolshevik Party in 1915 and after the October Revolution she was appointed People's Commissar for Social Welfare. In 1919, she founded the Zhenotdel (Women's Department), set up to improve the conditions of women's lives, fight illiteracy and educate women about the new marriage, education and workplace laws. For Kollontai, the liberation of women would take place through women's entry into the waged workforce. But she was also sympathetic to their demands for erotic equality and saw clearly the connection between economic and sexual

30 Letter of 27 January 1917

freedom – freedom she asserted in her own life at great personal and political cost. Kollontai's political downfall came at the Tenth Party Congress in 1921 where, with her lover Alexander Shlyapnikov, she led the Workers' Opposition which argued against the Party leadership for greater autonomy for trade unions in the running of the economy and the abolition of the NEP (New Economic Policy). Dismissed by Lenin and Trotsky as Anarcho-Syndicalism, the Workers' Opposition was routed. In 1923, Kollontai was sent into political exile as Soviet Ambassador to Norway; this marked the end of her political influence. Today, Kollontai is known for the advocacy of free love but this is a simplification and only part of the story. She thought that changes in attitudes to sex and sexual equality could only come about with wage parity, communal childcare and the sharing of housework. This is beginning to happen for Zhenya in 'Three Generations'. Zhenya's casual attitude to sex is not something that Kollontai endorses – with more time and leisure, Zhenya will be able to attend to the demands of 'Winged Eros', Kollontai's term for heterosexual love based on erotic attraction and a shared commitment to the building of a new society. It is a great tribute to Kollontai that in the midst of revolutionary upheaval and civil war, she lived a life in which the personal was political. She paid a heavy price for it. Her writings continue to find a growing readership with successive generations of feminists and radicals

Vera Inber (1890–1972) was born in Odessa in 1890. Her father Moshe owned a scientific publishing house, Matematika, and was a cousin of Leon Trotsky who when young lived in their Odessa apartment when Vera was a baby. After living in France and Switzerland, Inber returned to Russia in 1914. She began to write poetry as part of the Constructivist group who advocated poetry reduced to streamlined formulae so as to be comprehensible to the masses. 'Five Nights and Days', a poem written in 1924 in memory of Lenin who died that year, brought Inber public acclaim. At this time, she wrote perceptive stories about the position of children in Soviet society which included 'Lalla's Interests'. She is best known for her moving account written during the siege of Leningrad and published, in 1944, as *A Leningrad Diary*. This brought her patriotic fame. Vera Inber died in Moscow 1972.

Three Genersations

from *Love of Worker Bees* by Alexandra Kollontai
(translated by Cathy Porter)

'But now let's talk about my problem, shall we,' said Olga Sergeevna, interrupting herself in that dry clear voice of hers which reminded me of her mother's compelling tones. 'The problem is my daughter, Zhenya. I'd like you to have a word with her. It may well be that there is something I just don't understand, and that this is just the inevitable crisis between the generations.

'But it may be something else; possibly Zhenya really has been corrupted by the abnormal conditions of her upbringing. Even as a very little girl she was being carted from one place to another, with her grandmother, with me, with friends. Over the past few years she's lived in a factory, fully involved in factory life, she's gone to work at the Front, taken part in the recent production drive, and naturally she's experienced many things which in the past girls of her age would only have heard about. Perhaps this is all as it should be, and one just has to face it, but on the other hand . . .

'Oh if only you knew how utterly confused I've been these last few weeks – I just don't know what's right and what's wrong! It used to make me so happy that Zhenya was so unprejudiced and that she faced up to life so boldly; she could extricate herself from any sort of practical difficulty, she was not intellectually equivocal, she was honest to the point of naïvety, it often seemed to me, and now suddenly . . .

'Well, briefly the facts are these. You know that when I was studying abroad I met Comrade Ryabkov, whom I nursed back to health in Davos. Since that time we have been living as man and wife. Of course, I'm considerably older than he is, and you might say he was my pupil, but in all these seven years together we've been very happy. When we returned together in 1917 we both helped to establish the power of the soviets.

'You know what a sunny disposition Comrade Ryabkov has – he's a true proletarian by temperament and a totally uncompromising person by nature. I don't need to tell you what kind of a worker he is either, everybody knows about that. I thought there was no cloud in our relationship and that everything was happy and simple between us.

'Last year when we settled in Moscow I decided Zhenya should live with us. She's a Party worker, as you know, although she's only just twenty. She's a tireless, passionate girl – just like her grandmother. And she has a good reputation in her district.

'You know our housing allocation; one room for three people. We're cramped but that's unavoidable in the present circumstances, and besides we're very rarely at home, especially me. I am frequently out of town visiting factories. When, after such a long separation, Zhenya did move in with us, she immediately established a close relationship with us. It was exceptionally friendly. I didn't feel at all like her mother, and just being with her made me feel young. Her energy, her laughter, and her youthful self-confidence were so infectious.

'Comrade Ryabkov got on with her splendidly too, and I was delighted, as I had feared that they wouldn't take to each other. But Zhenya and Andrei became excellent comrades, and I would send them off together to the theatre, or to meetings and public conferences. We lived together, amicably and harmoniously, and what pleased me most of all was that Andrei became so much more cheerful and fell ill less often.

'That was all fine until . . . until something happened which changed everything . . . '

Olga Sergeevna broke off suddenly, as if it was too painful for her to continue. I waited, while Olga Sergeevna looked over my shoulder out of the window.

'Well, Olga Sergeevna,' I said at last, 'I would suspect that what happened is distressing but inevitable – Zhenya and Comrade Ryabkov slept together. But, come on, what's so dreadful and sordid about that? You really must try to understand that sort of thing.'

'Oh, but it's not that! It's not that at all!' Olga Sergeevna interrupted me hastily. 'No, it's just that afterwards I felt I could suddenly see into his and Zhenya's minds . . . '

'And what did you see there?'

'Oh, it was a kind of heartlessness which I found utterly incomprehensible, a calm confidence in their own rights in the matter – there was something cold and rational about it, a kind of cynicism. You see, there's no love involved, no passion or regrets, nor any desire to end the situation. It's as if everything is just as it should be, and it's only me who doesn't understand and is behind the times.

'Sometimes their behaviour strikes me as the most utterly contemptible moral laxity and incomprehensible promiscuity, but then I'm assailed by doubts and wonder if it really is me who is behind the times. After all, my mother didn't understand my emotional crisis. And so that's why I'm asking you to help me to make sense of things.'

Olga Sergeevna then told me that her daughter had come to see her at work and had asked her mother for a ten-minute interview because, as she said, 'There's no other way of getting hold of you, mother.'

Very calmly, and without preamble, she had informed her mother that she had all the symptoms of being pregnant. Olga Sergeevna had been utterly aghast at this, and involuntarily exclaimed, 'But by whom?'

'I don't know,' Zhenya had replied. Her mother had concluded that she did not want to tell her, but something about this news had devastated her.

Zhenya asked her mother's advice on how to arrange an abortion (the new abortion law had just come into effect), and wanted the papers to take to the appropriate department. She didn't want a baby, she didn't have time for one.

Olga Sergeevna hadn't told her husband of Zhenya's news, as she regarded this as Zhenya's personal affair, and she could always tell him herself if she wanted to. But there was something, some unconscious anxiety about the whole thing, which preyed on Olga Sergeevna's mind. Doubts began to stir in her, and details of their life together started taking on a wholly different light.

Olga Sergeevna despised herself for these thoughts and tried to drive them from her mind, but they persisted and prevented her from getting on with her work. And they persisted so obstinately that one evening in the middle of a conference she pretended to be unwell, went home – and there she had found her daughter and her husband in each other's arms.

'You know, it wasn't so much the facts of the case which stunned me at the time, it was what happened afterwards. Andrei simply grabbed his hat and walked out, and when I blurted out to Zhenya, "But why did you tell me that you didn't know by whom you were pregnant?" she replied quite calmly: "I'll say again what I said then – I don't know whose baby it is. It might be Andrei's and it might be the other one." '

' "What do you mean, the other one?" '

' "Well, these past few months I've been involved with another man – nobody you know." '

'Can you understand how flabbergasted I was at this news? Zhenya then told me that even when she was taking parcels to the Front she was already having sexual relationships. But the thing I found most bewildering and shocking was that she declared quite openly that she did not love anyone and had never done so.

' "But why did you sleep with men then? Is it because you're really so attracted to them physically? You're still so young; why, it's not normal at your age!"

' "How can I put it, mother? For a long time I was really just physically attracted to men, as you probably understand the term anyway. That is, until I met this other man, the one I've been involved with over the past few months, although it's all over now. But I liked the men I slept with, and they liked me. That way it's simple, and it doesn't tie you to anything.

' "I can't understand what you're so upset about, mother. It would be different if I was prostituting myself or being raped. But this is something I do quite voluntarily, of my own free will. We stay together as long as we get on with each other, and when we no longer do, we just part company and nobody gets hurt. Of course, I'm going to lose two or three weeks' work because of this abortion, which is a pity, but that's my own fault and next time I'll take the proper precautions." '

When Olga Sergeevna asked her how, after everything she'd said, she could have two relationships at the same time, and why she should want to anyway, since she did not love anyone, Zhenya replied that it had been a coincidence. The other man attracted her emotionally, but treated her like a baby, and refused to take her seriously, which had infuriated her. It was her feelings of outrage that had led her to take up with Andrei, whom she felt to be a kindred spirit, and whom she loved as a friend and with whom she always felt happy and comfortable.

'And do they know about each other?' Olga Sergeevna had asked her.

'Yes, of course. I don't see that I have anything to conceal from them. They don't have to sleep with me if they don't like it. I have my own life to live and Andrei doesn't mind,' she had replied. 'Oh, the other man got angry about it and started to give me ultimatums, but of course he came round in the end. Anyway, I've left him now. I lost interest in him, he was so crude. I really don't like that sort of person.'

Olga Sergeevna had then tried to point out how unacceptable this frivolous attitude to sexual relationships was – frivolous about life, and about people in general.

But Zhenya had argued back, saying, 'Look, mother, you say that my behaviour is shabby, that you shouldn't sleep with people you don't love, and that my cynicism is driving you to despair. But just tell me honestly, if I was a boy, your twenty-year-old son, who had been at the Front and had generally led an independent life, would you be so horrified to hear that he had been sleeping with women he liked? I don't mean with prostitutes he'd bought, or with little girls he'd seduced, because I agree that *is* shabby, but with women he liked and who liked him too. Would that really horrify you so much? Admit it, it wouldn't, would it? So why are you in such a state of despair about what you describe as my immorality? I assure you, I'm exactly the same sort of person, and I'm perfectly well aware of my obligations and my responsibilities to the Party.

'But I don't understand what the Party, the Revolution, the devastation of the country, the White Guard, and everything else you've been talking about have to do with the fact that I sleep with Andrei and with someone else at the same time? I couldn't possibly have a baby, I know that. It would be terribly wrong at this time, when there are so many political problems. I'm quite well aware of that, and at the moment I certainly don't intend to be a mother. But as for everything else . . . '

'But what about me, Zhenya?' cried Olga Sergeevna. 'Did you never consider how *I* might react to your relationship with Andrei?'

'But how can it make any difference to you?' Zhenya objected. 'It was you who wanted us to be close to each other, and you were so pleased that we were friends. Where are the boundaries of intimacy? Why is it all right for us to experience things together, enjoy ourselves together, but not sleep together? It's not as if we've taken anything from you – Andrei still worships you as he has always worshipped you, and I certainly haven't robbed you of one iota of his love for you. Anyway, what does it matter to you? It's all the same to you, you never have the time for that sort of thing.

'Besides, mother, do you really want to tie Andrei to your apron strings so that he can't have a life of his own without you knowing about it? That really would be a terribly possessive attitude. It must be grandmother's bourgeois upbringing coming out in you! Anyway, you're being so unfair! In your day you lived your own life, so why shouldn't Andrei now?'

What had upset and angered Olga Sergeevna most of all was that neither her daughter nor her husband had shown any signs of remorse, just saw everything as quite natural, simple and not worth discussing. It was only with the greatest condescension to her, as someone who didn't really understand things, that Andrei and Zhenya had laboriously made a few superficial remarks about how sorry they were that everything had worked out like this, and how regretful that they had made life so unpleasant for her.

But she had been only too painfully aware that neither Zhenya nor her gentle sincere Andrei truly considered themselves to be in the wrong. Both of them constantly repeated variations on the theme that nothing had changed, and that she was viewing the whole thing quite needlessly in these tragic dimensions. Nobody, they assured her, wanted to cause her any pain or unhappiness, but if it was really upsetting her so much they would both agree to call it a day, although they couldn't imagine what difference that was going to make.

It was because she was plunged in this chaos of ideas and emotions that Olga Sergeevna had decided to ask for my advice and for some clarification of the matter. Was this nothing more than wanton promiscuity, unchecked by any sort of moral standards? Or was it some quite new phenomenon created by new lifestyles? Was this in fact the new morality? We discussed these questions at great length.

'What I find most painful about the whole thing,' said Olga Sergeevna, wearily leaning on her shapely arm in a gesture which reminded me of Maria Stepanovna, 'is that they're so totally cold and rational, like two old people with no emotions left. I could understand it if Zhenya loved Andrei and he loved her, and even if it did make me unhappy (because I do love Andrei very much, you know) I wouldn't have this unpleasant taste in my mouth, this feeling of physical nausea. To put it quite bluntly, I have grown very hostile towards Andrei and Zhenya – I cannot understand how they could have treated me so unscrupulously, with so little regard for my feelings and reactions. Do you know, it's shaken my faith as to whether these two people are capable of loving at all. They both keep telling me that they love me, but what do they mean by love when they cause me so much unhappiness and inflict it casually too, without any qualms or remorse. I really think they must be emotionally deficient in some way. I don't understand either of them.

'Once, I couldn't help reproaching Zhenya, and she just retorted: "Well, didn't you conceal your relationship with my father from his wife? Didn't you lie too?" But then surely that's the whole point – there's an enormous difference there that Zhenya can't grasp and won't understand. First of all, I never loved M's wife, who was like a total stranger to me. I never had any deep feelings for her and I only spared her the truth for humane reasons. Secondly, I loved M, loved him passionately, no less than his wife did, if not more. Our feelings gave us both equal rights over him, and my justification then was the power of my love for him and the suffering he caused me.

'But in this case, you see, there's nothing – no love, no suffering, no remorse, nothing. Only a sort of icy self-confidence and an insistence on their right to seize happiness however and wherever they may find it. That's what I find so dreadful, the fact that they seem to lack any warmth or kindness, even the most rudimentary sensitivity to others! And yet they call themselves communists!'

I couldn't help laughing at this somewhat illogical conclusion; and Olga Sergeevna also smiled shamefacedly, admitting that this conclusion did not really follow from her previous accusations.

When at last we said goodbye, we agreed that I should see Zhenya within a day or so.

It was two days later, in the morning, that Zhenya came to see me – she worked in her district all day and in the evenings. She was a slender girl, very tall, with a lively face and a small head that reminded me of her grandmother's. She looked rather pale and had dark circles under her eyes. Her hand when I shook it was cold and damp, and she'd obviously not yet fully recovered from her operation. She had a simple direct manner, and started to speak at once.

'I expect the main thing that surprises you is that I sleep with men just because I like them, before I've had time to fall in love with them. But don't you see, you have to have *leisure* in order to fall in love – I've read enough novels to know just how much time and energy it takes to fall in love and I just don't have the time. At the moment we've got a really enormous load of work on our hands in our district. Come to that, have we ever had any spare time over these last few years? We're constantly in a rush and our heads are always full of other things.

'Of course, sometimes you have periods when you're less busy and then you suddenly realise that you like someone. But as for falling in love, there's no time for that! Just as soon as you've grown really fond of each other he'll be called to the Front or shoved off to some other town. Or else you have so much work to do that you forget all about him. That's why you cherish the few hours when you *can* be together, and then you both enjoy it. It doesn't commit you to anything, and the only thing I'm always afraid of is catching some venereal disease. But actually if you look someone straight in the eye and ask him whether he's got it or not, he'll never lie to you. There was one man who liked me very much, I think he even loved me, and when I asked him it was terribly hard for him to admit it and I could see how upset he was. But in the end we didn't sleep together, and he knew I would never have forgiven him if we had.'

Zhenya had lovely wide-open eyes, and she gave an impression of utter directness and honesty.

'But tell me, Comrade Zhenya,' I said. 'If you can tell me that, how is it that you did not tell your mother everything immediately? Why did you conceal your relationship with Andrei from her all those months?'

'Well, I didn't think it concerned her, that's why. If I had fallen in love with Andrei and he had loved me, then of course I would have told her all about it, and I would probably just have gone out of her life. I wouldn't want to do anything to make her unhappy. But it wasn't as if there was anything that could possibly have robbed her of Andrei's affections! Why doesn't she understand that! If it hadn't been me it would only have been somebody else, and she really can't tie Andrei to her apron strings, or prevent him seeing anyone else or getting involved with other women, can she? I simply can't understand her!

'She's not at all upset by the fact that I'm friends with Andrei, that he talks to me more than to her and that he's closer to me emotionally. But as far as she's concerned, the fact that I slept with him means that I'm taking Andrei away from her. But mother has no time to sleep with him – it's true, she just hasn't the time! Anyway, Andrei is nearer my age than mother's, we share the same tastes, and really the whole thing is so natural . . . '

'But maybe, without really being aware of it, you actually have fallen in love with Andrei?' I interrupted her.

Zhenya shook her head. 'I don't know what you mean by love, but my feelings for him aren't anything like what I understand love to be. If you love a person, then you want to be together all the time, you want to sacrifice everything for his sake, you think about him, you worry about him. But if you suggested that I set up permanently with Andrei, I'd say thanks a lot, but no. Oh, he's a pleasant person, and it's nice to be with him because he's so frail and so cheerful about it, as mother probably told you. But I get bored if I have to spend too much time with him, and then I prefer Abrasha. Not that

I love him either, I never did, although Abrasha did have some sort of hold over me. I used to be at his beck and call and there was nothing I could do about it!'

Zhenya frowned and thought for a bit. Then she suddenly brightened again. 'The thing that upsets mother so much is that I don't love any of them and that she sees it as 'immoral' and abnormal for someone of my age to be sleeping with men I don't love. But I think mother is wrong, and that things are much simpler and better this way. I remember how, when I was a child, mother was always rushing between Konstantin and my father, eating her heart out and tormenting herself over the whole thing. Everyone suffered, Konstantin and my grandmother too. Why, even now I can hear my grandmother's voice ordering my mother to make some decision. 'Stop being such a coward,' she used to say, 'You must make your choice and come to a decision.'

'But mother was quite unable to decide, since she loved both of them and they both loved her. They were all so unhappy and made each other so wretched that they eventually started hating one another, and finally parted as enemies.

'As for me, I don't part with anyone as an enemy – when I stop liking them that means it's over, and that's all there is to it. Whenever someone starts to act jealously I always remember how wretched mother was and how jealous Konstantin and my father were of each other, and I tell myself that I wouldn't go through that for anything. I don't belong to anybody, and they'll just have to accept that!'

'But do you really mean to say that you've never loved anyone, and don't love anyone now?' I asked her. 'Quite apart from anything else, I doubt whether your definition of love is terribly plausible. It sounds as if you've got it out of books!'

'But what makes you think that I don't love anyone?' said Zhenya in honest amazement. 'What I said was that I didn't feel any love for the men I slept with. I certainly didn't say that I didn't love anyone . . . '

'Would you mind if I asked who you do love, then?' I said.

'Who do I love? Why, my mother, more than anyone else in the whole world. There is nobody like my mother – in some ways she's more important to me than Lenin. Anyway, she is completely special, and I couldn't exist without her. Her happiness means more to me than anything else . . . '

'And yet you've put paid to your mother's happiness and almost broken her heart. How do you reconcile that with what you've just said?'

'Look,' replied Zhenya thoughtfully, 'if I'd dreamt for one moment, if I'd known that mother would take it this way and that it would make her so miserable, I expect – no, I'm *sure* – I would never have done it. But I really imagined that she was above that sort of thing and that she saw things in the same way as Andrei and I did, and wouldn't pay much attention to it all. Now I realise how wrong I was, I feel terribly sad, much sadder than she realises . . . '

For the first time during our conversation the tears welled up in Zhenya's eyes. Much embarrassed, she wiped them away with the tips of her fingers, trying not to let me see them.

'I would give my life for mother, and those aren't just empty words, that's how I feel about her. She herself can tell you how much I suffered when we thought that she had caught typhus. But do you know what I find so especially painful now? I'm very, very sad for mother, and furious with myself for being so foolish and for being unable to understand, anticipate, or even guess that the whole business would affect her like this. I can't think of anything now that I wouldn't give for this not to have happened. But despite all this, deep down I still feel that mother is wrong and that Andrei and I are right. There must be some other interpretation of the whole thing which will make it all clear and simple and stop everyone being so unhappy. Then we'll all be able to continue as friends and no one will despise anyone.

'You see, however deeply I love mother, I feel for the first time in my life that she is terribly wrong, and that . . . Oh, that's what is so painful for me! I'd always considered mother to be utterly infallible, and now that's been shaken and I've lost all the old faith that mother was above everything and everybody and that she understood every-thing. It's dreadfully painful – I don't want to stop loving or trusting her, because how could I ever believe in other people if I did that? Oh, you can't imagine how unhappy all this has made me, and not for the reasons that my mother thinks either. It's all so sad . . . '

Zhenya no longer tried to conceal the large tears that ran down her cheeks and fell on to her frayed black skirt.

We talked about how best to resolve the situation. Zhenya had already decided to move into a hostel with some of her girl friends, and would be going there in a few days' time. She was only anxious as to how her mother and Andrei would cope without her constantly being there, for the whole tedious business of seeing to the provisions rested on her.

'I'm quite sure that mother won't eat properly,' she said disconsolately. 'If someone isn't there to take care of her and push food at her she'll go the whole day without eating. And Andrei's just as bad. I can't imagine how they're going to manage without me, they're both as helpless as children. Of course I can call on them and do everything I can, but it won't be the same. I'm busy too, you know. Everything is so much simpler when you all live together.'

She sighed, and went on talking about her mother and Andrei in a sober, maternal voice, as though she was dealing with children.

When it was time to say goodbye, I said, 'I'm so glad that I shall be able to reassure your mother now about everything, and tell her how much you love her. What upset her particularly was the idea that you were incapable of strong, healthy emotions, and that you were too rational about things.'

Zhenya smiled. 'Well, she can rest easy about that, because I'm quite sure I'll get myself into some stupid scrape again because of men! I'm not her daughter and my grandmother's granddaughter for nothing, after all! Anyway, there are people whom I love now, whom I love very much, other people besides mother. There's Lenin, for instance – don't smile, I mean it! I love him far more than all the men I like and have slept with. I'm always beside myself for several days whenever I know I'm going to see him and hear him talk – I'd give my life for him too!

'And there's Comrade Gerasim, do you know him? He's our district secretary. Now there's a man for you! I love him too, I truly love him and even if he's not always correct I'll always submit to him because I know that his intentions are good. Do you remember when there was that scandal about him last year? I didn't sleep for nights, and what a fight we put up for him! I mobilised the entire district to support him. Yes, I love Gerasim,' Zhenya concluded with conviction, as if trying to vindicate herself and her feelings.

'Well, I must be running off now. We've got some urgent local work to do, and now that I've been elected secretary of our cell' (she said this with some pride), 'there's even more work to do. Oh, how good life would be if only mother could understand and accept things.' She sighed again, a deep childish sigh.

'I'll get in touch with mother. Please, do try to convince her that Andrei is all hers, that I need him about as much as I need this table here. Do you think she'll understand and go on loving me? I'm so terrified of losing her love – I couldn't live without mother, without her love. It's so awful that this whole business is affecting her work too. Say what you like, I never want to fall in love like mother did! How would you ever find the time to work?'

It was on this note that Zhenya disappeared out of the door. I remained sitting where I was, wondering who was right, whose view would be taken up by the new generation, this emerging class grappling with these new ideas and feelings.

Behind the door I could hear Zhenya's youthful laugh and her cheerful voice, saying, 'Well, friends, I'll see you this evening! You mustn't delay me now, I'm late as it is, and we have so much work to do!'

Lalla's Interests

by Vera Inber (translated by Joanne Turnbull)

The lift was old and very lonely in its cage. Embittered by incessant tottering from floor to floor, it had begun snapping the gate shut with a vicious click and whimpering on the way down like a wounded wolf. Sometimes it went out of service altogether and sulked between floors, glowering at people trudging up the stairs.

For chaperon the lift had Yakov Mitrokhin, someone's eleven-year-old son. He had appeared from the yard; the night watchman had taken to him and he to the lift. In accordance with his instructions from the house-manager's office, Yakov Mitrokhin did not allow anyone into the lift unaccompanied. He took everyone up himself and exacted from each, again as per his instructions, a fee of five kopeks.

During the long evening hours, while a blizzard hissed, howled and ran riot outside, Yakov Mitrokhin, ever at his post by the lift and waiting for people who had gone to the theatre or to see friends, would reflect upon life. He would reflect upon life, upon the fact that his felt boots were full of holes, that his adoptive father, the night watchman Mitrofan Avdeyich, hit hard – and, worse, for no reason, and that it would be nice to find a pencil and take up book learning. Again and again he would examine the lift's mechanism, its inner workings, its seats, its buttons. One button in particular, a little red one: press it hard and the lift would stop dead. Very interesting.

In the evenings, when the grown-ups were out at the theatre or sitting quietly at home, giving their guests tea, boys in fur hats and sheepskin coats from all over the yard would come by for some talk with Yakov Mitrokhin. He was even visited, on occasion, by a velvet-bonneted six-year old by the name of Lalla. Lalla's mother, a stout woman resembling a round chest of drawers, was deeply distressed by this friendship and always said, 'Why he's nothing but a waif, Lalla, wipe your nose! He could kill you or kidnap you, don't suck your thumb! Isn't there anyone else you'd rather play with?'

When Yakov Mitrokhin heard remarks like that, he would snort reproachfully, but he never said anything.

Lalla's nanny, a venerable old lady, was even more distraught: 'Lallachka, stop this foolishness, don't you even look at him! To think what you've found: a little lift boy, when your papa's writing desk is covered in leather and you drink hot cocoa every day. A treasure, you say? Don't be silly! He's not your sort!'

But little Lalla, fair and round as a button, invariably walked past Yakov Mitrokhin as close as she could, and smiled up at him.

One day downstairs by the lift, on the wall where people usually put up announcements to do with the building, there appeared one more:

All children what live in this house are invited to a meeting tomorrow after 5 under the stairs where the old coat is laying. Very important things will be said. Enter free. The ones not from this house will have to pay (two licorice sticks).

The announcement was unsigned.

The first to notice it was Lalla's mother. She read it through her pince-nez, then with her naked eye, and immediately rang the bell of the house-manager's office on the second floor. The house-manager's deputy emerged.

'What can you be thinking of, Comrade Pelageyaitis?' said Lalla's mother. 'How can you permit such a thing?' She jabbed the notice with her reticule. 'Our children are being corrupted while you stand idly by! Why don't you say anything? Of course, my Lalla won't go, but that's not the point, what about the principle?'

Comrade Pelageyaitis blinked, blew his nose and took exception: 'I don't see anything wrong, ma'am. Children have a right to co-organise themselves for the protection of their professional interests.'

Lalla's mother spluttered with indignation and clenched her teeth: 'What interests can they possibly have when their noses are always running? I'm quite sure this is the work of that boy Yury from apartment eighteen. His father's a senior secretary.'

Senior secretary Seleznyov, a gloomy man with bad kidneys, looked askance at the announcement and thought: 'I can see that's Yury's writing. Who he'll be when he grows up, I don't know! An adventurer like that Pilsudsky.'

The children seemed not to notice the announcement. Only the stairs became unusually grubby with the marks of small boots, while the demand for liquorice sticks at a nearby co-operative rose so sharply that a fresh supply had to be laid in.

The night passed uneventfully, but the morning turned anxious.

To begin with the milkmaid arrived with the news that out-of-doors there was such a snowstorm you couldn't see an inch in front of your face and she'd nearly harnessed her horse the wrong way round, in consequence of which milk had gone up a kopek. A sense of trouble brewing hung over the house. But Seleznyov still went to the office with a dietetic lunch in his briefcase, while Lalla's mother set off for private-trader Lapin's to see about this complication with the milk.

The children sat in their rooms and kept suspiciously quiet.

A little after five, when most parents – weary from the office, the blizzard and lunch – were resting, *Pravda* or *Izvestiya* slipping from their limp hands, small shadows began flitting down the stairs, clearly bound for the place where the old sheepskin coat was lying.

Lalla's mother, having stood in line at Lapin's for an hour and ascertained that milk had indeed gone up and that there was no cottage cheese at all, was resting on the ottoman amid a quantity of pillows, mostly round, some as large as automobile wheels, others as small as saucers. In the kitchen, Lalla's nanny was arguing with the washerwoman about God.

The central heating was quietly snuffling. Suddenly a door slammed.

Lalla's mother jumped up, only to discover that little Lalla – Yelena Yegorovna Antonova – had disappeared.

Lalla's mother threw something on, stormed across the hall and rang the bell. The door was opened by Senior Secretary Seleznyov himself, holding a hot-water bottle: 'My Lalla is gone, and Yury, too, I imagine,' said Lalla's mother. 'They're having a meeting under the stairs, professional interests, but all they'll wind up with is pneumonia.'

'My Yury's not here,' Senior Secretary Seleznyov replied peevishly. 'Must have gone, too. I wouldn't be surprised if this was his doing. Let me put my coat on.'

They walked out together and started down. Just then the decrepit lift began to groan, hobbling down from the seventh floor. Seeing the two of them on the stairs, Yakov Mitrokhin stopped the machine, clicked open the gate crisply and said: 'F'you please.'

Downstairs, meanwhile, the little room – where the old sheepskin coat was lying and the street-watering hose hibernating – had become so jammed with children you couldn't take a deep breath. The air was thick with the smell of liquorice.

Yury Seleznyov was standing on an old chair and getting ready to preside. His assistant, Viktor, aged twelve and not a party member, kept running up to him with questions.

'Yury, there's a girl from another yard here with a baby. Can the baby give her its vote or not?'

Just then the baby began to vote all by itself, so loudly they were all nearly deafened.

'Comrades,' Yury tried to scream over it, 'comrades, I hereby inform you that in order to vote you must be able to walk! Anyone else must abstain. Votes are not transferable. Please put your name down if you'd like to speak – we don't have much time – about the problem of re-electing parents.'

Lalla, pale, eyes sparkling, squeezed her way through to Viktor and said quietly, 'Put my name down, too. I want to speak. Write: "Lalla from the fifth floor".'

'What do you want to speak about, comrade?'

'About prickly woollies, so we won't have to wear them any more. And lots of other things besides.'

Yury waved a liquorice stick and began: 'Comrades, I'd like to say a few words. All sorts of people – metalworkers, shop assistants, even bootblacks – have a union to protect them from exploitation, but we children can't do anything like that. Every parent, whether father or mother, and especially if he has bad kidneys, does whatever he wants with us. This can't go on. I suggest we present a list of demands and devise slogans in keeping with the times. Who's in favour? Against? Abstentions?'

'Yakov Mitrokhin's name is down next,' Viktor announced, 'to speak about not letting them box our ears. But he's not here.'

Yury frowned knowingly and said, 'Must be busy. He wouldn't run off for no reason. It's obviously something important. Leave him on the list.'

The meeting was hectic. Many problems were raised, all of them so pressing that no one could keep quiet. They talked about the fact that parents think too much of themselves and even forbid children to play in the corridor in communal apartments, which is absolutely intolerable. They talked about the fact that washing one's shoes in puddles was necessary, and about all sorts of other things.

For the first time ever, the protection of children's interests was put on a professional footing.

The lift hung between the third and fourth floors for an hour and a half. Lalla's mother banged and bustled about in vain and Senior Secretary Seleznyov clutched the small of his back, while Yakov Mitrokhin kept insisting that the lift's insides were in a bad way and he couldn't do anything about it: the lift would hang there a while, then start up again all by itself.

When Lalla's mother, half dead from worry and the tense wait, finally returned to her round pillows, she found Lalla sitting at her father's writing desk. With a large blue pencil on a large sheet of paper she was painstakingly tracing out a slogan evidently devised at the meeting: CHILDREN, BE CAREFUL WHEN ELECTING PARENTS!

Lalla's mother was so horrified she turned pale green.

The next day she received a letter via Lalla's nanny. To her surprise, the bedraggled envelope contained something round. She opened it. Inside was a bright, sticky five-kopek coin. The note said:

Ma'am, I'm giving you back your five kopeks for the lift. To be fair, I held you there on purpose so as your daughter Lalla could speak about all her interests.

For illiterate Yakov Mitrokhin,

Yury Seleznyov

Nina Berberova

In 1922, Lenin drew up a list of intellectuals that he wanted exiled – he berated Stalin for not getting the job done swiftly enough! **Nina Berberova** (1901–1993) was on the list and was sent into exile that year.[31] One of the finest chroniclers of Russian émigré life, she is best known for her short fictions *Cape of Storms* and *Billancourt Tales*[32] and her autobiography, *The Italics are Mine*.[33] Her fiction, which was written in Russian but first published in French, was translated into English in the 1960s because Jacqueline Kennedy Onassis, who had read her books in French, brought them to the attention of a US publisher. *The Italics are Mine*, is a wonderful portrait of a generation of writers and intellectuals surviving as best they can, keeping their culture alive and trying to engage in a dialogue with the culture of France, the country they live in. A difficult task given the inclination of French intellectuals to view what was happening in the Soviet Union through rose-tinted spectacles:

> 'In the years 1925–35, despite the suicides of Esenin and Mayakovsky, the difficulties of Ehrenburg, the disappearance of Pilniak and the rumours about Gorky's troubles, the faith that the USSR would bring the young postwar world and in particular the art of the left a renewal, a support, unseen perspectives, was in the West stronger than all the vacillations and doubts. This was particularly

31 For this and much more, see Lesley Chamberlain's *Lenin's Private War: The Voyage of the Philosophy Steamer and the Exile of the Intelligentsia*, London and New York, 2007
32 Billancourt is the area of Paris where a lot of Russian émigrés lived; many worked in the Renault car plant there. Some of the finest writing in *The Italics are Mine* describes the Allied bombing of Billancourt, *Bil'yankur* as it came out in Russian, during World War II.
33 *The Italics are Mine*, Vintage, 1993

so in France (and possibly in the USA), where people, when they want not to know something, manage to do it with impunity.'[34]

In 1950, Nina Berberova emigrated to the United States where she began an academic career, teaching Russian literature at Yale and Princeton. It was only in the 1960s under *glasnost* that she was published in Russia. The themes of her writing – of displacement, emigration and survival – continue to resonate with readers today.

'The Destruction of the Intelligentsia'
from *The Italics are Mine* by Nina Berberova
(translated by Philippe Radley)

I see a dining room, living rooms and a hall in the uninterrupted motion of familiar faces, young and old, near and far. In the dining room all are still eating and drinking, in the hall there are four couples dancing who have miraculously borrowed somewhere all the fashionable dances of a Europe as distant as a dream. People feast their eyes on them, stand in doorways, greedily drink in the novel syncopations of the foxtrot, and look at the figures swaying and fused together. Someone smells of l'Origan, someone says something in French, someone drinks a glass of champagne – don't ask whence it comes: perhaps from the Eliseev cellar (a bottle fell in a far-off corner), perhaps from the distributor of the Central Committee of the party, perhaps from grandmother's closet. We sit on a couch in the living room, people walk past us, do not look at us, do not speak with us: they long ago understood that we were not interested in them.

At dawn he takes me home, from Moika to Kirochnaya. At the house gates we stand for several minutes. His face is near my face, and my hand is in his hand. In those moments a bond arises between us, which with every hour will grow stronger.

That winter I think only a pretext was necessary to give people the appearance of a festive occasion. The 'Russian Christmas' of 7 January reminds me anew of a kind of whirling in the Eliseevs' house, of

34 *The Italics are Mine*, op. cit., p. 278

music and a crowd. At about three o'clock Khodasevich and I walked through deep snow to his entrance, and sat till morning at his window, looking at Nevsky: the clarity of this January dawn was unusual, the distant became clearly visible, with the railroad-station tower behind the roofs, and Nevsky itself was empty and clean; only at Sadovaya was there a glimmer, a solitary street lamp that did not want to die out, but then it too went out. When the stars disappeared (at night it seemed that they hung very near – you could reach them with your hand) and a pale sunlight flooded the city, I left. The deep seriousness of that night had altered me. I felt that I had become other than I was. That words had been uttered by me which I never had spoken to anyone, and that words had been said to me which I had never heard before. And that conversation had turned not on our mutual happiness, but on something completely different, in the key not of 'happiness' and 'unhappiness' but of magic, of a new dual reality, his and mine.

Another (and I believe the last) soirée was at Zubov's place, on the eve of the Russian New Year. Count Valentin Zubov was still at that time the director of the Institute of the History of Art, which he had founded and which continued to bear his name. It was again the same ones who gathered in the huge, frozen halls of his palace (on St Isaac's Square). Some rooms were so cold breath was visible while in others fireplaces were aflame. Again couples swirled and swayed, again chandeliers burned, and some venerable servants watched us with scorn and disgust.

It was now the beginning of spring. Before this, on 2 March, Khodasevich had finished 'Not by my mother, but by a peasant woman of Tula' (the first four stanzas had lain untouched since 1917). Everything began to flow somehow at once, the sun shone, water dripped from the rooftops, there was ringing in the courtyards and gardens. He went to buy galoshes at the Sennoy market and for this sold the herrings he had just received from the House of Scholars. In haste he bought galoshes one size larger than necessary, shoved in them the draft of his poem and came to my place. In a year, in Berlin, the draft was found in one of the galoshes – I have kept it till now.

That day several people gathered at my place; the second room, which had become icy cold in winter, was opened, heated, tidied up. There (it was Glinka's study) for the first time he recited 'Not by my mother', recited it (the draft was already in one of the galoshes) by heart and, at the request of everyone, twice. That day we did not read 'in a circle' – no one wanted to read their verse after his.

At the very beginning of February had come the Serapions' 'jubilee': one year of their official existence and the coming out of the miscellany *Ushkufniki*, which Nikolai Chukovsky published and in which Tikhonov, Nikolai Chukovsky himself, I and someone else were represented. And in April, still in that same Mikhailovsky Square on a bench, Khodasevich said to me that two tasks lay before us: to be together and survive. Or perhaps: to survive and be together.

What did 'survive' then mean? Something physical? Moral? Could we at that time foresee the death of Mandelstam on a heap of refuse, the end of Babel, the suicides of Esenin and Mayakovsky, party politics in literature aimed at destroying two if not three generations? Could we foresee twenty years of silence on Akhmatova's part? The destruction of Pasternak? The end of Gorky? Of course not. 'Anatoly Vasilievich will not allow it': this opinion about Lunacharsky was then in the air. But if Anatoly Vasilievich is himself poisoned? Or even if he dies a natural death? Or if he is removed? Or if he decides one day not to be a communist aesthete any more but to become a hammer, forging the Russian intelligentsia on the anvil of the Revolution? No, such possibilities dawned on no one, but doubts that it would be possible to survive swarmed in those months for the first time into Khodasevich's thoughts. That for no reason one would be seized, jailed, and annihilated seemed then unthinkable, but that one would be crushed, tortured , have his mouth shut and either be forced to die (as later happened with Sologub and Gershenson) or to leave literature (as Evgeny Zamiatin, Mikhail Kuzmin and for twenty-five years Victor Shklovsky were forced to do) began dimly to take on more distinct shapes in one's thoughts. Only a few could follow Briusov into membership of the Communist Party; others could for a short time clutch at the triumphal chariot of the futurists. But the rest?

Many times subsequently this 'concept of survival' came to me in its most diverse aspects, bringing with it a whole rainbow of overtones:

from the conception 'not to be devoured' of a beast, to the ancient 'self-affirmation in the face of destruction'; from the instinctive 'not to be caught by the enemy' to the lofty 'deliver oneself of the final Word'. Both the low and lofty often have one root in man. Both to grab on to a blade of grass as you hang over an abyss and to give the manuscript of your novel to a foreigner leaving Moscow for the West have one and the same foundation.

It was an April day in Mikhailovsky Square, the square in which in the winter the searchlights' rays chased us, and I decided now to set out for the Neva to look at the flow of ice, not with him but alone: the Ladoga wind these spring days was dangerous for Khodasevich. He had lost count of his illnesses and others still lay in wait for him. Once, in 1915, he feared tuberculosis of the bone and he had permanent chest trouble. From the Moscow life of 1918–20 and a three-year period of malnutrition (or rather hunger) he had got furunculosis, of which he was barely cured and which still threatened him. He was thin, pale, weak; he had to take care of his teeth; he tired of carrying rations – though God knows how light they were, feather-weight. Among them were herring (which he did not eat), matches, flour. He would sell the herring at the Sennoy market, buy cigarettes. He bought cocoa on the black market.

In the winter a parcel was sent me from Northern Ireland (yes, it turned out that in the world there was such a country!) by a cousin who in 1916 had married an Englishman. This parcel was a real event. On a sled, together with father, I brought it from the customs house and opened it, or rather ripped open the heavy package wrapped in matting. On the grand piano we spread out: a wool dress, a sweater, two pairs of shoes, a dozen pairs of stockings, a piece of lard, soap, ten bars of chocolate, sugar, coffee, and six tins of sweet condensed milk. Right then – as I was, all bundled in my fur coat and huge shawl – I took hammer and nail, made two holes in one of the cans and, without stopping, drank in one burst the thick sweet liquid. To the bottom of the can. (Twenty-five years later, in Paris, having opened the first package I received from America after the war in 1945 – it was from Mikhail Karpovich, the Harvard professor of Russian history – which contained almost the same things, I ripped open the blue soap wrapper, took out the soap and kissed it.) To the bottom, that first time, like a beast. We later hung the empty tins on the stove-pipe to catch the liquid soot that was spoiling my books. Out of the matting we fashioned a floor rag. Nothing was wasted.

Now the Hoover ARA[35] parcels began to come. It is frightful and shameful now to read how Gorky asked Frenchmen, Americans, Englishmen, even Germans to help the hungry population of Revolutionary Russia. When a face was deathly pale, some rosy shade came to it because of lard, cocoa and sugar. The parcels gave us hope of survival. We existed from parcel to parcel. Heating for warmth ceased as it was spring, and we moved on to heating for cooking. On the other hand, the poverty of our dress became more noticeable in sunlight; in the winter all escaped notice: Pyast's soles tied by string were not conspicuous, nor the turned jacket of Zamiatin, nor the patches on Chukovsky's trousers, nor Zoshchenko's field jacket worn to a sheen. Every week living became a little more frightful. Yes, it got warm and it was possible to settle in two rooms, remove one's boots and not count each log, open the windows and hope that in a month there would at least be something at the distributor's; but along with this in different people in different ways there began to appear the sense of a possible end – not so much a personal one but a kind of collective abstract one, one which, however, did not practically impede one's staying alive; not a *physical* end certainly, because the NEP[36] continued to play its role and the 'rosey tint' appeared in faces here and there, but perhaps some *spiritual* end. The end appeared in the air at first like some kind of metaphor, collective and abstract, which became clearer from day to day. It was said that soon everything would close up – that is, private publishing houses – and that 'all' would be turned over to Gosizdat. It was said that in Moscow censorship was even more severe than with us, and that in Petersburg it would soon be the same. It was said that in the Kremlin, in spite of Anatoly Vasilievich Lunacharsky, a decree on 'literary politics' was being prepared which Mayakovsky was ready to transpose swiftly into verse. From Moscow someone brought the

35 American Relief Administration
36 New Economic Policy

rumour that somewhere a call to order had been made by someone to someone and that it smacked of a threat . . . With frosts and blizzards, all had held together somehow, but presently everything started flowing, ran in streams, there was nothing to hold on to, all was running somewhere. Don't delude yourself, fellow writers; not 'somewhere' but in a very definite direction where we will have no place, where most probably we will not survive.

Now, looking back at those months, I see that destruction of the intelligentsia came not in a straight path but in a tortuous one, through a period of brief flowering; that the way was not simple through that flowering, that some people at the same time both flowered and perished, and made others perish, without being themselves aware of it; that a little later there would be hundreds of sacrifices and later still tens of thousands: from Trotsky through Vororsky, Pilniak, the formalists and fellow travellers to the futurists and young workers and peasant poets who bloomed to the very end of the twenties, serving the new regime wholeheartedly. From bearded elders, members of the Philosophical Society of the beginning of the century, to the members of the Association of Proletarian Writers, who had invented, at the right time it then seemed, the slogan about the debasement of culture but were killed like everybody else. Destruction came not personally to each one who was being destroyed, but as a group destruction of a whole profession, carefully planned. Poets were destroyed as a class *as planned*. In parallel fashion not things, but planned things, began to be produced . Mandelstam was destroyed *as a class*, Zamiatin was forbidden to write *as a class*. Literary politics (to the end of the thirties) was a part of general politics – at first of Lenin – Trotsky, then of Zinoviev – Kamenev – Stalin, and finally of Stalin – Ezhov – Zhdanov. And in the end three kinds of people were destroyed: those who were born around 1880, those who were born around 1895, and those who were born around 1910.

Thin and weak physically, Khodasevich all of a sudden began to display an energy not in keeping with his physical make-up on preparations for our departure abroad. Since May 1922 the distribution of passports for abroad had begun in Moscow; this was one of the consequences of the general policy of the NEP. Passports for our departure came into our hands – numbers 16 and 17. I would be curious to find out who got passport number 1. Perhaps Ehrenburg?

Khodasevich made the decision to leave Russia, but he certainly did not foresee that he was leaving for ever. He made his choice; only a few years later he made a second one: not to return. I followed him. If we had not met and not taken the decision then to 'be together' and 'survive', he undoubtedly would have remained in Russia: there is no possibility, not even the slightest, that he would have gone abroad alone. He probably would have been sent at the end of 1922 to Berlin, in the group that included Berdyaev, Kuskova, Evreinov and others banished from Russia as enemies of the people: his name, as we later learned, was on the list of those to be exiled. I would have remained of course in Petersburg. Having made his choice for himself and me, he arranged it so that we came out together and survived – that is, survived the terror of the thirties, in which almost certainly I would have perished. My choice was *him* and my decision was to follow him. One can now say that we saved each other.

A passport was issued to me in Moscow. I went there in the middle of May at the summons of Khodasevich, who had gone there to petition for permission to leave for himself and me. I did not recognise Moscow: now it was the capital of the new state, the streets were black with people, everything all around was growing and being created, shooting up, coming alive, being born anew, pulsating. From morning to evening we went to fill out questionnaires, hand over papers, sit in waiting rooms. Two signatures were needed for permission to leave: Yurgis Baltrushaitis, the Lithuanian ambassador in Moscow and an old friend of Khodasevich's, gave one and the other came from Anatoly Vasilievich. On the passports there was the enquiry 'reason for the trip'. The replies supplied were: for a health cure (on Khodasevich's passport), for completion of education (on mine). I was represented by a photograph with a round face, round eyes, a round chin, and even a round nose. When this roundness came to me, I did not notice. Now, forty-five years later, in my slightly Indo-Chinese face there is no roundness whatsoever.

While we were in Moscow there was a literary evening at the Union of Writers on Tverskoy Boulevard, and there Khodasevich read his new verse ('I don't believe in earthly beauty', 'She was misty and anonymous', 'Evidence', 'A stranger passes by'), verse about love; and Gershenson and Zaitsev and others (not to mention his brother Misha and Misha's daughter, Valentina Khodasevich, the artist) looked at me with unconcealed curiosity. We dropped in on the Zaitsevs later in the evening, in an alley near the Arbat; they were also preparing to go abroad for a 'health cure'. From that day date my relations with Boris and Vera, which have lasted more than forty years . At their place I saw Pavel Muratov, one of the most remarkable men I have ever met; our friendship exercised a tremendous influence on me – strange though it seems – only later, when it came to an end. We sat at the Zaitsevs in the midst of open suitcases and trunks, books piled on tables. It looked as if we were to find ourselves in Berlin at the same time.

The writers' bookstore at that time was (if I am not mistaken) somewhere near Strastnoy Boulevard. We went there. Nikolai Berd-yaev stood at the counter and 'did business', it was his day. There were books in manuscript (those for which it had been impossible to find a publisher) and old editions, rare copies and newly published journals and brochures. Then, we went to visit Misha. He was twenty-one years older than Khodasevich, and a famous counsellor at the Moscow Criminal Court. He came with us to the station (we were returning to Petersburg). There I went back to my parents' house, while Khodasevich stayed at the house next door, on Kirochnaya , in Georgy Annenkov's flat. Three days later we left for Riga.

On the eve of our departure he lay on my bed, I sat at his feet, and he spoke about the past, which suddenly in those last weeks had moved so far from us, supplanted by the present. It would move off still further, he said, as if looking into his future. I asked him to write down something as a remembrance: the groundwork for an autobiography, perhaps, a calendar of his childhood and youth. He sat down at my desk and began to write, and when he had finished he handed me a piece of cardboard, a calendar of his life, which is now in my archives.

Now his past was before me, his life *before* me. I read this record many times in succession then. It was for me a substitute for an album of family photographs , it illustrated a book dear to me, and as such I loved it. To this piece of cardboard he then and there added his comic

'Don Juan's Catalogue' – this list amused me for a long time:

> Evgenia
> Aleksandra
> Aleksandra
> Marina
> Vera
> Olga
> Alina
> Natalia
> N. N.
> Madeleine
> Nadezhda
> Evgenia
> Evgenia
> Tatiana
> Anna
> Ekaterina
> N.

At the station, bewildered, confused, sad, troubled, stood my father and mother. Our departure was kept secret; this Khodasevich wanted. I said goodbye neither to Ida nor to Lunts, and said nothing to Nikolai Chukovsky. Petersburg receded from me – in rail entanglements, pump houses, empty cars (40 MEN. 8 HORSES. BRIANSK – MOGILEV), the Admiralty needle – part of my childhood mythology. This year receded, having begun in one June and ended in another, a year without which I would not have been I, a year bestowed on me that filled me to the brim with feelings, thoughts, a year that ploughed me anew, that taught me to approach people (and a man), that inspired me, and brought my youth to an end. Poor Lazarus was now so rich that he was preparing already to begin distributing everything he had acquired – and much more – right and left.

In the freight car in which we were taken across the border at Sebezh, Khodasevich said to me that he had an unfinished poem with him. Here are those lines:

> In Moscow I was born. I never saw

The smoke above a Polish roof.
My father never left a grain of Polish soil
For me to cherish as a sacred proof.

I, Russia's stepson, what am I to Poland,
What do I know of her? – I could not understand . . .
All I possess are eight slim volumes,
And they contain my native land.

Your fate is to accept the yoke,
To live exiled in bitterness and woe.
But I have packed my Russia in my bag,
And take her with me anywhere I go.

Our knapsacks lay around us on the floor of the freight car .

Yes, there was his Pushkin, of course – all eight volumes. But I already knew then that I would never be able completely to identify with Khodasevich, I wouldn't even try to: Russia was not for me just Pushkin. She always lay outside literary categories; then (as now) she lay in historical categories, if by history one understands not only past and present but future as well. And we spoke – he and I – about other unfinished verse and about my perhaps continuing a narrative poem begun by him, but which he felt he was unable to finish:

Here is a story, it came to me
Entire, definitely and clearly,
While in my hand lay
Your obedient hand.

I took a piece of paper and a pencil and while the train moved slowly from one frontier checkpoint to another I added to his four lines my four:

Thus from your warm palm
Into my palm blood overflowed
And I became alive and perceptive,
And this was your love.

Ilya Ehrenburg

It is not surprising that a writer who survived fifty years in Soviet Russia is viewed with suspicion in the West. This is the case of **Ilya Ehrenburg** (1891–1967), who became active in the Bolshevik Party after the 1905 revolution and managed to outlive Stalin! Ehrenburg's survival is partially explained by the fact that he spent much of his life outside the Soviet Union – in exile in Paris and Vienna before and after the 1917 Revolution and as a war journalist in Spain during the Civil War (1936–9). In France, he met Lenin and became good friends with Picasso, Apollinaire, Léger and Modigliani. In Vienna before the First World War, Ehrenburg edited copies of *Pravda* to be smuggled into Russia. He had conversations on art with Trotsky who dismissed the poets he liked as decadent. After the Revolution, Ehrenburg went back to Paris where he lived from 1925 writing a series of novels that caricatured wealthy capitalists, the best known being *The Life of the Automobile* whose targets were Andre Citroën and Henry Ford. Reporting from Spain on the Civil War, Ehrenburg became a passionate defender of the Republican cause. Back in Russia during the Second World War, Ehrenburg wrote almost daily for the *Red Star* newspaper. His patriotic, anti-German articles were loved by Russian soldiers. An order was passed not to use copies of Ehrenburg's articles for rolling cigarettes! For his wartime efforts, he was awarded the Lenin Prize in 1944. But Ehrenburg, never content as a member of the establishment, was always looking for ways to provoke the censor. After the death of Stalin, he quickly tested the waters with his novel *The Thaw*. With its portrayal of a corrupt 'little Stalin' factory boss and its references to the anti-semitic hysteria of the 1950s, *The Thaw*, published in 1956, gave its name to an entire era in Soviet history. Ehrenburg's last years were spent writing *People, Years, Life*, his memoirs. The book contain eloquent pages in defence of Ehrenburg's contemporaries Tsvetaeva, Mandelstam, Pasternak, Babel, Meyerhold, Tatlin and many more. They are a unique window on twentieth-century history.

'Hares of All Lands, Unite'

from *First Years of Revolution 1918–21, Volume II of People, Years, Life* by Ilya Ehrenberg (translated by Anna Bostock in collaboration with Yvonne Kapp)

Although V. L. Durov did not approve of the Futurists he was himself an eccentric, and the opening production at his children's theatre had an eccentric title: *Hares of All Lands, Unite!* I remember the occasion very well indeed. At the beginning, a hare held up a large wooden book-cover inscribed with the words DAS KAPITAL. He turned the pages, then summoned some other hares, of whom there were at least twenty. In the next scene there was the model of a palace on the stage; it was guarded by rabbits holding rifles. Hares pushing a toy cannon came running out from the wings: they fired the cannon at the rabbits and, having routed them, hoisted a red flag over the palace.

The curtain was raised and lowered by a bear-cub in a blue smock.

The children's delight was indescribable; pale and thin, they laughed to split their sides. And after the curtain had fallen the hares and rabbits came round to the front, and that intermingling of actors and audience of which the producer of *Dawn* dreamed took place. (On entering the theatre the children were given small pieces of carrot with which they later seduced the actors.)

This part of the show took half an hour, but it required lengthy preparatory work. Durov explained to me from the start that he meant to overthow a number of false ideas about animals. For example, it was traditionally believed that hares were cowards, and also, in Russian folklore, that they were squint-eyed; consequently it had to be shown that hares could fire a cannon.

Durov was then fifty-seven years old. He was Russia's most famous clown. I had seen him in the circus as a boy and had carried away a memory of a funny man in brightly coloured clothes wearing a multitude of fantastic medals. Long before I was born the brothers Durov had been the favourites of all Russia. Chekhov had laughed at the antics of Vladimir Durov's mongrel Zapyataika. It may well be that the clown I saw as a child was not Vladimir Durov but his brother Anatoly, who at first was the more popular. Originally the brothers appeared together; later they quarrelled. Vladimir began billing himself as 'Durov the Elder', Anatoly as 'The Genuine Durov'. (He died before the Revolution and left instructions in his will that the same words – The Genuine Durov – should be inscribed on his gravestone.)

In any case, by the time I met Vladimir Durov he was Durov the One and Only. Members of the circus section of TEO tried to lure him to join them, but he was absorbed in his animals. I remember the occasion when he first came to see me: would we help him to organise a theatre for children in his house in Bozhedomka? He talked about the works of Pavlov, about conditioned and non-conditioned reflexes; he gave the impression, not of a famous clown, but of a venerable professor.

I was invited to one of the first rehearsals. Durov was trying to cure the hares of their nervousness; this was not easy. Although, according to him, animals were governed by various reflexes, whereas, unless Descartes was mistaken, man thinks and therefore is, there is much in common between the behaviour of men and animals; in particular, it is easier to intimidate the boldest of men than to make a hero out of a coward. Durov used to say that if a worm crawls away from a chicken, the chicken will eat it, but if, on the contrary, the worm crawls towards the chicken, the chicken will retire hastily. (There is, by the way, a Russian proverb – 'Brave before sheep, a sheep himself before a brave man' – which was not invented by hares or chickens.) The rehearsals took place at night. Durov patiently fed the principal performer – a most charming hare – with carrots, and the trainer's hand withdrew timorously all the time. As for the cannon, it frankly ran away from the hares. At the end of two or three weeks the hares realised that they were stronger than anyone. Durov called this method of training 'fear deception'.

Carrots played the dominant part in the producer's work. They were placed between the pages of the book, and in order to get a piece of carrot a hare had to pull the cord which made the cannon go off.

During rehearsals it transpired that rabbits had nothing against headgear, while hares broke formation if made to wear anything on their heads. Durov gave in, and the hares stormed the palace bareheaded.

Someone supplied Durov with carrots; the bear-cub, however, had a hard time. I applied to MPO for permission to issue rations to the bear-cub as a member of the cast. Although the rations were small, the cub grew and its smock was soon too small for it. Durov wanted me to get some cotton material for another smock. In vain did I tell him that this was extremely difficult, that I had spent months getting a pair of trousers for myself and that the bear-cub could perfectly well appear without a smock. In the end we got the material.

Durov was terribly upset by the death of a young elephant, called Baby, that he had temporarily housed in the Zoological Gardens. There was no coal. Baby caught cold and died. It weighed about three tons; the meat was shared out among the zoo staff. But Durov kept repeating: 'You never knew Baby . . . Baby had extraordinary gifts'. Five years later he wrote: 'My best, my true, devoted comrade died, my Baby died, a child I had brought up and invested with a part of my soul.'

The second item on the bill was a scene which Durov had first produced at the beginning of the century under the title *The Hague Peace Conference*. Now the name was different. Sworn enemies – a wolf and a goat, a cat and a rat, a fox and a cock, a bear and a pig – sat next to each other round a table.

Durov explained to me in detail how he had prepared this scene. The cage containing the rat was equipped with casters and hung all over with bells; it was lowered on rails from the table to the basket containing the cat. The clatter of the cage and the ringing of the bells frightened the cat, and it gradually began to be afraid of the rat, whereas the rat grew bolder every hour. Durov trained the other performers in the same way. The strong ceased to be confident of their invulnerability and the weak were cured of their fears. On this basis, 'peaceful coexistence' was established.

During the winter of which I am speaking I often saw Durov, tried to help him and became extremely attached to him. Later we met rarely, but he amused, delighted and inspired me on each occasion.

He was one of the most fantastic men I have ever met. In the circus ring he wanted to preach and teach, gave scientific explanations, talked about reflexes, and at the same time came out in his dazzling costume driving dogs four-in-hand or riding on a pig. At home in Bozhedomka, where his visitors included eminent scientists such as Chelpanov and Bekhterev, he would suddenly interrupt a serious discussion with a clown's jest. He was a poet by nature, and he found poetry in the world of four-legged actors.

He often became muddled when talking to people. He was apt to confuse materialism with Tolstoyanism and Marxism with Christianity. He signed his theoretical works 'Durov, Self-Taught Man'. But he was truly at ease with animals. He wanted human beings 'to feel a personality in the animal, conscious, thinking, rejoicing and suffering'.

Fantastic plans took shape in his head.

In one of his books he quotes the text of a letter received in August 1917: 'The Naval General Staff has considered Mr Durov's suggestion that he should train animals, to wit, sea lions and seals, for purposes of naval warfare, and regards the suggestion as highly interesting.' The letter was signed by the Naval Chief of Staff, a rear-admiral. One can easily guess the state of mind of the naval command at that time if it seriously hoped to use trained seals against German submarines.

Later, everything settled down again. No one was tempted any longer by the idea of mobilising seals. In 1923 Durov was sent on an official mission to Germany, where he picked up some sea lions. He thought very well of them and rated them higher than dogs. I remember being taken by him to the pool and introduced: 'This is Ilya Grigoryevich, poet and friend of animals.' The sea lions came out, began to applaud with their fins and drenched me in icy water. Meanwhile Durov was saying: 'You ought to see the convolutions of their brains!'

He was convinced that human beings did not understand animals. Why did the Russians say 'blind as a hen'? A hen could see a hawk long before a man did. Stubborn as a donkey? Not a bit of it: the donkey was mercilessly exploited and only occasionally offered passive resistance. The pig was the cleanest creature and wallowed in the mud only in order to rid itself of parasites; housed in a clean place, it would score points over many human beings.

Why had his proposal to use sea lions against submarines been turned down in the end? Why had no one given consideration to his plan for setting fire to bombers with the help of tame eagles? Say what you will, people were very difficult to deal with.

Many years earlier Durov had fallen ill and made a will giving instructions that if he died, animals should escort him to the cemetery. The church regarded this wish as blasphemous. Alas, people did not understand that animals had souls. Ten or fifteen years later, the word 'soul' had disappeared, to be replaced by 'reflexes'. Yet people still went on smiling sceptically. For example, physiologists claimed that dogs could not distinguish colours. Durov was indignant: 'All my dogs, even complete beginners, puppies, can tell a green ball from a red one.'

Anna Ignatyevna, Durov's wife, was very fond of animals. Yet he once told me, sadly, that only monkeys, dogs, cats and parrots were allowed into the bedroom. Badgers or geese, for instance, were excluded. 'It isn't right . . . it isn't fair.'

Once he came to see Lunacharsky with his usual sort of request: would Lunacharsky sign this paper? Lunacharsky said he must think it over. Then Durov's favourite, the rat Finka, jumped out of his pocket and stood on its hind legs in front of the People's Commissar. Lunacharsky, who was afraid of rats, shouted, 'Take it away!' Durov only sighed: 'Sorry, Anatoly Vasilyevich, I can't do that. It's pleading on behalf of its comrades. Solidarity, you know.'

Ten years later he appeared at the Coupole in Paris with another rat and was most surprised when women started screaming hysterically; he tried to explain that this rat was an artiste, but no one listened.

When he went out to dinner he would talk about science and progress, and then suddenly he would pull out of his pocket, together with his handkerchief, a raw fish or a lump of meat: all his pockets were crammed with titbits for animals.

As he looked at people, he thought of animals. Describing how his toy terriers, when pleased, smiled and wagged their behinds, he added: 'The way feelings are expressed is very often the same. Take the wagging of the behind. I have often noticed, particularly at dances, that a young man going up to ask a lady to dance will wag his behind quite unmistakably.'

When he and Anna Ignatyevna came to Paris we took them to a dance-hall in the rue Blomet which was frequented by Negro students, artists and models. Durov watched the dancing couples with great attention and suddenly cried out with delight: 'My dear, look how they rub their bellies together! It's the same reflex as parrots.'

Anna Ignatyevna said to my wife: 'I was hoping to buy a few dresses in Paris, but Volodya has bought a giraffe. Giraffes are awfully expensive and, besides, it's got to travel in a special truck.'

Durov adored his chimpanzee Mimus, and reported to me in detail on his progress: 'Mimus has learnt to pronounce syllables. He can say several words. He's beginning to write; the only letter he's really sure of is 'o', but now I'm teaching him 'ж'.

Then a disaster occurred. Durov was to go on tour to Minsk. He took special care of Mimus and never showed him in the ring, but he took him along to make sure he was looked after. The ape, who had already been ill several times before, caught a cold which developed into pneumonia. Durov told me how it died: 'He slept in my bed at the hotel. It's the most difficult thing to house-train an ape. A kitten will behave properly very soon. But apes are so absent-minded. They know they ought to go out, but they're distracted by something amusing, and so they make a mess. But not Mimus. I saw him get up, take some toilet paper and go towards the chamber pot. He never got there: he died on the way.' And there were tears in Durov's eyes.

I have already said that it was sometimes difficult to understand his view of the world; but he hated war and spoke of this both in the circus ring and at scientific gatherings. In 1924 he wrote: 'Soviet Russia was the first to take a bold initiative in the matter of disarmament and is still openly calling on other nations to follow its example.' (It is sad to think that thirty-six years have gone by, that a war such as history had never known has taken place and that Durov's words read as if they had been copied from today's newspapers.)

Durov's whole life was one of poetry and eccentricity. At a scripture examination in the third form of the Moscow Military Gymnasium,

Vladimir Durov, son of a nobleman, walked into the examination hall on his hands. The examiners had not heard of the medieval *jongleurs* and sent the impudent boy packing.

In his old age Durov was surrounded by scholars; Professors Kozhevnikov and Leontovich wrote a preface to one of his books. One might ask: What was there in common between Durov and a clown? And yet he remained a circus man to the end, cursing the ring, yet unable to live without it.

When Durov died in the summer of 1934, the funeral procession moved off from Bozhedomka towards the circus. Thousands of people came to bid farewell to a clown who had amused many generations.

But the dogs listened, sniffed and waited. The sea lions waited. The raven waited, uselessly repeating his name: 'Voronok . . . Voronusha.' Durov did not come. We shall not look upon his like again.

At the beginning of 1921 he and I were driving from TEO to Bozhedomka, pulled along by the emaciated but still cheerful camel. Suddenly Durov said: 'Why do they keep saying "clown, clown"? Let me tell you a secret: clowns are the most serious people.'

Emma Goldman
&
Alexander Berkman

In 1919, the anarchists **Emma Goldman** (1869–1940) and **Alexander Berkman** (1870–1936) were with two hundred and forty-six others deported to the Soviet Union from the United States. The *Buford*, on which they sailed, landed in Finland on the 16 January 1920. Four days later they were in Soviet Russia – for Berkman it was 'the most sublime day of my life'. Berkman and Goldman spent almost two years in Russia – they arrived full of expectations and faith in the revolutionary process that they were convinced would usher in a new, egalitarian society and were left crushed by what they experienced as a cruel, despotic dictatorship. They both wrote of their time in Russia: Berkman in *The Bolshevik Myth* and Goldman in *My Disillusionment in Russia* and *Living My Life*, an autobiography. In these years crucial decisions were taken by the Bolsheviks that restricted political and artistic freedom, curtailing the role of soviets and trade unions. This was at a time when the Civil War was being won and it was no longer credible for the Bolsheviks to use the excuse of the Civil War to restrict liberties and impose severe discipline throughout society; on the contrary, it would, at this time, have been possible to reintroduce freedom of association, of the press, etc. In their writings, Berkman and Goldman, whose deep friendship lasted a lifetime, convey these extraordinary months when the future of the Revolution was still in the balance and discussion and debate were still possible – though not for much longer. The events of Kronstadt in March 1921 convinced Berkman and Goldman that they had to leave Russia. They could not accept the brutal way in which the Bolsheviks dealt with the striking workers and sailors in Petrograd and Kronstadt. The Red Army took back the Kronstadt fortress after ten days of ferocious fighting with many casualties on both sides – though many more sailors and workers were killed, sent into exile or into forced labour. The events of Kronstadt convinced Lenin and the government that they had to abandon War Communism and introduce the NEP. Goldman writes about the Tenth Congress of the Communist Party which took place at the same time as the siege of Kronstadt:

> Lenin unexpectedly changed his inspired Communist song for an equally inspired paean to the New Economic Policy. Free trade, concessions to the capitalists, private employment of farm and factory labour, all damned for over three years as rank counter-revolution and punished by prison and even death, were now written by Lenin on the glorious banner of the dictatorship. Brazenly as ever he admitted what sincere and thoughtful persons in and out of the Party had known for seventeen days: that 'the Kronstadt men did not really want the counter-revolutionists. But neither did they want us.' The naïve sailors had taken seriously the slogan of the Revolution: 'All power to the Soviets,' by which Lenin and his party had solemnly promised to abide. That had been their unforgivable offence. For that they had to die.[37]

Convinced that the Revolution was over, Goldman and Berkman left Russia in December 1921. In the train to Lithuania, Goldman writes: 'December 1, 1921! My dreams crushed, my faith broken, my heart like a stone.'

The Bolshevik Myth, first published in 1925, is a reworking of the material in the diary Berkman kept during his stay in the Soviet Union – though there are important differences between the book and the diary, which has never been published.[38] Bertrand Russell to whom Berkman sent a copy of *The Bolshevik Myth* replied in June 1925 that he had read the book with great interest and that 'my judgement of the Bolsheviks is substantially the same as yours; I went through the same disenchantment, having come with the same hopes'. It remains one of the important books on the Russian Revolution.

37 *Living My Life*, London, 2006, pp. 507–8
38 See the introduction to *The Bolshevik Myth* by Nicolas Walter, London, 1989.

John Reed burst into my room . . .

from *Living My Life* by Emma Goldman

John Reed had burst into my room like a sudden ray of light, the old buoyant, adventurous Jack that I used to know in the States. He was about to return to America, by way of Latvia. Rather a hazardous journey, he said, but he would take even greater risks to bring the inspiring message of Soviet Russia to his native land. 'Wonderful, marvellous, isn't it, E. G.?' he exclaimed. 'Your dream of years now realised in Russia, your dream scorned and persecuted in my country, but made real by the magic wand of Lenin and his band of despised Bolsheviks. Did you ever expect such a thing to happen in the country ruled by the tsars for centuries?'

'Not by Lenin and his comrades, dear Jack,' I corrected, 'though I do not deny their great part. But by the whole Russian people, preceded by a glorious revolutionary past. No other land of our days has been so literally nurtured by the blood of her martyrs, a long procession of pioneers who went to their death that new life may spring from their graves.'

Jack insisted that the young generation cannot for ever be tied to the apron-strings of the old, particularly when those strings are tightly drawn around its throat. 'Look at your old pioneers, the Breshkovskayas and Tchaikovskys, the Chernovs and Kerenskys and the rest of them,' he cried heatedly; 'see where they are now! With the Black Hundreds, the Jew-baiters and the ducal clique, aiding them to crush the Revolution. I don't give a damn for their past. I am concerned only in what the treacherous gang has been doing during the past three years. To the wall with them! I say. I have learned one mighty expressive Russian word, *razstrellyat* [execute by shooting]!'

'Stop, Jack! Stop!' I cried; 'this word is terrible enough in the mouth of a Russian. In your hard American accent it freezes my blood. Since when do revolutionists see in wholesale execution the only solution of their difficulties? In time of active counter-revolution it is no doubt inevitable to give shot for shot. But cold-bloodedly and merely for opinion's sake, do you justify standing people against the wall under such circumstances?' I went on to point out to him that the Soviet Government must have realised the futility of such methods, not to speak of their barbarity, because it had abolished capital punishment. Zorin had told me that. Was the decree revoked, that Jack spoke so glibly of standing men against the wall? I mentioned the frequent shooting I heard in the city at night. Zorin had said that it was target practice of *kursanty* [Communist students at the military training-school for officers]. 'Do you know anything about it, Jack?' I questioned. 'Tell me the truth.'

He did know, he said, that five hundred prisoners, considered counter-revolutionists, had been shot on the eve the decree was to go into force. It had been a stupid blunder on the part of over-zealous Chekists and they had been severely reprimanded for it. He had not heard of any other shootings since, but he had always thought me a revolutionist of the purest dye, one who would not shirk any measure in defence of the Revolution. He was surprised to see me so worked up over the death of a few plotters. As if that mattered in the scales of the world revolution!

'I must be crazy, Jack,' I said, 'or else I never understood the meaning of revolution. I certainly never believed that it would signify callous indifference to human life and suffering, or that it would have no other method of solving its problems than by wholesale slaughter. Five hundred lives snuffed out on the eve of a decree abolishing the death-penalty! You call it a stupid blunder. I call it a dastardly crime, the worst counter-revolutionary outrage committed in the name of the Revolution.'

'That's all right,' said Jack, trying to calm me; 'you are a little confused by the Revolution in action because you have dealt with it only in theory. You'll get over that, clear-sighted rebel that you are, and you'll come to see in its true light everything that seems so puzzling now. Cheer up, and make me a cup of the good old American coffee you have brought with you. Not much to give you in return for all my country has taken from you, but greatly appreciated in starving Russia by her native son.'

I marvelled at his capacity to change so quickly to a light tone. It was the same old Jack, with his zest for the adventures of life. I longed to join in his gay mood, but my heart was heavy. Jack's appearance had brought back memories of my recent life, my people, Helena and those dear to me. Not a word from anyone had reached me in two months. Uncertainty about them added to my depression and restlessness. Sasha's letter, suggesting that I come to Moscow, put new energy into me. Moscow was much more alive than Petrograd, he wrote, and there were interesting people to meet. A few weeks in the capital might help to clarify the revolutionary situation to me. I wanted to go immediately. I had already learned, however, that in Soviet Russia one does not just buy a ticket and board a train. I had seen people standing in queues for days and nights to obtain a permit for their journey and then again wait in long lines to purchase their tickets. Even with the helpful co-operation of Zorin it required ten days before I could leave. He had arranged for me to be in the party of Soviet officials going to Moscow, he informed me. Demyan Bedny, the official poet, would be there and he would place me in the Hotel National. Zorin was as obliging as ever, though somewhat distant.

Free Speech is a Bourgeois Prejudice

from *Living My Life* by Emma Goldman

Lenin's auto rushed at furious speed along the congested streets and into the Kremlin, past every sentry without being halted for *propusks* [permission to enter]. At the entrance of one of the ancient buildings that stood apart from the rest, we were asked to alight. An armed guard was at the elevator, evidently already apprised of our coming. Without a word, he unlocked the door and motioned us within, then locked it and put the key into his pocket. We heard our names shouted to the soldier on the first floor, the call repeated in the same loud voice at the next and the next. A chorus was announcing our coming as the elevator slowly ascended. At the top a guard repeated the process of unlocking and locking the elevator, then ushered us into a vast reception hall with the announcement: 'Tovarishtchy Goldman and Berkman.' We were asked to wait a moment, but almost an hour passed before the ceremony of leading us to the seat of the highest was resumed. A young man motioned us to follow him. We passed through a number of offices teeming with activity, the click of typewriters, and busy couriers. We were halted before a massive door ornamented with beautifully carved work. Excusing himself for just a minute, our attendant disappeared behind it. Presently the heavy door opened from within, and our guide invited us to step in, himself vanishing and closing the door behind us. We stood on the threshold awaiting the next cue in the strange proceedings. Two slanting eyes were fixed upon us with piercing penetration. Their owner sat behind a huge desk, everything on it arranged with the strictest precision, the rest of the room giving the impression of the same exactitude. A board with numerous telephone switches and a map of the world covered the entire wall behind the man; glass cases filled with heavy tomes lined the sides. A large oblong table hung with red; twelve straight-backed chairs, and several armchairs at the windows. Nothing else to relieve the orderly monotony, except the bit of flaming red.

The background seemed most fitting for one reputed for his rigid habits of life and matter-of-factness. Lenin, the man most idolised in the world and equally hated and feared, would have been out of place in surroundings of less severe simplicity.

'Ilich wastes no time on preliminaries. He goes straight to his objective,' Zorin had once said to me with evident pride. Indeed, every step Lenin had made since 1917 testified to this. But if we had been in doubt, the manner of our reception and the mode of our interview would have quickly convinced us of the emotional economy of Ilich. His quick perception of its supply in others and his skill in making the utmost use of it for his purpose were extraordinary. No less amazing was his glee over anything he considered funny in himself or his visitors. Especially if he could put one at a disadvantage, the great Lenin would shake with laughter so as to compel one to laugh with him.

His sharp scrutiny having bared us to the bone, we were treated to a volley of questions, one following the other like arrows from his flint-like brain. America, her political and economic conditions –

what were the chances of revolution there in the near future? The American Federation of Labor – was it all honeycombed with *bourgeois* ideology or was it only Gompers and his clique, and was the rank and file a fertile soil for boring from within? The IWW – what was its strength, and were the anarchists actually as effective as our recent trial would seem to indicate? He had just finished reading our speeches in court. 'Great stuff! Clear-cut analysis of the capitalist system, splendid propaganda!' Too bad we could not have remained in the United States, no matter at what price. We were most welcome in Soviet Russia, of course, but such fighters were badly needed in America to help in the approaching revolution, 'as many of your best comrades have been in ours'. 'And you, Tovarishtch Berkman, what an organiser you must be, like Shatoff. True metal, your comrade Shatoff; shrinks from nothing and can work like a dozen men. In Siberia now, commissar of railroads in the Far Eastern Republic. Many other anarchists hold important positions with us. Everything is open to them if they are willing to co-operate with us as true *ideiny* anarchists. You, Tovarishtch Berkman, will soon find your place. A pity, though, that you were torn away from America at this portentous time. And you, Tovarishtch Goldman? What a field you had! You could have remained. Why didn't you, even if Tovarishtch Berkman was shoved out? Well, you're here. Have you thought of the work you want to do? You are *ideiny* anarchists, I can see that by your stand on the war, your defence of "October", and your fight for us, your faith in the soviets. Just like your great comrade Malatesta,[39] who is entirely with Soviet Russia. What is it you prefer to do?'

Sasha was the first to get his breath. He began in English, but Lenin at once stopped him with a mirthful laugh. 'Do you think I understand English? Not a word. Nor any other foreign languages. I am no good at them, though I have lived abroad for many years. Funny, isn't it?' And off he went into peals of laughter. Sasha continued in Russian. He was proud to hear his comrades praised so highly, he said; but why were anarchists in Soviet prisons? 'Anarchists?' Ilich

39 Errico Malatesta, Italian anarchist journalist, friend of Mikhail Bakunin.

interrupted; 'nonsense! Who told you such yarns, and how could you believe them? We do have bandits in prison, and Makhnovtsy,[40] but no *ideiny* anarchists.'

'Imagine,' I broke in, 'capitalist America also divides the anarchists into two categories, philosophic and criminal. The first are accepted in the highest circles; one of them is even high in the councils of the Wilson Administration. The second category, to which we have the honour of belonging, is persecuted and often imprisoned. Yours also seems to be a distinction without a difference. Don't you think so?' Bad reasoning on my part, Lenin replied, sheer muddle-headedness to draw similar conclusions from different premises. Free speech is a *bourgeois* prejudice, a soothing plaster for social ills. In the Workers' Republic economic well-being talks louder than speech, and its freedom is far more secure. The proletarian dictatorship is steering that course. Just now it faces very grave obstacles, the greatest of them the opposition of the peasants. They need nails, salt, textiles, tractors, electrification. When we can give them these, they will be with us, and no counter-revolutionary power will be able to swerve them back. In the present state of Russia all prattle of freedom is merely food for the reaction trying to down Russia. Only bandits are guilty of that, and they must be kept under lock and key.

Sasha handed Lenin the resolutions of the anarchist conference and emphasised the assurance of the Moscow comrades that the imprisoned comrades were *ideiny* and not bandits. 'The fact that our people ask to be legalised is proof that they are with the Revolution and the Soviets,' we argued. Lenin took the document and promised to submit it to the next session of the Party Executive. We would be notified of its decision, he said, but in any event it was a mere trifle, nothing to disturb any true revolutionist. Was there anything else? We had fought in America for the political rights even of our opponents, we told him; the denial of them to our own comrades was therefore no trifle to us. I, for one, felt, I informed him, that I could not co-operate with a regime that persecuted anarchists or others for the sake of mere opinion. Moreover, there were even more appalling evils. How were we to

40 Independent Ukrainian peasant revolutionaries led by Nestor Makhno

reconcile them with the high goal he was aiming at? I mentioned some of them. His reply was that my attitude was *bourgeois* sentimentality. The proletarian dictatorship was engaged in a life-and-death struggle, and small considerations could not be permitted to weigh in the scale. Russia was making giant strides at home and abroad. It was igniting the world revolution, and here I was lamenting over a little blood-letting. It was absurd, and I must get over it. 'Do something,' he advised; 'that will be the best way of regaining your revolutionary balance.'

Lenin might be right, I thought. I would take his advice. I would start at once, I said. Not with any work within Russia, but with something of propaganda value for the United States. I should like to organise a society of Russian Friends of American Freedom, an active body to give support to America's struggle for liberty, as the American Friends of Russian Freedom had done in aid of Russia against the tsarist regime.

Lenin had not moved in his seat during the entire time, but now he almost leaped out of it. He swung round and stood facing us. 'That's a brilliant idea!' he exclaimed, chuckling and rubbing his hands. 'A fine practical proposal. You must proceed to carry it out at once. And you, Tovarishtch Berkman, will you co-operate in it?' Sasha replied that we had talked the matter over and had already worked out the details of the plan. We could start immediately if we had the necessary equipment. No difficulty in that, Lenin assured us; we would be supplied with everything – an office, a printing outfit, couriers, and whatever funds would be needed. We must send him our prospectus of work and the itemised expenses involved in the project. The Third International would take care of the matter. It was the proper channel for our venture, and it would afford us every help.

In blank astonishment we looked at each other and at Lenin. Simultaneously we began to explain that our efforts could prove effective only if free from any affiliation with known Bolshevik organis-ations. It must be carried out in our own way; we knew the American psychology and how best to conduct the work. But before we could proceed further, our guide suddenly appeared, as unobtrusively as he had left, and Lenin held out his hand to us in goodbye. 'Don't forget to send me the prospectus,' he called after us.

Back in Petrograd

from *The Bolshevik Myth* by Alexander Berkman

At the home of my friend M—, on the Vassilevsky Ostrov, I met several men and women, sitting in their overcoats around the *bourzhuika*, the little iron stove which they kept feeding with old newspapers and magazines.

'Doesn't it seem incredible,' the host was saying, 'that Petrograd, with great forests in its vicinity, should freeze for lack of fuel? We'd get the wood if they'd only let us. You remember those barges on the Neva? They had been neglected, and they were falling to pieces. The workers of the N— factory wanted to take them apart and use the lumber for fuel. But the Government refused. 'We'll attend to it ourselves,' they said. Well, what happened? Nothing was done, of course, and the tide didn't wait for official routine. The barges were swept out to sea and lost.'

'The Communists won't stand for independent initiative,' one of the women remarked; 'it's dangerous for their regime.'

'No, my friends, it's no use deluding yourselves,' a tall, bearded man retorted. 'Russia is not ripe for Communism. Social revolution is possible only in a country with the highest industrial development. It was the greatest crime of the Bolsheviki that they forcibly suspended the Constituent Assembly. They usurped governmental power, but the whole country is against them. What can you expect under such circumstances? They have to resort to terror to force the people to do their bidding, and of course everything goes to ruin.'

'That's a good Marxist talking,' a Left Socialist Revolutionist rejoined, good humouredly; 'but you forget that Russia is an agrarian, not an industrial country, and will always remain such. You Social Democrats don't understand the peasant; the Bolsheviki distrust him and discriminate against him. Their proletarian dictatorship is an insult and an injury to the peasantry. Dictatorship must be that of Toil, to be exercised by the peasants and the workers together. Without the co-operation of the peasantry the country is doomed.'

'As long as you have dictatorship, you'll have the present conditions,' the Anarchist host replied. 'The centralised State, that is the great evil. It does not permit the creative impulses of the people to express themselves. Give the people a chance, let them exercise their initiative and constructive energies – only that will save the Revolution.'

'You fellows don't realise the great role the Bolsheviki have played,' a slender, nervous man spoke up. 'They have made mistakes, of course, but they were not those of timidity or cowardice. They dispersed the Constituent Assembly? The more power to them! They did no more than Cromwell did to the Long Parliament: they sent the idle talkers away. And, incidentally, it was an Anarchist, Anton Zhelezniakov, on duty that night with his sailors at the palace, who ordered the Assembly to go home. You talk of violence and terror – do you imagine a Revolution is a drawing-room affair? The Revolution must be sustained at all costs; the more drastic the measures, the more humanitarian in the long run. The Bolsheviki are Statists, extreme governmentalists, and their ruthless centralisation holds danger. But a revolutionary period, such as we are going through, is not possible without dictatorship. It is a necessary evil that will be outlived only with the full victory of the Revolution. If the left political opponents would join hands with the Bolsheviki and help in the great work, the evils of the present regime would be mitigated and constructive effort hastened.'

'You're a Sovietski Anarchist,' the others teased him.

*   *   *

Almost every *otvetstvenny* [responsible] Communist is gone to Moscow to attend the Ninth Congress of the Party. Grave questions are at issue, and Lenin and Trotsky have sounded the keynote – militarisation of labour. The papers are filled with the discussion of the proposed introduction of *yedinolitchiye* [one-man industrial management] to take the place of the present collegiate form. 'We must learn from the bourgeoisie,' Lenin says, 'and use them for our purposes.'

*   *   *

Among the labour elements there is strong opposition to the new plan, but Trotsky contends that the unions have failed in the management of industry: the proposed system is to organise production more efficiently. The labour men, on the contrary, say that the workers had not been given the opportunity, extreme State centralisation having taken over the functions of the unions. *Yedinolitchiye*, they claim, means complete charge of factory and shop by one man, the so called *spets* [specialists], to the exclusion of the workers from management.

'Step by step we are losing everything we've gained by the Revolution,' a shop committee-man said to me. 'The new plan means the return of the former master. The *spets* is the old *bourzhooi*, and now he is coming back to whip us to work again. But last year Lenin himself denounced the plan as counter-revolutionary, when the Mensheviki advocated it. They are still in prison for it.'

Others are less outspoken. This morning I met N—, of the *Buford* group, a man of intellectual attainment and much political acumen. 'What do you think of it?' I asked, anxious to know his view of the proposed changes.

'I can't afford the luxury of expressing an opinion,' he replied with a sad smile. 'I have been promised a place on a commission to be sent to Europe. It's my only chance of joining my wife and children.'

*   *   *

4 April – A beautiful, bright Sunday. In the morning I attended the burial of Semyon Voskov, a prominent Communist agitator killed on the front by typhus. I had met him in the States, and he impressed me as a fine type of revolutionist and enthusiastic devotee of the Bolsheviki. Now his body lay in state in the Uritsky Palace, and high tribute was paid the dead as an heroic victim of the Revolution.

Along the Nevsky the funeral procession wended its way to the Field of Mars, marching to the strains of music and the singing of a choir from Archangel. Thousands of workers followed the hearse, line after line of men and women from shop and factory, tired toilers, in a spiritless, mechanical way. Military salutes were fired at the grave, and eulogies pronounced by several speakers – rather official, I thought; all too partisan, lacking the warm personal note.

The huge demonstration, arranged by the Petrograd Soviet of labour unions within twenty-four hours, as I was informed, seemed a striking proof of organisation. I congratulated the chief Committee man on the quick and efficient work.

'Done without my leaving the office,' he said proudly. 'The Soviet decision was wired to every mill and factory, ordering each to send a certain contingent of its employees to the demonstration. And the thing was ready.'

'It was not left to the choice of the men?' I asked in surprise.

'Well,' he smiled, 'we leave nothing to chance.'

Returning from the Voskov funeral I met another procession. Two men and a woman walked behind a pushcart on which stood a rough, unpainted pine coffin, holding the dead body of their brother. A young girl, leading a little child by the hand, was wearily following the remains to its last resting place. Three men on the sidewalk stopped to watch the tragic sight. The mourners passed in silence, the picture of misery and friendlessness – black cameos sharply etched on the bright day. In the distance crashed the martial music of the Bolshevik funeral and long lines of soldiers in parade dress, their bayoneted guns glistening in the sun, marched to the Field of Mars to pay honour to Voskov, Communist martyr.

Victor Serge
&
Panaït Istrati

The extracts that follow are taken from Victor Serge's epic autobiography *Memoirs of a Revolutionary*. Never one to accept the Party line, Serge spent his twenty years in the Soviet Union defending all those – Anarchists, Trotskyists, trade unionists – who fell foul of the regime.

Born in Brussels in 1890 to anti-Tsarist Russian exiles, **Victor Serge** was directly involved in the major political conflicts of the first half of the twentieth century. In 1913, he was sentenced in France to five years for his alleged involvement in the robberies of the Anarchist Bonnot Gang. Released from prison in 1917, Serge travelled to Russia in exchange for Bruce Lockhart and some anti-Bolshevik prisoners. During the Civil War, he served as a machine gunner in a special defence battalion, joined the Communist Party and collaborated with Zinoviev in the founding of the Communist International (Comintern). Already at this time, Serge was interceding with the Cheka on behalf of left oppositionists and Anarchists who had fallen foul of the regime. The harsh repression by the government of the Kronstadt Uprising in 1921 confirmed Serge's doubts about the new regime. At the height of the Uprising, Serge met with the Anarchists, including Emma Goldman and Alexander Berkman, in an attempt the find a peaceful solution to the crisis – the nightly meetings took place at the Petrograd home of Serge's father-in-law Alexander Russakov. Already in 1921, Russakov was identified as a trouble-maker to be dealt with at a later date.

After Kronstadt, Serge became a member of the Left Opposition led by Trotsky. Expelled from the Party, Serge was sent into internal exile and forced to leave the Soviet Union in 1936. He went to Paris, where he was the Paris correspondent of the POUM, a Spanish Trotskyist Party (which George Orwell also belonged to) that supported critically the Republic in the Civil War. When the Germans occupied Paris, in 1940, Serge escaped south. He was able to sail on the last ship out of Marseille (André Breton and Claude Levi-Strauss were also on board) and arrived in 1942 in Mexico City. As John Berger wrote: 'The essence of Victor Serge and his books is to be found in his attitude to the truth . . . Serge never saw anybody as an anonymous agent of historical forces. He could not write even of a passer-by without feeling the tension between the passer-by's inner and outer life.' In November 1947, Serge died in Mexico City of a heart attack. Having no nationality, no Mexican cemetery could legally take his body, so he was buried as a 'Spanish Republican'.

A close friend of Victor Serge, **Panaït Istrati** (1884–1935), known as the Maxim Gorki of the Balkans, was during his lifetime a world-famous writer. His most well-known novel, *Kyra Kyralina*, was translated into many languages and brought Istrati fame and wealth – which he rapidly spent with enthusiasm. A committed Communist, he visited the USSR three times – twice in the company of his great friend Nikos Kazantzakis whose novel *Toda-Raba* describes their trips, friendship and painful falling out over the Russakov Affair. As a result of the heroic efforts of Istrati and Serge, Russakov was acquitted in the first trial to excited and vociferous cheers from the working-class audience. After an appeal by the prosecution, a second trial was held in which Russakov was sentenced to three months forced labour. In June 1929, having failed to get justice for Russakov, Istrati went to Paris, where he was widely acclaimed and much loved in left-wing circles (Romain Rolland had for a long time supported Istrati and his work), determined to tell what he saw as the truth about the Soviet Union. In November 1929, he published the three volumes of *Towards the Other Flame* (*Vers l'Autre Flamme*). In fact Istrati wrote only the first volume, *After Sixteen Months in the USSR*, the second volume, *Soviet 1929*, was written by Victor Serge, the third *Russia Unveiled*, by Boris Souvarine [41] – Istrati claimed authorship of the three volumes since his name would maximise sales;

41 In 1931, a translation of *Russia Unveiled/La Russie Nue* was published with Istrati as its author – in fact, this is not the case. In his *Souvenirs*, Souvarine writes how it was the promise of a holiday in the south of France (together

it was also the case that Serge was still in the USSR and it would have been extremely dangerous for him to be credited with authorship of a document that had been smuggled out by Istrati's lover, Marie-Louise Baud-Bovy. Never translated into English *After Sixteen Months in the USSR* is an essential document – written at a time when Stalin's grip on power was tightening and open opposition was becoming very risky. The three volumes are not consistent; Istrati writes from a moral commitment to Communism and cannot accept the acts of brutality and cruelty he sees being done to individuals, Souvarine's critique is much more empirical and based on his close reading of the daily Soviet and bourgeois press; for him the Soviet state under Stalin is moving away from socialism not towards it,[42] Serge's viewpoint is different again: he is also a vehement critic of Stalin but sees his errors as reversible – at this time, he still had faith in the Communist Party and believed that under a different leadership (e.g. Trotsky) a return to the original values of the Revolution was possible.[43] Disillusioned by Trotsky's sectarianism, Serge abandoned these beliefs in 1936. It is the variety of opinions expressed in *Towards the Other Flame* that makes the book so compelling: it is written by three individuals who twelve years after the Revolution felt obliged to figure out for themselves and for their readers what had gone wrong. After its publication, Istrati fell out with his Communist friends who branded him a 'Trotskyist' or even a 'Fascist'. Abandoned and isolated, Istrati returned to Bucarest where he died in 1935.

---

with a summer suit!) that convinced him to write *Russia Unveiled*; he agreed to write it on the condition that Istrati also wrote a volume. I am not aware of there being an English translation of Istrati's volume, *After Sixteen Months in the USSR*.

42 Already in November 1917, Souvarine had written: 'It is to be feared that, for Lenin and his friends, "the dictatorship of the proletariat" must be a dictatorship of the Bolsheviks and their leader. This could become a terror of the Russian working class, and eventually, the global proletariat . . . ' This from a man who was a member of the Comintern until his expulsion in 1924 for supporting the left-wing opposition to Stalin.

43 An excellent guide to Serge's politics and life is Susan Weissman's *Victor Serge: The Course is Set on Hope*, London, 2001

Anguish and Enthusiasm: 1919–20

from *Memoirs of a Revolutionary*
by Victor Serge (translated by Peter Sedgwick)

I end this chapter in the aftermath of the Second Congress of the International, in September and October of 1920. I have the feeling that this point marked a kind of boundary for us. The failure of the attack on Warsaw meant the defeat of the Russian Revolution in Central Europe, although no one saw it as such. At home, new dangers were waxing and we were on the road to catastrophes of which we had only a faint foreboding. (By 'we', I mean the shrewdest comrades; the majority of the Party was already blindly dependent on the schematism of official thinking.) From October onwards significant events, fated to pass unnoticed in the country at large, were to gather with the gentleness of a massing avalanche. I began to feel, acutely I am bound to say, this sense of a danger from inside, a danger within ourselves, in the very temper and character of victorious Bolshevism. I was continually racked by the contrast between the stated theory and the reality, by the growth of intolerance and servility among many officials and their drive towards privilege. I remember a conversation I had with the People's Commissar for Food, Tsyurupa, a man with a splendid white beard and candid eyes. I had brought some French and Spanish comrades to him so that he could explain for our benefit the Soviet system of rationing and supply. He showed us beautifully drawn diagrams from which the ghastly famine and the immense black market had vanished without trace.

'What about the black market?' I asked him.

'It is of no importance at all,' the old man replied. No doubt he was sincere, but he was a prisoner of his scheme, a captive of his system, within offices whose occupants obviously all primed him with lies. I was astounded. So this was how Zinoviev could believe in the imminence of proletarian revolution in Western Europe. Was this perhaps how Lenin could believe in the prospects of insurrection among the Eastern peoples? The wonderful lucidity of these great

Marxists was beginning to be fuddled with a theoretical intoxication bordering on delusion, and they began to be enclosed within all the tricks and tomfooleries of servility. At meetings on the Petrograd front, I saw Zinoviev blush and bow his head in embarrassment at the imbecile flattery thrown in his face by young military careerists in their fresh shiny leather outfits. One of them kept shouting, 'We will win because we are under the command of our glorious leader, Comrade Zinoviev!' A comrade who was a former convict had a sumptuously coloured cover designed by one of the greatest Russian artists, which was intended to adorn one of Zinoviev's pamphlets. The artist and the ex-convict had combined to produce a masterpiece of obsequiousness, in which Zinoviev's Roman profile stood out like that of a proconsul in a cameo bordered by emblems. They brought it to the President of the International, who thanked them cordially and, as soon as they were gone, called me to his side.

'It is the height of bad taste,' Zinoviev told me in embarrassment, 'but I didn't want to hurt their feelings. Have a very small number printed, and get a very simple cover designed instead.'

On another day he showed me a letter from Lenin that touched on the new bureaucracy, calling them 'all that Soviet riffraff'. This atmosphere was often exacerbated, because the perpetuation of the Terror added an element of intolerable inhumanity. If the Bolshevik militants had not been so admirably straight, objective, disinterested, so determined to overcome any obstacle to accomplish their task, there would have been no hope. But on the contrary, their moral greatness and their intellectual standing inspired boundless confidence. I therefore realised that the notion of double duty was fundamental and I was never to forget it. Socialism isn't only about defending against one's enemies, against the old world it is opposing; it also has to fight within itself against its own reactionary ferments. A revolution seems monolithic only from a distance; close up it can be compared to a torrent that violently sweeps along both the best and the worst at the same time, and necessarily carries along some real counter-revolutionary currents. It is constrained to pick up the worn weapons of the old regime, and these arms are double-edged. In order to be properly served, it has to be put on guard against its own abuses, its own excesses, its own crimes, its own moments of reaction. It has a vital need of criticism, therefore, of an opposition and of the civic courage of those who are carrying it out. And in this connection, by 1920 we were already well short of the mark.

A notable saying of Lenin's kept rising in my mind: 'It is a terrible misfortune that the honour of beginning the first Socialist revolution should have befallen the most backward people in Europe.' (I quote from memory; Lenin said it on several occasions.) Nevertheless, within the current situation of Europe, bloodstained, devastated and in profound stupor, Bolshevism was, in my eyes, tremendously and visibly right. It marked a new point of departure in history.

World capitalism, after its first suicidal war, was now clearly incapable either of organising a positive peace, or (what was equally evident) of deploying its fantastic technological progress to increase the prosperity, liberty, safety and dignity of mankind. The Revolution was therefore right, as against capitalism, and we saw that the spectre of future war would raise a question mark over the existence of civilisation itself, unless the social system of Europe was speedily transformed. The fearful Jacobinism of the Russian Revolution seemed to me to be quite unavoidable, as was the institution of a new revolutionary State, now in the process of disowning all its early promises. In this I saw an immense danger: the State seemed to me to be properly a weapon of war, not a means of organising production. Over all our achievements there hung a death sentence; since for all of us, for our ideals, for the new justice that was proclaimed, for our new collective economy, still in its infancy, defeat would have brought a peremptory death and after that, who knows what? I thought of the Revolution as a tremendous sacrifice that was required for the future's sake, and nothing seemed to me more essential than to sustain, or rescue, the spirit of liberty within it.

In penning the above lines, I am no more than recapitulating my own writings of that period.

Deadlock of the Revolution 1926–28

from *Memoirs of a Revolutionary*
by Victor Serge (translated by Peter Sedgwick)

Joffe had, now that his mind was made up, written at great length. First he affirmed his right to commit suicide: 'All my life I have been of the opinion that the political man has the duty to depart at the right time . . . having most assuredly the right to abandon life at that moment when he is aware that he can no longer be useful to the cause which he has served . . .Thirty years ago, I adopted the philosophy that human life has no meaning except in so far as it exists in the service of something infinite – which for us is humanity. Since anything else is limited, to work for the sake of anything else is devoid of meaning . . . ' There followed a reasoned affirmation of faith, so great that it went beyond reason itself, appearing almost puerile: 'Even if humanity should have an end, this end will be in an epoch so distant that for us humanity should be considered as an absolute infinity. And if like me one believes in progress, one can well imagine that, with the disappearance of our planet, humanity will be able to find another, younger one to inhabit [. . .]. In this way, all that has been accomplished for its benefit in our time will find reflection in centuries to come . . . ' The man who wrote these lines, prepared to seal them with his own blood, here touched on heights of faith where neither reason nor unreason counts any longer: there has been no better expression of the revolutionary's communion with all mankind in all ages.

'My death is a gesture of protest against those who have reduced the Party to such a condition that it is totally incapable of reacting against this disgrace' (the expulsion of Trotsky and Zinoviev from the Central Committee). 'Perhaps these two events, the great one and the little' (Joffe's own suicide) 'in occurring together, will reawaken the Party and halt it on the path that leads to Thermidor . . . I should be happy to think so, for then I would know that my death was not in vain. But, though I have the conviction that the hour of awakening will sound one day for the Party, I cannot believe that it has already

287

sounded. In the meantime, I have no doubt that today my death is more useful than the prolongation of my life.'

Joffe addressed certain friendly criticisms to Trotsky, exhorted him to intransigence against orthodox Leninism, authorised him to make changes in the text of the letter before publishing it, and entrusted him with the care of his widow and child. 'I embrace you firmly. Farewell. Moscow, 16 November 1927. Yours, A. A. Joffe.'

The letter signed, the envelope closed and placed in full view on the writing table. Brief meditation: wife, child, city; the huge eternal universe; and myself about to go. The men of the French Revolution used to say: Death is an everlasting sleep . . . Now to do quickly and well what has been irrevocably decided: press the automatic comfortably against the temple, there will be a shock and no pain at all. Shock, then nothing.

The path of agitation was closed to Joffe because of his sickness. For the last time at his funeral we breathed in the salty air of times long past. The Central Committee had arranged two o'clock as the time for the departure of the procession which would accompany the body from the Commissariat for Foreign Affairs to the Novodevichy cemetery; working people would not be able to come as early as that. The comrades delayed the removal of the body for as long as they could. At about four o'clock a crowd, singing and slowly tramping through the snow, and bearing a few red flags, went down towards the Bolshoi Theatre. It already numbered several thousand people. We went along Kropotkin Street, the old Ostozhenka. Long ago, on this very road, I had seen Kropotkin off to the selfsame cemetery, accompanied by quite different victims of persecution; now our own persecution was beginning, and I could not but see a secret justice in this.

Tall, aquiline profile, wearing a cap, collar of his light overcoat raised, Trotsky walked beside Ivan Nikitich Smirnov, thin and blond, still People's Commissar of Postal Services, and Christian Rakovsky. Georgian militants of imposing military appearance in their tightly belted blue overcoats escorted this group. A poor and grey cortege, free of pomp, whose soul vibrated and whose chants rang with defiance. At the approaches to the cemetery, the incidents began.

Sapronov, his aged, emaciated face framed in a mane of bristling white (at the age of forty), passed along the ranks: 'Keep calm, comrades, we mustn't let ourselves be provoked . . .We'll break through the barrier.' A man who had organised the Moscow rising of 1917 was now organising this painful struggle at the cemetery. We marked time for a moment in front of the high battlements of the gateway; the Central Committee had issued an order that only twenty or so persons be allowed to enter.

'Very well,' replied Trotsky and Sapronov, 'the coffin will go no farther and the speeches will be delivered on the pavement.' For a moment it looked as though violence would break out. The representatives of the Central Committee intervened, and we all went in. For one last instant the coffin floated above men's heads in the cold silence, then it was lowered into the pit. Some functionary, whose name I forget, presented official condolences from the Central Committee. Murmurs were heard: 'That's enough! Why doesn't he clear off?' It was so ponderous. Rakovsky towered over the crowd, stout and smooth-shaven; his words snapped out, carrying a great distance: *'This flag – we will follow it – like you – right to the end – on your tomb – we swear it!'*

Old Russia! A tall, ornate tower, red and white, rising over the Novodevichy convent into a clear blue sky above, its architecture ablaze. Here lie great mystics and Chekhov, rich merchants named Bukharin and Evgenia Bosch. A silver birch carries a small plaque, 'Here lies P. A. Kropotkin'. Opulent tombs are in granite, while on others small gilded domes rest on chapels. Later, in the time of industrialisation, many of these were destroyed to use the materials for construction.

The country at large did not hear Joffe's pistol shot, and his last message remained secret. The country knew nothing of our *Platform*, an illegal document. We had copies of these texts circulated, and the GPU came at night to search our quarters for them. The reading of either of them became an offence punished by imprisonment – in contravention of all legal procedure, be it noted. Official Russia was organising the tenth anniversary of the October Revolution: congresses, banquets, etc. Foreign delegates, hand-picked by the

Communist Party, the Friends of the USSR and the Secret Service, poured into Moscow. Among them were two young Frenchmen, ex-Surrealists, singularly upright in character and unflinchingly acute in intelligence, Pierre Naville[44] and Gérard Rosenthal[45] They had come with me to keep watch over Joffe's body. I took them to see Zinoviev and Trotsky. The interview with Zinoviev took place in the little apartment of Sachs-Gladnev, an old Marxist scholar who was a timid, fastidious man, myopic and bearded up to his eyes. Storks in white silk were in flight upon a Chinese tapestry. On his bookshelves, the twenty-five volumes of Lenin. The two French comrades questioned Zinoviev on the prospects for the Opposition in the International. Zinoviev said, more or less, 'We are starting the Zimmerwald movement all over again. Think of Europe at war and that handful of internationalists gathered in a Swiss village; we are already stronger than they were. We have cadres practically everywhere. In our time, history moves faster . . . '

As we went out, Naville, Rosenthal and I exchanged glances, all somewhat horrified by this crude approach. Did Zinoviev believe what he told us? I think so, more or less. But he had besides a second and a third set of possibilities kept in reserve, and these he did not disclose. Poor Sachs-Gladnev, our host for that day, disappeared in 1937, classified as a 'terrorist.'

44 Pierre Naville: French Surrealist in the 1920s. Invited (with Rosenthal) to the tenth anniversary of the Revolution in 1927, Naville was introduced by Serge to Trotsky and returned to France a Trotskyist.

45 Gérard Rosenthal: editor of the French Surrealist *Oeuf dur* in the 1920s. Joined the Left Opposition after his return from Moscow and became Trotsky's French lawyer. Active in the Maquis in World War II.

The Years of Resistance, 1928-33

from *Memoirs of a Revolutionary*
by Victor Serge (translated by Peter Sedgwick)

At this point I should have dealt at length with the Soviet writers whose life I shared; with their resistance, timid and stubborn at once, to the smothering of their creative freedom; with their humiliations and their suicides. I should have outlined portraits of remarkable men. I have no space to do so, and of these men, some are still alive. In speaking of them I might put them in danger. What I must tell here briefly is the tragedy of a literature of mighty spiritual sources, strangled by the totalitarian system – and also the diverse reactions evoked by this tragedy in men supremely gifted for creative work, whether poets or novelists.

Poets and novelists are not political beings because they are not essentially rational. Political intelligence, based though it is in the revolutionary's case upon a deep idealism, demands a scientific and pragmatic armour, and subordinates itself to the pursuit of strictly defined social ends. The artist, on the contrary, is always delving for his raw material in the subconscious, in the preconscious, in intuition, in a lyrical inner life that is rather hard to define; he does not know with any certainty either where he is going or what he is creating. If the novelist's characters are truly alive, they function by themselves, to a point at which they eventually take their author by surprise, and sometimes he is quite perplexed if he is called upon to classify them in terms of morality or social utility. Dostoyevsky, Gorky and Balzac brought to life, all lovingly, criminals whom the Political Man would shoot most unlovingly. That the writer should involve himself in social struggles, have enriching convictions, that his potency will increase to the extent that he identifies himself with the rising classes, thus communicating with masses of individuals who carry within them a precious potential – all this does not significantly alter the simple psychological truths that I set out above. Is it possible for one man to be both a great politician and a great novelist at the same time, uniting in one personality Thiers and Victor Hugo, Lenin and Gorky? I doubt it, given that the two temperaments are profoundly incompatible, and anyway, history has not yet achieved such a success. Under all regimes writers have adapted to the spiritual needs of the dominant classes and, depending on the historical circumstances, this raised them to greatness or maintained them in mediocrity. Their adaptation, in great periods of interior and spontaneous culture, was full of contradictions and fertile torments. The new totalitarian states, imposing on their writers narrow ideological directives and absolute conformism, succeed only in killing the creative faculty within them. Between 1921 and 1928 Soviet literature had its glorious season of full flower. From 1928 onwards it declines and dies out. Doubtless they go on printing – but what gets printed?

Max Eastman found the right expression for it: 'Writers in uniform'. The conscription and uniforming of Russia's writers took several years to complete; creative freedom disappeared side by side with freedom of opinion, with which it is inseparably bound. In 1928 or 1929 the Leningrad writers were on the point of protesting openly against the censorship, the press campaigns of slander and threats, and the administrative pressure. I was consulted and thought we should. Gorky, when asked, 'Do you think, Alexei Maximovich, that the time has come to get ourselves deported?' replied, 'Yes, it's time.' I also heard him make the following joke: 'In the old days, Russian writers only had the policeman and the archbishop to fear; today's Communist official is both at once. He is always wanting to lay his filthy paws on your soul.' Nothing was done, apart from interviews with high officials (who offered reassurances) and routine acts of petty cowardice. When the press denounced Zamyatin and Pilnyak as public enemies, the first for a biting satire on totalitarianism, the other for a fine realist short novel, full of suffering (*Mahogany*), my writer friends voted whatever was required against their two comrades, only to go and ask their pardon, in private. When, at the time of the technicians' trial, the Party organised demonstrations in favour of the execution of the culprits and unanimous votes for the death penalty, the writers voted and demonstrated like everybody else – this although they numbered men who knew what was going on and were troubled by it, such as Konstantin Fedin, Boris Pilnyak, Alexei Tolstoy, Vsevolod Ivanov and Boris Pasternak.

During the Ramzin trial, the Leningrad Writers' Union summoned me to an important meeting. Knowing that it was to concern itself with demanding executions, I did not go. A member of the Bureau came to see me.

'Doubtless you were ill, Victor Lvovich?'

'Not at all. I am on principle opposed to the death penalty in our country at this present time. I think that the revolver has been abused in such excess that the only way of restoring any value to human life in the USSR would be to proclaim the abolition of the death penalty in accordance with the 1917 Programme. I request you to take note of this statement.'

'Certainly, certainly. In that case, will you kindly take note of our resolution, unanimously carried, on the trial of the Industrial Party, and give us your approval with your reservation about the death penalty?'

'No. I think that trials are the affair of the courts, not of the unions.'

And yet . . . nothing happened to me. Two schoolmistresses who adopted the same attitude (I did not know them) were forthwith expelled from their union, hounded from their jobs, arrested as counter-revolutionaries and deported. The worst of it all was that after having gone to so much trouble to obtain an outcry for bloodshed, the Central Committee reprieved the condemned men.

Every time this sort of voting took place, the writers felt a little more domesticated. Our social tea-gatherings were divided into two parts. From eight to ten at night conversation was conventional and directly inspired by the newspaper editorials: official admiration, official enthusiasm, etc. Between ten and midnight, after a few glasses of vodka had been drunk, a kind of hysteria surfaced, and conversations – now diametrically at odds – were sometimes punctuated by fits of anger or weeping. Face to face, no more official-speak, but instead an alert critical intelligence, a tragic sorrow, a Soviet patriotism coming from souls being flayed alive.

Andrei Sobol, an outstanding novelist and a good revolutionary (ex-convict), had killed himself at the same time as Sergei Yesenin, in

1926. There were several suicides of young folk; I remember that of Victor Dmitriev and his wife. On 14 April 1930, Vladimir Mayakovsky fired a bullet into his heart. I wrote of this (in Paris, anonymously): 'This death comes after eighteen leaden months of stagnation in literature: not one work in this period – not a single one! – but plenty of frenzied campaigns against one writer or other, lots of major and minor excommunications and recantations of heresies in abundance. We were unable to hold on to this artist, that much is clear. Enormous publicity, official recognition, financial rewards were not enough for him precisely because of the portion of lies and the great emptiness they concealed. He was a wonderful 'fellow traveller'; he wasted his best talents in a weary quest for God knows what ideological line, demanded of him by petty pedants who made a living out of it. Having become the most-requested rhymester of hack journalism, he suffered at sacrificing his personality to this daily drudgery. He felt that he was going to the dogs. He never stopped justifying himself and pleading that it was 'a surrender to superior force . . . ' Mayakovsky had just joined Leopold Averbach's Association of Proletarian Authors. In his last poem, 'At the Top of My Voice!' he wrote of '*the petrified crap of the present* . . . '

I know that he had spent the previous evening drinking, bitterly justifying himself before his friends who kept telling him harshly, 'You're finished; all you ever do is piss out copy for the hacks.' I had only held one conversation of any significance with him. He was annoyed at a long article I had devoted to him in *Clarté* at a time when he was unknown in the West. 'Why do you say that my Futurism is no more than Past-ism?'

'Because your hyperboles and shouts, and even your boldest images, are all saturated with the past in its most wearisome aspects. And you write:

> 'In men's souls
> Vapour and electricity . . .

'Do you really think that's good enough? Surely this is materialism of a peculiarly antiquated variety?'

He knew how to declaim before crowds, but not how to argue.

'Yes, I'm a materialist! Futurism is materialist!' We parted cordially, but he became so official that I never met him again and most of the friends of his youth dropped him.

I no longer saw anything of Gorky, who had come back to the USSR terribly changed. My near relatives, who had known him since he was a youth, had stopped seeing him since the day he refused to intervene on behalf of the five condemned to death in the Shakhty trial. He wrote vile articles, merciless and full of sophistry, justifying the worst trials on grounds of Soviet humanism! What was going on inside him? We knew that he still grumbled, that he was uneasy, that his harshness had an obverse of protest and grief. We told each other: 'One of these days he'll explode!' And indeed he did, a short while before his death, finally breaking with Stalin. But all his collaborators on the *Novaya Zhizn* [New Life] of 1917 were disappearing into jail and he said nothing. Literature was dying and he said nothing.

I happened to catch a glimpse of him in the street. Leaning back alone, in the rear seat of a big Lincoln car, he seemed remote from the street, remote from the life of Moscow, reduced to an algebraic cipher of himself. He had not aged, but rather thinned and dried out, his head bony and cropped inside a Turkish skullcap, his nose and cheekbones jutting, his eye sockets hollow like a skeleton's. Here was an ascetic, emaciated figure, with nothing alive in it except the will to exist and think. Could it, I wondered, be some kind of inner drying, stiffening and shrinking peculiar to old age, which had begun in him at the age of sixty? I was so struck with this idea that, years later in Paris, at the very time when Romain Rolland, then sixty-five, was following exactly the same spiritual path as old Gorky, I was inexpressibly reassured by the humanity and clear-sightedness of André Gide, and I thought gratefully of John Dewey's honest perspicacity.

After this encounter I tried to see Alexei Maximovich but was barred at the door by his secretary (GPU), a robust character with pince-nez, generally despised and singularly well-named since he was called Kriuchkov – i.e., Hook.

Boris Andreyevich Pilnyak was writing *The Volga Falls to the Caspian Sea*. On his worktable I saw manuscripts under revision. It had been suggested to him that, to avoid banishment from Soviet literature, he should remodel *Mahogany*, that 'counter-revolutionary' tale of his, into a novel agreeable to the Central Committee. This body's Cultural Section had assigned him a co-author who, page by page, would ask him to suppress this and add that. The helpmate's name was Yezhov, and a high career awaited him, followed by a violent death: this was the successor to Yagoda as head of the GPU, shot like Yagoda in 1938 or 1939. Pilnyak would twist his great mouth: 'He has given me a list of fifty passages to change outright!'

'Ah!' he would exclaim, 'if only I could write freely! What would I not do!' At other times I found him in the throes of depression. 'They'll end up by throwing me in jail . . . Don't you think so?' I gave him new heart by explaining that his fame in Europe and America safeguarded him; I was right, for a while. 'There isn't a single thinking adult in this country,' he said, 'who has not thought that he might be shot . . . ' And he related to me details of killings that he had picked up while drinking with tipsy executioners. He wrote a wretched article for *Pravda* on some technicians' trial, received a passport for travel abroad on Stalin's personal recommendation, visited Paris, New York and Tokyo, and came back to us dressed in English tweed, with a little car of his own, dazzled by America.

'You people are finished!' he told me. 'Revolutionary romanticism is out! We are entering an era of Soviet Americanism: technique and practical soundness!' He was childishly pleased with his fame and material comforts . . .Thirty-five years of age, books like *The Naked Year*, *Ivan and Maria*, and *Machines and Wolves* behind him, a love for and familiarity with the lands of Russia, goodwill towards the powerful . . . He was tall, an oval head, strong features, a Germanic type, very egotistical and very human. He was criticised for not being a Marxist, for being a 'typical intellectual', for having a national and peasant vision of the Revolution, for emphasising instinct above reason . . .

Shortly before my arrest we took a long car trip together to enjoy vistas of sunshine and unsullied snow. Suddenly he slowed down and turned to face me, his eyes saddened: 'I do believe, Victor Lvovich, that one day I too will put a bullet into my head. Perhaps it's what I ought to do. I cannot emigrate like Zamyatin: I could not live apart from Russia. And I have the feeling that as I come and go there is a gun in my back, held by a pack of blackguards . . . '

When I was arrested he had the courage to go and protest to the GPU. (He disappeared without trial in 1937, quite mysteriously: one of the two or three real creators of Soviet literature, a great writer translated into ten languages, disappeared without anyone in the Old World or the New – except myself, and my voice was stifled – enquiring after his fate or his end!) One critic has said that the works he had written with Yezhov 'shout the lie and whisper the truth'.

The star of Count Alexei Nikolayevich Tolstoy was climbing gently to its zenith. I had met him in Berlin in 1922, an authentic counter-revolutionary émigré, negotiating his return to Russia and his future royalties. Highly esteemed by the educated classes under Tsarism, a discreet liberal and honest patriot, he had fled with the White forces from the Revolution. He was a decent stylist and now and then a good psychologist, skilful enough to adapt to the public taste, to turn out a successful play or a novel of contemporary interest. In character, manner and morals he was really a high Russian lord of olden days, loving beautiful things, good living, polite literature, cautiously liberal opinions, the odour of power and, what is more, the Russian people: 'our eternal little muzhik'.

He invited me out to his villa at Dietskoe Selo, where his furniture came from the Imperial palaces, to hear the first chapter of his *Peter the Great*. At this time he was not particularly well regarded, and was deeply distressed by the sight of the devastated countryside; he conceived of his great historical novel as a defence of the peasant folk against tyranny as well as an explanation of the present tyranny in terms of the one of the past. A little later, the analogy he drew between *Peter the Great* and the General Secretary turned out to be strangely satisfying to the latter. Alexei Tolstoy, too, now began to protest aloud, when he was in his cups, that it was almost impossible to write in such an oppressive atmosphere. He told the General Secretary himself as much, in the course of a writers' reception, and the General Secretary drove him home in his car, reassured him, lavished on him pledges of friendship . . . On the following day, the press stopped attacking the novelist: Alexei Tolstoy was revising his manuscripts.

Today he is the official 'great writer' of Soviet Russia. But has he ever enquired after the fate of Boris Pilnyak or so many others who were his friends? The quality of his writings has sunk quite incredibly, and falsifications of history can be found in them on a scale that is simply monstrous. (I am thinking of a novel of his about the Civil War.)

Three men far removed from this rising official celebrity used to meet in an old cottage in Dietskoe, and through them I made contact with a different set of values. These were representatives of the Russian intelligentsia of the great period from 1905 to 1917. The ancient, shabby interior of the place seemed pervaded through and through with silence. Andrei Bely and Feodor Sologub would be playing chess. Sologub, the author of the novel *The Petty Demon*, was in his last (the sixty-fourth) year of his life: a small man of an astounding pallor, his oval face well proportioned, his forehead high, bright-eyed, timid and introverted. Since the death of his wife he had been delving into mathematics for some proof of an abstract form of immortality. His work had been concentrated variously on the mystical world, the sensual world and the Revolution. His utterances displayed a childish ingenuity, and it was said of him that all he lived on now was 'his big secret'. In the visionary eyes and passionate voice of Andrei Bely an inextinguishable flame still burned. He was fighting for his imprisoned wife and writing his autobiography, *At the Frontier of Two Epochs*; he lived even now in a state of intellectual fever. Ivanov-Razumnik, now failing, his face cadaverous and his suit threadbare, would from time to time emit some mordant observation; he was allowed to deal only with subjects of literary scholarship, writing his study of Shchedrin until he disappeared.

The Russakov Affair

from *After Sixteen Months in the USSR,* Volume 1 of
Towards the Other Flame, by Panaït Istrati
(translated by Pete Ayrton and Sarah Martin)

Everyone knows what the *Communist Party* is: a weapon of struggle for the taking of power by the proletariat, whose controls are in Moscow. But do workers know what the *Red Trade Unions* are?

Before the war, unions were neither red nor white nor black, there were just trade unions full stop to fight the employers. *Against whom in the USSR do the Red Unions fight? What is the reason for their existence, for their tremendous power in this country where employers are merely a memory?*

It is this: they exist to control *all the means* by which a worker can earn his living and to hand out work depending on the mindset of whoever wants to earn his crust. It is through the Red Unions that the Party lays down the law in the factory, the workplace, the workshop, the office, housing, *everywhere*. No one can find a job except through the union. Once expelled from the union, all that remains is to blow your brains out: all ways of making money, of earning a livelihood are closed off.

Imagine the terrible power given to men who have been taught in schools that *morality* and *honesty* are 'bourgeois prejudices', and that only *materialism* really exists on earth. It's worth considering that even if Communist education taught exactly the opposite, it would still be a social disaster to hand over the majority of the population to the arbitrary power of a very small minority of men who, after all, cannot be angels.

That said, let the curtain rise:

On 1 February this year, demoralised and beaten down, I had completed my arrangements to leave Russia and I was in my room in the *Passage Hotel* in Moscow, when Victor Serge, very calm but white as a sheet, entered.

'Now,' he said falling into a chair, 'it's our turn to be eaten up.' And he read me a telegram his family had just sent to him from Leningrad. It referred to a horrible article that had appeared the day before in the most important regional newspaper of the Party, the *Leningradskaïa Pravda*, the *Pravda* of Leningrad. Exposed to public condemnation, old man Russakov was denounced as an enemy of the proletariat. His immediate arrest and exemplary punishment were called for. What punishment? Well, the title of the article made that clear: *Kalganovskaïa porada*, meaning 'Just Like Kalganov'. Now Kalganov, the son of a landowner and the assassin of the president of a co-operative, had just been shot, a few weeks ago.

His arms dangling, Victor Serge, as he stared at the floor, seemed crushed.

'Come on,' I told him. 'You can't make me believe that there is anyone in the world who can mix up our old Russakov with the white Kalganov. It's a sinister joke.'

He looked at me with dulled eyes: 'Old boy . . . You now know this country better than almost anyone, but no one wanted to tell you how far the power of evil can go. We tried to spare you this. Now evil is throttling you in spite of our efforts. Why did you not leave a week ago?'

'What's this all about?'

'This is how it goes: in the USSR, when you take on an isolated individual, it's OK; you stand a chance. But when it's an *organisation* or *several individuals* that attack someone, as is the case today, the man is a goner. It's very far from a fight of equals.'

We went to get the article. Here it is word for word:

Just Like Kalganov

A few weeks ago, Alexander Kalganov was shot in Moscow. The son of a former landlord, he had killed Karavaiev, the president of the housing co-operative. The execution of Kalganov was a brutal warning to kulaks and nepmen[46] whose activity is on the increase.

---

46 People promoted under the New Economic Policy. By now, the NEP was no longer government policy and nepmen were no longer welcome.

But it would seem that Kalganov's end did not have the desired effect on everyone.

On the 26th of this month, comrade Maria Svirtsiéva, a member of the housing management committee of 19 Jéliabov Street, entered the apartment of Citizen Russakov to take stock of the repairs that had just been completed. Citizen Russakov, the lead tenant, approached Svirtsiéva and rudely asked the purpose of her visit. On her answering that she had come as a member of the management committee, he attacked her shouting: 'The committee is full of crooks and that includes you.'

In support of Russakov, there came from the rooms he occupied three women and an elegantly dressed man who also started to insult Svirtsiéva. When Svirtsiéva asked the citizen close to her by what right he was threatening her, he answered that he was a writer and beyond the law. Then, fingering the order of the Red Flag that Svirtsiéva wore, the writer exclaimed: 'People who wear that kind of order we have killed by the truck load!'

The verbal stage of the aggression was short. One of the women, the daughter Russakov, grabbed Svirtsiéva by the shoulder, while Russakov slapped her in the face. The five of them, with Russakov in the lead, dragged Svirtsiéva along the corridor to the hallway, hitting her with whatever was at hand. Russakov hit Svirtsiéva with his fist, his daughter with an unknown heavy object, and the 'writer' attempted to rip off the Red Flag medal. Svirtsiéva fainted and only regained consciousness on the stairs covered in gobs of spit.

Helped by the tenants of the house, Svirtsiéva went to the Pérovskaïa hospital where a doctor noted serous bruising on her body, traces of blood, bruises and scratches. Her dress was torn and the order of the Red Flag bent.

Who is Russakov? Of the eleven rooms in his apartment, he rents out *nine and on these he speculates to the hilt*. In one of the rooms he rents out live *two Romanian komsomols* whom he had also repeatedly punched and terrorised: so much so that they were afraid to go to the relevant authorities. In the house meetings, Russakov always puts forward *clearly anti-Soviet views*, makes trouble, creates problems and tries to disrupt the meetings. He has come from France where he owned a hat workshop.

And who is Svirtsiéva? Here are a few facts of her biography clearly defined by class. A manual worker with 20 years on the shop floor; one of the organisers of the first Women's Congress in 1918. During the Civil War, she fought in the Red Army cavalry. She then worked underground in Poland. For her military valour, she received the order of the Red Flag. She is a member of the Leningrad soviet and the Party.

These are the class biographies of the aggressor and of the victim. There is no doubt that in the poorly lit corridor of a *bourgeois apartment* a clearly defined class brawl took place.

Russakov is made from the same clay as the executed Alexander Kalganov. Sworn enemy of the proletarian society, frustrated in his profit-making activities, he took his fury out on the militant Svirtsiéva. The aggression of Russakov with his fists, like Kalganov with his flick-knife, is an attempted attack of kulaks and nepmen against our rank and file and our creative labour.

Proletarian opinion demands the immediate arrest of Russakov. What is needed is an exemplary trial that carries as strong a warning as the trial of Kalganov in Moscow.

The enemies of the proletariat who attack our militants with fists and knives over housing and domestic issues must be severely punished.

The Russakov Affair must be removed from the shadowy corridor of a *bourgeois apartment* and taken to an exemplary trial followed by a harsh sentence so that others will be dissuaded from such conduct.

Tower

(*Leningradskaïa Pravda*, 31 January 1929)

So *proletarian opinion demanded the immediate arrest of Russakov*, whom comrade Tower describes as we have just read, *without ever having met or questioned him, knowing nothing about how he lives, without ever having set foot in his dwelling where the act of aggression is meant to have taken place.*

I ask forgiveness from the workers who read me; but such a 'proletarian opinion ' concocted by *Tower, Dower* or *Fower*, I can't take any more seriously than the 'opinion' which is expressed in the bourgeois press, democratic or reactionary, but with their very own *Towers*.

'Now,' said Victor Serge, 'what follows is: an avalanche of "motions" from factories and other work places; the arrest of the old guy, of my companion and possibly of myself; our expulsion from the dwelling that they have been wanting to take from us for such a long time; and then "an exemplary trial and sentence".'

'Now,' I said, 'we shall unpack our bags, prolong our visas and our train tickets, and delay our departure until further notice: what do you say, dearest?'[47]

'Just what I was thinking myself.'

What joy, in adversity, to have by one's side a very dear life companion!

We deliberated how best to act as swiftly as possible. The first priority was to prevent the arrest of Russakov, which would lead to other arrests and unleash a raft of populist articles, well known in the USSR, which are fed to the masses and allow those in power to *hold on*.

Just at this moment Victor Serge got the first letter from home. The truth: it's a complete stitch-up: Victor's wife has been beaten, bloodied by punches to the face that the Red Army cavalry woman Svirtsiéva let rip at their home in Jéliabov Street. We make haste!

In Moscow at the time, coming back from the border with Mongolia where he had been sent by the Soviet Government, was Dr Nikolaenko, anarchist and *a man*. He knew Russakov better than I did. He had been interned with him in Marseille and he also had been part of the group exchanged for French hostages. A rare document, a photograph of that period, featured him as well as Russakov, Victor Serge and some other political detainees, in front of their prison door surrounded by Senegalese soldiers.

47 On the trip Istrati is accompanied by Marie-Louise Baud-Bovy, his Swiss lover.

(Later on, a comrade judge to whom we presented this proof of the revolutionary past of Russakov disputed its authenticity claiming to our great amusement that *the Senegalese did not seem black enough to him!*).

At the *Petit-Paris*, this oasis of free discussion in tyrannical Moscow, Pierre Pascal, like Serge a son-in-law of Russakov, Dr Nikolaenko, Victor Serge and I put our heads together. Pascal and the doctor are doubtful.

'Nothing to be done. We can only let ourselves be eaten up.'

'But,' I said, 'at least we can thrash around energetically, like when one falls into the water.'

'It depends what you mean by "thrash around". In Soviet waters, too much movement leads to swift suffocation.'

But Victor Serge concurs with me and we agree to bombard the authorities with telegrams that each writes as they see fit.

Here are the wires sent from Moscow, the 1 February 1929:

From Dr Nikolaenko:

TO THE EDITORIAL OFFICE OF THE *PRAVDA* OF LENINGRAD

HAVING KNOWN FOR OVER TWENTY YEARS, THROUGH OUR LIVES AS ÉMIGRÉ COMMUNISTS IN FRANCE, THE REVOLUTIONARY WORKER RUSSAKOV, I FIERCELY PROTEST AGAINST THE LIBELLOUS ARTICLE BY TOWER AND DEMAND AN IMPARTIAL INVESTIGATION.

Pierre Pascal sends a similar telegram to the *Pravda* of Leningrad.

Victor Serge telegraphs:

TO THE EDITORIAL OFFICE OF THE *PRAVDA* OF LENINGRAD

I PROTEST AGAINST THE DISGRACEFUL AND LIBELLOUS CAMPAIGN WAGED IN THE *PRAVDA* OF LENINGRAD UNDER THE SIGNATURE OF TOWER AGAINST THE OLD WORKER, POLITICAL ÉMIGRÉ RUSSAKOV. THIS CAMPAIGN CONCLUDES A SERIES OF PETTY PROVOCATIONS COMING FROM A 'KOMSOMOLSKA' [young Communist] OF SMOLENSK WHOSE SOLE AIM IS TO OBTAIN A ROOM, PROVOCATIONS WHICH HAVE RESULTED IN AN ATTACK AGAINST MY WIFE IN HER OWN HOME.

Mine read:

from *After Sixteen Months in the USSR*

TO THE PRESIDENT OF THE TSIK[41] KALININ

THE *PRAVDA* OF LENINGRAD HAS PUBLISHED UNDER THE TITLE 'JUST LIKE KALGANOV' A LIBELLOUS ARTICLE AGAINST THE OLD REVOLUTIONARY WORKER RUSSAKOV, WHOM I KNOW WELL AND WHOSE INNOCENCE IS EASY TO PROVE, WHICH CONSTITUTES AN UNACCEPTABLE ENCOURAGEMENT TO LEGAL AND OTHER PERSECUTIONS. DUE TO LEAVE THE USSR WITHIN FORTY-EIGHT HOURS, I APPEAL TO YOUR SPIRIT OF JUSTICE AND DEMAND FOR THIS FAMILY OF WORKERS A PUBLIC APOLOGY.

TO THE *PRAVDA* OF LENINGRAD

ON THE SUBJECT OF THE ARTICLE 'JUST LIKE KALGANOV' WHICH YOU PUBLISHED, I WOULD BE GRATEFUL IF YOU CONSIDERED THE FOLLOWING: I KNOW THE RUSSAKOV FAMILY FROM HAVING LIVED WITH THEM IN LENINGRAD. I AM TOTALLY CONVINCED NOT ONLY OF THEIR INNOCENCE, BUT ALSO OF THE PERSECUTIONS THEY ARE SUBJECT TO AND BE AWARE THAT I AM PREPARED TO ACT WITH ALL MY STRENGTH, HERE AND ABROAD, AGAINST SUCH DISGRACEFUL ACTS.

These telegrams were sent in the afternoon and evening. The one for Kalinin caused great agitation among the post-office workers who, alas, knew me well for having often of late sent protests to Moscow. But I had until now not bothered the president of the union. Where was he to be found? Everyone asks themselves. One boss is called after another. Phone calls are made left and right.

'There is a telegram for Tovarishtch Kalinin.'

'Send it to the Central.'

The workers laugh to themselves. I do the same though my heart had not expected so low a blow and had no desire to laugh.

The next day, from ten onwards, I get the first sign of a reaction. And what a reaction! The Moscow bureau of the *Leningradskaïa Pravda* asks me, incredulous, *if it is really me* who sent such a telegram to a great regional headquarters of the Party; in Leningrad they cannot believe it.

I can no longer contain myself. Forgetting that I am phoning from

48 The TSIK was the Central Executive Committee of the Soviet Union.

a hotel corridor, I rage like a man who has nothing to lose since all faith has been lost.

'You think that you are the victim of a hoax? You are so little used to see people fight back?'

'No . . . but . . . "to act here *and abroad*"', "*disgraceful acts*" . . . It seems a bit over the top to us.'

'It seems a bit over the top to you. Well, bastards. Crooks! Murderers of workers! Yes, they are *disgraceful acts* that you are committing and I will protest here and abroad.'

I scream in this way for at least ten minutes, not letting anyone interrupt me – if someone is still listening. The doors of the corridor opened. I feel more than I see eyes wide open take a quick look at me and disappear.

Finally, I am stopped by the editor saying: 'Fine, Comrade Istrati, I will report back what you have just told me. But, I have nothing to do with it.'

When I get back to my room I find my partner content, totally happy to know that someone has howled his revolt against tyranny. However, Victor Serge, who is also there, is terrified: 'Well. Until now no one has had the audacity to throw in the face of the Soviets what you have just told them almost in public. For any of us, it would be Siberia – no less.'

Hard to believe that the first effect of social progress is that you can no longer shout between brothers in struggle the words that the most backward bourgeois scream daily at each other: *murderer! crook!* without risking a trip to some Siberia or other. What does it mean, this right to criticise, right to control, this professed ability of a worker to express himself, to act in ways only made possible by a revolutionary republic? Is it progress or barbarism worthy of the Inquisition if suspended rights, the most dreadful of crimes, the most heinous abuses of power flourish like a vipers' nest in the sun, attack and consume men in funereal silence.

I tell in detail this moment in my life with all it contains of bravery, not to boast since I am one of the defeated but so that working and revolutionary humanity can learn as much as possible in preparation for tomorrow's struggles.

Having kept quiet for eight months, I am not here to get upset over my revolt. Eyes I will never forget, voices that still thunder in my heart, have placed on my shoulders responsibilities that crush me and that I can no longer bear. I see appear on the page the image of men gaunt, skeletal, with the look of madmen, shaking from anger as much as hardships, who tell me: 'From how our *Pravdas* write about you, we will know whether, when abroad, you kept your word or are just a scoundrel.'

These men were not 'whites'. They were political émigrés, these *polit-emigrants*, wrecks of fascism, who in their tens of thousands roam the Soviet Union, where the worst villains live it up at the Lux, because 'they follow the right line'. And one of those ninety-kopeck-a-day wanderers shouted to me: 'Tell our comrades over there that they must always defend the USSR at the cost of their lives and die defending it. But they should avoid doing like us: they should not come here, *if they are revolutionaries*, to taste the bread of the Revolution.'

This was one of those 'moaners' like Russakov.

'Yes, I protest against the injustice!' he cried out. 'Why am I a revolutionary? If I was one of those who bend and keep quiet, I would now not be here and I would be better off obeying the bourgeois rather than the soviets, since I lacked nothing in my country except the right to speak. And I did not know, taking refuge here, that the right to speak dies under all dictatorships.'

I spend the 2nd of February glued to the phone, going over – for the judges, for the media and for the presidency – what Russakov was really like. I tell them the life of the man and the revolutionary, and give an accurate version of the crime committed by the hysterical woman decorated with the order of the Red Flag. Everywhere I end with: *If I am lying and you prove to me that Russakov is the 'counter-revolutionary' described by Tower, I am fully prepared to be shot at the same time as him.*

Hopefully, that made my position clear.

With the article in our pockets, we went to visit some of our editor friends who always wanted me to write for their publications. The editorial staff of *Kosomolskaïa Pravda* – the most important Moscow paper after *Pravda* – receives me with cries of joy.

'So, you have something for us?'

'Yes, I have an article for you. Here it is. It is restrained, not long, and it would be good if you could run it immediately, *without making any changes*. It's a very serious business: I count on you.

A quick look at my article and heads drop. Still, they promise to run it as it stands.

You will see how they kept their word. I publish here the article to allow the reader to grasp the arbitrary nature of life under Communism, of how impossible it is for a worker to defend himself when an organisation overwhelms him with lies.

(Everything in *italic* is a cut made by the editors.)

The Russakov Affair

For a year now, I have been travelling all over the USSR. Quite a few times, I have passed through Leningrad. *On a few occasions, I rested with a friend, a French writer, in the midst of a family of good people.* There, I learnt of the worries and joys of a real Russian proletarian who has for a long time fought misery in many of the ports of the world, in Hamburg, in New York, in Buenos Aires, in Marseille. Expelled from Russia in 1905, *because of the pogroms and the repression*, he had settled in France. He lived there for many years, getting just enough food on the table, by the work of his hands, for his seven children (I know six of them personally) and giving over his evenings to the Russian sailors' trade union. At the time of the intervention in Russia, the political activity he was engaged in brought about his expulsion from France with his whole family. He arrived in Petrograd in the middle of the winter of 1919 as a 'Bolshevik hostage' exchanged for French officers who had been arrested in Russia. *At the height of the famine and mortal danger, this old worker happily brought six of his children to the country of the Revolution.*

In Leningrad, he, in turn, set up *children's homes, was manager* of a large children's home installed in the *Hotel Europe*, and ran a laundry. Then, he was out of work for quite a while. For the last two years, he has been a worker at the Samoïlova clothes factory. He has over forty years of work experience. He is still full of energy and retains from his activist past an open and courageous way of expressing himself.

His name is Alexander Ivanovitch Russakov. He lives in Leningrad, 19 Jéliabov Street, KB/4.

I left his family on 30 December. I know it well. I have seen how they live. I knew about its little problems. I knew that a komsomolka who lived in the same building was *forcing him for months* to undergo trials and *denounced him as a criminal* to take from him a room – more exactly a corner in the passage, behind a bathroom – where he sleeps. I know that the housing crisis is serious in the USSR and that stories like this, *unfortunately*, are not infrequent. But in due course I am told about a revolting article that appeared in the Leningrad *Pravda* of 31 January under the title 'Just Like Kalganov' to do with this business. I get it translated word for word. *I meet here two French writers, Victor Serge and Pierre Pascal, who have lived in Russia for a long time and who know well the worker Russakov. I meet a doctor I have known for a long time, the Dr N— who has known Russakov for twenty years. We agree together that the Leningrad* Pravda *article is an act of immense moral aggression. I ask myself how such an act can occur in the second capital of the USSR. How is it that one can slander, hound and give up to the contempt and hostility of the population as a criminal and counter-revolutionary, an old revolutionary worker whose past and present are beyond reproach.* The *Pravda* article describes him as a kulak, nepman and counter-revolutionary! *Three* unacceptable and dangerous lies. *I did not know that it was possible to play with words in this way. The article also calls him a 'speculator'. Fourth lie. As the 'former owner of a hat workshop in France'. Fifth lie. As the persecutor of 'two Bessarabian young communists'. Sixth lie. To say nothing of the tone and conclusions of the author, who compares Russakov to a recently shot assassin.*

He and his family are accused of having knocked about a communist who entered his apartment. Unfortunately for those who fabricated this story, I know only too well those who are involved. *This incident began with acts of violence carried out against a young woman, moral and cultivated, the wife of my friend, who I know to be incapable of carrying out acts of violence against anyone. She was insulted, provoked and hit, in her home, by a person unknown to her who had entered from outside without permission. If the person who deliberately provoked this incident herself later suffered, should she not blame herself??*

If an old worker or his loved ones can, for a few moments, be made to lose control, who is to blame. All patience has its limits.

For months, the worker Russakov was the target of continual harassment by the komsomolka in question, who went so far as to denounce him to the criminal militia. In the four cases, brought one after the other against him, the tribunals ruled in his favour. [Here, the editors make me say exactly the opposite: 'The tribunals ruled against him!!!'] He addressed – *without any result* – *in person* the editorial board of the Leningrad *Pravda*, asking that an end be put to this petty persecution. *My friend Victor Serge warned in person two members of the communist cell (Jakt) in the building to whom he had already sent a few months ago a written complaint.* All these actions served no purpose. In fact; they went unanswered!

I am upset to find in one of the capitals of the revolution such behaviour. I am upset to see komsomols and communists behave in this way towards a worker. I am sad to see the press involved in so unspeakable a campaign against a worker. I ask for light to be shed on this affair. I demand a public reparation for the worker Russakov who has been slandered in public.

PS The scandal goes on. This article finished, I learn that Russakov was already, within twenty-four hours, expelled from the trade union that was to defend him, and thrown out of the factory, *which will condemn him to misery till the end of his days! Obviously, he is without any defence.* As an old worker, I demand for him a public reparation.

Moscow, 2 February 1929

As you can see they had not been shy of mutilating my article and even of making me say that 'the tribunals ruled *against* Russakov' when in fact my text said exactly the contrary. And this is not a typo – 'against' is a different word from 'for' even in Russian. Then, not withstanding the urgency, the seriousness of the matter and what they had promised me, my article handed in on the afternoon of the 2nd only appeared on the 5th and attributed to me an atrocity.

Even so, it shook things up. There was no precedent; two of the most important voices of the Party hurled at each other contradictory versions of a social drama. One ran with: 'Just Like Kalganov', the other answered with: 'The Russakov Affair'. And to whom is due this amazing achievement? A 'without party', a 'foreigner'!

One has to admit that the *Komsomolskaïa Pravda* softened their position by adding to my article *an editor's note* which demanded 'an investigation and clarity'. And the next day, they corrected the misleading error. They refused any concession on the deleted passages. From their point of view, Russakov could now die: I had obtained on his behalf everything that the Soviet media was able to do for a worker for whom any Tower could demand the death sentence in ten newspapers every day.

This I did not know. I still gave my all. I rushed everywhere in 35 degrees of cold, in a spring overcoat like one of these ninety-kopeks-a-day 'polit-immigrants', despite the *thirteen thousand roubles* in royalties paid to me over fifteen months that I had freely spent in my usual way.

In my rush through editorial offices to save the life of a man and the livelihood and reputation of two families, I will never forget the interview with the famous Communist journalist Koltsov.[49] We were on very friendly terms. He welcomes us, Victor Serge and me, in his office at the *Ogoniok*. We outline the case to him. He listens to us calm, friendly and slightly blasé, since he is the man who knows all there is to know about these things.

On my plea that he acts fast and with all his authority, he says: 'Fine, but to do that I need to study the case in detail, assess the documents . . . One week, fifteen days will go by.'

'But,' I answer, 'in Leningrad the factory "motions" and the workers' meetings of the housing committee are asking for Russakov to be shot without trial.

49 The most famous Soviet journalist of his time, Mikhail Koltsov later travelled to Spain to report on the Spanish Civil War, while also working for the Soviet Secret Police (NKVD). He knew Ernest Hemingway who used him as a model for Karkov in *For Whom the Bell Tolls*. In 1937, Koltsov published an article criticising some aspects of Stalin's endless purges. Arrested in January 1940, Koltsov was shot on 2 February.

'Without trial he won't be shot. But he can be shot after a trial. What can we do?' And showing me a stack of files on his desk: 'Look at what awaits me, just *this morning's arrivals.*'

There are around fifty. Victor Serge has a look at five or six and comes upon *two suicides because of bureaucratic persecution.*

In most of our households, Koltsov says, housewives scald each other with boiling water. Some are the wives of former people's commissioners.

Well, I thought: nice, your dictatorship.

Claude McKay
&
Langston Hughes

The visits of **Claude McKay** (1889–1948) and **Langston Hughes** (1902–67) to the Soviet Union were landmarks in their lives – the visits feature prominently in their respective autobiographies, *A Long Way from Home* and *I Wonder as I Wander*. Encouraged by Lenin's view[50] that the struggle against racial oppression was central to the revolutionary process in America, both went to Soviet Russia with high hopes – it was a promised land for African Americans, to be favourably compared with the slavery and segregation of the USA. However, both writers made it very clear to their Russian hosts that they were visiting Russia as individuals and not as 'token' Black Americans. Neither writer joined the American Communist Party: both thought that Party membership would limit their intellectual freedom.

Although McKay's visit (1922–3) was much earlier than Hughes's (1932–3), his assessment was the more critical. McKay was thrilled at the welcome he was given: 'Never in my life did I feel prouder of being an African, a black, and no mistake about it. Unforgettable, that first occasion upon which I was physically uplifted. I had not yet seen it done to anybody, nor did I know it was a Russian custom . . . ' (*A Long Way from Home*, London, 1985, page 168)

But he still refused the role of spokesman for Black Americans his hosts were keen to cast him in. Later on, in 1930s, events in the Soviet Union made a deep impression on McKay. He rejected the views of those intellectuals who argued that 'as Russia is a proletarian state we should suspend criticism of its mistakes and criticise only the fascist-dictatorship manoeuvres which menace the social progress of the

50 See his speech on 'The Negro Question' given to the Second Congress of the Third Communist International, 1920.

world.' This was not a position McKay could share; he was 'against all dictatorships, whether they are social or intellectual. I believe in the social revolution and the triumph of workers' democracy not workers' dictatorships.' His ideas on the need not to subsume race oppression into class oppression found little resonance during his lifetime. They were rediscovered and reclaimed by the Black Power movements of the late 1960s and early 1970s.

A leading member of the Harlem Renaissance, Langston Hughes sailed in 1932 to Russia with twenty-two other black actors and activists to make a film, *Black and White*, that would portray the oppression of African Americans in the American South and show, in contrast, the Soviet Union as the champion of the oppressed and coloured people of the world. Whilst Hughes and his comrades were in Moscow, there was a rapprochement between the USA and the USSR: part of the deal was that the USSR would cease its propaganda among American blacks. The film project was immediately cancelled and the cast sent home. Hughes, who was in the unusual position of having roubles earned from the royalties of his book sales in the Soviet Union, remained in Moscow and in September 1932 travelled to Central Asia – the cities he visited included Tashkent, Samarkand and Bukhara. In Ashkhabad, Hughes came across Arthur Koestler who was touring Central Asia at the invitation of the Comintern. Koestler describes this tour in *The Invisible Writing*, the second volume of his autobiography. At that time Koestler was a much more committed Communist than Hughes; he writes: 'Hughes at that time was deeply sympathetic towards the Soviet regime, but as far as I remember not a Party member. He was a poet with a purely humanitarian approach to politics – in fact, an innocent abroad.'

Once back in the US, Hughes wrote extensively about his time spent in Central Asia: he wrote magazine articles, the short book *A Negro Looks at Central Asia* and *I Wonder as I Wander*, written in 1956. With hindsight, it is easy to see that Hughes's writing on the ethnic minorities in Central Asia is too uncritical, since it was written at a time when there was already great hardship and racial oppression in the Soviet Union. But for Hughes (and McKay), the comparison was with the condition of Black people in the American South and by those standards they saw progress in the Soviet Union.

The Pride and Pomp of Proletarian Power

from *A Long Way From Home* by Claude McKay

The Bolshoi Theatre in Moscow presented a pageantry of simple proletarian pride and power on the night of the opening of the Congress of the Communist International. The absence of the primitive appeal of gilded pomp made the manifestation even more sublime and awe-inspiring.

I had received a pass to attend the great opening of the Congress. When I succeeded in getting into the vast Bolshoi auditorium, Martin Anderson Nexö, the author of *Pelle, the Conqueror,* waved to me to come and sit beside him. He was seated in the centre front of the hall. But an usher grabbed me, and before I could realise where I was going, I was being handed from usher to usher like an object that was consigned to a special place. At first I thought I was going to be conducted to the balcony, but instead I was ushered on to the platform to a seat beside Max Eastman and just behind Zinoviev. It seems as if the curious interest the crowd focused upon me had prompted Zinoviev to hoist me up there on the platform.

Zinoviev asked me to speak and I refused. Max Eastman pleaded: 'Do speak! See how the people are looking at you; they want to hear you.' I said that if they had given me notice beforehand I might have prepared a few phrases, although speaking was not my speciality. But I wouldn't stand up before the Bolshevik élite and that vast eager crowd without having something prepared to say. Eastman said: 'Just tell them you bring greetings from the Negro workers of America.'

'But,' said I, 'I have no mandate from any American Negro workers to say that. There is an official mulatto delegate; perhaps he has a message from the Negro workers.'

I said to Eastman, 'Why don't you speak?' He said he would like to if they would ask him. Certainly the American Communists had in Max Eastman the finest platform personality to present. Unlike me, he was as pure a Marxist as any of them there and had given the best of his intellect to serve the cause of Communism and extol the Soviets in

America. But because of petty jealousy they cold-shouldered Eastman in Moscow. Perhaps if they had been a little diplomatic about him, he probably would be one of them instead of a Trotskyist today.

I told Zinoviev that I came to Russia as a writer and not as an agitator. When his messenger interpreted what I said, Zinoviev's preacher face turned mean. He was most angry. But I did not mind. My personal triumph had made me aware that the Russians wanted a typical Negro at the Congress as much as I wanted to attend the Congress. The mulatto delegate was a washout. He was too yellow. I had mobilised my African features and won the masses of the people. The Bolshevik leaders, to satisfy the desires of the people, were using me for entertainment. So why should I worry about Zinoviev's frown? Even though he was president of the great Third International, I knew that there was no special gift I could get from Zinoviev after the entertainment was over and ended. I could never be a radical agitator. For that I was temperamentally unfit. And I could never be a disciplined member of any Communist party, for I was born to be a poet.

And now I was demanded everywhere. Sometimes I had to participate in three different meetings in one day: factory meetings, meetings of soviets, youth meetings, educational conferences in colleges and schools, the meetings of poets and writers, and theatrical performances. I was introduced to interesting sections of the new social and cultural life of Moscow and Petrograd.

I was always asked to speak, and so I prepared a few phrases. The Russians adore long speeches, which it did not interest me to make. And so they lengthened mine by asking a lot of questions. I had listened to the American delegates deliberately telling lies about conditions in America, and I was disgusted. Not only the Communist delegates, but radical American intellectuals really thought it was right to buoy up the Russians with false pictures of the American situation. All the speeches of the American delegates, the tall rhetoric, the purple phrases, conveyed fundamentally a common message, thus: 'Greetings from America. The workers of America are groaning under the capitalist terror. The revolutionary organisations have been driven underground. But the American Communist Party is secretly organising the masses. In a few years we will overthrow American capitalism and join our forces with the Russian Communists. Long live the Revolution . . . ' I heard the chairman of the American delegation say: 'In five years we will have the American revolution.'

The Russians from these speeches pictured the workers of America as denied the right to organise and the rights of free assembly and free speech, as denied representation in Congress, as ridden down by American cossacks, banished in droves from their homes to the Siberias of the Far West, with their imprisoned and exiled leaders escaping to Canada and Mexico and working underground to over-throw the capitalist system. Briefly, the American situation, as they understood it, was similar to that of Russia under the Tsarist regime just before the Revolution.

The police raid on the illegal Communist Party meeting in the beautiful woods of Michigan had been spread all over the Russian newspapers. Everything about that funny raid was so Tsarist-Russian-like that the Russians really believed that it was typical of American conditions.

Truly, I could not speak such lies. I knew that the American workers in 1922 were generally better off than at the beginning of the World War in 1914. I was aware, of course, that labour organisation in this country was far below the standard of labour organisation in England, Germany and France, that American labour was not organised as a political weapon, that in some sections of the country and in certain industries labour was even denied the right to organise, and that radicals were always baited. But Leavenworth was not Siberia. And by no stretch of the imagination could the United States be compared to Tsarist Russia.

How, then, could I stand before the gigantic achievement of the Russian Revolution and lie? What right had I to tell these people, who had gone through a long death struggle to conquer their country for themselves, that the American revolution was also in travail? What could *I* presume to tell them? I told them that it was a great honour for me to be there to behold the triumph of their great revolution. I told them that I felt very insignificant and dumb before that wonderful thing. I said that I had come to Russia to learn something, to see with my own eyes and try to write a little of what I had seen.

Invariably I was questioned: 'And what about the American revolution?' When I replied I thought it was a long way off, the audiences did not like me to say that. I must admit that the Russians in those days were eager to be deceived. I remember that I was asked to attend a large and important meeting of Young Communists. When I had finished talking the president got up and said: 'Comrade, we appreciate what you feel about our revolution, but we want you to tell us about the American revolution. When will there be the American revolution?'

It was a direct question and I answered directly. I said that I could not prophesy about an American revolution; but that perhaps if the American ruling class started a wholesale suppression of labour organisations, if the people had to read radical literature in secret, if the radicals had to hold all their meetings in secret, if the liberals and radicals who agitated for more civil liberties and the rights of the working class were deported to the Philippines, then possibly in ten or fifteen years America might develop a situation similar to that in Russia in 1905.

The interpreter, a comrade commander in the navy, asked if he should translate me literally. I said, 'Word for word.' And when he had finished there was no sound of applause. That was the first time that I was not applauded when I spoke, but I preferred that.

The young president of the Young Communists took the platform: 'Comrade,' he said, 'you are a defeatist. The American revolution cannot be so far away. But if that is your opinion, we command you at once to do your part and help make the revolution.' I said to the interpreter: 'Tell the young comrade that I am a poet.'

After the meeting my friend Comrade Venko said to me: 'You should have told them the American revolution is right around the corner. That's what they want to hear.' (He had lived many years in England and had acquired some Anglicisms.) I said, 'You know I read somewhere that Lenin said that it is necessary to face facts and tell the truth always.'

'Yes, comrade,' said Venko, 'but Lenin is Lenin and we are just ordinary mortals.'

Yet in spite of my obstinacy I was still everywhere demanded. When the American Negro delegate was invited to attend meetings and my mulatto colleague went, the people asked: 'But where is the *chorny* (the black)?'

The mulatto delegate told me: 'Say, fellow, you're all right for propaganda. It's a pity you'll never make a disciplined Party member.'

'Bigger shots than you have said the same thing,' I replied. Zinoviev had referred to me as a non-partisan. 'My destiny is to travel a different road.'

We were sitting in on the discussions as to whether there should be an illegal or legal Communist Party in America, and on the Negro in American life. I was there not only as a writer, but I was given the privileges of a special delegate. One thing sticks in my memory about that American delegation in Moscow. It had the full support of the Finnish Federation and the Russian Federation of America. The representatives of these organisations voted *en bloc*, rallying to the support of an illegal party. The argument of the Yankee representatives of the legal group was unanswerable, but they were outvoted every time by the foreign federations. The Finnish and the Russian federations were not only the most highly organised units of the American party, but, so I was informed, they contributed more than any other to the party chest. They controlled because they had the proper organisation and the cash.

I said to the mulatto delegate: 'That's what Negroes need in American politics – a highly organised all-Negro group. When you have that – a Negro group voting together like these Finns and Russians – you will be getting somewhere. We may feel inflated as *individual* Negroes sitting in on the councils of the whites, but it means very little if our people are not organised. Otherwise the whites will want to tell us what is right for our people even against our better thinking. The Republicans and the Democrats do the same thing. They give a few plum places to leading Negroes as representatives of the race and our people applaud vicariously. But we remain politically unorganised. What we need is our own group, organised and officered entirely by Negroes, something similar to the Finnish Federation. Then when you have your own group, your own voting strength, you can make demands on the whites; they will have more respect for your united strength than for your potential strength. Every other racial group in America is organised as a group, except Negroes. I am not an organiser or an agitator, but I can see what is lacking in the Negro group.'

I listened to James Cannon's fighting speeches for a legal Communist Party in America. Cannon's manner was different from Bill Haywood's or Foster's. He had all the magnetism, the shrewdness, the punch, the bag of tricks of the typical American politician, but here he used them in a radical way. I wondered about him. If he had entered Democratic or Republican politics, there was no barrier I could see that could stop him from punching his way straight through to the front ranks.

I think Trotsky was the first of the big Russians to be convinced that there should be a legal Communist Party in America, then Rakovsky and finally Zinoviev, a little reluctantly. Bukharin was for the illegal group. He said: 'Remember what Jack London has told us about the terror and secret organisation in America in his *Iron Heel*.' That was so rare that I had to smile. While Cannon was informing the Russians about actual conditions in America, Bukharin was visualising the America of Jack London's *Iron Heel*. Bukharin always did make me think of that line about some men having greatness thrust upon them. I believe that Lenin said of Bukharin, as Frank Harris said of H. G. Wells, that he could not think. Yet Bukharin was the author of *The A B C of Communism*, which once had a big vogue among the radicals.

At last even I was asked my opinion of an illegal Communist Party in America. I tried to get excused, saying that as I was not an official delegate or a politician, but merely a poet, I didn't think my opinion was worth while. But as my colleague the mulatto was for the illegal party, I suppose they needed a foil. So then I said that although I had no experience of the actual conditions of social life in Tsarist Russia, I believed there was no comparison between them and American conditions today. There were certain democratic privileges such as a limited freedom of the press and a limited right of free speech that our governing classes had had to concede because they were the necessary ingredients of their own system of society. And American radicals could generally carry on open propaganda under those democratic privileges. Our Upton Sinclairs, Eugene Debses, Max Eastmans and Mother Joneses might be prosecuted and imprisoned for a specific offence against the law, but they were not banished for their radical ideas to an American Siberia. And I said I thought that the only place where illegal and secret radical propaganda was necessary was among the Negroes of the South.

What I said about the Negroes of the South was more important than I imagined, and precipitated the Negro Question. The Negro Question came under the division of the Eastern Bureau, of which Sen Katayama was an active official. Because of his American experience and his education among Negroes, Sen Katayama was important as a kind of arbiter between black and white on the Negro Question. It was an unforgettable experience to watch Katayama in conference. He was like a little brown bulldog with his jaws clamped on an object that he wouldn't let go. He apparently forgot all about nice human relationships in conference. Sen Katayama had no regard for the feelings of the white American comrades, when the Negro Question came up, and boldly told them so. He said that though they called themselves Communists, many of them were unconsciously prejudiced against Negroes because of their background. He told them that really to understand Negroes they needed to be educated about and among Negroes as he had been.

Think not that it was just a revolutionary picnic and love feast in Moscow in the fifth year of Lenin! One of the American delegates was a southerner or of southern extraction. An important Bolshevik facetiously suggested to him that to untangle the Negro problem, black and white should intermarry. 'Good God!' said the American, 'if Jesus Christ came down from Heaven and said that in the South, he would be lynched.' The Bolshevik said: 'Jesus Christ wouldn't dare, but Lenin would.'

Also I remember Walton Newbold, who was the first Communist candidate elected to the British House of Commons. Saklatvala, the Indian Parsee, had announced himself a Communist only after he had been elected as an independent, but Walton Newbold was the first candidate of the British Communist Party. Just after his election to Parliament, Newbold came to Moscow, while the Fourth Congress of International Communism was in session. For any reader who might not understand why a Communist member of the British Parliament should go to Moscow, I may explain that by the parallel of a cardinal going to Rome after receiving his hat. It was a big day for the little insignificant delegation of British Communists when Newbold arrived in Moscow. Of that triumphant arrival, one incident sticks more in my memory. I was informed that a member of the Chinese Young Communists, who was attending the Congress, met Newbold in the lobby of the Lux Hotel. He went up to Comrade Newbold to congratulate him and began: 'Comrade Newbold – '

'Hello, Chink,' Newbold cut in.

'But Comrade Newbold, I am not a Chink.'

'Who told you that you weren't?' said Comrade Newbold as he turned away.

In a little while the incident had flashed like an arrow through Communist circles in Moscow. The young Chinese was a member of an old Chinese clan and had been educated in America. At that time Bolshevik eyes were fixed on China. Chinese soldiers made up some of the crack units of the Red Army when Great Britain was supporting the White war against the Reds and tightening the blockade against Russia. I remember Radek's saying to me: 'We are pinning our hopes on China more than any other country. If we can make China Red, we will conquer the world.'

I don't know if that incident of the young Chinese and the first Communist member of the British Parliament ever reached the ears of the big Bolsheviks. I do know, however – I got it from a good source – that the big Bolsheviks gave Newbold a hell of a skating over the Communist ice of Moscow. Newbold returned to the Parliament of British gentlemen and finally drifted over to the capitalist side.

I was asked to write a series of articles on the Negro group for *Izvestia*, the Moscow organ of the Soviets. Thus I came to meet Steklov, the editor-in-chief. Steklov was a huge man with a leonine head, more picturesque than intelligent. He told me that he was interested in Negroes being won over to the cause of Communism because they were a young and fresh people and ought to make splendid soldiers. I didn't relish that remark out of the mouth of a Communist. So many other whites had said the same thing – that Negroes made good cannon fodder when they were properly led – led by whites to the black slaughter. That filled me with resentment. The head of the French General Staff had proclaimed to the world the same thing, that France with its African empire had an army of a hundred million. When Trotsky, the chief of all the Bolshevik fighting forces, talked to me about Negroes he spoke wisely. Trotsky was human and universal in his outlook. He thought of Negroes as people like any other people who were unfortunately behind in the march of civilisation.

Karl Radek was one of the Big Five of the Politbureau, which decided Bolshevik policy in those days. He invited me to dinner at his apartment in the Kremlin along with the Negro delegate of the American CP. Radek wanted to know if I had a practical policy for the organisation of American Negroes. I said that I had no policy other than the suggestion of a Negro *Bund*, that I was not an organiser or an agitator and could not undertake or guarantee any practical work of organisation.

The Negro delegate said that I was a poet and a romantic. I said I was not as romantic as he and his illegal party with their secret names and their convention in the wilds of Michigan. Radek laughed, and as I looked at his face set in a thick circle of hair I thought how much he resembled a red spider. Radek said that the Communists should adopt a friendly attitude to all writers who were in sympathy with the Soviets. For example, Upton Sinclair, he thought, would be a valuable asset to the revolution if the Communists knew how to handle and use him. The mulatto said that Upton Sinclair was a bourgeois Socialist.

'Oh, no, no,' said Radek, 'I insist that is not the attitude to take. Upton Sinclair is a powerful writer with an enormous influence, and the American Communists should make use of his influence, even though Sinclair is not a Communist. Now with our Gorky – ' At this point an infant wailed and Radek said, 'My baby comes first.' He left the room, to return a few minutes later with the maid, who brought in the baby. Radek and Mrs Radek kissed and fondled the child. The maid then brought the child to the mulatto, who touched its hand and patted its hair. From the mulatto she brought the child to me, but it shrank away, hid its face, and began to cry. Radek was interested and told the maid to take the child to the mulatto again. The mulatto took the child in his arms and it stopped crying, but when the maid tried me again, the child hid its face and cried. The maid retired with the child, and Radek said: 'Now I understand the heart of the difference between white and black in America. It is fear. The Americans are like children, afraid of black complexion, and that is why they lynch and burn the Negro.' I told Radek that his deduction was wrong; that in the South, where Negroes were lynched and burned, the black complexion was not a strange thing to the whites, and that the majority of the children of the better classes of the South were nursed from their birth by black women, and that those children were extremely fond of their black foster mothers. Radek said that that was a strange thing.

Turkmenian Flamenco

from *I Wonder as I Wander* by Langston Hughes

Arthur Koestler asked me one day why in Moscow I did not join the Communist Party. I told him that what I had heard concerning the Party indicated that it was based on strict discipline and the acceptance of directives that I, as a writer, did not wish to accept. I did not believe political directives could be successfully applied to creative writing. They might well apply to the preparation of tracts and pamphlets, yes, but not to poetry or fiction, which to be valid, I felt, had to express as truthfully as possible the *individual* emotions and reactions of the writer, rather than mass directives issued to achieve practical and often temporary political objectives. Koestler agreed with me that it was very difficult to write both politically and individually at the same time, especially when the political lines were applied from above by bureaucrats who had no appreciation of creative impulses. But he said that, at certain historical periods, collective social aims might be worthy of transcending individual desires. However, Koestler did not press the point nor try to change my position.

In Turkmenistan, outside of official conferences and statistical sessions, Communism was hardly mentioned. I don't believe I ever heard Yeah Man say the word *communism*, although I am sure he was a loyal Red Army officer who enjoyed the achievements of the Revolution. In Moscow, where we twenty-two Negroes had been hailed so widely and where propaganda relative to the Negro's hard lot in America was played up, almost everyone took for granted that all Negroes were, or eventually would be Communist Party members, so it was seldom discussed with us there either. But good Muscovite Party members were usually amazed when they found out that only one of our number claimed Party membership.

Once I gave as my reason for not joining the Party the fact that jazz was officially taboo in Russia, being played only at the déclassé Metropol Hotel, and very badly there.

'But jazz is decadent bourgeois music,' I was told, for that is what the Soviet press had hammered into Russian heads.

'It's my music,' I said, 'and I wouldn't give up jazz for a world revolution.'

The Russians looked at me as if I were a decadent bourgeois writer and let it go at that. But they liked my jazz records as much as I did, and never left the room when I played them.

While I was in Moscow my third book of poems, *The Dream Keeper*, was published in the United States. When copies reached me, I gave one to Ivy Litvinoff, the cultivated Englishwoman who was most gracious to members of our movie group, and whose husband later became Soviet Ambassador to Washington. Mrs Litvinoff said that she liked my poems, all save those in the religious group. When I informed her that they were based on the old folk forms of the spirituals, she said that such poems had no place in the class struggle and were not worthy of a Party member. When I told her I was not a Party member, she asked why, and I gave her the same reasons I gave Koestler. She said gently that she felt I should be a Party member, that the Party needed me. But, oddly enough, I heard later that she herself was not a Communist, although her husband stood high in Party councils. At any rate, Ivy Litvinoff was not dogmatic, and did not run my spirituals through so harsh a wringer as some of the American Communists did.

The party given for our Writers Brigade on the Kolhoz Aitakov had nothing to do with the Communist Party, so far as I could tell.

The Kolhoz had only ten Communist Party members. There were forty or fifty men at least at our party, and that many more milling around outside after the room was filled. I supposed only eight of the ten Communists were there, since two members on the farm were women, and there were no women present that evening. Turkoman women did not share the social life of the men.

After supper the party folks started arriving, mostly on foot, but some galloping up on stunted Asiatic ponies, and some riding high on camels. Most of the Turkomans were big fellows, and their tall shaggy Karacul hats made them look enormous. In soft boots and padded robes and baggy trousers, that night they looked to me for all the world like figures out of Omar Khayyám's poems or the *Arabian Nights*. There were fierce old fellows with black moustaches, stout pincushion farmers in two or three padded gowns, Mongol-like youths with slanted eyes, and paler lads who looked like Persian figures on old vases or drawings on parchment scrolls. A couple of shepherd boys came garbed exactly as if they had stepped out of the Book of Moses. Their black Karacul hats alone saved them being Sunday-school characters of my Protestant youth, perhaps bearing the Lamb of God.

Balls of melons hung from the rafters in groups like yellow balloons and gave the room a sweet smell. But as the place filled up, clouds of smoke from the odd-smelling mahorka tobacco, which the men smoked wrapped in newspaper cones, gave off a ranker olfactory atmosphere, mixed with the scent of sheepskin and camelskin and sand and padded robes. Windows and doors were tightly closed for after sundown it got cold outside. Everyone sat on well-worn but beautiful old Bokhara rugs that Park Avenue might envy, drinking tea from bowls that went from mouth to mouth, around and around in the customary ritual. Koestler got away off on the edge of the crowd so that he would not be in the main circle of tea-bowl passing, and thus could avoid drinking from bowls that dozens of strange moustaches had touched. I had given up on this problem weeks before, so I sat in the middle and drank from everybody's bowl. But fortunately Kikilov with his cough went to squat beside Koestler and share his bowl.

The men all sat on the floor. There was very little walking around, and no cocktails, wine or hard liquors, just tea. Although I didn't understand a word of anything, I observed that as the tea bowls went around and around, the party was becoming more lively. Groups of men began laughing and joking together, and others shouted over a forest of heads to friends across the room. In all this hubbub, it was impossible to get from Kikilov via Koestler any accurate idea of what anyone might be saying, so I gave up trying, and started talking in English plus signs to those around me, which amused them no end. I would say to a fellow who handed me a tea bowl, 'Man, why didn't you bring your girlfriend?' And outline with my hands the shape of a woman. Whereupon, he would answer God only knows what, but I would laugh, and everybody would laugh. Somebody would roll me a mahorka cone, and around would come another tea bowl. The next day when I ran into some of these fellows digging irrigation ditches, they greeted me like an old buddy. We had made friends.

There was a roaring fire outside on the ground and over it hung a copper pot big enough to hold a giant genie. It was full of boiling water from which the smaller teapots were continually replenished. There seemed to be a party going on in the yard, too. It was alive with shadow shapes in the chilly night. After a while some fellows arrived with long-necked two-string lutes and a shout went up. These were the *bakhshis*, favoured singers of the region, who had come from another oasis to entertain us. And in a few minutes they had my hair standing on my head. Spanish gypsy music at its wildest never surpassed theirs.

Twang went one of the shaggy-hatted men on his lute, then sang softly in a semi-recitative a few short phrases, whereupon he threw back his head and, without warning, uttered one of the loudest, longest, most spine-chilling cries I ever heard. This was followed by a song that must have been about the end of time, for surely nothing else could inspire such a wail or such a song. Succeeding verses were interspersed with lesser wails from time to time as someone else in the crowd would utter a similar musical howl. I never heard madder music anywhere, utterly weird and blood-curdling, a kind of cross between the Chinese scale at its strangest and gypsy flamenco at its wildest. To start a song the leader might make an odd clucking sound in his throat a few times, pluck a string, rock, hum, cluck again, then finally in a high monotone, begin a line. Sometimes two men sang together, sometimes they took turns, sometimes one or two fellows sitting cross-legged facing each other on the floor contributed a verse or punctuated a song with a single long cry. But most of the singing was solo, with high drawn-out ear-splitting wails to accentuate the interlude.

I could have listened all night to this singing, but in due time food arrived, and the music gave over to feasting. Just before the food was brought in, a number of men left. Perhaps they had not contributed to the feast, or maybe there was not enough to go around.

We had not had much to eat on that farm all day, mostly camel stew and melon. But now in our honour, tonight they had slaughtered a sheep and made piles of hot unleavened bread in flat round discs. I was hungry, so when two men brought in a huge copper drum filled with steaming mutton swimming in juice, I was happy. Another kettle followed of the same fare, and in two groups we gathered around them on the floor. Pleasant heat and a fine aroma arose from the pots, into each a single large wooden spoon was dipped, filled with broth, and offered to Koestler and me first, then a spoonful each to Kolya and Kikilov. This was the first course, each man taking his turn at a spoonful of soup right out of the kettles. There were fifteen or twenty men and only two spoons. Turkoman hospitality, even to spoons, is based on sharing.

By now the food kettles had cooled enough for our hosts to reach in with bare fingers and pick up chunks of meat and tear them into smaller bits which they dropped back into the soup. This was so that we might more easily dine from these common bowls without having to pull the meat apart ourselves. Politely, the Turkomans motioned for Koestler and me to help ourselves, so we put our hands into the warm liquid and fished around until we found a nice piece of mutton, pulled it out and ate it. Then everyone else dived in, too, and some-times there were several hands in a pot at once until all of that sheep was gone. Then we soaked the bread in the juice until the juice was gone, too. Full and happy, about three o'clock in the morning, I rolled up in a rug and went to sleep.

Viktor Ardov

Writer of film scripts and short stories, **Viktor Ardov** (1900–76) published his first prose collection in 1921. A regular contributor to the satirical magazine *Krokodil*, Ardov wrote with dark humour about the problems of censorship and the pitfalls of communal living. In 1933, he married the well-known actress Nina Antonovna Olshanskaya and their Moscow home, 17 Bolshaya Ordynka, became a meeting place for many stars of Russian culture including Bulgakov, Zoshchenko, Pasternak, Shostakovich, Brodsky and Solzhenitsyn. Viktor and Nina were close friends with Anna Akhmatova. In 1941, *The Shining Path*, a film for which Arlov wrote the script, won the Stalin Prize presented by Stalin himself. Arlov used the fact that Stalin viewed his work favourably to try to protect Akhmatova; between 1934 and 1966 she stayed for long periods in the Moscow apartment. It was here that, in May 1956, she met by accident her son Lev Gumilev who was visiting the Arlovs after fourteen years in labour camps; he had no idea his mother was there. In fact, 17 Bolshaya Ordynka is known as the Akhmatova House. The sculpture outside the Akhmatova House is based on a drawing by Modigliani, who was also her lover.

The Bloodthirsty Profession

by Viktor Ardov (translated by Grigori Gerenstein)

A shy young man entered the office, politely wiped his feet on the doormat, jerked his shoulders to adjust his jacket, and gave a delicate cough.

The denizen of the office, who sat at a wardrobe-like desk, raised his head and looked at the young man.

'Oh, it's you. Good. I've got some work for you . . . Take a seat . . . I'll show you. I've got it written down somewhere. Here we are.

Look, my dear fellow, when are you going to bump off this Professor Mokin?'

'As soon as he finishes his invention. I've got people following him. As soon as he writes it all down we'll . . . '

'But you can't. It's too early, my dear boy. Let us see his machine in action first. Then we'll be perfectly justified in finishing him off. Not before.'

'Well, perhaps you're right. We can wait.'

'Definitely! Another thing, it would be a good idea if Zherebtsov broke a leg. You know, your province is full of pot-holes, ditches – it shouldn't be difficult. Will you organise for him to break a leg?'

'Yes, sir. We can do it.'

'Now it would help if that woman – what's her name? – Prilipaeva – also died. Only quietly, without fuss, without causing suspicion, if you see what I mean.'

'Oh yes, of course!'

'See to it, will you? Now, what are we going to do with Uprelov's money? The only way I can see is to burgle him. Yes, the simplest way to get hold of his money is to burgle him. Can you do that?'

'I don't see why not. We can burgle him. He shares a flat with some old crone. I'll send a couple of boys. Should be easy.'

'That's that then. Now, Katushkevich. You know what? I think the best way to get rid of him is to infect him with some disease. Cholera, for instance, or malignant anthrax.'

'May I object, sir, if you don't mind? Cholera or anthrax won't do. If we had to organise an epidemic, cholera would be perfect, but for one person typhoid fever is best. Especially spotted. The fever, I mean . . . '

'All right, let it be typhoid fever. It's all the same to me. Just make sure you don't forget. Find a couple of bacilli and all that. So, that's Katushkevich. Now, Karasuke. Shall we poison him? Yes, I think we'll poison him. Put some cyanide in his food, or maybe rotten fish will do the trick.'

'Sure. We'll slip him a rotten sturgeon in the canteen.'

'Lovely. Well, keep me posted, dear boy. I expect a report from you next week. Incidentally, let Utyatin die as well. To hell with him. One more, one less doesn't make much difference, but I'll feel much safer without him. That's all for now. See you.'

There is no reason for the reader to be terrified by the viciousness and cynicism of the above conference. I swear it's not the conspiracy of a criminal gang but only . . . corrections to a film script.

Striving after Friendship

by Viktor Ardov (translated by Grigori Gerenstein)

It transpired that the empty room had been given to a professor. The inhabitants of the communal flat were flattered by the rank of their new neighbour, although nobody knew him personally.

On the morning the professor moved in, the front door opened unusually wide to let through a rampant mattress, and behind it the professor's wife, anxious, her hat askew, her arms loaded with bundles. Klavdia Nikiforovna, who lived in the last room down the corridor, stood in the entrance hall offering her smile by way of welcome.

'At long last!' Klavdia Nikiforovna said. 'I simply couldn't wait. I thought, at least there'll be other intellectuals in the flat.' Lowering her voice, she added, 'Without you I've been literally suffocating here . . . such a rough lot . . . all workers. Greetings to the professor.'

In half an hour, Klavdia Nikiforovna put her head through the professor's door. The head turned, inspecting everything, and whispered, 'One more thing: don't trust the Katins. Their room is the first off the entrance hall. He drinks and she has a lover and a temper.'

In the evening, when the professor and his wife sat in their already tidied room, something rustled in the keyhole and in five seconds their door opened slightly. Again Klavdia Nikiforovna put her head through the door.

'I see your kettle's been boiling. Come and have tea with me. You're welcome, without ceremony, as neighbours and intellectuals.'

The professor declined politely, pleading fatigue.

In the morning the professor's wife noticed the disappearance of a basket she had left in the corridor. The basket turned up on the back stairs, considerably misshapen.

'I put it there,' Klavdia Nikiforovna said drily. 'You refuse me friendship, turn up your nose at my tea . . . In general you seem to have an inflated idea of yourself as a professor. So you've no right to clutter up the corridor!'

During the next three days Klavdia Nikiforovna tried to do mischief to her new neighbours. She put water in their paraffin, hid their crockery, stole their mail, dirtied their furniture and used many other similar devices to avenge her rejected friendship. On the fourth day, quite unexpectedly, Klavdia Nikiforovna's head once again appeared in the professor's room.

'Why is your kettle taking so long to boil? Maybe there's water in your paraffin? You can come and have tea with me. It isn't proper that we intellectuals should be complete strangers. I feel ashamed before people.'

Once again the invitation was declined. Klavdia Nikiforovna at once resumed hostilities with a view to offering peace in a week.

The third stage of the struggle for friendship took a somewhat less intense course. Klavdia Nikiforovna molested the professor lazily, without fancy, as if from habit.

Once, right in the middle of this agony of hostility, the professor had a party. The sight of the jolly guests, their cheerful voices, the bustle of the hosts aroused envy in the entire block of flats.

There was a sharp knock on the professor's door.

'Citizens! It's pretty selfish of you,' they heard Klavdia Nikiforovna's voice. 'It's pretty boorish of you to leave your galoshes in the corridor to make puddles for us!'

After five minutes the knock and the shout were repeated. The guests lapsed into an awkward silence.

The professor's wife went to the kitchen. Trying to contain herself she said to Klavdia Nikiforovna, 'What do you want from us?'

Klavdia Nikiforovna picked up the professor's boiling kettle and emptied it into the sink.

Trembling, the professor's wife repeated, 'What do you want from us?'

'I want to be friends with you. Invite me to your party,' Klavdia Nikiforovna said calmly, and stretched her hand towards the tray carrying the professor's plates.

'Never!'

Without haste Klavdia Nikiforovna chose a cup and threw it to the floor.

'My God . . . What is this? Never!'

Klavdia Nikiforovna lifted a pile of saucers from the tray.

The professor's wife pressed her fingers to her temples. She could hear the renewed conversation in her room. A row would be too loud and it would embarrass her before her guests.

'All right,' the professor's wife said. 'I give in. Will you come to my party?'

Klavdia Nikiforovna gave her a contemptuous look and, slowly and neatly, put the saucers back on the tray.

'In a minute,' she said cheerfully. 'I'll just change into something more dressy. After all, you've got a lot of intellectual strangers in there.'

In twenty minutes she knocked, this time quietly and delicately, and entered the professor's room, freshly powdered and wearing a lace collar.

'May I introduce,' the professor's wife said, closing her eyes and firmly pressing her hands together, 'our neighbour.'

Klavdia Nikiforovna smiled, demonstrating her gold tooth.

'Oh, so many people! I won't shake hands individually. I'll just say a general how-do-you-do.'

Walter Benjamin

Walter Benjamin (1892–1940) was one of the great philosophers and cultural critics of the twentieth century. A committed Marxist, Benjamin went to Russia in the winter of 1926/7. He went at a time of *relative* prosperity in Moscow, when the benefits of the NEP (New Economic Policy) were beginning to be felt – there was food to be bought and fuel available for heating. In his essay 'Moscow' Benjamin imbibes the city as he walks through it. One feels that he is being as sympathetic as possible to the Revolution while at the same time knowing that it was not a process that he could wholly identify with. It was because he saw so clearly the discipline the Party demanded of intellectuals that Benjamin could not join. The time when those who held different points of view could debate in print and in public was coming to an end.

> Today it is official doctrine that subject matter, not form, decides the revolutionary or counter-revolutionary attitude of a work. Such doctrines cut the ground from under the writer's feet just as irrevocably as the economy has done on the economic plane . . . In Russia the process is complete: the intellectual is above all a functionary, working in the departments of censorship, justice, finance, and, if he survives, participating in work – which, however, in Russia means power. He is a member of the ruling class.'[51]

For all the sympathy Benjamin had with the teeming life he brilliantly observed in the Moscow streets, he cherished his status as 'freelance' intellectual, a status as much in danger in the West as in Russia. Empathy combined with lucidity explains the appeal of Benjamin's writing, which continues to grow rapidly since his suicide fleeing the Nazis on the French–Spanish border in 1940. He reminds

51 *Reflections*, New York, 1978, p. 120

us that it is possible for an intellectual to remain independent in an age of mass technology and totalitarianism.

'Moscow'

from *Reflections: Essays, Aphorisms, Autobiographical Writings* by Walter Benjamin (translated by Edmund Jephcott)

In the street scene of any proletarian quarter the children are important. They are more numerous there than in other districts, and move more purposefully and busily. Moscow swarms with children everywhere. Even among them there is a Communist hierarchy. The 'Komsomoltsy', as the eldest, are at the top. They have their clubs in every town and are really trained as the next generation of the Party. The younger children become – at six – 'Pioneers'. They, too, are united in clubs, and wear a red tie as a proud distinction. *'Oktiabr'* ('Octobrists'), lastly – or 'Wolves' – is the name given to little babies from the moment they are able to point to the picture of Lenin. But even now one also comes across the derelict, unspeakably melancholy *besprizornye*, war orphans. By day they are usually seen alone; each one on his own warpath. But in the evening they join up before the lurid façades of movie houses to form gangs, and foreigners are warned against meeting such bands alone when walking home. The only way for the educator to understand these thoroughly savage, mistrustful, embittered people was to go out on the street himself. In each of Moscow's districts, children's centres have been installed for years already. They are supervised by a female state employee who seldom has more than one assistant. Her task is, in one way or another, to make contact with the children of her district. Food is distributed, games are played. To begin with, twenty or thirty children come to the centre, but if a superintendent does her work properly, it may be filled with hundreds of children after two weeks. Needless to say, traditional pedagogical methods never made much impression on these infantile masses. To get through to them at all, to be heard, one has to relate as directly and clearly as possible to the catchwords of the street itself, of the whole collective life. Politics, in the organisation of crowds of such children, is not tendentious, but as natural a subject, as obvious a visual aid, as the toy-shop or doll's house for middle-class children. If one also bears in mind that a superintendent has to look after the children, to occupy and feed them, and in addition to keep a record of all expenses for milk, bread and materials, that she is responsible for all this, it must become drastically clear how much room such work leaves for the private life of the person performing it. But amid all the images of childhood destitution that is still far from having been overcome, an attentive observer will perceive one thing: how the liberated pride of the proletariat is matched by the emancipated bearing of the children. Nothing is more pleasantly surprising on a visit to Moscow's museums than to see how, singly or in groups, sometimes around a guide, children and workers move easily through these rooms. Nothing is to be seen of the forlornness of the few proletarians who dare to show themselves to the other visitors in our museums. In Russia the proletariat has really begun to take possession of bourgeois culture, whereas on such occasions in our country they have the appearance of planning a burglary. Admittedly, there are collections in Moscow in which workers and children can quickly feel themselves at home. There is the Polytechnic Museum, with its many thousands of experiments, pieces of apparatus, documents and models relating to the history of primary production and manufacturing industry. There is the admirably run toy museum, which under its director, Bartram, has brought together a precious, instructive collection of Russian toys, and serves the scholar as much as the children who walk about for hours in these rooms (about midday there is also a big, free puppet show, as fine as any in the Luxembourg). There is the famous Tretiakov Gallery in which one understands for the first time what genre painting means and how especially appropriate it is to the Russians. Here the proletarian finds subjects from the history of his movement: *A Conspirator Surprised by the Police*, *The Return from Exile in Siberia*, *The Poor Governess Enters Service in a Rich Merchant's House*. And the fact that such scenes are still painted entirely in the spirit of bourgeois art not only does no harm – it actually brings them closer to this public. For education in art (as Proust explains very well from time to time) is not best promoted by the contemplation of 'masterpieces'. Rather, the child or the proletarian who is educating himself rightly acknowledges very different works as masterpieces from those selected by the collector. Such pictures have for him a very transitory but solid meaning, and a strict criterion is necessary only with regard to the topical works that relate to him, his work and his class . . .

Bolshevism has abolished private life. The bureaucracy, political activity, the press are so powerful that no time remains for interests that do not converge with them. Nor any space. Apartments that earlier accommodated single families in their five to eight rooms now often lodge eight. Through the hall door one steps into a little town. More often still, an army camp. Even in the lobby one can encounter beds. Indoors one only camps, and usually the scanty inventory is only a residue of petit-bourgeois possessions that have a far more depressing effect because the room is so sparsely furnished. An essential feature of the petit-bourgeois interior, however, was completeness: pictures must cover the walls, cushions the sofa, covers the cushions, ornaments fill the mantelpiece, coloured glass the windows. (Such petit-bourgeois rooms are battlefields over which the attack of commodity capital has advanced victoriously; nothing human can flourish there again.) Of all that, only a part here or there has been indiscriminately preserved. Weekly the furniture in the bare rooms is rearranged – that is the only luxury indulged in with them, and at the same time it is a radical means of expelling 'cosiness', along with the melancholy with which it is paid for, from the house. People can bear to exist in it because they are estranged from it by their way of life. Their dwelling place is the office, the club, the street. Of the mobile army of officials only the baggage train is to be found here. Curtains and partitions, often only half the height of the walls, have had to multiply the number of rooms. For each citizen is entitled by law to only thirteen square meters of living space. For his accommodation he pays according to his income. The state – all house ownership is nationalised – charges the unemployed one ruble monthly for the same area for which the better off pay sixty or more. Anyone who lays claim to more than this prescribed area must, if he cannot justify his claim professionally, make manifold amends. Every step away from the preordained path meets with an immeasurable bureaucratic apparatus and with impossible costs. The member of a trade union who produces a certificate of illness and goes through the prescribed channels can be admitted to the most modern sanatorium, sent to health resorts in the Crimea, can enjoy expensive radiation treatment, without paying a penny for it. The outsider can go begging and sink into penury if he is not in a position, as a member of the new bourgeoisie, to buy all this for thousands of rubles. Anything that cannot be based on the collective framework demands a disproportionate expenditure of effort. For this reason there is no 'homeliness'. But nor are there any cafés. Free trade and the free intellect have been abolished. The cafés are thereby deprived of their public. There remain, therefore, even for private affairs, only the office and the club. Here, however, transactions are under the aegis of the new *byt* – the new environment for which nothing counts except the function of the producer in the collective. The new Russians call *milieu* the only reliable educator.

For each citizen of Moscow the days are full to the brim. Meetings, committees are fixed at all hours in offices, clubs, factories, and often have no site of their own, being held in corners of noisy editorial rooms, at the cleared table of a canteen. There is a kind of natural selection and a struggle for existence between these meetings. Society projects them to some extent, plans them, they are convened. But how often must this be repeated until finally one of the many is successful, proves viable, is adapted, takes place. That nothing turns out as was intended and expected – this banal expression of the reality of life here asserts itself in each individual case so inviolably and intensely that Russian fatalism becomes comprehensible. If civilising calculation slowly establishes itself in the collective, this will, in the first place, only complicate matters. (One is better provided for in a house that has only candles than where electric light is installed but the supply of current is interrupted hourly.) A feeling for the value of time, notwithstanding all 'rationalisation', is not met with even in the capital of Russia. 'Trud', the trade-union institute for the study of work, under its director Gastiev, launched a poster campaign for punctuality. From earliest times a large number of clockmakers have been settled in

Moscow. They are crowded, in the manner of medieval guilds, in particular streets, on the Kuznetsky Bridge, on Ulitsa Gertsena. One wonders who actually needs them. 'Time is money' – for this astonishing statement posters claim the authority of Lenin, so alien is the idea to the Russians. They fritter everything away. (One is tempted to say that minutes are a cheap liquor of which they can never get enough, that they are tipsy with time.) If on the street a scene is being shot for a film, they forget where they are going and why, and follow the camera for hours, arriving at the office distraught. In his use of time, therefore, the Russian will remain 'Asiatic' longest of all. Once I needed to be wakened at seven in the morning: 'Please knock tomorrow at seven.' This elicited from the hotel porter the following Shakespearean monologue: 'If we think of it we shall wake you, but if we do not think of it we shall not wake you. Actually we usually do think of it, and then we wake people. But to be sure, we also forget sometimes when we do not think of it. Then we do not wake people. We are under no obligation, of course, but if it crosses our mind, we do it. When do you want to be wakened? At seven? Then we shall write that down. You see, I am putting the message there where he will find it. Of course, if he does not find it, then he will not wake you. But usually we do wake people.' The real unit of time is the *seichas*. That means 'at once'. You can hear it ten, twenty, thirty times, and wait hours, days, or weeks until the promise is carried out. Just as you seldom hear the answer 'no.' Negative replies are left to time. Time catastrophes, time collisions are therefore as much the order of the day as the *remonte*. They make each hour superabundant. Each day exhausting, each life a moment.

Travel by street car in Moscow is above all a tactical experience. Here the newcomer learns perhaps most quickly of all to adapt himself to the curious tempo of this city and to the rhythm of its peasant population. And the complete interpenetration of technological and primitive modes of life, this world-historical experiment in the new Russia, is illustrated in miniature by a street-car ride. The conductresses stand fur-wrapped at their places like Samoyed women on a sleigh. A tenacious shoving and barging during the boarding of a vehicle usually overloaded to the point of bursting takes place without a sound and with great cordiality. (I have never heard an angry word on these occasions.) Once everyone is inside, the migration begins in earnest. Through the ice-covered windows you can never make out where the vehicle has just stopped. If you do find out, it is of little avail. The way to the exit is blocked by a human wedge. Since you must board at the rear but alight at the front, you have to thread your way through this mass. However, conveyance usually occurs in batches; at important stops the vehicle is almost completely emptied. Thus even the traffic in Moscow is to a large extent a mass phenomenon. So one can encounter whole caravans of sleighs blocking the streets in a long row because loads that require a truck are being stacked on five or six large sleighs. The sleighs here take the horse into consideration first and then the passenger. They do not know the slightest superfluity. A feeding sack for the nag, a blanket for the passenger – and that is all. There is room for not more than two on the narrow bench, and as it has no back (unless you are willing so to describe a low rail), you must keep a good balance on sharp corners. Everything is based on the assumption of the highest velocity; long journeys in the cold are hard to bear and distances in this gigantic village immeasurable. The *izvozshchik* drives his vehicle close to the sidewalk. The passenger is not enthroned high up; he looks out on the same level as everyone else and brushes the passers-by with his sleeve. Even this is an incomparable experience for the sense of touch. Where Europeans, on their rapid journeys, enjoy superiority, dominance over the masses, the Muscovite in the little sleigh is closely mingled with people and things. If he has a box, a child or a basket to take with him – for all this the sleigh is the cheapest means of transport – he is truly wedged into the street bustle. No condescending gaze: a tender, swift brushing along stones, people and horses. You feel like a child gliding through the house on its little chair . . .

In the Red Army Club at the Kremlin, a map of Europe hangs on the wall. Beside it is a handle. When this handle is turned, the following is seen: one after the other, at all the places through which Lenin passed in the course of his life, little electric lights flash. At Simbirsk, where he was born, at Kazan, Petersburg, Geneva, Paris, Cracow, Zurich,

Moscow, up to the place of his death, Gorki. Other towns are not marked. The contours of this wooden relief map are rectilinear, angular, schematic. On it Lenin's life resembles a campaign of colonial conquest across Europe. Russia is beginning to take shape for the man of the people. On the street, in the snow, lie maps of the SFSR[52] piled up by street vendors who offer them for sale. Meyerhold uses a map in *D.E.* *(Here with Europe!)* – on it the West is a complicated system of little Russian peninsulas. The map is almost as close to becoming the centre of the new Russian iconic cult as Lenin's portrait. Quite certainly the strong national feeling that Bolshevism has given all Russians without distinction has conferred a new reality on the map of Europe. They want to measure, compare, and perhaps enjoy that intoxication with grandeur which is induced by the mere sight of Russia; citizens can only be urgently advised to look at their country on the map of neighbouring states, to study Germany on a map of Poland, France, or even Denmark; but all Europeans ought to see, on a map of Russia, their little land as a frayed, nervous territory far out to the west . . .

Anyone entering a Russian classroom for the first time will stop short in surprise. The walls are crammed with pictures, drawings and pasteboard models. They are temple walls to which the children daily donate their own work as gifts to the collective. Red predominates; they are pervaded by Soviet emblems and heads of Lenin. Something similar is to be seen in many clubs. Wall newspapers are for grown-ups schemata of the same collective form of expression. They came into being under the pressure of the civil war, when in many places neither newspaper nor printing ink was available. Today they are an obligatory part of the public life of factories. Every Lenin niche has its wall newspaper, which varies its style among factories and authors. The only thing common to all is the naïve cheerfulness: colourful pictures interspersed with prose and verses. The newspaper is the chronicle of the collective. It gives statistical reports but also jocular criticism of comrades mingled with suggestions for improving the factory or appeals for communal aid. Notices, warning signs and didactic

52 Soviet Federated Socialist Republic

pictures cover the walls of the Lenin niche elsewhere, too. Even inside a factory everyone is as if surrounded by coloured posters all exorcising the terrors of the machine. One worker is portrayed with his arm forced between the spokes of a driving wheel, another, drunk, causing an explosion with a short circuit, a third with his knee caught between two pistons. In the lending room of the Red Army bookshop hangs a notice, its short text clarified by many charming drawings showing how many ways there are of ruining a book. In hundreds of thousands of copies a poster introducing the weights and measures normal in Europe is disseminated throughout the whole of Russia. Meters, litres, kilograms, etc., must be stuck up in every pub. In the reading room of the peasant club in Trubnaia Square the walls are covered with visual aids. The village chronicle, agricultural development, production techniques, cultural institutions are graphically recorded in lines of development, along with components of tools, machine parts, retorts containing chemicals displayed everywhere on the walls. Out of curiosity I went up to a shelf from which two Negro faces grimaced at me. But as I came nearer, they turned out to be gas masks. Earlier, the building occupied by this club was one of the leading restaurants in Moscow.

The erstwhile *séparées* are today bedrooms for the peasants of both sexes who have received a *komandirovka* to visit the city. There they are conducted through collections and barracks, and attend courses and educational evenings. From time to time there is also pedagogical theatre in the form of 'legal proceedings'. About three hundred people, sitting and standing, fill the red-draped room to its farthest corners. In a niche a bust of Lenin. The proceedings take place on a stage in front of which, on the right and the left, painted proletarian types – a peasant and an industrial worker – symbolise the *smychka*, the clasping together of town and country. The hearing of evidence has just finished, an expert is called on to speak. He and his assistant have one table, opposite him is the table of the defence, both facing sideways to the public. In the background, frontally, the judge's table. Before it, dressed in black, with a thick branch in her hand, sits the defendant, a peasant woman. She is accused of medical incompetence with fatal results. Through incorrect treatment she caused the death of a woman in childbirth. The argumentation now circles around this case in monotonous, simple trains of thought. The expert gives his report: to blame for the mother's death was the incorrect treatment. The defence counsel, however, pleads against harshness; in the country there is a lack of sanitary aid and hygienic instruction. The final word of the defendant: *nichevo*, people have always died in childbirth. The prosecution demands the death penalty. Then the presiding judge turns to the assembly: Are there any questions? But only a Komsomol appears on the stage, to demand severe punishment. The court retires to deliberate. After a short pause comes the judgment, for which everyone stands up: two years' imprisonment with recognition of mitigating circumstances. Solitary confinement is thus ruled out. In conclusion, the president points to the necessity of establishing centres of hygiene and instruction in rural areas. Such demonstrations are carefully prepared; there can be no question of improvisation. For mobilising the public on questions of Bolshevik morality in accordance with Party wishes there can be no more effective means. On one occasion, alcoholism will be disposed of in this way, on others fraud, prostitution, hooliganism. The austere forms of such educational work are entirely appropriate to Soviet life, being precipitates of an existence that requires that a stand be taken a hundred times each day.

Theodore Dreiser

Theodore Dreiser (1871–1945) is best known for his novel *Sister Carrie*. A member of the New York avant-garde in the 1910s, Dreiser was friends with Max Eastman and Emma Goldman and supported the birth-control movement of Margaret Sanger. The great success, both critical and commercial, of *An American Tragedy*, published in 1925, made Dreiser the darling of the American left and encouraged him publicly to support the right of free speech for socialist, anarchist and other radical groups. In 1927 he was invited by the Soviet Government to attend the celebration of the tenth anniversary of the October Revolution. Dreiser was too much of an individualist not to question Soviet claims of making a (uniformly) better day for all. He felt the need to record the truth as he had experienced it:

> A musician playing in a restaurant in Rostov, a seaport on the Don River, insisted that the police and the Communists were too officious and superior, even brutal at times. 'They talk about how terrible things were under the Tsar, but I lived under the Tsar,' he said, 'and the soldiers and officials weren't any worse than these people. Then you couldn't say a word against the
> ; now you can't say a word against these fellows!'[53]

Like many of the radicals from the West who made the journey to the Soviet Union in the 1920s, Dreiser returned home to an economic depression brought about by economic policies that favoured the interests of the rich. This led him to speculate that in the new Russia it might 'be possible to remove that dreadful sense of social misery in one direction or another which has so afflicted me in my life in

53 *Dreiser Looks at Russia*, pp. 122–3. Published in New York 1928, the book is a thoughtful mix of his enthusiasms and his criticisms.

344

America ever since I have been old enough to know what social misery is'.

Dreiser wanted to be positive about what he saw in the Soviet Union in contrast to the political, economic and racial inequalities in the US. As the depression got worse, Dreiser became more politically involved – more and more of his time was spent campaigning against what he saw as the crimes of capitalism. His final political protest was to join the American Communist Party in July 1945, five months before his death.

Propaganda Plus

from *Dreiser Looks at Russia* by Theodore Dreiser

ONE of the most amazing, and, at times, disagreeable, phases of life in Russia as I saw it was the endless outpour and downpour of propaganda, not only in regard to the principles and practices of Communism as organised and interpreted by Marx, Engels, Liebknecht, Lenin, Trotsky and others, but in the same breath the modernisation and industrialisation as well as defence from foreign attack of all the Russias from Poland to the Pacific, the Arctic to Afghanistan. Overnight, as it were, the leaders at Moscow and all their enthusiastic disciples and followers would like to educate, train, house and modernly equip all of these fine Russians! And so schools, schools, schools. And factories wherever they can get the money and the machinery wherewith to equip them. And barracks, barracks, barracks, and soldiers, soldiers, soldiers, always marching and singing or being trained somewhere. And on top of all this, books, books and pamphlets by the millions. And most, not all, relating to propaganda in one form or another. (For Zane and Ethel and Rex[54] have arrived. So fear not.) Talk about our American advertising programs! Really, I never saw its equal anywhere, – almost a nightmare of propaganda.

The first posters I came upon were on the Russian–Polish frontier,

54 Zane Grey, Ethell Lilian Voynich and Rex Stout, writers popular in America

in the border station at Negoralje. The station walls were plastered with them. And when I questioned a fellow-traveller – a most agreeable and mentally diversified Belgian, by the way – he explained that they were all of a paternalistic and benevolent character and represented at its best the Government's desire to educate and uplift the masses everywhere.

'And you will never get rid of them,' he added, 'as long as you are in Russia, anywhere. They will come to haunt you. You will probably get good and sick of them. These here,' and he waved an inclusive hand, 'are designed to show the peasant what ten years of revolution have done for him. Miles of others, as you go along, will picture what the Communist Government intends or wishes to do, or what the Russian worker or peasant can do for himself. It's the greatest advertising company in the world, I think.'

And now I agree, for I never was rid of them. From Leningrad to Tashkent, from Poland to the heart of Siberia, from Odessa to Samarkand, there they are – or were, in every station, hotel, Government post office, Government or co-operative store, factory, office building, theatre, home even, the endless posters of this most ambitious of governments urging (never commanding, really) the people to do this and that, from combing their hair to swatting flies, washing out the stables and milk pails, cleaning the babies' milk bottles, opening the windows of sickrooms, ploughing with tractors, fertilising with the right fertilisers, building with the right lumber, eating the right food – oh, Lord, hold me! I feel myself spinning around!

One of these posters which this very good Belgian was kind enough to translate for me showed a peasant woman sitting under a hay wagon, her little boy at her feet, reading a book. The legend accompanying the picture set forth news of the fairyland of wonders that the knowledge of reading would bring to those who would only trouble to learn to read. In the background of this same poster, in a small cloud in the distance, glowered the envious, opposed and threatening figure of the Tsar and his royalist friends, all wretchedly caricatured and literally gnashing their teeth, because of the peasant woman's intention to educate herself, I assume.

Another poster in this same station – and one that I found all over Russia – done in flaming red, by the way – showed a massed group of young and valiant Communist workers, guns in hand, bayonets fixed, standing as a Red wall against an approaching storm of capitalistic ills, pictured in this instance as a mass of black water overhung by tumultuous and sinister clouds, in their turn composed of greedy and sensuous and selfish faces and eyes and hands. It was quite vivid. Still another presented an accusing finger levelled directly at me, a face behind it. The legend, according to my friend, urged all citizens and peasants to connect with and work for the various local committees for either the uplift of the village or the nation-at-large. We have the same type of poster over here. It usually reads: 'This means you!'

But this was a bare beginning. Wherever I went, there they were. Pictures or charts relating to every conceivable type of thing – cooking, washing, exercising, cleaning the house, getting rid of fleas and dirt, packing fruits or vegetables for shipment or preservation; mixing different kinds of grain or vegetables for animal or human food; pruning trees; running the automobile or caring for the horse; making the right sort of roof for the winter; arranging the right sort of ventilation in summer; showing the right sort of clothing for baby or school child; showing the proper arrangement of a new town; showing methods of building a cellar or a silo – a thousand and one things in connection with the life of the people. I sometimes wondered how the poor Russians made out under it all – why they were not smothered under the downpour.

For, in addition and all over Russia, in every street and on every other corner, in all of the cities and small towns, and even in the hamlets, stations, post offices and general stores (or co-operatives, as they are called), hundreds of books, pamphlets, magazines on what and how to do for sale – and costing very little. 'How to be a Carpenter'. 'How to be a Chauffeur'. 'How to be an Engineer'. 'Stenography in Ten Lessons'. 'Mirakowsky on Draughtsmanship'. 'Mirakowsky on Architecture'. 'Mirakowsky on Surveying'. 'The Principles of Building'. 'Soil Diagnosis and Crop Rotation'. 'The ABC of Gardening'.

It was amazing, the endless variety of these things, and in the most unexpected places – on a stand outside a church, on Sunday! In all the public markets, next to stands selling pickled pigs' feet or second- or eighth-hand furniture. One man in Baku had a table of pamphlets resting on the back of a wholly stationary donkey. He had driven it to market with this load. And except for an occasional flick of an ear or a swish of a ropelike tail, no disturbing motion. You might examine the stuff at your leisure. No danger of the store moving off, not even of lying down.

But my purpose is not to laugh, neither to rhapsodise. For propaganda, however valuable to the Russians – and I know it to be a great and valuable thing in this instance – is to the American visitor at least a pest. For all they are talking about or urging we already have. And at times I could not help wondering whether the Russians themselves did not get a little weary of it. For there is so terribly much of it. You never hear the last of it anywhere. Take the programme for industrialising Russia. Lord, the endless pother! Russia must be industrialised. This machine (and here is a picture of it) will do the work of fifteen or one hundred and fifteen men. (And here are the men.) Twenty-five or one hundred such machines in one factory can and will produce so and so many bales of something. (And the bales are shown, and the machine, or a chart with heavy black lines indicating how many machines in how many days or hours will do what.) And these have to hang in every factory, office, depot, market, hotel, or be tacked on the side of every box car, freight station, street car, truck, or what not. Well, guess how much you might like the sight of them after a time! And not only that, but lectures by radio as well as in person in every Red or Lenin Corner throughout the land. And there is no end to Red or Lenin Corners throughout the land. They compete with arc lights and mail boxes.

By the way, these Lenin Corners are used not only for industrial as well as political and educational instruction, but they have a military or national defence meaning as well. For in every apartment house, club, factory, shop, school or residence, or wherever citizens can be gotten together, the young and old are instructed not only in the doctrines of Marx and the virtues of communal life as practised in Russia today but the dangers of a world war against Russia. Also the need of the masses sticking together, learning to use rifles, bombs, machine guns, as well as to practice first aid and self-help in times of disaster. And almost invariably, in the same corners, or nearby in an adjacent room, practice in all these matters is actually furnished for a half or three-quarters of an hour each day to all who can be induced to come, men and women, girls and boys. And many of the employees of every institution or business do come. It is by now almost a religious duty.

And here quite all are taught, and under glowing pictures of Marx and Stalin and Lenin – no longer any of Trotsky – and cartoons or lithographs, most lurid in colour, of enormous, hoglike plutocrats with their fat heels on the necks of chained workers lying at their feet. And other cartoons, usually that one of the Red workers repelling the oncoming horde of plutocrats. And mottoes: Workers of the World Unite! Down with Plutocracy! Remember the White Guards! The Red October! And always some comrade nightly to lecture or explain, firing the masses with pictures of the danger in which they stand. Here also, however, educational programmes are undertaken, illiteracy liquidated – lessons on dietetics, sanitation, the care of children, etc., furnished; even lessons in some trade or art delivered. And in addition the radio, with lectures, speeches, songs coming over. Never, never anywhere indeed have I seen the equal of it. There is something strange, almost mystic, in the present fever of these people to consolidate their gains, make themselves sure that what they have attained shall not be taken away from them. And possibly, who knows? Some epochal mystic urge behind or below it all. Who knows?

In this connection I must speak of the press, for while every city and town in Russia has one or more papers, presumably permitted to reflect the news and the political or social changes of the region in which they appear, nevertheless they do not really do so by any means. For *Pravda* and *Izvestia*, two daily papers of Moscow, and both organs of the Communist Party – and in their turn inspired by the executive heads of the Government, or rather the Communist Party – are again, and from another point of view, the exemplars for every other paper in Russia outside and inside Moscow. What they say – and not only that but the very way they say it – is repeated all over

Russia by all of the other papers, yet as original news or opinion. So true is this that in Tiflis, or Tashkent, or Chita, or Perm, wherever you chance to be, you will read – and that from one to ten days after these two Moscow papers have printed them – facts or policies or Government declarations with not a trace of deviation from the opinions expressed in these same papers in Moscow. Communistic team work, one might call this. Only a little dull.

In this connection I took a particular interest in the Communists' repeated declaration that in Russia there was absolute freedom for the press to think and say what it chose – criticise the Communist rule if it chose – and followed it up with many personal enquiries and examinations. That is, I would have the same paper – quite often the same items – read to me by two different assistants at different times, and when they were not together. But at no time did I find any news or criticism or opinion of any kind that was not safely held within the lines of *Izvestia* or *Pravda* and always with the intellectual slant directed by the central group in Moscow. For, as I have said, the Government will not tolerate any unfavourable criticism, not so much of itself as of Communism. Communism can do no wrong.

Worse, in order to control and direct all thought and conclusions, and to bias the same in favour of Communism, no news from within or without Russia may appear which does not tend to glorify the principles of Marx and Lenin, and by the same token belittle all other theories or principles which in any way conflict. Thus, all news from anywhere else on earth must show that all other governments are really oppressive mechanisms in the hands of capitalists, and constantly being used to betray and enslave labour; also that labour in other lands is oppressed, restless and constantly seeking to free itself from the shackles of capitalism. So every little strike or labour decision, favourable or unfavourable to Communism, or any slump or rise in prices unfavourable to the mass, or any fact in connection with the extravagance or waste of the rich anywhere outside Russia was, as I soon found, played up in the local paper everywhere in Russia as of the greatest significance, while at the same time any fact in connection with the industrial or social improvement of the Russian worker in Russia was set forth at length. Could the Catholic Church do better? Has it ever? It is faced, let me tell it, by a new, and, I think, for it, fatal, competitor.

But never, never anywhere, a single word to the effect that anything is wrong or badly done in Russia by the Communists; no complaint of lack or error, say, unless the same chances to be generally known by hearsay or commented on in Moscow in *Pravda* or *Izvestia* or is in process of being remedied, when, of course, it will be the remedial process that will be emphasised.

To tell the truth, after the first month or six weeks I found myself either irritated or bored by this persistent harping on the bright Communistic scene within Russia as opposed to the dark capitalistic world without, when, as any outsider could see, it was so much at variance with the truth. Yet, the Communists, like the capitalists and the religious organisations the world over, are entitled (are they not?) to make their side good – 'put it over', as we say. And as between the lies of the British and American capitalists and their selfish propaganda for purely personal and plutocratic reasons or those of the Catholic Church in regard to its descent and merits and those of the self-sacrificing Communists, I vote for the Communists and am willing to leave the matter there and trust to the future. Of course, from one point of view, this pro-Communistic exaggeration is obviously and often offensively biased or dishonest, but from another not. For there is anti- or underground opposition to Communism in Russia, too, and that has to be met. And when I recalled the various lying and mass-befuddling articles and preachments in regard to Russia foisted by a capitalistic opposition the world over upon an all too gullible citizenry, I knew I had no particular kick coming. One may meet sword with sword, may one not? Besides, I do not charge them with much downright lying and I do insist they have a valuable something which tends to evoke exaggeration to a degree.

In regard to the amusements of the country, however – theatres, moving pictures, opera – this business of propagandising as well as censoring, or censoring as well as propagandising, was not so pleasing to me, its results as I saw them tending to limit or tame the stage in a too disagreeable manner. All the more so because Russia certainly has able producers, both in the legitimate theatre and in the movies –

Stanislavsky, Meyerhold, Tairov, in the theatre; Eisenstein and several others in the moving-picture world. But the Communists' restless concern for the welfare of the future mind of Russia, their determination to reeducate all of the citizens of the land, young and old, to their way of thinking causes them to insist upon colouring and twisting all art, where possible, to their way of thinking. The result thus far is that there is neither art for art's sake nor knowledge for its own sake in Russia – any more than there is in the Catholic Church or Christian Science or Mohammedanism. Both are for one purpose, and one purpose only – the confirmation and so establishment of Communism. Thus up to now, in quite all Russian cities, the plays of Strindberg, Ibsen, some of Shakespeare's (such as *Julius Caesar* or *Macbeth*), Chekhov's *Cherry Orchard* and *Three Sisters*, a number of Schiller's plays as well as others of Hauptmann, Sudermann and Shaw, are taboo. And, as I said before, for various reasons. Too grim, or too sad or, according to Communist opinion, celebrating royalty or nobility at the expense of the peasant. My own two plays, *The Hand of the Potter* and *An American Tragedy*, were entirely agreeable to Stanislavsky, who would have liked to produce them, but the Communist censors would have none of them. They were, as I heard, too grim.

Again, plays that glorify religion or dwell too heavily on love or sex are mostly taboo, the latter being supposedly beneath the interest of a really concerned Communist – or his disciple, any Russian. And so apart from the opera *Carmen*, still being done in different parts of Russia, I saw not one play, and only two second-class movies, dealing with love or sex. These related themes were, as I understood it, considered beneath the interest of a nation called upon to straighten out the economic miseries of the world.

On the other hand, when it comes to what the Communists do want, they are just as annoying and pestiferous, never for an instant losing an opportunity to preach a doctrine or to teach a lesson. Thus in Leningrad I saw one of Schiller's plays, *The Robbers*, edited and furnished with a prologue and an epilogue in order to make it teach independence to the rising youth of Russia. In the same city I saw *Uncle Tom's Cabin* with little Eva left out and Simon Legree shot by a young negro introduced into the play especially for this purpose, who saw it as his duty to avenge the brutal treatment of Uncle Tom and Eliza by Legree. And when I asked the reason I was told that the Russian youth of the day were too tame and needed to be taught independence and opposition to tyranny. Now shouldn't that be telegraphed to Harriet Beecher Stowe?

And in the same way, quite all over Russia revolution is lauded while anything which tends to emphasise the submission of one class to another in society is out. In consequence, the stage and cinema abound in pictures of the fighting that took place between the revolutionists and the capitalist classes, but never with any that criticise, let alone satirise, any phase of Communist doctrine.

Again, education, in its most direct or school forms, and being as it is in the hands of the State, is little more than a weapon or machine for the inculcation of the theories of Marx – a means for assuring the stability of the State and for creating a type of human being who will fit in with and continue the theories of Marx. In other words, all education is and must be class-conscious and Marxian. You know the old saw about giving you the child until six or seven years of age and then letting any take him who will. Well, obviously the Communists in Russia like the Catholic Church in the rest of the world, America included, understand, believe, and act on that. Having taken the child out of the hands of the religionist and practically out of the hands of his parents – since they begin with him in the public nurseries and kindergartens – they have decided to inculcate the principles of Communism from the cradle up. And to this end, in all the day nurseries all over Russia, where parents can and (as in the instance of the vast number of working men and women who go into the factories at half-past seven or eight o'clock and do not return to their homes until four o'clock or after) must leave their children while they work, you will find, and this opposite children lying in cradles or still crawling about on their hands and knees, not only red flags hung upon the walls, so that the colour and form of the same will presumably become familiar and so a memorable thing, but pictures of Lenin, with a red factory chimney behind him, his working cap awry, his solid, square-toed, working shoes firmly placed upon the hard cobblestone paving, his attitude that of a man about to make an address.

And with that as a beginning, the good work goes on and on, the nurseries, kindergartens and schools being little mills for the grinding out of Reds, desirable or undesirable as they may be. Not a spelling or a reading or a writing or geography or history or grammar lesson or a class exercise or diversion but is connected in some way with Communist theory and practice. For how easy, in connection with the spelling of words and the inculcation of their meaning, to spell and explain a few words directly bearing on Communism and its aims. The word 'commune', for instance, or 'communist', or 'individualist', or 'capitalist', or 'king', or 'idler', or 'worker', or 'parasite', and how these things or persons are directly connected with the Russian state and its problems. Will the Catholic hierarchy please take note?

And there is the reading lesson, best read from a Communist paper – the *Pravda*, say – with all that that implies. Or the geography lesson, with maps of other countries and the data concerning the same, the forms of government and lives of their people, and the difficulties the same have had with kings and queens, capitalists and idlers who oppressed and enslaved them.

As early as six or seven, I was told, the schoolchildren of Russia today begin to listen to talks on current events and facts in connection with Russia's recent history, and by the time they are in the fourth or fifth grade there are regular periods devoted to events in other countries – England, France, China, America – and the social conditions which give rise to these events. And there are, of course, patriotic Communist songs and Communist school societies. Each school also has its 'collective' committee of students elected by the rest to carry out self-management, in which the children are trained by actual example in the processes of Soviet Government. And, in addition, each school has its Octobrist, Pioneer and Konsomol organisations, all preparatory for the Communist Party, and these are for kindergarten, grade school, and high-school ages.

But, oh, those little schools! In little cabins in the villages, tucked away in the snow and under the bleak, grey sky of Russia! I can see them now, with so many lumbering jackdaws in the trees outside. And the little Russian boys and girls, with their straps of books, coming and going, morning and evening. In a way today these same schools are really sub-branches of the Communist Party, with the children graduating from one sub-Communist organisation to another until at last, if they can prove themselves worthy of it, they are taken into the Party itself. But what of it? Are not Americans being taught the perfection of capitalism, the Italians that of Fascism, the Spaniards that of Catholicism, and so on. Yet do not believe that the Communist Party is easy to get into! If one is not proletarian-born, one is admitted only after long and severe tests of one's merit and fitness. There are still less than a million Communists in the whole of Russia's hundred and fifty million population, and they must have more, of course, in the future.

Also, in connection with the national assumption that Russia, as the head and front of the Communist movement in the world, is called upon to sovietise the world, comes all the serious and gloomy propaganda in connection with that military preparation that is now afoot. For all over Russia there is at present a constant military stirring, which keeps one thinking of war all the time. In fact, you are never done with the sight of soldiers marching or drilling, practising with machine guns or cannon, or horses or ambulances, stretchers, first-aid kits, and what not else that chances to be a part of present-day military training – aeroplanes for one thing. I saw this wherever I went, and not since the days of Germany before the war have I seen anything quite like it. On the other hand, the general statement reiterated by all officials and Communists is that there is only a defence army of some five hundred and twenty thousand men, with such equipment, and no more, as is necessary to protect the country. Well, if Russia has an army of only five hundred and twenty thousand men, it is the most effectively distributed and active army that I have ever seen. For in every city and town of any size all over the great empire, but more especially where its borders march with the seas or those of another nation, soldiers, soldiers, soldiers – in Leningrad, Archangel, Perm, Omsk, Tomsk, Irkutsk, and all along the Chinese and Polish frontiers, at Baku and Batoum and Tiflis and Vladikafkaz, between the Black and Caspian Seas, and all along the northern shores of the Black Sea, particularly in Poti, Adler, Suchum, Sochi, Feodosia, Yalta, Sevastopol, and Odessa. And well clothed and well armed, too, with barracks, machine guns, cannon, gas masks, bombs, army trucks and trains, aeroplanes, and what not else.

But most ominous of all, I think, is the additional propaganda which goes with keeping a great nation in the mood and the faith that such a war is inescapable, and that the very intensive internal labour and accessory preparation is necessary in order for Russia to be ready. Posters, pamphlets, radio talks and lectures by the GPU and others to convince the populace that not only is it necessary to have the army in question, but worse – or better, as you please – a large civilian population – in fact, all the able-bodied men and women who are not in the army – trained to fight or nurse or to help in some other military fashion with the necessary military equipment to take up the struggle along with the army in case Russia is attacked.

And so, as I have said, in every Lenin Corner, or in an adjoining room, a rack or shelf for guns, bombs, gas masks, first-aid kits, and I know not what else, all intended as a part of a school or class for war – a local or neighbourhood or industrial training in attack and defence.

Ilf and Petrov

Both from Odessa, **Ilya Ilf** (pseudonym of Ilya Fainzilberg) (1897–1937) and **Yevgeni Petrov** (pseudonym of Yevgeni Katayev) (1903–1942) met in Moscow working on the railroad workers' newspaper *Gudok* (*Whistle*): other writers on the paper included Mikhail Bulgakov and Yuri Olesha. Their first collaboration was the best-seller *The Twelve Chairs*, a satire on the NEP, which featured Ostap Bender, the amoral conman who travels the Soviet Union in search of jewellery hidden in one of the chairs. At the end of the book, Bender is murdered by his companion Ippolit Matveyevich, who eventually discovers that the diamonds have already been found. So successful was *The Twelve Chairs* that Ilf and Petrov were obliged to resurrect Bender for the sequel, *The Little Golden Calf*. In this book, Bender blackmails the millionaire Koreiko and ends up with a million roubles – which is illegal to spend in a Communist country. Bender considers donating the money anonymously to the Minister of Finance but decides to flee to Romania. On the border, he is robbed by Romanian guards and left only with a medal, the Order of the Golden Fleece. Not a work likely to pass the censors, *The Little Golden Calf* was only published after an intervention by Gorky. A huge international success, the book brought Ilf and Petrov financial independence but not artistic freedom. A third volume in which Bender is sent to a hard-labour camp and is transformed into a model citizen was, unfortunately, never written. 'How Robinson Was Created', written in 1932, chronicles the difficulties Ilf and Petrov had over the years with the censors. Unavailable for many years under Stalin's rule, the works of Ilf and Petrov were republished during the Thaw in the 1960s. For many growing up in that period, their availability was symbolic of the new intellectual freedom. It is estimated that by 1993 sales of their works exceeded forty million copies in Russian alone.

How Robinson was Created

by Ilf and Petrov (translated by Ellendea Proffer)

The editorial board of the illustrated bi-weekly *Affairs of Adventure* felt the lack of artistic works capable of attracting young readers.

There were some manuscripts around, but none of them was right. There was just too much drivelling seriousness in them. To tell the truth, rather than attracting young readers, they depressed their spirits. And the editors wanted to attract them.

In the end they decided to commission a serial novel.

The editorial errand-boy rushed off with a note to the writer Moldavantsev, and the very next day Moldavantsev was sitting on the bourgeois couch in the editor's office.

'You understand,' droned the editor, 'it should be entertaining and fresh, full of interesting adventures. In general, we need a Soviet *Robinson Crusoe*. Something that the reader can't put down.'

'A *Robinson* – can do,' said the writer laconically.

'Not just a *Robinson*, but a *Soviet Robinson*.'

'What else! Not a Romanian one, for example!'

The writer was not loquacious. Obviously, he was a man of action.

And, indeed, the novel was ready on the agreed-upon date. Moldavantsev didn't stray too far from the great original. They wanted a *Robinson*, they got a *Robinson*.

A Soviet youth suffers a shipwreck. A wave carries him to a deserted island. He's alone, defenceless in the face of mighty nature. Dangers are everywhere: beasts, lianas, the approaching rainy season. But the Soviet Robinson, full of energy, conquers all the obstacles which appear so unconquerable. Three years later a Soviet expedition finds him flourishing. He's dominated nature, built a little house, surrounded it with a green ring of gardens, raised rabbits, has sewn himself a Russian shirt from gorilla tails and has taught a parrot to wake him in the morning with the words: 'Attention! Take off the blanket, take off the blanket! We're starting morning exercises!'

'Very good,' said the editor, 'the stuff about the rabbits is just superb. Completely contemporary. But, you know, the basic idea of the work isn't quite clear to me.'

'Struggle of man with nature,' reported Moldavantsev with his usual brevity.

'But there's nothing Soviet in it.'

'But what about the parrot? He replaces the radio. An experienced announcer.'

'The parrot's good. And the ring of gardens is good. But one gets no sense of Soviet public spirit here. Where, for example, is the local committee? The leading role of the unions?'

'How can there be a local committee? The island's supposed to be deserted.'

'Yes, quite true, deserted. But there must be a local committee. I'm not an artist of the word, but if I were you I'd put one in. As a Soviet element.'

'But the whole plot is based on the idea that the island is deserted . . . '

At this point Moldavantsev happened to glance into the editor's eyes and stopped cold. Those eyes were so springlike, one even sensed in them the empty blueness of March, and he decided to compromise.

'Actually, you're right,' he said, raising his finger. 'Of course, why didn't I see it right away? Two people survive the shipwreck: our Robinson and the head of the local committee.'

'And also two regular members,' said the editor coolly.

'Oy,' squeaked Moldavantsev.

'Nothing to oy about. Two regular members and one woman activist, who collects dues.'

'Why a dues collector too? Who's she going to collect dues from?'

'From Robinson.'

'The committee head can collect Robinson's dues. That's all right for him.'

'In that you are mistaken, Comrade Moldavantsev. That's absolutely objectionable. The head of the local committee should not be misused for such trivial things as running around collecting dues. We are trying to combat just such things. He should spend his time on serious leadership work.'

'Well, then there can be a dues collector. That's even better. She'll marry either the committee head or Robinson. More entertaining to read.'

'Not worth it. Don't lapse into trashiness, into unhealthy eroticism. Let her collect the dues and keep them in a fireproof safe.'

Moldavantsev squirmed on the couch.

'With all respect, a fireproof safe can't be on a desert island!'

The editor gave it some thought.

'Wait a minute,' he said, 'you've got a terrific section in the first chapter. The wave washes up various things along with Robinson and the local committee.'

'An axe, a rifle, a compass, a barrel of rum and a bottle of anti-scurvy medicine,' recited the writer.

'Cross out the rum,' said the editor quickly, 'and then what's the point of the scurvy medicine? Who needs that? Better to have it be a bottle of ink! A fireproof safe is vital.'

'You're crazy on the subject of that safe! The membership dues can just be kept in the hollow of the baobab tree. Who's going to steal them?'

'What do you mean, who? What about Robinson? The head of the committee? The regular members? The store commission?'

'The store commission also survives?' asked Moldavantsev cravenly.

'They survive.'

Silence ensued.

'Maybe the wave also washes up a meeting table?!'

'Positively! We have to create the conditions for people to work in. Give them a pitcher of water, a bell, a tablecloth. The wave can wash up whatever kind of tablecloth you like. Either red or green. I'm not interfering with creativity. But the first thing you've got to do, old man, is show the masses. A broad cross-section of working people.'

'The waves can't wash up the masses,' said Moldavantsev obstinately. 'That goes completely against the plot. Just think a minute! The waves suddenly wash up several thousand people! We'd be laughing stocks.'

'But actually, a little healthy, cheerful, life-loving laughter never hurts,' enthused the editor.

'No! A wave can't do that.'

'Who needs a wave?' said the editor in sudden amazement.

'How else are the masses to land on the island? It's a deserted island, you know.'

'Who says it's deserted? You're getting me mixed up. It's clear. There's an island, better – a peninsula. That way it's calmer. And on it occur a series of entertaining, fresh, interesting adventures. Union work is being carried on, sometimes badly. The activist exposes a series of defects, for example, in the area of dues collection. The broad cross-section helps her. And the repentant committee head. At the end you can show a general assembly. That will be really effective artistically. There, that's it.'

'What about Robinson?' gibbered Moldavantsev.

'Yes. Good you reminded me. Robinson bothers me. Throw him out completely. An absurd, completely unjustified sniveller.'

'Now everything's understood,' said Moldavantsev in a funereal tone, 'everything will be ready tomorrow.'

'That's all. Go create. By the way, you have that shipwreck at the start of the novel. You don't need it, you know. Do it without the shipwreck. It'll be more riveting that way. Right? Good. Goodbye.'

When he was alone, the editor began to laugh happily.

'Finally,' he said, 'I'll have a work that's both a real adventure and a genuine work of art as well.'

Permissions

Every endeavour has been made to locate the copyright holders of the texts included here. Please would any copyright holders we were unable to locate get in touch with Harbour Books?

'An Ex-Capitalist' and 'A Theorist of Revolution', from *Six Weeks in Russia in 1919* by Arthur Ransome © Arthur Ransome Literary Estate

'Perhaps it is for the best', extract from *Memoirs of a British Agent* by Robert Bruce Lockhart © Pen and Sword Books Limited

'Alone in Petrograd', extract from *The Russian Countess* by Edith Sollohub © Edith Sollohub 2009, 2010. Reproduced by permission of Impress Books.

'Blockade', from *Story of a Life, Volume 4: Years of Hope* by Konstantin Paustovsky, translated by Manya Harari and Andrew Thomson. Published by Harvill Press. Reprinted by permission of the Random House Group Limited.

'Family Man', from *Tales from the Don* by Mikhail Sholokhov, translated by Valentina Brougher and Frank Miller, with Mark Lipovetsky, and included in *50 Writers: An Anthology of 20th-Century Russian Short Stories* and selected, with an introduction by Mark Lipovetsky and Valentina Brougher, translated and annotated by Valentina Brougher and Frank Miller (Academic Studies Press, Boston, 2011), pp. 193–9. Permission granted by Academic Studies Press.

'Mr Harrington's Washing', from *Ashenden: or the British Agent* by Somerset Maugham © the Royal Literary Fund. Permission granted by United Agents LLP on behalf of the Royal Literary Fund.

'Rasputin', from *Rasputin and Other Ironies* by Teffi, published by Pushkin Press. Original Russian text © Agnès Szydlowski. Translation copyright © 2014 by Anne Marie Jackson

'They got her to scrub the deck!' from *Memories: From Moscow to the Black Sea* by Teffi, published by The New York Review of Books. Copyright © Agnès Szydlowski. Translation copyright © 2016 by Robert Chandler and Irina Steinberg

'*Diary: 1920*' (excerpts) by Isaac Babel, in *Russian Literature of the 1920s*, edited by Carl R. Proffer, translated by Nicholas Stroud. Copyright © by Ardis. Published in 1987 by Ardis Publishers, Peter Meyer Publishers, Inc. www.overlookpress.com/ardis.html. All rights reserved

'Letters from Russia', from *The Collected Papers of Bertrand Russell: Volume 15: Uncertain Paths to Freedom: Russia and China 1919–22* eds Richard A. Rempel and Beryl Haslam. Copyright © Routledge, 2000. Reproduced by permission of Taylor and Francis Books UK and the Bertrand Russell Peace Foundation.

'The Outgoing Letter N37' by Lev Lunts, included in *The Terrible News*, published by Black Spring Press. Translation and collection © Grigori Gerenstein 1991

'Pelageya' & 'The Hat' by Mikhail Zoshckenko, from *Russian Short Stories from Pushkin to Buida*, edited and translated by Robert Chandler, Penguin Classics, 2005. Introductory material and notes copyright © Robert Chandler, 2005.

'Electrification', 'Domestic Bliss', 'Crisis', 'Nervous People' & 'An Incident on the Volga' by Mikhail Zoshckenko, from *The Galosh and Other Stories*, Angel Books, 2000. Translations, introduction and notes copyright ©Jeremy Hicks 2000

'The Secret of the Cheka', from *Mess-Mend: The Yankees in Petrograd* by Marietta Shaginian, translated by Samuel Cioran. Copyright © 1991 by Ardis. Published in 1991 by Ardis Publishers, Peter Meyer Publishers, Inc. www.overlookpress.com/ardis.html. All rights reserved

'Three Generations', from *Love of Worker Bees* by Alexandra Kollontai, Virago Press, 1997. Translation copyright © Cathy Porter 1999. Reprinted by permission of Virago, an imprint of Little, Brown Book Group (UK Rights). Used with permission of Academy Books, Chicago (USA Rights).

'Lalla's Interests' by Vera Inber, from *Russian Short Stories from Pushkin to Buida*, edited by Robert Chandler, Penguin Classics, 2005. Introductory material and notes copyright © Robert Chandler 2005.

'The Destruction of the Intelligentsia', from *The Italics are Mine* by Nina Berberova. Original title *Kursiv moi*, published in France under the title *C'est moi qui souligne*. Original publisher Editions Actes Sud, Arles © Actes Sud, 1989

'Anguish and Enthusiasm: 1919–1920', 'Deadlock of the Revolution: 1926–1928' 'The Years of Resistance: 1928–1933' from *Memoirs of a Revolutionary*. Copyright © 1951 by Editions du Seuil. Translation copyright © 2012 by the Victor Serge Foundation. Reprinted by permission of the estate of Victor Serge.

'Turkmenian Flamenco', from *I Wonder as I Wander* by Langston Hughes. Copyright © Langston Hughes, 1956. Reprinted by permission of David Higham Associates.

'The Bloodthirsty Profession' & 'Striving after Friendship' by Viktor Ardov, included in *The Terrible News*, published by Black Spring Press. Translation and collection © Grigori Gerenstein 1991

'Moscow' (excerpts), from *Reflections: Essays, Aphorisms, Autobiographical Writings* by Walter Benjamin. English translation copyright © 1978 by Houghton Mifflin Harcourt Publishing Company. Reprinted by permission of Houghton Mifflin Harcourt Publishing Company. All rights reserved

'How Robinson was Created' by Ilf and Petrov. Copyright © 1987 by Ardis. Published in 1987, in *Russian Literature of the 1920s*, edited by Carl R. Proffer, translated by Ellendea Proffer. Published in 1987 by Ardis Publishers, Peter Meyer Publishers, Inc, www.overlookpress.com/ardis.html. All rights reserved